Reader's Digest

MYSTERIES
OF THE ANCIENT
AMERICAS

Reader's Digest

MYSTERIES
OF ANCIENT
THE
AMERICAS

THE NEW WORLD BEFORE COLUMBUS

The Reader's Digest Association, Inc. Pleasantville, New York • Montreal

MYSTERIES OF THE ANCIENT AMERICAS

Project Editor: Joseph L. Gardner
Project Art Editor: Gilbert L. Nielsen

Senior Editors: Monica Borrowman, Kaari Ward
Associate Editor: Noreen B. Church
Research Editors: Hildegard Anderson, Mary Jane Hodges
Picture Researcher: Margaret O. Mathews
Art Associate: Renée Khatami
Assistant Editor: Carol Davis
Editorial Assistant: Ann Purdy

Contributing Researcher-Writers: Sara Solberg, Jozefa Stuart
Contributing Copy Editor: Susan Converse Winslow
Indexer: Jane Whipple

Contributing Writers: Martha Fay, Charles Flowers, Jill L. Furst,
   Peter T. Furst, Warren Hoge, Edward Kern, John Mason,
   Wendy Murphy, Donald Pike, Stephen W. Sears

Principal Adviser
and Editorial Consultant
   Michael D. Coe
   Department of Anthropology
   Yale University

Board of Consultants
   Alan Lyle Bryan
   Department of Anthropology
   University of Alberta

   Richard L. Burger
   Department of Anthropology
   Yale University

   Linda Cordell
   Department of Anthropology
   University of New Mexico

   James B. Griffin
   Museum of Anthropology
   The University of Michigan

   Peter David Joralemon
   Curator, The Wray Collections
   Scottsdale, Arizona

   Richard S. MacNeish
   Department of Archeology
   Boston University

   Mary Ellen Miller
   Department of The History of Art
   Yale University

   Michael E. Moseley
   Field Museum of Natural History
   Chicago

   Irving Rouse
   Department of Anthropology
   Yale University

   Alan R. Sawyer
   Department of Fine Arts
   University of British Columbia

   Dean R. Snow
   Department of Anthropology
   State University of New York
   at Albany

READER'S DIGEST GENERAL BOOKS
Editorial Director: John A. Pope, Jr.
Managing Editor: Jane Polley
Art Director: Richard J. Berenson
Group Editors: Norman B. Mack, John Speicher,
David Trooper (Art), Susan J. Wernert

The acknowledgments and credits that appear on pages 308–310 are hereby made a part of this copyright page.

Library of Congress Cataloging in Publication Data
Main entry under title:

Mysteries of the ancient Americas.

   Bibliography: p.
   Includes index.
   1. Indians—History.   2. Indians—Antiquities.
3. Indians—Origin.   4. America—Discovery and
exploration.   5. America—Antiquities.   I. Reader's
Digest Association.
E58.M97   1986   970.01   84-15038
   ISBN   0-89577-183-7

Introduction

History's most surprising encounter, perhaps, was that between the Europeans who followed in the wake of Columbus and the native inhabitants of the New World. The conquering Spaniards viewed the complex, sophisticated Aztec and Inca civilizations with disbelief; surely these people could not have achieved such cultural heights without outside inspiration — from other, earlier European visitors or transpacific wanderers from Asia. The native Americans, for their part, too often regarded the intruders with haughty disdain and paid for their unwariness by falling easy prey to superior technology and clever strategy.

The reasons for such misconceptions have puzzled historians for centuries, and the answers have been sought in an avalanche of books, pamphlets, and commentaries. The editors of Reader's Digest here take a fresh look at the story. Unlike most histories of the New World, this book *ends* — not *begins* — with Columbus and follows a topical instead of a chronological approach.

"Voyagers of Legend," the first of seven major sections, presents the confusing evidence and lingering doubts about pre-Columbian visitors — Egyptians, Phoenicians, Israelites, Welsh, Irish, Japanese, Chinese, and, finally, the Vikings, who we now know arrived 500 years before Columbus. "In Search of Early Man" reviews the highly controversial timetable for the arrival of the first Americans from Asia, at least 27,000 years ago, and outlines their development of hunting and farming skills. As long as 3,000 years ago, we learn in "Stirrings of New World Civilizations," people as far apart as the bayous of the lower Mississippi Valley, the Andean highlands of Peru,

and the humid forests of Gulf Coast Mexico were fashioning distinct cultures — two of which, at least, would leave substantial legacies to their successors. The flowering of the Maya culture in the first millennium A.D. in the region anthropologists call Mesoamerica (parts of modern-day Mexico and the Central American states) and the impressive accomplishments of the Adena/Hopewell/Mississippian peoples of North America over some of the same centuries are described in "Pyramid Makers and Mound Builders."

Some breathtaking achievements of New World peoples are featured in "Ancient Artisans and Master Builders," two picture portfolios that serve as showcases for works of high artistry and astonishing engineering skill. "Lost Cities" offers in-depth studies of Mexico's Palenque, New Mexico's Pueblo Bonito, Colombia's Buritaca 200, and Peru's Chan Chan. "Of Gods and Men" reveals some shocking facts about the Aztec religion and highlights the persistence of ancient mystical beliefs.

By no means are the mysteries all solved, the wonders all discovered; tomorrow's headline can announce a newly discovered Maya tomb or a previously unknown Andean culture. Nor are scholars and scientists agreed on the record of the past, for this is a field rife with conflicting evidence and passionate controversy — all of which makes for fascinating reading.

Read this book from cover to cover, savor it a chapter at a time, or dip into its profusely illustrated pages at random. You will find fascinating stories, startling facts, enduring puzzles, imaginative solutions wherever you turn. This is history — but not as you learned it in school.

The Editors

CONTENTS

LOST CITIES

OF GODS AND MEN

Time Line of the Ancient Americas

	NORTH AMERICA	MESOAMERICA	SOUTH AMERICA
3000– 2000 B.C.	Coppersmiths *(to 1000 B.C.)*	Maya Pre-Classic Era *(2000 B.C.–A.D. 300)*	Valdivia pottery on Ecuador coast
1200		Olmec *(to c. 300 B.C.)*	
1000	Poverty Point culture *(to 500 B.C.)*		
800			Chavín de Huantar *(850–200 B.C.)*
500	Adena *(to A.D. 200)*		
200		El Mirador occupied *(c. 200 B.C. to A.D.150)*	
100 B.C.	Hopewell *(to A.D. 350)*		Tiahuanaco *(to A.D. 1200)* Moche *(to A.D. 750)*
A.D. 100		Teotihuacán flourishes *(to c. 650)*	
200		Palenque occupied *(to c. 820)*	
300	Anasazi *(to 1300)*	Maya Classic Era *(to 900)* Monte Albán Classic Era *(to 1000)*	
500			Tairona *(to 1500)*
800	Mississippian *(to 1500)*		
900	Pueblo Bonito constructed *(c. 920–1150)*	Toltec Maya *(987–1526)*	
1000	Vikings reach North America		Chimú *(to c. 1470)*
1300	Chaco Canyon abandoned	Aztec *(1350–1519)*	
1400	Key Marco, Florida *(to 1700)*		Inca *(c. 1438–1532)*

VOYAGERS
OF
LEGEND

VISITORS FROM LANDS BEYOND

The New World's resplendent civilizations were beyond the creative capacity of the native population, said the conquistadors. Where had the inspiration come from? Egypt? Phoenicia? Visitors from Outer Space?

We were amazed and said that it was like the enchantments they tell of in the legend of Amadis, on account of the great towers and temples and buildings rising from the water, and all built of masonry. And some of our soldiers even asked whether the things that we saw were not a dream. . . . there is so much to think over that I do not know how to describe it, seeing things as we did that had never been heard of or seen before, not even dreamed about."

Thus wrote Bernal Díaz del Castillo of the day in 1519 when he stood with Cortés and his conquistadors and glimpsed, for the first time, the great Aztec capital of Tenochtitlán, the site of Mexico City today. The Spaniards were awed. The best-traveled of the soldiers thought Tenochtitlán's marketplace greater and better run than those of Constantinople or Rome or any other city they had seen. Cortés admitted to his king that the royal palaces of the emperor Moctezuma (Montezuma) far exceeded anything in Spain.

The reports of Cortés and Pizarro and others who took part in the Spanish Conquest caused intense speculation in Europe about the identity and origin of the peoples who had created these glittering civilizations — and if, in fact, they were the creators. Only a

few years earlier this had not been considered a mystery. Christopher Columbus died believing his landfalls were the Indies on the rim of Asia, far across the Ocean Sea, and he called the people he encountered Indians, an identifiable (if not well known) Old World population. Balboa's crossing of the Isthmus of Panama and his discovery of the Pacific in 1513 finally furnished proof that this was not some part of Asia but something entirely different — a New World.

The concept of a populated New World created a problem for the faithful. The Old Testament story of the Creation credited the descendants of the three sons of Noah with peopling Asia, and Africa, and the Aegean coastline (Europe) but left the origins of the inhabitants of the Americas unaccounted for. A dual Creation, a second Garden of Eden in the new-found continents, was heresy; thus the Indians could only have come to the New World from the Old.

But how does one account for their cultural achieve-

The Spanish invaders, led by Cortés (under the number 18), file toward Tenochtitlán, seen in the distance. The flourishing capital of Aztec Mexico took the conquerors by surprise and caused speculation about the origins of New World peoples.

18

Entrada de
Cortes En Me
xico Por la Cal
sada de S. Anto
nio Abad.

ments? For centuries theorists have proposed that pre-Columbian visitors from Egypt, from Phoenicia, from Wales, or from Scandinavia must have sparked the development of civilization in the Americas. More romantic writers have seen the possibility of wandering colonists who were forced to seek refuge because of some catastrophe in the classical world.

Adding to the mystery is the prevailing lack of historical records that could date and document the growth of the Indian cultures. Local legends have the vague symbolism of myth, at least to us, and they can be interpreted in many different ways. They are as likely to foster as to deny the possibility of cultural dissemination from the ancient worlds already known to Westerners at the time of the discovery of America.

The old controversies still rage. Did civilization rise unaided in the Americas, or did the early explorers and conquistadors come upon a transplanted Old World culture? Will man, wherever he may live, inevitably develop along a fairly predictable cultural path, or do the massive structures and sophisticated art of the Americas prove that influences must have somehow swept westward from Europe and the Middle East? Those who argue the latter theory are known as diffusionists, proponents of the notion that the world's cultures must have had a "single common cradle of all civilizations" — as one of them has described it.

We will see that they find many disparate bases for their arguments — similarities in the construction of pyramids, the practice of mummification, religious parallels in the worship of the sun, even specific motifs in art and apparent borrowings in myth. But few contemporary diffusionists have theorized with the creative abandon of one of the best-known adherents of the "Egyptian connection," the stubbornly determined Augustus Le Plongeon, a 19th-century French antiquarian and adventurer.

The Egyptian Connection

To understand Le Plongeon at all, we must remember that the true extent of Egyptian civilization itself was only beginning to be understood by the late 19th century, a period that witnessed the coming of age of archeology as a respectable science. While Egyptologists were painstakingly puzzling over the latest finds along the Nile, Le Plongeon, camped out in the hot, mosquito-infested Yucatán Peninsula with his devoted young wife, was investigating the artifacts and hieroglyphics of the vanished Maya civilization.

His translations of inscriptions have remained unique. In 30 years of single-minded, fanatical study in the field, he compiled a history entitled *Queen Moo and the Egyptian Sphinx,* allegedly the factual chronicle of Maya colonization of the Nile no less than 11,500 years ago. This is, of course, a reversal of the usual diffusionist pattern; according to Le Plongeon, influence ran from west to east, from the New World to the Old, and thence to the shores of the Indian Ocean.

His search for evidence of contact was not confined to the study of murals, sculptures, and hieroglyphics. Maya temples, he divined, were laid out in the shape of the Egyptian letter for "M," called *ma,* which signified "place, country, and by extension, the Universe."

A bitter antagonist in debate, Le Plongeon was more likely to attack those who questioned his theories than to share the evidence for his conclusions. This attitude, perhaps, was to make it all the more difficult for later diffusionists to receive a respectful hearing from traditional academics and scholars. In the preface to his book *Queen Moo* the eccentric theorist wrote, "In questions of history theories prove nothing." Yet, since he was secretive and iconoclastic to a fault, others were to find that, for him, theories were everything. He declared that a Maya sculpture depicted a scene from the Old Testament. Furthermore, he noted that a carved zigzag motif near a line on a Yucatán lintel gave ample proof that the Maya had used the telegraph. He suggested that one third of the Maya language was "pure Greek . . . the dialect of Homer" and found traces of Assyrian as well. Yet another intercultural contact could be inferred from his contention that the last words of Jesus were not spoken in Aramaic, the mother tongue of Jesus and his disciples. Rather than " My

The Negroid features of the colossal stone heads that are unique relics of the Olmec culture suggest to some that Africans visited Mexico's Gulf Coast three thousand years ago.

The graceful lotus motif decorating the neck of the Inca vessel, left, is also found on the frieze of the Great Ball Court at Chichén Itzá, Mexico. Above, the towering 15th-century B.C. granite columns at Karnak, Egypt, reveal a similar floral design.

God, my God, why hast thou forsaken me," Le Plongeon claimed that Jesus said, in Maya, "Now I am sinking, darkness covers my face."

By the end of his life Le Plongeon's credibility was, for all practical purposes, bankrupt, but he was defiant to the last. Speaking before an American audience in 1881, he said, " . . . since I felt that I was abandoned by ALL, notwithstanding ALL wanted to procure from me GRATIS what had cost me so much time, labor and money to acquire, I made up my mind to keep my knowledge, so dearly purchased, to destroy some day or other my collections, and to let those who wish to know more about the ancient cities of Yucatán, do what I have done. . . ."

Le Plongeon was, perhaps, a fantasist. And yet his questioning curiosity was something of an inspiration to cooler heads: "Who carried the Maya to the country of Helen? . . . Were they emigrants from this Western continent? Was not the tunic of white linen . . . used by the Ionian women . . . the same as the *uipil* of the Maya females of to-day. . . ?" It was exactly the kind of restless imagination essential for delving into the shadowy American past and pursuing its often illusory leads.

A more eminent and cautious explorer of these mysteries was Sir G. Elliot Smith, a highly respected Australian brain anatomist writing about Egypt in the early part of the 20th century. Smith knew the value of factual evidence. He and his followers collected an impressive body of materials to support his thesis that all civilizations of the globe had originated in the high culture of the Nile — to be carried by the "Children of the Sun" throughout the world.

In his books, Smith theorized that this "Heliolithic" culture first reached the Americas during the Egyptian 21st Dynasty, or about 1000 B.C. Smith's fundamental

The striking kinship between artistic motifs may indicate that two very different cultures came in contact with each other. The sacred eye of Horus, above, was one of the most common religious symbols of ancient Egypt. The god Horus was often associated with the ruling pharaoh. The remarkably similar eyes on the intricately worked Peruvian feather hat, right, are as boldly stylized as the Egyptian design. It was probably worn by a priest or warrior for ceremonies.

line of argument seems to have been based on the practice of mummification, which he saw as originating in Egypt and then diffusing across Africa to India, Indochina, Polynesia, and finally, to the Pacific shores of the American continents. It was not just the mummification, but the specific practices, that he found to be persuasive, including the embalming of the dead. The one obvious exception on his path of diffusion was China, where the practice of mummification was unknown. But Smith ingeniously proposed that the existence of jade, pearls, and gold in burials there implied the influence of mummification, for these precious objects were believed capable of forestalling decomposition of the corpses.

Among other provocative bits of "evidence," Smith cited a ball court in the Maya city of Chichén Itzá with its running motif of lotus blossoms, which was a traditional design in Egyptian art. On a prehistoric monument at Copán, Honduras, Smith noted a carving resembling an elephant — an unlikely theme in an isolated Central American setting. These similarities between American and Old World art were widely debated in academic circles.

In the mid-19th century, the brilliant and accomplished authority on Mexico's pre-Columbian history, Abbé Charles Stephen Brasseur de Bourbourg, also connected Mexico and Egypt, but from a different per-

spective. After decades of laboriously deciphering Maya codices, this French priest suddenly realized that perhaps they were all myth. What he had introduced to the world as chronicle was, he began to feel, an allegory. But of what?

The answer he found would startle the academic world and alter his reputation for conservative, deliberate research. Without the advantage of Smith's list of cultural parallels, Brasseur de Bourbourg began to speculate about the Egyptian influence, largely because of the resemblances between Egyptian pyramids and those of Mexico. His *Quatre Lettres* settled the issue, so far as he was concerned. There was a common cultural source: the fabled lost continent of Atlantis. Atlantean colonists, he claimed, first came to America, then traveled eastward to create the monumental civilizations of Egypt and the Old World.

Brasseur de Bourbourg's studies of linguistics led him to the "astonishing discovery" of seemingly Germanic words in the language of the Maya. One word, he suggested, even showed a possibility of British influence. In addition he equated the Egyptian God Horus with Quetzalcoatl, the feathered serpent god of ancient Mexico. However, he was not able to assemble evidence that would persuade the skeptical, though most historians and archeologists of his time did not condemn him.

Perhaps we are wrong to hold the man to contemporary standards of scholarship. His works were probably more persuasive as flights of fevered imagination than as history, but Brasseur de Bourbourg and his contemporaries did not have access to the growing anthropological evidence that we possess today.

When, for example, the Indian-born R. A. Jairazbhoy published his *Ancient Egyptians and Chinese in America* in 1974, he culled his supporting evidence from the most recent archeological findings. He documents, for example, 21 parallels to be found in the myths and religious practices of ancient Egypt and Mexico. In both cultures, a deity is assigned to "eat" the sins of men after they made a confession; in both, a mythic figure has the odd characteristic of a double twisted rope issuing from his mouth. On a more mundane level, Jairazbhoy saw meaningful likenesses in daily life: the sport of wrestling, the existence of a phallic cult, the aristocratic delight in dwarfs, the building of stepped pyramids. From these and other cultural similarities, he proposed that Egyptian contact occurred less than 1,200 years before the birth of Christ, perhaps during the 20th-Dynasty reign of Ramses III.

Most of Jairazbhoy's parallels have been known and discussed by diffusionist thinkers. But he also found additional likenesses in religious ritual. He seems to be the only one who noted that the Egyptian custom of including small strips of papyrus in burials has a striking resonance in the Aztec ritual of placing bunches of paper with the dead. However, few of the parallels he found between Egyptian and Mexican cultures have been confirmed by archeological data — though some of these similarities were reported by Spanish chroniclers in the 16th century.

The Search for Answers

What are we to make of these insights, from Le Plongeon's intuitive theories to Smith's carefully argued views, from Brasseur de Bourbourg's almost mystical inspirations to Jairazbhoy's cultural resemblances? Why has the Egyptian connection always seemed so immediately plausible to so many different kinds of people? Could all the similarities have occurred solely as the result of mere coincidence?

To date, most scholars are not convinced that any contact has been persuasively documented, even when some of the parallels are so suggestive. Diffusionists see indications of Egyptian influence, but their opponents believe that the evidence is slender, contradictory, and isolated. The issue remains unresolved until scientists can point to a local artifact of definite Old World provenance as "hard" evidence for contact.

Moreover, it has been convincingly argued that mummification need not have been spread from a single source. It is a practical way to dispose of the dead in many climates. And the attendant rituals, in the widely scattered areas of the world where mummification has been practiced, are known to be different from ones practiced by the Egyptians in almost all cases.

As for the existence of similar customs or art styles or building patterns, it can be argued that each is a response to a similar cultural need. The idea of building a stepped pyramid, for example, is obvious enough to have occurred to more than one civilization wanting to build an impressive-looking temple. Other similarities such as linguistic parallels are often in the ear of the theorist, and picture-writing, too, lends itself all too easily to individual interpretation.

Generally accepted historical records, however, often conflict with the speculative. For example, the kingdom of Ramses III, it is now known, was surrounded by enemies, and was largely occupied in de-

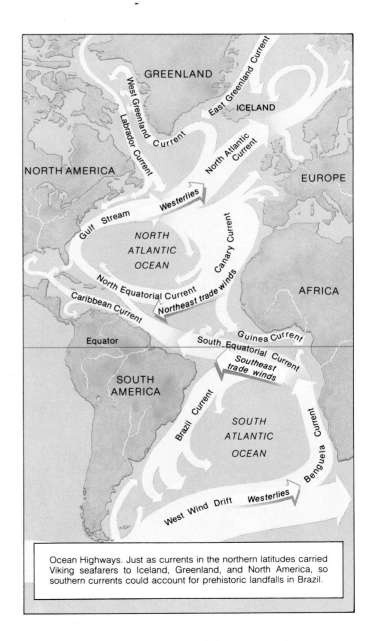

Ocean Highways. Just as currents in the northern latitudes carried Viking seafarers to Iceland, Greenland, and North America, so southern currents could account for prehistoric landfalls in Brazil.

fending its borders. It was not likely to mount colonial or exploratory expeditions to other parts of the world.

Proof of expeditions across the formidable Atlantic is also critical to the argument. Although at least one modern explorer thinks that he has proved the possibility of transoceanic travel in ancient times (see box below), possibility is not necessarily probability. Nor would Egyptians be the most likely candidates, because their ships were more suited to river and coastal travel than to the open sea.

Such a crossing would have been more within the known capabilities of the early voyagers of the great seas, the Phoenicians. To some thinkers, it has seemed almost inevitable that these sailors, whose maritime daring often dazzled the less adventurous cultures of the ancient Mediterranean, would have sailed on to America simply because it was there.

To one 19th-century writer, the Phoenicians no doubt encountered the New World "in joyous gladness" having followed " . . . still the star-tracery on the azure wall of the external Dome, and their Apollo daily sinking on his Western couch, and with his last glance, beckoning them as it were, still to follow on his path, — this knowledge and their Religious adoration, directed them in safety to that Virgin land where the glorious Sun from Creation's dawn, had never beamed upon a human foot-print, until their own had kissed the untouched Floridian Shore!"

But what is the evidence for Phoenician travels to the American shores? To diffusionists who find the likelihood compelling, the technology of these famous seafarers is in itself a powerful argument. Unlike their less-skilled contemporaries, the Phoenicians built merchant ships that were mainly wind-propelled, relying on oars only when necessary. By 600 B.C. the Phoenicians had ships that could carry 50 to 100 tons, making them equal in capacity to the Portuguese caravels of the 15th century. There are historical accounts of Phoenicians making voyages around the tip of Africa and to the "Tin Isles," perhaps a reference to Britain's Cornwall. Of all maritime peoples in the Old World, it is unquestionably true that these daring seamen were

The Ra Expedition

"People are apt to duplicate each other's feats, given the same environmental conditions," says Thor Heyerdahl, who is world famous for his courageous attempts to duplicate possible voyages of the ancient past. A fervent advocate of the speculative approach, Heyerdahl believes it worthwhile to investigate the *possibility* of transoceanic travel in earlier eras. Inspired by the similarity of reed boats in Egyptian art to contemporary craft in South America and elsewhere, he decided to test out the theory that reed sailing vessels could have crossed the Atlantic from Africa to the Americas. Because Heyerdahl believed the papyrus plant had become extinct in Egypt, he had 12 tons of 10- to 12-foot-long sun-dried reeds brought from Ethiopia to Giza. There, Buduma tribesmen from Lake Chad, who still use a boat rather like the Egyptian model, built a 50-foot craft, *Ra I,* named for the sun god.

In May 1969, with a crew of seven, Heyerdahl set sail from Safi, Morocco. His boat was stocked with food and water in 160 ceramic jars modeled on prototypes in the Cairo Museum. More than 2,600 miles and about two months out to sea, severe storm damage convinced Heyerdahl to abort the trip.

The following year *Ra II* was built by Aymara Indians brought from Lake Titicaca, where totora-reed boats are a familiar means of transportation. Ten feet shorter than *Ra I,* this vessel was to make the 3,270-mile trip from Safi to Barbados in 57 days, arriving soaked but virtually undamaged. This success, Heyerdahl thinks, countered several objections to theories of ancient transoceanic travel. The reeds did not deteriorate, as many skeptics had predicted. The combination of winds and currents made possible an average speed of 65 statute miles a day. *Ra II* rode out breaking seas in a full gale. Heyerdahl noted that reed boats were the most highly developed type of water craft being used in the New World when the Spaniards explored the coast of Peru. Was the basic design, he asks, a legacy from Egyptian seamen who had braved the Atlantic millennia before?

Egyptian wall paintings of reed boats, like the one above dating from a New Kingdom period (1554–1304 B.C.) tomb, fired Heyerdahl's imagination. Here seamen maneuver a sailing vessel similar to Ra II, *which is shown opposite.*

the most capable of crossing the uncharted Atlantic.

If so, what traces have been found of their visit? Again, there are cultural parallels that pique the curiosity. Were the Phoenicians, who practiced child sacrifice, responsible for teaching this fairly unusual, as well as shocking, practice to the Gulf Coast Olmec? Does an Olmec relief carving depict an ancient Phoenician, since the figure is bearded and sports the up-turned shoes worn in the eastern Mediterranean? Can the numerous monumental stone Olmec heads with Negroid lips and noses be taken as proof that the Phoenicians brought along their black slaves on the lengthy voyages to America?

An American underwater archeologist, Robert Marx, has proposed a visit by 2nd-century B.C. Romans to the coast of Brazil. In 1976 a Brazilian diver found two intact amphorae, tall storage jars of the type carried on long ocean voyages, on the muddy bottom of Guanabara Bay, about 15 miles from Rio de Janeiro. Since then, Marx has found thousands of pottery fragments and more than 200 necks from similar amphorae. Is this evidence of ancient trade contact, or was a heavily laden Roman vessel blown off course after venturing past the Strait of Gibraltar into the Atlantic?

Among the best-known of the transatlantic diffusionists is Barry Fell, professor emeritus of biology at Harvard. His *America B.C.* (1976) and other works rely on inscriptions found primarily in New England to prove that not only Phoenicians but also Celts, Arabs, Egyptians, and still others ventured to the New World. His method is to employ the esoteric skills of epigraphy, the complex and very demanding art of deciphering little-known ancient inscriptions.

Fell has applied his craft to some of the most controversial archeological finds and amateur discoveries in America, such as the Davenport Tablet found in Iowa in 1877, which is considered a hoax by most archeologists. Fell claims that he has been able to decipher three languages on the tablet: Egyptian hieroglyphics, Libyan, and Iberian Punic. However, most of his translations have dealt with inscriptions that he identifies as Celtic Ogam, clusters of short bars along a single line.

The dramatic 1970 voyage of Ra II, *shown breasting the Atlantic above, succeeded because Peruvian Indians understood boat-building skills like those of ancient Egyptians. Above left, a reed boat sails in Lake Titicaca; left, doomed Ra I rises near the Giza pyramids.*

The bearded Phoenician oarsmen depicted on an Assyrian relief (c. 700 B.C.), above, are typical of their culture. The pre-Columbian incense burner, right, featuring a bearded face with Semitic features, was unearthed in Guatemala. Some scholars speculate that the Mesoamerican artist must actually have encountered a Mediterranean seafarer.

The Paraiba Stone Controversy

In 1872 slaves working on a Brazilian plantation near the Paraiba River were reported to have uncovered four pieces of a stone tablet inscribed with unknown characters. A copy of the inscription but not the stone itself reached Dr. Ladislau Netto, Director of the Museu Nacional in Rio de Janeiro. After diligent study, Netto announced that the inscription recorded a visit to Brazil by Phoenician mariners centuries before the time of Christ. Unfortunately, neither the tablet nor the sender was ever located and Netto's translation was ridiculed by the academic establishment of his day.

A century later, however, an American scholar, Cyrus H. Gordon, took a new look at the Paraiba inscription — and came up with some startling conclusions. The text, he claimed, contained expressions and grammatical forms unknown to linguistic students of the 19th century. How, then, could forgers have produced such a text? Gordon's translation reads, in part: "We are sons of Canaan from Sidon, from the city where a merchant (prince) has been made king. He dispatched us to this distant island. . . .We sailed from Ezion-geber into the Red Sea and voyaged with ten ships. We were at sea together for two years around Africa. Then we got separated by the hand of Baal and we were no longer with our companions." He dates the accidental landfall in Brazil to the 6th-century B.C. reign of Hiram III of Tyre. Not all scholars accept Gordon's hypothesis; there are, as he himself acknowledges, "too many unanswered questions."

Ogam, he says, was used in northeastern America from 800 to l00 B.C. But other linguistic "evidence" has convinced him that the Phoenicians annexed Massachusetts briefly, perhaps around 400 B.C. He has also listed links between Egyptian hieroglyphics and the written language of the Micmac Indians of eastern Canada.

In these and his many other arguments for early European influence upon the development of American cultures, Fell has been accorded a wide audience; as he has written, " . . . it is plain that the word we bring is something that young people have longed to hear." However, many scholars find Fell's conclusions lacking in sufficient proof.

Many of the rock markings Fell cites as evidence to support his theories could just as easily be the work of natural forces, say his critics. The few remains in New England that might be remnants of settlement have been shown to be root cellars no more than a few centuries old.

Yet the search continues. Frequently, we will read that an outdoorsman, a farmer, or a construction worker will suddenly turn up a stone covered with weird, indecipherable markings. Northeastern America seems to be richly blessed with such seeming artifacts, and the diffusionists are tireless in looking for that tablet or boundary stone that will prove, once and for all, that Phoenicians or Egyptians or some other Old World culture sent representatives to pre-Columbian America.

The search is part of a well-established tradition. In the 18th century Ezra Stiles, then Yale College president, argued that strange characters found on a rock near Dighton, Massachusetts, were "Phoenician 3,000 years old." At an Indian mound near Tennessee's Bat Creek, a puzzling tablet found in the 19th century was adjudged by some to be Canaanite writing dating back to the 1st or 2nd centuries A.D. Other discoveries have gained varying degrees of public acceptance. Some have been found to be the work of skillful pranksters, others have been declared works of nature, and a few are still pored over by puzzled epigraphers.

Why does this passion exist to find the hidden link with the civilizations of classical history? Is it the desire to explain the unknown by means of the known? Is it, as some have suggested, a form of cultural arrogance, with the implication that the peoples of America must have been innately inferior to the great nations of the "cradle of civilizations" in the Middle East? Or is there a reverse motive, a desire to show that American cultural achievements rank with those of the classical world because they derive from a shared origin?

In certain episodes of the past, we can surmise less than idealistic motives for the promotion of unusual theories about pre-Columbian transatlantic contacts. One 16th-century account, for example, credits the discovery of the New World to the Portuguese official João Vaz Corte Real in 1472. Nationalism, it seems, was responsible for this claim. Certain Portuguese historians, protective of their country's known mastery of

the seas in the 15th century, sought to add the discovery of America as the appropriate next step in a series of brilliant accomplishments such as the circumnavigation of Africa and the tracing of a sea route to India.

Other accounts of the late 16th century mention the supposed New World voyages of two European pirates, Didrik Pining and Hans Pothorst, and the explorations of a navigator, Johannes Scolvus (Jan of Kolno), who might have come from Poland. So far as is known, such references were produced by writers who wanted to out-Columbus Columbus, after the fact. As American historian Samuel Eliot Morison has written, "Whilst there is no reason to believe that the pirate pair discovered anything, it is possible that Scolvus sailed around Cape Farewell, Greenland, and looked into Davis Strait [to the west]."

Somehow, the whole subject has long had irresistible appeal to the charlatan and the forger. One of the most successful fictions of the 16th century was a navigation map with commentary, published in Venice in 1558 by Nicoló Zeno. The text, he claimed, was based on accounts written in the 14th century by his ancestor, Antonio Zeno, who had, along with his brother (also called Nicoló), sailed off to "Frislanda, Eslanda, Engrouelanda, Estotilanda and Icarìa," — presumably stepping-stones on the route to North America. Unfortunately, the later Zeno did not cover his tracks very well, and it has been easy to show that much of his map

Chalked for easier reading, this petroglyph under a cliff overhang in Wyoming County, West Virginia, has been identified as an ancient Celtic Ogam inscription by well-known *diffusionist Barry Fell. Lit by the late December sun at winter solstice, it reads in part, says Fell, "At the time of sunrise a ray grazes the notch on the left side on Christmas Day."*

was copied from earlier maps of Iceland and the Faroes.

Factual evidence for the claim, moreover, is nonexistent. One investigator dismissed the whole tale as an example of "family pride and . . . personal vanity," and concluded, "Zeno's work has been one of the most ingenious, most successful, and most enduring literary impostures which has ever gulled a confiding public."

But why did it find such favor in the popular imagination? Although there has been a steady stream of archeological discoveries from ancient American sites within the past few decades, and although recent scientific techniques add to our ability to infer answers from fragments of bone or cloth or pottery, the theory of cultural dissemination still has appeal.

Perhaps the ultimate diffusionist, at least so far, is the enormously popular Swiss writer Erich von Däniken, whose imaginative reach goes back much farther in time and space than any of those who have proposed an Egyptian or Phoenician connection. According to him, not only culture but the race of man was engendered as the result of visits from ancient astronauts.

It is von Däniken's contention that these beings from outer space were sufficiently humanoid in form to mate with earthlings and pass on their genius genetically. Evidence of these visits by ancient astronauts is to be found in the art and legends of pre-Columbian civilizations. (Quetzalcoatl was of course one of these ancient astronauts.) In a relief at Palenque, Mexico, von Däniken sees the carved figure of an extraterrestrial visitor seated in his rocket rather than the typical depiction of a Maya nobleman long accepted by many eminent archeologists. In a secret tunnel in Ecuador are golden treasures crafted by cosmic gods, which he suggested should not be photographed for fear that the flashbulb would set off a synchronized laser-beam booby trap and collapse the site. Statues of Toltec warriors at Tula, he claims, hold ray guns of advanced design, not spear throwers as scholars had previously thought.

Yet von Däniken, an apparently insatiable traveler, does not rely on art alone for his inferences. In the pitted limestone of the Yucatán Peninsula, he finds evidence of early blast-offs; the numerous sinkholes, he contends, are craters formed by rocket exhaust.

It is in Peru that von Däniken claims to have found

Armed with ray guns, ancient astronauts, left, are honored in these 10th-century 18-foot-tall pillars at Tula, Mexico, claims writer Erich von Däniken; traditional scholars see Toltec warriors with spear throwers. An Olmec relief from southern Mexico, above, is usually identified as a man in a jaguar headdress; von Däniken sees an extraterrestrial in a space helmet.

Seen from the air, giant intaglio figures, one measuring 180 feet, in the desert near Blythe, California, resemble shapes at

Nazca, Peru. Von Däniken has proposed that prehistoric man tried to communicate with beings from outer space.

greatest support for his imaginative theories about the acculturation of the Americas. Archeologists are the first to admit that this intriguing, eerily beautiful country may hold a wealth of information in archeological sites yet to be uncovered. There are great gaps in the historical record to date, and ancient cultures, their very existence unsuspected, have come to light within recent memory.

One of the most bewildering areas near the southern coast of Peru is the brown level plain at Nazca, crisscrossed by long straight lines that, from the ground, seem to end on the far horizon. Scattered among the trapezoidal and triangular lines are huge shapes clearly delineated in the unchanging desert. These gigantic figures, highly stylized, depict birds, a monkey, and other animals, many of which actually exist in the eastern Andes, hundreds of miles away.

What is the meaning of this sprawling, abandoned plain, with its reverberations of the strange and secret? Despite the many important studies that these enigmatic lines have prompted, particularly the work of German mathematician Maria Reiche, they are still "mysteries of the desert," as she calls them.

Before such conundrums, diffusionists like von Däniken believe that entirely new approaches are essential: "The story of Man's origins is instilled into him in the form of a pious fairy story." And thus he interprets the lines at Nazca as landing fields for ancient spacecraft. For the imaginative von Däniken is more likely to base his conclusions upon familiarity with the ideas of physicists than with the conventional notions that find

acceptance among most traditional archeologists.

Whatever his evidence, von Däniken is only the most recent, and perhaps most widely kown, representative of the thinking that seeks an explanation for the glorious diversity of the American past in the likelihood of outside influence.

The controversy over transoceanic migration will not soon be laid to rest. The typical diffusionist looks for resemblances between American and Old World cultures as proof of interpenetration. On the other hand the Americanist, or isolationist, using a very different approach, almost automatically dismisses apparent similarities as, to use the academic term, "convergences." In this view, cultures sometimes develop along similar lines, and the resulting art or ritual or social organization may coincidentally arise in completely isolated civilizations.

In support of their point of view, the Americanists are likely to stress the negative. That is, why are only some similarities readily apparent? Why, they ask, would a highly sophisticated European-based culture bring an art motif or a religious rite to the New World but neglect to spread such essentials of Western daily life as the use of wheeled vehicles? Why must so much be inferred, so little proved? Why did the allegedly wanderng Egyptians, Phoenicians, Celts, and visitors from outer space leave no verifiable evidence behind, when ancient sites all over the Americas are chock-full of local ceramics, bones, ornaments, and waste products? As one writer has wryly commented, these early visitors must have been remarkably courteous in cleaning up their litter.

MIRRORS OF CULTURE

Remarkable similarities between the cultural relics of the Far East and the ancient Americas suggest to some that there were transpacific voyages in the distant past. Could the Chinese or Japanese have discovered America?

Dim as the past may be, the obscurity is deepened by our own inability to see properly. We wear the blinders of cultural bias. Thus most North and South Americans tend to look across the Atlantic to the Old World as the cradle of civilizations, but it is around the rim of the broad Pacific Ocean that we find suggestions of earlier contact between the ancient peoples of Asia and the native Americans of thousands of years ago.

Archeologists and anthropologists have documented numerous similarities between contemporaneous cultures on or near the Pacific coasts of the American and Asian continents. As we shall see, many curious motifs in ancient American art, so odd as to seem unique when seen in isolation, might in fact reflect Asian themes.

Had the centuries, then, seen an acceptance of the existence of America on the part of knowledgeable thinkers in the countries of the Far East? Did ancient adventurers from such highly successful and distinctive civilizations as China, India, and Japan not only know about the Americas but also visit and influence the natives living there?

For the definitive answer, archeologists must discover an "oopart," or "out-of-place-artifact." Perhaps, for example, some fortunate scholar will find a fragment of Japanese pottery buried in an Ecuadoran grave. A simple Buddhist talisman might be hidden in one of the presumed numerous sites still to be explored by professional archeologists. To date, however, no such artifact has been found — at least not one that has received the respect of traditional scholars in this field. The debatable possibility of transpacific contacts in pre-Columbian times has been pieced together from ancient Chinese annals, such lore as the currents and wind patterns of the inappropriately named Pacific, and most important of all, parallels in art motifs that have been described as cultural mirrors.

One of the most intriguing indications of Asian influence upon ancient America was discovered along the coast of Ecuador in 1956. There, on a slope adjacent to the barren salt flats near the fishing village of Valdivia, an archeologist uncovered a type of pottery not found elsewhere in the New World. Manufactured about

Posed with the dignity of an eastern Buddha, this 6th-century wooden Maya figure sports a handlebar moustache, as do some ancient Chinese funerary figurines. This Mexican artifact might indicate Oriental contact with the Americas.

5,000 years ago, Valdivia ware was then the oldest known pottery in America. These early inhabitants of Valdivia were most probably hunters, fishermen, and gatherers. They lived largely on food from the sea, as evidenced by the shell fishhooks and pebble sinkers found among the fragments of pottery.

Unlike the work of other contemporary pre-Columbian cultures, such as the peoples to the north in Mexico and to the south in Peru, Valdivian pottery is characterized by a diversity of shapes and decorative techniques — a style that has been called "incongruous." Suddenly, it would seem, a highly developed and varied body of ceramic work appears in the archeological record, virtually out of nowhere. Simpler ware, indicating a line of development, is not in evidence at the Valdivia site.

What explains this burst of artistic inspiration and technical competence in a fairly isolated, seemingly unimportant coastal settlement? The answer might well lie more than 8,000 nautical miles away across the Pacific, in the Japanese islands of Honshu and Kyushu. Pottery found at Valdivia bears a striking resemblance to pottery of the Jomon culture of Japan made in the same period, about 3000 B.C. For example, a unique type of castellated rim found on a red-clay incised vessel in Valdivia has been found to exist in great quantities at Jomon sites. It is rare anywhere else in the world, so far as is known for this time period. But perhaps even more significant to scholars interested in Valdivia and its history is the fact that Jomon ceramics are clearly part of a tradition that can be traced back to simple vessels as old as 9,000 years (7000 B.C.). In other words, what is missing in Valdivia has been discovered in Japan, a tradition of pottery-making that can be seen evolving over several millennia. The flowering of technique and esthetic appeal that seems inexplicable in Valdivia is, by contrast, shown to be a slow, progressive development in the islands of Japan.

To archeologists Betty J. Meggers and Clifford Evans, who investigated the Valdivia potsherds, the answer to this puzzle was obvious. They proposed that the art of pottery-making was introduced to Valdivian villagers by Japanese fishermen who made an unexpected landfall in Ecuador some 4,000 years before the Vikings reached the shores of North America. How likely is such contact? No doubt the Jomon fishermen were fearless on the water and had learned how to survive the vicissitudes of the Pacific. Typhoons are born not far to the south of Japan, and some of the Pacific's strongest currents race near the southern shore of Kyushu. Possibly, blown off course and far from home, a boatload of Jomon fishermen found themselves in a current traveling slowly, but insistently, north of Hawaii, southeastward down the North American shore, and then southward to Ecuador. How could anyone survive such a rigorous and lengthy voyage that would have taken months? Supporters of diffusionist theory point out that these ancient sailors

The Oriental look of this round-bellied, almond-eyed Mexican terracotta figure (1400–1150 B.C.) helps to fuel the debate about possible influence from the Far East. Could it be modeled on a Japanese Sumo wrestler? Diffusionists find another Oriental tradition represented on a Moche ceramic vessel. Above right, a fisherman retrieves a fish from a restrained bird, much as Japanese fishermen have used cormorants for centuries. Below right, an Inca ruler appears in state with the two symbols of Andean power, the litter and the parasol. In Asia, too, these privileges were granted only to the elite.

would have been inured to exposure to the elements and would probably have known how to cope with hunger and thirst on long sea voyages.

If this is so, it raises a question in many minds. Why not other indications of contact? Perhaps other evidence decayed, or perhaps it has simply not been found yet. Perhaps it was only in the making of pottery that the Jomon fishermen saw a cultural gap that could be closed with relative ease. In any event, samples of pottery from Valdivia and from Jomon sites show such a great number of decorative and technical parallels that diffusionists feel these similarities cannot be explained as mere coincidence.

Whether or not the amazed villagers of the Valdivia

region in fact looked up one day to find the exhausted Jomon fishermen bearing gratefully toward shore, it was to be some 3,500 years before another major trans-pacific contact might have occurred.

According to the 7th-century Chinese records of the Liang Dynasty kept by the historian Li Yen, a Buddhist priest named Hui-Shen had sailed eastward from China to the land of Fu-Sang in the 5th century A.D. The priest reported that the kingdom of Fu-Sang was a peaceful, if strange paradise, without armies or taxes. The Fu-Sang tree provided the inhabitants with food and bark for the making of cloth and paper. Copper was used, but not iron, and neither gold nor silver was treasured.

Unlike many tales of adventure-filled sea journeys and marvelous discoveries of lands beyond the horizon, Hui-Shen's account is convincingly down-to-earth. The priest paid attention to all manner of domestic details, almost as if he were accurately scouting the land for missionaries to follow. He noticed carts pulled by horses and cattle and that the people kept herds of deer and made a "creamy substance . . .out of their milk." He remarked about red pears that could be eaten year round and the abundant supply of grapes. He reckoned the maritime journey to be approximately 20,000 li, about 7,000 nautical miles, which indeed is close to the distance the Chinese would have to travel to reach North America.

Once again, there are those who will argue that the currents across the northern Pacific could easily have swept a ship toward the Alaskan shore and then southward to a landfall in Mexico or "our own fair California," as one proud writer has surmised. (How Hui-Shen returned to China to tell his tale, however, is not as easily explained.)

It is not difficult to match some of Hui-Shen's descriptions with what is known of life along the coasts of the Americas in the 1st millennium A.D. The Fu-Sang tree is not unlike the century plant found in the Americas, and we know that copper was used in Mexico but not iron. On the other hand, wheeled carts and beasts of burden were unknown in Mexico, and the fruit of the century plant is neither pear-shaped nor red.

The story was debated back and forth during the 19th century, with critics concluding that if Fu-Sang ever existed it best described an island off the shore of Japan; Fu-Sang became a poetical term for Japan in Chinese literature. At the 1875 meeting of the International Congress of Americanists held at Nancy in France, Fu-Sang was on the agenda and provoked a heated argument. The exasperated delegate from Austria, Frédéric de Hellwald, hoped that "the Congress of Nancy would render a true service to science in declaring that it holds the Fu-Sang theory to be a scientific sea serpent and in forbidding it to infest henceforth the latitudes of Americanism."

The "blown across" theory was a favorite explanation for Pacific as well as for Atlantic crossings. In 1827

What could be more tranquilly Oriental than this bedecked deity emerging from a lily as do some Eastern divinities? Yet this clay figure (A.D. 700–900) is a Maya work.

an Englishman, John Ranking, revealed an unbridled imagination by calling his work *Historical Researches on the Conquest of Peru and Mexico in the Thirteenth Century by Mongols, Accompanied with Elephants.* In it he claimed that the Inca civilization of Peru owed its origins to ships' crews of the 13th-century Chinese emperor Kublai Khan, whose armada, intended for the conquest of Japan, was scattered by a great storm. Surviving vessels were blown, along with their elephants, across the Pacific. Another 19th-century writer proposed an alternate theory. In 1836 he suggested that a party of Koreans, to escape their tyrannic conquerors, had abandoned their homeland to found a colony across the sea. After a nine-week voyage, the Coreans (as the writer styled them) discovered a new land. "This land [called] Santini, very reasonably, supposes to be America," he wrote. "This information . . . tends to prove beyond the possibility of a doubt, that the Coreans were the first that visited the new world from Asia."

An even more curious tale of a transpacific crossing involved the young conqueror Alexander the Great of Macedonia. According to the story, after Alexander died suddenly of a fever in 323 B.C., his powerful fleet of many ships headed east from the Persian Gulf, only to vanish into thin air. The theorist has suggested that the remnants of his lost fleet later turned up on the shores of America where the survivors established great civilizations.

Are these tales of daring just so many colorful legends that have sprung up over the centuries, like the claim that Coronado's men sighted strange ships, with figureheads of golden pelicans, at the Colorado River in 1540? Or like the 16th-century report by a Franciscan friar who spotted "eight sail" of exotic ships near the Pacific coast of Mexico?

Artistic Parallels

Without tying their speculations to these or other specific accounts, scholars have indeed claimed support for the theory of contact between the Americas and Chinese or related Asian cultures. The Han Dynasty (202 B.C. to A.D. 220) has been especially appealing to transpacific diffusionists because a certain cylindrical tripod pottery dominant in that period was in use at roughly the same time in central Mexico and in the highlands of Guatemala. This distinctive form seems unrelated to other common pottery shapes in use in Mesoamerica. Teotihuacán ceramics sometimes have lids with rings, birds on the tops of lids, and other motifs that resemble vessels made during the Han Dynasty. In addition, the use of molds to make flat appliqués seems to point to Chinese influence.

Art is often a richer source of diffusionist evidence than technical invention. One can argue that similar implements found in widely separated cultures represent a functional answer to similar problems. Artistic motifs, on the other hand, by definition express the unique cultural perspective of a particular civilization.

Why would a highly stylized rendering, say, or an unusual mythological figure be found in the art of two apparently unrelated cultures?

Gordon Ekholm, a leading American transpacific diffusionist, has compiled intriguing lists of cultural similarities in support of his contention that "the several growth centers of early civilization in the Old World — Egypt, the Near East, India, and China — were variously interrelated." Asiatic influence, he believes, can be shown quite strikingly in the famous "wheeled toys" that have been uncovered in Mexico. The small clay figures of animals have puzzled scholars since they were discovered in ancient tombs in the 1940's. Why would a culture use the wheel in playthings and not apply its principle to the problems of everyday adult life? Could the ancient Americans have really been so blind as not to infer the large-scale employment of this tiny device? Leaving such questions aside, Ekholm decided that the so-called toys were, in fact, derived from the better-known cult chariots, similar miniature vehicles that were widely used in Bronze Age Europe and the Near East. The concept had reached China by the time of the Han Dynasty, usually in the form of two-wheeled little birds. Ekholm's compilations of historical connections also include Mesoamerican mirrors that resemble Chinese bronze mirrors, thin copper axes used as money by the Aztec that recall Chinese knife and ax currency, and clay stamps found in Mexico and Peru that seem to be functionless copies of seals from India or the Near East.

Robert Heine-Geldern, a colleague of Ekholm's and a distinguished Orientalist, has speculated that the Chinese of the Chou and Han dynasties undertook a period of maritime expansion that included planned voyages to and from the western hemisphere as early as 700 B.C. By about A.D. 200, India and other Asian lands had entered the trade, which "was never really interrupted until the 9th, or perhaps, the 10th century A.D. Why it finally ended, we do not know." Thus, for as long as 1,600 years, Asian vessels were supposedly making their way back and forth across the Pacific well before Columbus crossed the Atlantic. Did the adventurers bring with them their art, agriculture, calendars, writing, architecture, and perhaps even their philosophy about the universe?

The art of the Americas offers many intriguing par-

The "pensive prince" pose of a 7th-century Chinese Buddhist figure, above, appears often in Asian art as an attribute of divinity. The pose seems to be repeated in the Maya figure at right, which dates from about the same time.

allels. Lotus friezes carved in the 2nd century A.D. in the Amaravati region on India's east coast have an odd resemblance to water-lily friezes in Chichén Itzá's Temple of the Jaguars in the Yucatán. According to Heine-Geldern, it is significant that the root stalks, buried out of sight in a muddy lake bottom in nature, are depicted in both friezes as undulating ornamental creepers. In both the Mexican and Indian works, reclining human figures are shown grasping the vines with both hands. A similar representation has also been discovered at Uxmal in the Yucatán. Coincidence? Proof of cross-cultural esthetic influence? The answer depends on the likelihood that two artistic traditions would have created this unusual motif independently of each other. A Hindu-Buddhist sea-monster, the *makara,* is very like the so-called serpent of Maya art. Both creatures have wide open mouths, elephantine trunks, great teeth protruding powerfully from upper jaws, and, sometimes, fishlike bodies. In the art of India, Southeast Asia, Maya Mexico, and Guatemala, the monster is frequently shown disgorging a human from its mouth.

A complex three-headed monster in the Cham art of Cambodia may have been copied at Chichén Itzá. Palenque's Temple of the Cross has a cosmic tree in relief that stylistically resembles the cosmic tree in traditional Javanese shadow-play figures; in both cases, a demoniac face is shown in the tree's branches. Elephant-headed figures, perhaps derived from the popular Hindu god

Ganeśa, have been identified in a Oaxacan relief and a stone statue from El Salvador. Other stylistic affinities have been noted between rows of colonnettes used decoratively on panels of buildings in the Yucatán and those used as window gratings in ancient Khmer temples in Cambodia. This particular style may have been derived from lathe-turned wooden or stone prototypes. If so, the argument for Asiatic influence is further strengthened, for the lathe was not widely known in the ancient Americas.

Games, Customs, and Religion

In addition to artistic parallels, diffusionists have been puzzled by a wide range of cultural similarities, from religious ideas to the popularity of a board game. Some observers have remarked upon the resemblance of the Aztec game *patolli* to the Hindu Indian game *pachesi* (played today as the board game Parcheesi)—contests of chance that featured counters moved in a cross-shaped pattern. In both Mesoamerica and the cultures of Southeast Asia, political and social rank was often symbolized by thrones, litters, umbrellas, or fans mounted on poles. The Asian custom of divination from entrails was practiced in Peru. The Mexican belief in a succession of worlds, each to be destroyed by catastrophe and then replaced by a new world, is echoed in a Buddhist belief. The idea of hell and its torments is similar in Southeast Asia and in Mesoamerica.

Furthermore, considerable discussion has centered upon the similarities between the Hindu and Mexican calendar systems. Each is organized around certain mythological and religious associations; why would a god in Asia have the same associated animal attributes and religious concepts as his apparent counterpart in Mexico? Diffusionists feel that the sequential order of the gods' appearance in each calendar is so similar as to demonstrate conclusively that Asian ideas were transmitted to Mexico. They feel it persuasive that, for example, the gods of destruction in both pantheons are usually associated with the moon, while the deities of fertility are generally linked with the sun.

A diffusionist finds it significant that China shared with Peru many cultural practices: the building of great walls and elaborate terraces for agriculture, the placing of a coin or metal disk in the mouth of a corpse, the engineering of suspension bridges, the use of tally strings for mathematical computation and record-keeping. In fact, one scholar has even made a list of 95 Peruvian place names that he claims have no meaning in any local language, only in Chinese. Yet the accumulation of all these shared traits is still not sufficient to convince a majority of scholars.

Also, too much that is known about the Asiatic civilizations comes into conflict with diffusionist thinking because the dates do not meld properly.

What is known of the Chou Dynasty in China, which according to Heine-Geldern initiated contact, suggests that like Dynastic Egypt it was a land power,

Chinese Anchor Stones?

Skeptics will not believe that Chinese sailors discovered America before Columbus until an Asian artifact is found on the American soil. Would not Asian adventurers leave some evidence behind? In 1975 an exciting underwater find off the coast of Los Angeles seemed to some archeologists to be the long-sought crucial proof. Between 20 and 30 large stones, one of them weighing as much as half a ton, littered the sea floor at depths of 12 to 30 feet. Worked by human hands into such various geometric shapes as cylinders and doughnuts, the stones have grooves or drilled holes, evidently to secure ropes. According to one anthropologist, similar stones were common in the Far East from 500 to 1,000 years ago. But archeologist James R. Moriarity III was persuaded that an ancient Chinese vessel foundered at the site. Historian Frank J. Frost disagrees, contending that the stones were carved from shale indigenous to the California coast and suggests that 19th-century Chinese immigrants, many of them experienced fishermen, lost the anchors while fishing at sea. But the few existing period photos show only American iron anchors on immigrant craft. Once again, an archeological find seems to deepen rather than solve a mystery.

limiting its seagoing ventures to coastal voyages at best. The later Han Dynasty is believed to have utilized junks, some 60 feet long, but there is serious doubt as to their suitability for ocean voyaging. In 1974 Kuno Knöbl attempted to sail a replica of one of these junks, called *Tai Ki,* from Hong Kong to Mesoamerica. Its sailing performance was poor, and after its hull was riddled by wood-boring shipworms it had to be abandoned in midpacific. Even without this mishap, the vessels on which the *Tai Ki* was modeled appear to have had a poor chance of crossing 7,000 miles of ocean, and returning, on any kind of planned basis. Indeed, Chinese navigators did not venture as far as Ceylon in the Indian Ocean until the 4th century A.D. and did not make regular visits to Japan until the 6th century.

Some of the artistic parallels cited by diffusionists are separated not only by the wide Pacific but widely in time. For example, by what process would influences of China's late Chou style, which thrived in the years 700 to about 200 B.C., survive both time and distance to reappear in the Classic Veracruz decorative style of the years A.D. 500 to 1000? The similarities between art of the two periods is arresting, but the contribution of the donor culture seems to come much too early.

The determined diffusionist has a reasonable answer

The wheels of a toy deer or dog (Veracruz, A.D. 800–1200), above, may indicate Asian influence, since the wheel was not used in ancient America.

Some 200 years before this terracotta vase was made in Mesoamerica, similar decorative motifs were used on tripod vessels belonging to China's Han period (202 B.C.–A.D. 220).

The familiar dragon motif of Chinese art may have been the inspiration for the painted ceramic double flute, left, an unusual Veracruz artifact (Late Classic period c. A.D. 550–950).

29

to this problem of chronological fit. It is possible that an artistic style was continued in a perishable material, like wood, and that the gulf in time is only an apparent one. It can also be argued that the main aspect of the style in question passed along to the periphery of the donor culture, where it was maintained longer than in the heart of the civilization, and from there it was slowly diffused to the Americas. As for the absence of examples of a motif early enough in time in the donor culture, it has been proposed that the existence of earlier examples can be inferred, since related ideas are known to have existed for a long time.

Still, another major problem, the difficulty of breasting the treacherous Pacific storms and currents, coupled with the grueling length of the trip, also lends itself more to conjecture than to evidence. However, even scholars who think it unlikely that ancient inhabitants of Asia ever planned an expedition to the Americas are willing to concede that accidental trips could have taken place.

Thor Heyerdahl, the well-known writer-explorer who tested his theories by sailing across both the Pacific and the Atlantic in primitive-style crafts, took the sanguine view that "an ocean has pathways as alive as a river," unlike such other natural barriers to man's travel as desert, swamp, jungle, or tundra. He suggested that the prevailing winds and currents of the world's two great oceans form "conveyor-belts," which connect the land masses on both shores.

Heyerdahl contends that the uneasiness with theories of transpacific travel in ancient times on the part of some scholars might stem, at least in part, from their unfamiliarity with oceanography and marine geography. Despite what most people see when glancing at a map, for example, the path of the Japan Current up through the northern avenues of the Pacific is actually shorter and straighter than a route from Japan to Ecuador following the line of the Equator. Another little-understood factor is the role of the current in determining how far a boat must actually travel from one point to another. Heyerdahl notes that, although the "dead distance" from Peru to the Tuamotu Islands is about 4,000 miles, his experimental westward voyage on the raft *Kon-Tiki* required that he cross only 1,000 miles because "the ocean surface itself was displaced about 3,000 miles . . . during the time needed for the crossing." The same craft, reversing the trip, would have had to travel the equivalent of about 7,000 miles. He calculated that an aboriginal craft traveling a surface speed of 60 miles a day could make the crossing westward from Peru to the Marquesas in 40 days, but would need 200 days to accomplish the return voyage.

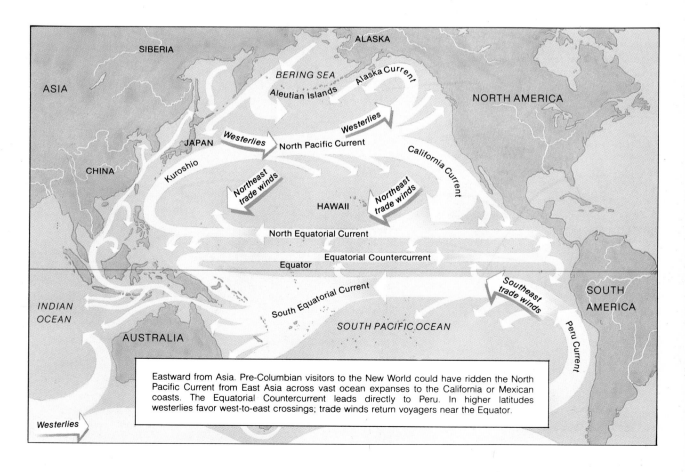

Eastward from Asia. Pre-Columbian visitors to the New World could have ridden the North Pacific Current from East Asia across vast ocean expanses to the California or Mexican coasts. The Equatorial Countercurrent leads directly to Peru. In higher latitudes westerlies favor west-to-east crossings; trade winds return voyagers near the Equator.

An 8th-century sculpture, above, at Copán, Honduras, looks very much like an elephant, though some scholars believe it is a macaw. At Uxmal, Mexico, odd projections from a stone frieze on an ancient Maya ruin, at right, suggest trumpeting elephants. How could the stonecutters have known about ancient elephants, such as the mammoth and the mastodon, which disappeared from the New World some 9,000 years earlier?

Heyerdahl, like many others who have come to respect the sailing lore that remains a live tradition in Polynesia today, feels that ancient sailors undoubtedly understood some of these "hidden" factors at work daily in the seas.

But did planned expeditions actually occur? If they did occur, as some claim, then why did they not provoke more than the mere ripple of legend and hearsay that has been noted in the Asiatic cultures? Most importantly, why are there so many improbable gaps? It is difficult for some to imagine that the Mesoamericans would enthusiastically embrace an imported Southeast Asian board game but not adopt the much more culturally significant art of ironworking. Some scholars find the list of correspondences between Asian and Mesoamerican cultures remarkable, but a similar list can be made of basic cultural factors that did not travel to the Americas. What they may have introduced to the New World, when taken together, is considerably less significant than what they could have introduced but did not. If they brought pottery designs with them, why not the potter's wheel? That most basic and useful agricultural tool, the plow, was used in Asia but not in pre-Columbian America. Nor did the architectural in-novation of the true arch reach the New World. The voyagers failed to introduce such basic Asian crops as rice and millet, nor did they bring with them their domesticated animals; the pig would surely have been welcomed by the protein-short Americans. On their return voyages, the visitors did not take away with them such staples as maize or tobacco, both of which were enthusiastically received in Asia when introduced after the Spanish Conquest; had they been introduced earlier, that fact would surely not have escaped the notice of the careful Chinese historians.

We might suppose that the Asian visitors could have decided to keep some of their technology secret or that certain aspects of Southeast Asian life would simply not appeal to Mesoamericans living in entirely different physical and social circumstances. As always, we can listen to those diffusionists who argue that the whole story cannot be known until a great many more archeological sites have been broken open and plumbed to their depths. Thus the search for evidence continues, as does the reinterpretation of known evidence in new and intriguing ways. Possibly the answer to this long-standing mystery may be uncovered in the next dig.

LOST TRIBES IN THE NEW WORLD

Could it be that native populations in the Americas were descended from ancient peoples of the Near East? Some claim that "white" Indians, the progeny of Welsh colonists, roamed the North American continent.

As the wary settlers of the American continent pushed their way stubbornly into the wilderness, out across the plains toward the sun that had just set in a blaze of color, they told stories about strange encounters in a new land. Sitting around the campfire at night, someone would begin a tale about "white" Indians who had been sighted among the crags of the next rugged mountain range.

In one man's version, these curious beings were thought to practice the rites of ancient Israel. Others reported that the Indians they had met spoke a language that evoked the rhythmical sounds of Welsh. One of these mysterious tribes, so the story goes, even cherished a printed Bible.

To some the conclusion was obvious. "White" Indians could exist only if earlier contact had been made by travelers from Old World countries. Europeans must have come to these shores and "gone native," or they had been captured, then forced or seduced into intermarriage. Their progeny would have become creatures of almost inconceivable complexity, still alive to the traditions of European culture but fundamentally adjusted to the demands of life in the dangerous, dramatically beautiful wilds of America.

Even down to the present, stories of "white" Indians live on in the folklore of some regions of the United States. This is not a matter of the occasional light-skinned native American, of the infrequent intermarrying that occurred along the leading edge of settlement of the West. Distinct tribes, living as integral communities, appear in the stories handed down from generation to generation of early settlers. They are "white," and they are "Indian," and the fascination with them underscores how little was actually known about the huge continent that was so quickly being tamed by the Old World's dogged invaders.

Perhaps the most popular of these tales centered on the figure of Prince Madoc ab Owain Gwynedd of Wales. The story, first published in 1584, relates that in the year 1170 Madoc and 120 of his followers fled a civil war in their homeland to make a new beginning across the sea. According to the tale, Madoc and his party landed at Mobile Bay, Alabama, and were thus the first Europeans to settle in America.

"Mint," the Mandan beauty at right, exemplified for 19th-century American artist George Catlin the "pleasing symmetry and proportion of features" that supported the many legends of Indians thought to have European forebears.

Catlin: Painter of the Mandan

"I set out alone, unaided and unadvised, re-solved . . .to rescue from oblivion so much of their primitive looks and customs as the industry and ardent enthusiasm of one lifetime could accomplish," wrote self-taught artist George Catlin. He spurned a legal career in Pennsylvania to brave the frontier and paint the little-known Plains Indians from 1830 to 1836. His naive, but heartfelt and detailed, portraits and action scenes would earn him fame in America and Europe, while introducing urban sophisticates to such tribes as the Sioux, Pawnee, and Comanche. But his "ardent enthusiasm" was reserved for the unusual Mandan, who lived in the upper regions of the Missouri River. Not only did this driven romantic find the women "exceedingly pleasing and beautiful," he also came to believe that their customs and looks clearly indicated an origin different from all other tribes, concluding that "they have sprung from some other origin than that of other North American tribes." He reported that they believed themselves to be "the *first* people created on earth" and was certain that they had "imperfect knowledge" of the great biblical flood, the fall of Adam and Eve, and the "appearance and death of a Saviour."

Catlin wrote that the horned headdress of Chief Four Bears resembled Old Testament Hebrew regalia.

It seems reasonable to assume that Madoc would have had the skill, and perhaps the inspiration, to make the ocean crossing. Seals from ancient Welsh ports show sturdy ships with square-rigged sails that were, no doubt, capable of making long journeys. It was an age of legend, and sailors must have been no less garrulous then than now. Perhaps this gossip of the trade fueled the desires of men whose national folklore celebrated a "magic Country beyond the looking glass of the sea."

Certainly, western Europe was fertile ground for the belief that Madoc's efforts were successful. And, since England's reigning House of Tudor was of Welsh origin, court historians were anxious to press Madoc's claim in order to assert England's New World priority over the Spanish. In 1584, Dr. Powel's *Historie of Cambria* affirmed that the Welsh prince not only discovered North America but also returned home to gather together "more of his own nation, acquaintance, and freends to inhabit that fayre and large countrie, [and] went thither againe." The historian also mentioned the use of "Brytish words and names" throughout Mexico and the report by Cortés that Moctezuma claimed descent from a race that "came from a generation very far, in a little island in the north."

Dr. Powel's account was popularized by many English writers, including Sir Walter Raleigh, whose *History of the World* (1614) notes that native Americans had been heard to use words derived from Welsh. England's renowned skeptic, Samuel Johnson, translated an ancient Welsh ode about Madoc into Latin. In the early 19th century, Robert Southey, who later became Poet Laureate, composed *Madoc:*

"But who can tell what feelings filled my heart,
　　When like a cloud, the distant land arose
Gray from the ocean; . . .when we left the ship,
　　And cleft with rapid oars, the shallow wave,
　　And stood triumphant on another world."

To the Welsh who began to settle in America during the 17th century, the story was made more credible by reports of Welsh-speaking natives. In 1666, Morgan Jones, chaplain to the Governor of Virginia and a Welshman, told of being captured on a trip to the Carolinas by the Tuscarora Indians. It was in "the British tongue" (that is, Welsh) that he learned he would be ransomed without harm.

It was perhaps the first of many such stories. Sometime in the 1660's, a Welsh sailor, washed ashore after a shipwreck in the Atlantic, conversed with North American Indians who not only spoke a form of Welsh but also referred to an ancestral homeland that could have been Great Britain. Travelers in the succeeding years would recount experiences that sounded similar on both significant points: use of the Welsh language and tradition of origin across the Atlantic.

In 1721, a Catholic priest, Father Charlevoix, heard from the Iowa Indians of the "Omans, three days jour-

Painter Catlin reported that the Mandan revered the 9-foot-tall wooden object, center, as symbolic of the "Big Canoe," in which a legendary white man alone survived a great flood. In *annual ceremonies, villagers followed this figure's ancient directive to sacrifice edged tools used in the building of the canoe to prevent a return of the flood waters.*

ney from them, [who] had white skins and fair hair, especially the women." Fourteen years later, a French explorer known to make scrupulous observations, the Sieur de la Verendrye, reached an unusual Missouri River tribe, the Mandan. He was certain that this light-skinned people, who lived in villages laid out with streets and squares, showed at least a trace of European ancestry. He thought he heard the names of Jesus and Mary spoken, and the men he left behind to study the Mandan language found affinities with "the dialect of Brittany," a language with words bearing a resemblance to Welsh.

Later visitors confirmed Verendrye's observations. One young Welshman reported that he saved his own life when captured by "white men in Indian dress" by addressing them in the language native to them, and to him — Welsh. A Louisiana Frenchman who had explored the Missouri told of Indians "rather of a yellowish complexion," many of them red-haired. One settler reportedly paid a visit to a "Welsh tribe" living on the west bank of the Missouri. A Captain Isaac Stewart, traveling up the Red River from the Mississippi, en-

countered "a nation of Indians, remarkably white and whose hair was a reddish colour." The women were beautiful, "high-browed, [with] blueish eyes and perfect lips." The elders of the tribe, according to the captain, said that their ancestors had come from a foreign country to the coast of Florida, and then the Spaniards had driven them toward the West.

Descendants of "White" Indians

Eventually, stories about "white" Indians conversant in the Welsh tongue were to be heard from the Missouri-Mississippi area, the Carolinas, Virginia, Kentucky, Tennessee, Alabama, Florida, and other nearby regions. The American folk hero Daniel Boone thought that a tribe of "Blue-Eyed Indians" he had met was probably related to the Welsh, "though I have no means of assessing their language." Others espied Welsh Indians from the Dakotas to Virginia, and from British Columbia to Mexico and Peru.

John Evans, a young Welshman specially commissioned by enthusiasts of the Madoc legend, traveled from London to America in 1792 to find the supposed descendants of the prince and his followers. He was to report: "In respect of the Welsh Indians, I have only to inform you that I could not meet with such a people, and from intercourse I have had with Indians from latitude 35 to 40 I think you may with safety inform our friends that they have no existence."

But there were dark hints that Evans had been bought off by the Spaniards, who did not want increased British interest in the area. His admission of failure to find "white" Indians did not kill the legend.

In 1804 two U.S. Army officers, Meriwether Lewis and William Clark, were commissioned by President Thomas Jefferson to explore the land included in the Louisiana Purchase. To aid them with their expedition, Jefferson sent Lewis a map of the Missouri River "as far as the Mandans," adding, "It was done by a Mr. John Evans by order of the Spanish Government." In late October of that year Lewis and Clark reported that they reached Mandan settlements, where they spent the winter among the Indians.

Archeological support for the tales of Welsh-speaking Indians has centered upon three ruined forts, apparently of pre-Columbian origin, on sites near Chattanooga — Old Stone Fort, Tennessee; De Soto Falls, Alabama; and Fort Mountain, Georgia. Considered to be unlike native construction in the region, they seem to date back to the 12th century, a few centuries before the Age of Exploration. The Tennessee site, in particular, with its walls and single gateway and moat fed by the Duck River, resembles ancient remains that have been studied in Wales.

Yet it is not in ancient stonework, but in the oral literature shared by Europeans and native Americans, that Madoc and the "white" Indians live on. Even the beloved governor of Tennessee's formative years, John Sevier, helped keep the story alive. He recalled that a Cherokee chief had told him of "the Whites [who] had crossed the Great Water and landed first near the mouth of the Alabama River near Mobile," before being driven off toward the "Muddy [Missouri] River."

What are we to make of these many legends? Do we simply accept the likelihood that history is what we choose to believe? The answer may lie in one's response to the memorial tablet, set up in 1953 at Fort Morgan, Mobile Bay, Alabama: "In memory of Prince Madoc, a Welsh explorer, who landed on the shores of Mobile Bay in 1170 and left behind, with the Indians, the Welsh language." It stands there today, a challenge to the passing doubter.

No such precise location has been marked out as the landing place for the Ten Lost Tribes of Israel. But, as the authors of one volume about early travelers and seafarers have pointed out with some exasperation, their presumed migrations crisscrossed the globe. "Virtually all the peoples on earth," they write, have been identified at one time or another with the vanished descendants of the tribes that rebelled against the rule of Solomon's son, Rehoboam.

According to biblical history, only those two tribes that remained loyal to the king, the tribes of Judah and Benjamin, survived the various invasions, conquests, and massacres that plagued the ancient Middle East. The other ten tribes were carried off by the Assyrians in the second half of the 8th century B.C. The Old Testament mentions the fate of these unfortunate tribes for the last time in 2 Kings 17:23: "So was Israel carried away out of their own land to Assyria unto this day."

This loss was not easily accepted. At times of intensified persecution, surviving Jews were likely to take up rumors of a great, growing Jewish empire somewhere to the east — the legacy of the Lost Ten. During the horrors of the Crusades in the 12th and 13th centuries, for example, many Jews tried to escape to this fabled haven. Their hopes were strengthened by the occasional appearance of self-described "ambassadors," who claimed to represent the Lost Tribes living in the Near East or Iran.

Inevitably, the Age of Exploration opened up new worlds of speculation about the whereabouts of the descendants of the tribes taken away to Assyrian captivity. Where had they gone when that infamous empire collapsed? Could a people that had endured so much in ancient history, and whose two fellow tribes survived such severe trials for the next two millennia, simply disappear from the face of the earth? Would *they* not have won out, even though tribes like the Hittites or the Huns or the Scythians seem to have vanished for all time?

Jewish Ancestors

In 1650, one answer was published, *The Hope of Israel* by Manasseh ben Israel, a rabbi in Amsterdam. He told of a Spanish-Jewish traveler, Antonio de Montezinos, whose Indian guide on a South American trip greeted him with "Shema Israel (Hear, O Israel)." Furthermore, the guide reported that many people "of the same origin" were living in the highlands near Quito, Ecuador. Manasseh dedicated a volume of his work to the English Parliament in the hope that Jews would be readmitted to that land. Biblical prophecy was deeply involved in the rabbi's motive, for he believed that the Messiah would not come until the Jews were scattered to all the ends of the earth. Oliver Cromwell received Manasseh in England and discussed his views, but in the end the rabbi's cause had limited success. General readmission was not granted, though some Jews were permitted to live in London and to establish a synagogue there.

Meanwhile, other religious interpretations were becoming confused with the aims of amateur anthropology. If the Jews had indeed survived, their existence on the American continent might prove that the God of Israel "is a God of truth and righteousness, and that whom he loves, he loves unto the end." Whether or not most observers were seeing what they wanted to see, or what a sincere faith gave them reason to hope to see, travelers in many parts of North and South America began to discover Old Testament customs in practice: ritual calendars, purification rites, circumcision, flood myths, sacrifices to gods, the veneration of a tribal ark. Native Americans were daily acting in ways that a European had previously encountered only in biblical stories about the earliest Jewish prophets and their families.

Numerous parallels were put forth in a book written in the late 18th century by James Adair, a trader in Indian territories for at least 40 years. In chants he heard among the Choctaw and the Chickasaw and their neighbors, he found the name Jehovah. According to Adair, the Indian phrase for dead or lost, "Illeht Kaneha," also meant "gone to Canaan," and the word for winter, "kora," was borrowed unchanged from the Hebrew. He reported that "when the Indians meet at night to gladden and unite their hearts before *Yohewah*," they sing over and over the Hebrew word for Messiah. He also saw Hebraic influence in the ritual oath of a witness before an Indian judge: "I have told you the naked truth, which I most solemnly swear, by this strong religious picture of the adorable, great, divine, self-existent name, which we are not to profane; and I likewise attest it, by his other beloved, unspeakable, sacred, essential name."

Early in the 19th century, a young member of Parliament, Edward King, Viscount Kingsborough, was struck by the beauty and mystery of a Mexican Indian codex, or manuscript, in the Bodleian Library at Oxford. He exhausted his fortune, and perhaps his life, in attempting to prove that the Lost Tribes of Israel were the ancestors of the Indians in Mexico. Nearly half of Adair's book was reprinted by the passionately convinced Kingsborough. But he sank the bulk of his fortune into the publication of nine magnificent volumes of Mexican codices, with commentary, entitled *Antiquities of Mexico*. Twice he was thrown into debtors' prison when he was unable to meet the bills of printers and paper manufacturers; on his release he doggedly continued his publishing efforts. In 1837, imprisoned a third time, he died at the age of 42. He was probably the victim of the infamous "prison disease" typhus, but his friends insisted that the cause of death was a broken spirit. Had he lived a year more he would have inherited his father's estate and a secure income.

Kingsborough, though his ideas were never to gain academic respectability, may indirectly throw some light, by his example, upon the fascination the Lost Ten have held for so many writers, explorers, amateur historians, and people of faith. As the 19th-century historian Hubert Howe Bancroft commented, " . . . we

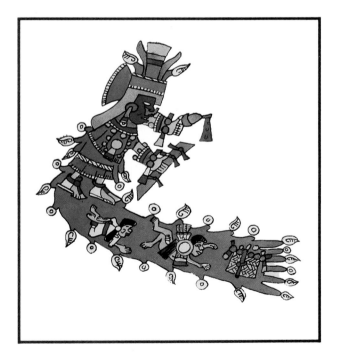

Lord Kingsborough was convinced that the Indians of Mexico were directly descended from Israel's Ten Lost Tribes. As proof, he spent his fortune on reproducing volumes of Aztec codices that, he claimed, illustrated biblical events. The two reproduced here are said to represent the story of Adam and Eve, left, and a primordial deluge, above.

should speak and think with respect of one who spent his lifetime and his fortune, if not his reason, in an honest endeavor to cast light upon one of the most obscure spots in the history of man."

But the story of the Lost Tribes is, for some people, painfully unresolved. Perhaps the disappearance of so many tribes is only too suggestive of the fragility of any nation, of any individual, in opposition to the impassive forces of history. It would be comforting, it might even be inspiring, if someone could prove that among the "white" Indians of the Americas there coursed the blood of the tribes of Reuben, Gad, Ephraim, Zebulun, Simeon, Dan, Asher, Manasseh, Naphtali, and Issachar.

Who Was Quetzalcoatl?

If the Welsh, if the Lost Ten, did not come to America and lose themselves racially in the genetic pools of certain native American tribes, perhaps they simply visited and left an arguably more significant part of themselves — a legend, a promise, a covenant with future generations. Who, otherwise, was the white god that Moctezuma imagined to have reappeared in the person of Cortés? Why is the feathered serpent god of Mexico, Quetzalcoatl, described as a white man who has promised to return and redeem all his followers? Why does the major god of Peru, Viracocha, also resemble a European? It is reasonable to speculate, as many have, that some very gifted human being came to America in ancient times, either by accident or design, and shared his more highly sophisticated knowledge with the native Americans he encountered. Later, perhaps when his sailing vessel was repaired, or he and his cohorts simply wanted to go home, he could have pushed off into the Atlantic, promising to return someday. Over the centuries, this homely event could easily gain the sacred proportions of myth. So, at least, runs a theory that has gained popularity with many laymen. It quite conveniently, of course, puts the European of the tale in the position of a godlike, if not actually divine, being.

There is, however, a serious flaw in the theories of the white-god-as-European. It is only after the Spanish Conquest that Quetzalcoatl is depicted as having a white skin, and then only in accounts provided by the Spaniards themselves. In local Aztec art, he is usually depicted as a feathered serpent or as a human wearing a mask or shown to have a black face, sometimes with yellow stripes and a red mouth. These are symbolic attributes; black, for example, was the color associated with priests. The god's sole link with the color white was equally symbolic. Quetzalcoatl was the personification of the planet Venus as both the Morning Star and the Evening Star. In the latter role, with its suggestions of the sun setting in the west, of the coming of the night and of, therefore, old age and decline and death, Quetzalcoatl was indeed identified with the color white, the hue of skeletons and corpses. Nothing

known of Aztec legend, though, implies that he had been a white man or a European in his human form on earth. Similarly, the Peruvian creator-god Viracocha was not revered by the Inca as a man from another race. Each of these deities, though spending a little while on earth among common men, was by definition non-mortal; each had mythical traits and attributes that had to do with spiritual meaning, not with genealogy.

But what about the beards? Would these not be highly unusual among the native Americans, who, most people assume never grow facial hair? Yet facial hair possessed in varying degrees by various tribes and individuals throughout the Americas could be, as some theorists have proposed, the result of intermingling with foreign populations, who passed on the trait. Ancient instruments designed for the removal of facial hair have been unearthed from Mexico to Peru. A ceramic figure from about A.D. 1000, found in Peru, shows a man using pincers to pluck out his beard hairs.

But to the anthropologist, the beard in pre-Columbian art is more a religious symbol than a literal fact of portraiture. It represented old age, of course, but may

In this illustration from a 16th-century Spanish manuscript, the great Mexican god Quetzalcoatl is light skinned and luxuriantly bearded, but it is unclear whether these attributes were part of the Indian legend or the invention of the Spanish.

About 1,000 years old, the Peruvian ceramic effigy vessel above shows a man plucking unwanted facial hair with a simple tweezers. The decorative gold pair at right, found in Colombia, is further indication that at least some pre-Columbian Indians could grow beards long before the possibility of intermarriage with European colonists.

have had other meanings as well. Stylized depictions of beards are believed to carry some association with ritual. Quetzalcoatl, before he was to leave earthly existence, "made his beard of feathers, of the red spoonbill and the blue cotinga. . . ." When he was shown as the creator of the human race, his beard was meant to symbolize his ancient precedence. And Moctezuma himself sported a light beard.

It is perhaps mere coincidence that both Mexican and Peruvian legends hinted that their national deities might return some day, much as Christ had promised to do. Could there have been an early Christian missionary who spread the teachings of the New Testament from the Mexican highlands down the Andean cordillera? Or, as some believe, did Christ himself become incarnate in the Americas and wander about — tall, white, bearded, fully robed — in an attempt to bring the Gospel to the uncomprehending natives?

In the first place, neither Quetzalcoatl nor Viracocha, by the lights of native believers, had been expected to "return." These promises were noted, long after the fact, by the Spanish chroniclers with wit enough to see the advantages of being taken as actors in the fulfill-

ment of prophecy rather than as greedy marauders. Clearly, the promulgation of this idea might be called the inspiration of a public-relations wizard; it has become so well known and deeply believed that it is not likely soon to be dislodged from the popular fancy. The Spaniards with their cannon and horses and ships that resembled houses on the sea may at first have appeared like supernatural beings, and we know that Moctezuma's waverings and despair cannot easily be explained as the conventional response of an all-powerful ruler dealing with a very small band of human adventurers. But there is little evidence that the Aztec ruler or anyone else in the land thought that the Spanish invasion was a promised Second Coming of the god Quetzalcoatl. As for possible pre-Columbian contact with Christian ideas, any such teaching, if it occurred, was dramatically unsuccessful.

Quite apart from the absence of New Testament thinking or church ritual, there is a startling contrast between the admonitions of the Prince of Peace and some of the favorite activities of Quetzalcoatl. For the Aztec god was worshiped in ceremonies in which tens of thousands of human beings were sacrificed and was

In a 19th-century painting the angel Moroni delivers the golden plates to Joseph Smith on a hillside in New York.

According to Mormon history, these plates told how their ancestors came to America from the "land of Jerusalem."

often portrayed as lustily tearing apart his enemies.

It is wishful thinking, then, or the legacy of Spanish political propaganda that keeps alive the belief that the native Americans were eagerly awaiting the coming of the white man in the 16th century. So far as is known today, the existence of such a being had never been imagined by the Aztec or Inca.

But we are discussing an age that either had no writing or had not known writing for very long and that apparently did not have our own insistence on setting down the facts in as much detail as possible. We are dealing with civilizations that might easily, as some think, have lost touch entirely with the cultural riches of their past. Or, perhaps, beliefs that were once strongly held had become confused, debased, and merely ritualistic as the native American tribes, for millennia, moved back and forth across the Americas, warring and intermarrying and assimilating ideas.

In that case, it is easier to understand why the history given in *The Book of Mormon* has not yet been documented by archeological evidence or echoed in native American folklore. This doctrinal work, which Joseph Smith said he translated from golden plates found in western New York State early in the 19th century, chronicles in detail the history of one people who came

from Israel to Mesoamerica. It does not, as some have mistakenly assumed, show the Lost Ten Tribes of Israel emigrating to America.

The Mormon story begins with an exodus to America immediately after the doomed attempt to build the Tower of Babel. The first group, called the Jaredites, left Nimrod's folly behind to cross the Pacific and found a great civilization, possibly in Mexico. The lesson of Babel must have been forgotten, however, for they defied the Lord and were eventually punished with total destruction, perhaps around 600 B.C. Nonetheless, other groups set out from Jerusalem for the New World at about the time of the Jaredite collapse. According to the story, followers of the prophet Lehi split when they landed in Mesoamerica. The Nephite faction became a ruling tribe in the area. At the same time, according to *The Book of Mormon,* some descendants of Judah arrived and eventually joined with the Nephites. These peoples were thought to have built many of the great pre-Columbian cities of Mesoamerica. The Lamanites, who became their bitter enemies, constituted a rival ruling tribe.

Like the Jaredites before them, both Lamanites and Nephites continually forgot the ways of God, and on more than one occasion they suffered the retribution of war, fire, and earthquakes. At one point, the newly resurrected Christ manifested himself before the Nephites and sent disciples to preach his message throughout the land. The Nephites and those they ruled proved incorrigible, however, and were finally wiped out in a horrendous battle near a "narrow neck of land" in Nephite territory. It is unclear how the golden plates reached New York State, where Smith would find them some 1,000 years later.

No other document, inscription, or legend now known shows a close correspondence with this account of the peopling of America, but there are tempting inferences that can be drawn from the evidence that does exist.

Was the myth of Quetzalcoatl a corruption of the tradition that Christ had visited America in pre-Columbian times? Some have seen a reference to the personified Morning Star in Revelation 22:16: "I Jesus have sent mine angel to testify unto you these things in the churches. I am the root and the offspring of David, and the bright and morning star." Attempts have been made to reconcile the radiocarbon dates of various sites in Mexico with *The Book of Mormon*'s chronicle of events. A form of ritual sacrifice practiced in veneration of the Mexican hunting god has been linked by some with the crucifixion, because the human victim, before being slain by a shower of arrows, would be lashed to a kind of cross-shaped bracket. It has been noted that native Americans confessed their sins before death, practiced a type of baptism, and sometimes went off on pilgrimages. In the *Popol Vuh*, a collection of traditional myths sacred to the Quiche Maya, there are many familiar-sounding tales: the miraculous parting of a sea when fugitives appear on its banks, a great deluge, the handing down of holy law to priests on a mountain.

These suggestive items, however, are not found convincing by traditional scholars of ancient America. They feel that each can be explained as coincidence, as *ex post facto* European influence, or as muddling of the evidence. A Mormon believer might not necessarily feel that the literal truth of the history of the Jaredites, Lamanites, and Nephites has to be (or can be) objectively proved.

The Mystifying Melungeons

What the warring tribes of Joseph Smith's golden plates have in common with the Welsh-speaking Indians and with the Lost Ten Tribes is, quite simply, that no descendants step forth today claiming kinship. Most of the lost tribes who have disappeared into the vast American continents are still "lost," with nothing but tradition and the written word to testify that they once existed.

In certain parts of America, however, there are small communities of people who seem, to their immediate neighbors, to be inexplicably different. These tiny populations are not lost, even if they are isolated, but their origins are lost, either because of policy or badly frag-

mented oral traditions. They may not see themselves as "white" or "Indian" or "black," and it may seem likely that they originated in lands across the sea and reached America within the not-too-distant past.

Along the Virginia-Tennessee border, for example, there still live groups of families in the sparsely settled mountains of Hancock County, Tennessee, who have become known as Melungeons, perhaps because they look to outsiders like a racial mixture, or *mélange*. These rather reclusive farmers have a rich store of folktales but do not know precisely how their forebears came to the area. Some claim that Melungeons were in Tennessee long before the local Indians and certainly before the coming of the European settlers.

Described as having reddish-copper skin, straight hair, thin lips, and narrow-shaped faces, these people have impressed observers with their air of caution, their quick intelligence, and their handsome features.

Are they part Portuguese, the descendants of a Portuguese fleet known to have been wrecked off the coast of North Carolina in 1665? Survivors could have easily made their way inland and found brides among the Cherokee. Are they part Spanish, descended from a band that deserted the forces of Hernando de Soto as he went west toward the Mississippi River Valley not far to the west? Are they part British, the remnants of Sir Walter Raleigh's storied Lost Colony on the Atlantic shore to the east? Could their ancestry go back to the Ten Lost Tribes, to the explorations of Prince Madoc, to the mysterious "Woodland People" whose civilization flowered nearby and then vanished, to a small group of Moors who are thought to have sailed from Portugal to South Carolina about the time of the American Revolution? At least one property rights case was won in a Tennessee court when the plaintiff's lawyer argued successfully that she was not black but kin with a "lost and hounded people, originally Phoenicians."

Here, then, is a mystery of a lost tribe in reverse, and the puzzling question of its origins continues to intrigue observers, who have seriously proposed all of the above possibilities as explanations. It must be said, however, that certain skeptical writers are more inclined to believe that this small group of Melungeons is really a clan descended from one or two Indians or blacks who intermarried locally. These "white" Indians, in that case, would be of very recent origin.

We remain in the sphere of unsolved mystery. Can we ever know for certain that so-called Lost Tribes did not actually travel to America and struggle to survive? Perhaps they were massacred, or perhaps they simply succumbed to the unfamiliar hardships of the new environment. Perhaps they made their peace with the new continent by assimilating gradually, and gratefully, so that in the end the only physical record of their having arrived would be the bluish-green eyes of a dark-skinned Indian child, or a pale cast to the skin of an entire tribe.

ISLANDS IN THE MIST

The search for legendary islands has intrigued men
from Plato's time to the present. But the fabled and exotic
Lemuria, Atlantis, and St. Brendan's Land of Promise
are yet to be discovered.

Christopher Columbus, that most celebrated of
adventurers, was pragmatic enough to mount a
complex expedition, an enterprising exercise in
preparing for the unknown. He was also politically
gifted enough to satisfy the aims of his backers while
cleverly allaying the fears of his sailors. That fortuitous
combination of virtues alone would not have enabled
him to succeed had he not also been "one of the greatest seamen of all time," according to his biographer
Samuel Eliot Morison. But a journey into the dark
regions far westward in the forbidding Atlantic must
also have had, even for Columbus, the aura of a dream.

Columbus most probably expected to encounter *In-
sula antilia septe citades* ("Antilia, the Isle of the Seven
Cities") on his route from the Canaries to "the Indies."
Scholars disagree over whether the canny explorer believed he would also find St. Brendan's legendary
"Land Promised to the Saints," which Prince Henry
the Navigator, Portugal's indefatigable patron of maritime daring, had sent some of his restless seamen to
locate in 1431. Predictably, there were those who believed that among the new lands discovered in the Age
of Exploration was one that would vindicate the classical tales of the lost continent of Atlantis. Some speculated that the Canaries, the Azores, and other islands of
the Atlantic were fragments of the vanished landmass.
Others believed that the New World in its entirety was
the long-lost site of Atlantean civilization.

The lack of factual evidence, however, did not deter
cartographers from simply sketching in many of the
fabled islands on the largely imaginative maps of the
15th century (and later), precisely delineating positions.
The Pizzi Nautical Chart of 1424 positions Antilia,
meaning "island opposite," westward of the Pillars of
Hercules at the entrance to the Mediterranean Sea. It is
shown as a large, rectangular island with its seven cities
clearly indicated — Vra, Marnlio, Cyodne, and the
like. The Pizzigani Chart of 1367 shows the island of
Mayda (Man, Mam), which still appeared on a published map as late as 1841. In a Portuguese book of
sailing directions dated 1514, a chapter on "Courses
for the Islands *not yet* discovered" gives instructions
for finding the *Septe citades* to the south of Newfoundland. Almost every 15th-century chart of the Atlantic

*The Cantino map of 1502, named for the envoy who secretly
commissioned it for an Italian map collector, presented the
New World with remarkable accuracy. The detail at right
shows the Antilles islands and northeastern South America.*

Circulus articus·

Occanus occidentalis

Terra del Rey de portuguall

Has antilhas del Rey de castella·

Est he o mar entre castella· τ portuguall

oda esta terra he descobert· p madado del Rey de castella·

Linha equinocialis·

Tropicus capricorni·

Mare occanus·

Solius antarticus·

depicted the islands of Lovo and Capraria, reputedly discovered by St. Brendan. These islands were found on maps as late as the 18th century.

It is all very well to say that cartographic standards were less restrictive in the days of the great maritime explorers; however, something other than the lack of accuracy is at work in the charts that purport to show the uncharted isles. "Here be sea serpents," was the phrase every schoolchild saw in Renaissance mapmaking, an admonition that dark forces lurk in the unknown. On the other hand, the "Islands *not yet* discovered," when drawn upon the map, give the message, "Here also be paradises," as if the mind of man insists that the unknown holds bright and lovely secrets, too.

A most charming account of blessed islands beyond the watery horizon is the *Navigatio Sancti Brendani,* the story of St. Brendan's voyage. Written perhaps as early as the 8th century, some 200 years after the holy father's death, the story became enormously popular all across Europe. It was translated into many languages and down through the centuries has been read with affection and wonder.

The Celtic saint is an appealing figure, quite apart from the poetic quality of many of his reported adventures. Evidently more activist than mystic, he is known to have founded two monasteries in Ireland in the mid-6th century, the more famous being Clonfert in County Galway. Historians believe that he probably organized trips by boat to the Hebrides, western Scotland, and possibly to Wales and Brittany.

But it is the *Navigatio,* an unlikely blend of the pious and the plucky, that memorializes Brendan as both an epic hero and a saintly explorer. In another work on the life of Brendan, *Vita Brendani,* he is portrayed as a no-nonsense religious leader who operates with directness and resolve. When some of the monks traveling with him are at odds about whether an object in the distance is a bird or a ship, Brendan says decisively, "Put an end to the discussion and turn the boat towards it."

Did this admirable adventurer actually make the extensive voyage described in the *Navigatio?* Since we know that the so-called Isle of St. Brendan and similar fantastic islands cannot have existed, at least not in the locations ascribed to them in legend and cartography, two possibilities seem likely. These places are either the stuff of fiction or they are actual locations now known under other names. Did the St. Brendan of the *Navigatio* sail only to imaginary lands that are accessible only to the pure in heart in a spiritually instructive tale, or did he and his followers come upon a more earthly landfall, such as the rocky shores of Newfoundland or the sandy beaches of coral isles in the Caribbean?

It can be argued that the *Navigatio* leaves itself open to either interpretation, as a brief summary of its narrative highlights illustrates. In search of the "Land Promised to the Saints," Brendan departs from Clonfert with 17 monks in a *curragh,* a characteristically Irish boat made with a wooden frame covered with animal hides. It probably had a square sail, but oars were the main source of locomotion.

Traveling at an exhaustingly slow pace, the expedition drifts to a steep, rocky island, then to an isle teeming with large, pure-white sheep. At Easter, the saint and his men mistakenly land on the back of a whale, which they take for an island. Just as they start a fire and are preparing breakfast, they feel the ground stir underfoot, and they scarcely have time to scramble back into the boat when the entire islet veers "off and downward."

As the days drag on, the group visits the island called Paradise of Birds, where avian choirs are "perpetually in their ears." Later they come to an island that seems to be a monastic hideaway where they break bread "with a community of twenty-four." Then the holy travelers, subject to the vagaries of tide and wind, helplessly skirt danger and experience novel mysteries: a fight between sea creatures, a patch of water so clear that many kinds of fish can be seen moving on the bottom like "flocks of sheep," a huge crystal column with a canopy the color of silver, and "a rugged island covered with slag . . . destitute of trees or grass. . . . On another day they see a high mountain rising

A 15th-century German account of St. Brendan's bold voyages to uncharted islands shows the abbot and his crew accidentally landing upon the back of Jasconius, the whale.

Could Ireland's beloved St. Brendan have crossed the fierce North Atlantic in a leather boat in the 6th century and landed safely in North America? In 1976–77, British author-sailor Timothy Severin, at right, and his daring crew set out on Brendan's route. Their 36-foot craft, the Brendan, *above, was built of tanned oxhides over an ashwood frame, according to medieval directions. In two spring-summer sailing seasons, the* curragh *braved gales, ice floes, and curious whales to travel the 2,600 miles from Ireland to Newfoundland.*

from the sea . . . smoke pouring from the summit."

In the seven years of this chronicle, Brendan's track would cross back upon itself often, so that many of the islands were revisited. At one point, the horrified monks encounter Judas Iscariot, enjoying a brief respite from his eternal punishment for the betrayal of Jesus. Finally, St. Brendan's patience and oft-expressed faith in the will of God find fruition. Emerging from the midst of a thick cloud, the band sees at last the "Land of Promise," bathed in a brilliant light. It is unlike any island they've visited during their grueling travels. "It was warm, fruitful, bathed in a seemingly endless autumn sunshine. They disembarked and pushed up country for 40 days, viewing the landscape on all sides. . . . Finally they stood on the bank of a great river which glided on into the interior." Brendan, whose imminent death is prophesied by a handsome young man they meet here, leads his followers home.

A chorus of birds, an encounter with a biblical character — these are elements of the fabulous or, at least, the metaphorical. But some interpreters have given the *Navigatio* a more serious reading. The crystal column is perhaps a poetic description of the great icebergs that loom up in the waters west of Greenland. The smoking

mountain might be the volcanic eruption of an island in the Arctic Ocean. The schools of fish in translucent waters could be the coral landscape of the Bahamas. The fog at journey's end brings to mind the fog off the Newfoundland Banks, and the broad expanses of that region, cut by a wide flowing river, resemble the *Navigatio*'s breathtakingly beautiful Land of Promise.

Whether the islands of St. Brendan were landfalls in the North Atlantic and Caribbean or nonexistent images of desire, they were a spur to exploration of the seas to the west. Perhaps Columbus was being purposely ambiguous when, casually referring to St. Brendan's alleged discoveries, he noted aboard ship in 1492 that "therein lay the Earthly Paradise."

Also fated to be lost in legend were the Seven Cities, which were as likely to be located in an imaginary "Brazil" as on the island of Antilia. The 1492 globe of Martin Behaim apparently gives the earliest acknowledgment of this tantalizing tale of escape. It was written on the globe that seven Portuguese bishops led Christian refugees to the island in flight from the Moorish occupation of the Iberian Peninsula, perhaps in 734. A number of other sources report European contact with Antilia in the 15th century. In more than one story, a

Portuguese ship is blown to the isle during a storm and the crew is astonished to find Portuguese-speaking natives. In one account, upon returning to the mainland, the crew discovers that the beach sand scooped up for use in their cook-box sparkles with grains of gold.

There are numerous references to the island throughout the Age of Exploration, a period of discovery that began about 1420 and ended some 200 years later. The references carry the trappings of romance rather than of fantasy — escape from religious persecution, transplanted civilization in a strange land, the familiar behind the horizon, perhaps even a kind of nationalistic pride for the seagoing Portuguese. In short, there seemed no reason to suspect that the well-chronicled island refuge did not exist. As late as 1498, Pedro Ayala, a Spanish ambassador in England, reported to the court of Ferdinand and Isabella that for the past seven years Bristol had dispatched from two to four ships a year "in search of the island of Brazil and the Seven Cities." Neither as Brazil nor as Antilia, however, has the Isle of the Seven Cities ever been found.

It is not surprising that this vast body of "documentation" of nonexistent islands leads only to more confusion, particularly in the matter of nomenclature. Today's Antilles islands in the Caribbean were so named because it was thought by many that Columbus's discovery of the West Indies was actually the discovery of Antilia. Some writers have mistaken references to "the island of Brazil" to indicate the Irish legend of the enchanted island of Hy-Brasil, or O'Brazil, which is a kind of Elysian Fields that floats about the north Atlan-

tic. Nonetheless, from the 14th through the 18th centuries, the island was supposedly glimpsed offshore by fishermen from Ireland's Aran Islands, seen by sailors coming round the Blaskets, and spotted in 1791 by an English sea captain. Professor Thomas J. Westropp of the Royal Irish Academy claimed to have sighted the fabled isle shimmering near the Irish coast in 1872. Part of the persistent appeal of this Gaelic legend may be that, to date, the tempting island has not yet been visited by man. There is some mystical boundary there — it is the land that we can sometimes see but never attain, not in this life.

Yet, as Samuel Eliot Morison has pointed out, attempts to find this land of promise had a practical re-

To dazzled Europeans, the New World sounded like a vestige of the lost Eden. Below, a detail from a highly imaginative 16th-century map shows Brazil as an earthly paradise. Brilliant watercolors of the time depict the parakeet, above, and the pineapple, right, soon prized as a superior fruit.

sult. Bristol merchants backed voyages to seek out Hy-Brasil; these were to have a connection with John Cabot's discovery of North America in 1497. In a sense, Hy-Brasil would be to Cabot what Antilia was to Columbus, the siren call of myth that would lead to major discovery in the real world.

Islands of escape — of the miraculous — of the unattainable. These beloved European traditions are not so well known to contemporary readers, on either side of the Atlantic. The seas are all too accurately charted, in our century.

Atlantis and Lemuria

But there is another type of "lost island" that endures, paradoxically, because it is not simply "lost" but "vanished." It is easier to believe in because it is more difficult to find, since its archetypal legend includes catastrophic destruction that would leave little evidence of the island's existence as a volcano erupts or the earth's crust splits open, and the billowing waters of the sea roll in, obliterating for all time a mighty civilization. So run the legends of Atlantis, a mystery that has tantalized Western minds since Plato first wrote about it. Equally catastrophic are the much later accounts of the popular Pacific counterpart of Atlantis, the continent of Lemuria, or Mu.

There are those who believe that the remains of Atlantis have already been discovered. Of course no inscriptions or currency attesting to its existence have been found, or the news would have become one of our century's journalistic coups. But evidence of the final destruction of sophisticated urban centers before the time of Plato, the 4th century B.C., has been found in more than one location, principally in the eastern end of the Mediterranean. To believe that one of these sites represents the Atlantis of legend is to believe that time, distance, narrative exaggeration, ambiguities of language, and man's credulity transformed a fairly minor local event into a disaster of global proportions.

Even in Plato's day the story was apparently not accepted as historical fact by other classical writers. The kingdom disappears "in a single day and night of misfortune" in Plato's *Timaeus,* but no such kingdom and no such event are chronicled in any earlier historical or mythological writings known to us. In the uncompleted *Critias,* Plato furnished a detailed description of an ancient metropolis that, under the patronage of the Greek god of the sea, Poseidon, was distinguished by great wealth, extraordinary achievements in engineering and administration, splendid architecture, and a strong commitment to virtue. His pupil Aristotle, however, commented on Atlantis, with what must have been a touch of irony, saying that "He who created it also destroyed it." It is in the *Critias* that we read that Zeus decided to punish Atlantis when the citizenry "began to behave themselves unseemly . . . taking the infection of wicked coveting and pride of power."

Whether destroyed by Zeus or Plato or natural agen-cy, Atlantis survived, even thrived, in the lore and literature of the West. The dawn of the Age of Exploration reawakened worldwide interest in the tale, and theorists combined the discoveries of the day with stories in the Bible, ancient writing, mythology, and archeological lore. As a result, Atlantis was sited in almost every part of the globe, undersea or in the desert, atop mountains or beneath the rubble of ruined cities. Nearly 50 major locations have been defended, with varying degrees of heat or playfulness, as the indisputable seat of the elusive civilization. During the last two centuries, more than 2,000 volumes devoted solely to the story of Atlantis have been printed and new sites continue to be proposed.

In 1968, an underwater structure was discovered on the sea floor near North Bimini, in the Bahamas. Its huge rectangular stones and other architectural features, including eroded marble and a stone with tongue-and-groove edges, fired the imagination of Atlantologists, but most geologists dismiss the find as an unusual natural rock formation. Also, catastrophe would not be necessary to explain the underwater location of the strange stones. Since the last ice age, the sea level has risen quite enough to cover the area, even assuming the site was on dry land in ancient times.

For some modern scholars, however, it is the Mediterranean island of Thera, now called Santorini, which seems most likely to be the source of the Atlantis legend, if indeed the tale was inspired by a historical event. In about 1500 B.C., the violent eruption of the Santorini volcano shattered the fertile island into three pitted isles, spewed ash over an area of more than 75,000 square miles, and generated tidal waves — possibly 300 or more feet high — which devastated the densely populated north coast of the island of Crete, some 65 miles away. Tsunamis, or giant waves, traveling as fast as 200 miles per hour, swept through the cities on the coast but spared the capital, Knossos. Volcanic debris rained down, killing people and livestock, ruining crops and poisoning the soil. Crete, the center of the Golden Age of the much-admired and influential Minoan civilization, suffered irreparable damage. Although the island did not sink beneath the waves, Minoan culture went into a decline from which it never recovered. Is that the kind of catastrophe that Plato, who wrote about civilization and its ideal forms, saw as worth the retelling?

Beneath the sea, on the other side of the world, lost between the tides of history — Plato's Atlantis and the versions conjured up by thousands of theorists over the centuries have one thing in common wherever they may be found: they are "sacred islands" of "marvelous beauty and inexhaustible profusion."

So it was that the lost kingdom of Lemuria, once widely discussed in serious scientific circles, would not long remain a featureless subcontinent, but would find adherents and would quite naturally inspire its own historians (long after the presumed fact) to recount wonders of nature and marvels of civilization.

It all began with a puzzle. The lemur, a quaint, round-eyed relative of the monkey, was thought in the 19th century to exist only in Madagascar, Africa, and Southeast Asia. A glance at the map shows that this habitational spread looks somewhat odd. Paleontologists, perhaps following the dictum that the simplest answer is likely to be the most accurate one, proposed that a land bridge must once have connected India and South Africa via the island of Madagascar. Hence, the "lost continent" of Lemuria was, in tentative fashion, given its name. Based on the geological knowledge of the time, scientists estimated that the land bridge had disappeared from 60 to 75 million years ago. Certain apparent resemblances between South African and Indian rock formations gave added weight to the theory.

The Lemurian land bridge was not the plaything of amateurs or fantasists. Darwin's most influential German adherent, the eminent zoologist Ernst Heinrich Haeckel, pondered the possibility that the human race might have had its beginnings on this drowned subcontinent in the Indian Ocean. A map of Lemuria was even included in his popular *History of Creation*, published in 1868. Other scientific thinkers found that the concept of the Lemurian land bridge fit nicely with their own speculations about the prehistoric movement of large masses of land.

Fascination with Lemuria was not confined to scientists, however. In the latter part of the 19th century the dynamic and irrepressible founder of Theosophy, Madame Helena Blavatsky, and her disciples began to present their theories regarding Lemuria. Although Madame Blavatsky thought Lemuria was situated in the Indian Ocean, her followers moved its location to the Pacific. It was peopled by a Third Root Race of the seven races she predicated for earthly history (including the Fourth on Atlantis). In the total Lemurian picture developed by Blavatsky and her disciples, we learn that native Lemurians were 27 to 30 feet tall, hermaphroditic, and in some cases, capable of seeing from the back of their heads by means of a third eye. In any event, this race did not survive.

In 1890, a New York newspaper published a letter that alerted fellow readers to a knowledge gap: "Who can offhand draw the lines of Lemuria? It is just as much a continent as the famed Atlantis, but who knows its former place upon the globe?"

In a 1929 effort to reconcile some of the conflicting lore, Max Heindel reported that the inhabitants of Lemuria were "guided more by internal perception than by external vision," for the atmosphere was so dense that objects were difficult to see. It was an epoch when the earth's fiery crust was just beginning to harden. Man had not yet developed speech, but he had the ability to mold his flesh and that of other creatures.

Finally, an Englishman named James Churchward was to furnish more than mere topographical detail about Lemuria. In 1926, when he was in his seventies, he published *The Lost Continent of Mu*, the first of many volumes he would write about the vanished land.

By his own account, Churchward, while serving in India in 1868, virtually stumbled on the truth when an aged priest in a temple helped him decipher some sacred tablets written "by the Naacals, either in Burma or the motherland. They told," he wrote, "how the Naacals had originally come from the motherland, the land in the center of the Pacific." Churchward discovered that the writings of "all the old civilizations," including 2,500 stone inscriptions some 120 centuries old found in Mexico, confirmed the tale: survivors from Lemuria had brought the tablets to Mexico. Furthermore, Churchward saw lithic remains of Mu on some islands of the Pacific, "notably Easter, Mangaia, Tonga-tabu, Panape, and the Ladrone or Mariana Islands," and, like those who subscribe to a more expansive form of diffusionist thinking, he found that symbols and customs are shared in "Egypt, Burma, India, Japan, China, South Sea Islands, Central America, South America and some of the North American Indian tribes."

Paradise on Earth

The immediate popularity of Churchward's books was not to be based on anthropological hypotheses. Much more fully than Plato had described Atlantis, he pictured "this earthly paradise" of Mu.

"Luxuriant vegetation covered the whole land with a soft, pleasing, restful mantle of green. . . . In valley places where the land was low, the rivers broadened out into shallow lakes, around whose shores myriads of sacred 'lotus flowers' dotted the glistening surface of the water, like varicolored jewels in settings of emerald green. Over the cool rivers, gaudy-winged butterflies hovered in the shade of the trees, rising and falling in fairy-like movements, as if better to view their painted beauty in nature's mirror. . . .

"At the time narrated, the 64,000,000 people were made up of 'ten tribes' or 'peoples,' each distinct from the other, but all under one government. . . . the people of Mu were highly civilized and enlightened. *There was no savagery on the face of the earth, nor had there ever been.* . . . The land of Mu was the mother and the center of the earth's civilization, learning, trade and commerce; all other countries throughout the world were her colonies or colonial empires."

This Golden Age would not endure. After a series of earthquakes, the great island "trembled and shook like the leaves of a tree in a storm." Fires from beneath the earth shot up to the heavens, waves flooded the plains, and the populous cities were destroyed. Mu sank into an abyss of fire, and 50 million square miles of water rolled over it, becoming its "burial shroud." Some few frightened survivors found themselves pitiably destitute upon the scattered promontories still visible above the boiling waves. The inhabitants of today's South Sea Islands, Churchward wrote, are the remote progeny of that "handful of human beings" who gazed upon a desolated world 13,000 years ago.

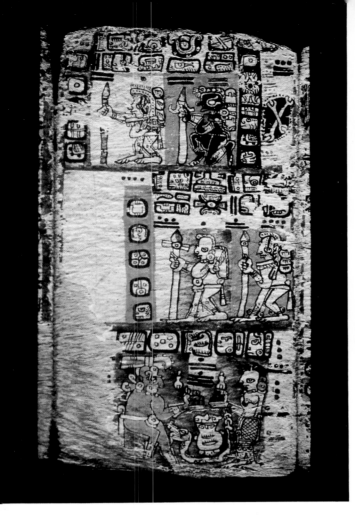

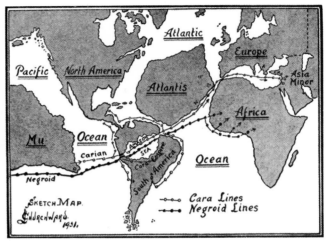

A page from the Troano Manuscript, a 13th-century Maya chronicle, left, was translated by James Churchward as a history of the lost continent of Mu. Above top, his 1931 sketch of the cataclysm that sank this "Motherland of Man" and, above, his map showing how refugees peopled the globe.

What was the immediate consequence of the loss of paradise? Churchward may be pointing to a moral here, for, as he puts it, "the survivors of the highest civilization descended to the lowest savagery which has continued on through the ages." Unprepared for the harsh facts of their new life, the remnants of the 10 great peoples now turned in desperation to cannibalism. Some chose to die rather than eat human flesh, but others "sank lower and lower until even traditions of their past, which at first were religiously kept and handed down to posterity, became dim and at last forgotten." Until Churchward himself happened upon the tablets, no man living had described the particulars of life in the world's true cradle of civilization.

Churchward was not destined, however, to remain sole possessor of the key to understanding Lemurian lore. After all, he had not reconciled his translated historical records with the presumed geological history; his Mu had inexplicably surfaced, not in the Indian Ocean, but thousands of miles eastward in the Pacific.

Clearly, the theory of the ancient land bridge in the Indian Ocean was taken out of the hands of scientists by mystics and other romancers who apparently gave full rein to inspiration or the stirrings of the subconscious. Academics, furthermore, had abandoned the concept of Lemuria by the last quarter of the 19th century. For one thing, the evidence involving lemurs

came to be seen as contradictory; lemur-like remains were found in America and Europe, but lemurs today are found only in Madagascar and the neighboring Comoro Islands. Contemporary theories of the prehistoric and continuing movements of the great land masses indicate that no "continent" or enormous island ever existed in any of the sites proposed for the "lost" kingdom of Lemuria.

In the end, it does not seem as if St. Brendan was alone in seeking out the earth's regions of promise, the islands of the blest. Churchward's Mu and Plato's Atlantis are lands of escape. These cities, these orderly and preeminently peaceful cultures, are not quite like any we have seen recorded in the history of man. Theirs is the architecture of dream.

It is interesting to note that tales of floating islands, of mist-shrouded continents, may have influenced the determined, highly practical luminaries of the Age of Exploration. One writer described their quest as follows: "Always mystery lay beyond the horizon. The spirit which tried to pierce it was a questioning spirit. And embedded in the mystery, as it turned out, was a continent." Men sent out frail ships on the dark little-known Atlantic and found continents and great civilizations that were to prove, to a certain way of thinking, as startling as an ancient metropolis of Atlantis or Mu. Legend was to be surpassed by the reality.

VINLAND
THE
GOOD

Was the land west of Greenland discovered by Leif the Lucky
actually North America? What are the clues? Is there proof?
Did Vikings name their discovery Vinland, "Wine-land,"
because of grapes growing wild there?

There was a man called Thorvald, who was the
father of Eric the Red. He and Eric left their
home in Jaederen, in Norway, because of some
killings and went to Iceland. . . ."

So begins the *Graenlendinga* (or *Greenlanders'*) *Saga*,
which celebrates the Viking discovery of lands westward across the storm-tossed North Atlantic. The un-
ruly Norseman and his son are forced to emigrate to
the recently settled outpost of Iceland, where Thorvald
dies. The son, repeating the misdeeds of the father, is in
turn banished, and later outlawed, from Iceland. Voyaging west, Eric (or Eirik) discovers and settles Greenland. The saga, originally an oral account that is believed to have been written down in about 1190, tells of
events that took place some 200 years earlier. The content is less the stuff of glowing legend than a personal
and detailed record of events, place-names, and genealogical relationships, some familiar to modern ears but
most not. Recounted by proud descendant or obliging
poet, the saga has the reassuring ring of only slightly
improved-upon truth.

By literary standards, the *Greenlanders' Saga* is considered to be neither so grand nor so sophisticated as
the later examples of the great Icelandic saga tradition.
If it were only the story of that aborted first settlement

of Greenland, it would long since have been forgotten.
But Eric the Red, outlaw son of an outlaw father, was
in turn the father of Leif Ericsson. And the saga describes, in an offhand, unsurprised manner, one of the
most remarkable sequences in the history of exploration: the unexpected sighting of North America by Leif
and his men 500 years before Columbus and subsequent attempts by the Norsemen to establish permanent settlements there.

To the bountiful and inviting country he explored
about the year 1000, Leif Ericsson gave the name Vinland ("Wineland"). The *Greenlanders' Saga* and a later,
slightly altered and longer version of the same events,
Eric's Saga, are together known as the Vinland Sagas.

Until the 1960's, in the absence of any material proof
that Norsemen had actually visited the New World,
scholars argued over the sagas' authenticity. Those inclined to the view that Vinland was not a myth but a

*Hunger for land forced Vikings to seek new homes overseas,
and they fanned out in many directions. This manuscript
illumination, made by English monks, shows a conquering
Danish host arriving in 9th-century England; other Norsemen later went to Iceland, Greenland, and North America.*

place of solid earth pointed to independent references of about the same period, in particular that of Adam of Bremen. Adam mentions Vinland in a history written around 1075, some 115 years before the *Greenlanders' Saga* was set down in writing. But as Magnus Magnusson (whose translation of the Vinland Sagas is used here) points out, Adam of Bremen "wrote some extremely silly things about other islands in the Atlantic . . . [of] Greenland, for instance, he says, 'The salt sea there gives the inhabitants a bluish-green appearance, and from this the country gets its name.' Adam of Bremen does not 'prove' the existence of Vinland — just the existence of a *story* about Vinland."

The Saga of the Greenlanders

Vinland also appears on maps, genuine and fraudulent (see page 57), but as with Adam of Bremen, these citings reflect nothing other than that Vinland was *thought* to exist. The sagas, in fact, were the only substantial references to Vinland, and so, attention naturally focused on them. Were they legendary or truthful, fanciful or accurate? Did they portray symbolic events or real ones? Did they represent the dreams of a people always seeking new lands, or did they chart the route to the New World? Clearly they were literary documents first and historical documents second, if at all. By modern standards, the two narratives — one of 9 chapters, the other of 14 — are imprecise (and occasionally contradictory) about such matters as distances and dates, numbers of ships and settlers, even who first caught sight of lands beyond Greenland. In *Eric's Saga*, Leif — an acknowledged Norse hero, the son of Greenland's founder, and a natural favorite — first sights the New World. In the *Greenlanders' Saga*, Bjarni Herjolfsson, a prosperous young merchant from Iceland, blown off course past Greenland while looking for his father, has that honor.

In addition to imprecision and discrepancies, large parts of the sagas have a fabulous air: a great stretch of white beach is called Wonderstrands, and the saga mentions gigantic salmon in great number, in a land "so kind that no winter fodder would be needed for livestock. . . ." The Norse regarded the New World as an Elysian land. The *Greenlanders' Saga* says Leif's party "went ashore and looked about them. The weather was fine. There was dew on the grass, and the first thing they did was to get some of it on their hands and put it to their lips, and to them it seemed the sweetest thing they had ever tasted."

Yet if the extravagance of the sagas' claims for Vinland or their vagueness about certain details caused many scholars to doubt Vinland's existence, others found these tales convincing and persuasive. They considered the saga accounts more than consistent with the practical possibilities for travel across the North Atlantic in the year 1000 and with the pattern of Viking expansion, conquest, and settlement at that time. It is a very logical, well-documented pattern.

By the year 1000, Norse sailors had already extended their range 1,500 miles to the west, and they had done it, like the Irish to a lesser extent before them, one landfall at a time. They sailed in open, beamy cargo boats called *knarrs* — the type illustrated opposite. That they should have continued their westward push and reached the New World seems in retrospect not just likely but almost inevitable.

The Norse impulse toward new territories was first manifest in the terrifying raids of Viking marauders, who swept down upon an astonished Europe in repeated lightning attacks. Beginning in the late 8th century with the pillage of Lindisfarne, an island monastery off the northeastern coast of England, the Vikings cut a swath across the Continent. They were port pirates — bearing down on coastal areas in their high-prowed longships, making intermittent stops to ravage the countryside, plunder the churches, and take prisoners for ransom. Before long, the Vikings sailed up the Seine to Paris and by way of the Pillars of Hercules into the Mediterranean, and they roamed up and down the rivers of Russia. To the more sophisticated Arabs they were known as a race of ferocious warriors.

Within a few generations, however, these campaigns of terror gave way to gentler enterprises. The lush valleys of France and the rich farmland of the British Isles proved as tempting to the Norse imagination as gold and silver. Hard on the heels of pirate raiders came invading farmers, who settled on the land. Although the savagery of the early Vikings was not forgotten, their more peaceable successors were rapidly absorbed into the existing cultures of western Europe. In France they were ceded the area known as Normandy, and in England they settled along the east coast. Eventually, Norman descendants of the Vikings conquered England in 1066. They also established a kingdom in southern Italy in the 12th century. Despite this Viking explosion, many land-hungry Norsemen remained behind in Scandinavia. In the latter part of the 9th century the more daring among them had already begun to venture farther west, out of the North Sea into the Atlantic, in search of new territory.

In about 860, sailors blown off course sighted a large and apparently uninhabited island some "seven days west of Norway." Hearing of this, a party of explorers led by Floki Vilgerdarsson set out from Norway. What they found were fish-filled fjords and green pastureland surrounding an icy, mountainous interior. There were no human inhabitants save for a handful of Irish monks, who departed when the pagan settlers arrived — they presumably sailed back to Ireland. The forbidding name — Iceland — that Floki gave the island did not deter migration; by 870, settlers began arriving in large numbers, and by 930, the island had virtually reached its natural limit, with 20,000 inhabitants occupying all of the arable land. Latecomers, such as Eric the Red and his father, Thorvald, found themselves in circumstances little better than those they had

Following an Arctic Mirage

The daring of Viking navigators of a millennium past has long been a source of wonder. Venturing westward into the North Atlantic, they entered one of the world's most dangerous oceans. Without compasses, fighting adverse winds and currents, they settled Iceland, discovered Greenland, and found North America 500 years before Columbus (map below). Moreover, these voyages of exploration, settlement, and trade were made in what in fact were no more than open boats — the small, beamy merchant craft called *knarrs,* which were of the same basic design and build as the swift longships the Vikings used in lightning raids and trading in European waters. The *knarr* was rather short and tubby by comparison, but just as seaworthy.

It was originally thought that the Viking discoveries of Greenland and America were the result of chance rather than design, due to dead-reckoning navigation or being blown off course by the North Atlantic's violent storms. However, a recent theory suggests that the Norsemen made use of a peculiar natural phenomenon of the region — that perhaps they were not sailing off into the unknown after all.

The Canadian geographer Leonard Sawatzky wondered how these storm-tossed sailors got home and then later made it all the way back again to settle: "I thought there was a much sounder basis, an explanation of human competence and logic." The solution he proposes is the so-called Arctic mirage, not uncommon in the higher latitudes. Under certain conditions of air, water temperatures, and weather, light waves are refracted, as if by a prism, so that they "bend" with the curvature of the earth (diagram below). Thus, a distant mountain peak or headland is "raised" high above the natural horizon, becoming visible from a greater distance than is normally possible. It may be that Eric the Red thus "saw" Greenland from the top of the 4,700-foot Snaefellsjökull, or Snaefells Glacier, an iced-over volcano on Iceland's west coast. And, since Eric the Red's first transatlantic landfall was probably the 6,000-foot Ingolfsfjeld, a glacier peak on Greenland's east coast, towering glaciers on both sides may have provided landmarks for crossings. It is possible that Eric's son, Leif the Lucky, also relied on the Arctic mirage to reach North America.

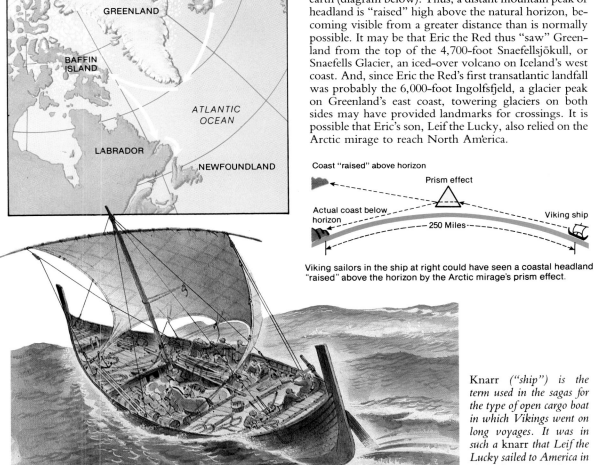

Viking sailors in the ship at right could have seen a coastal headland "raised" above the horizon by the Arctic mirage's prism effect.

Knarr *("ship") is the term used in the sagas for the type of open cargo boat in which Vikings went on long voyages. It was in such a* knarr *that Leif the Lucky sailed to America in about the year 1000.*

left behind, with good land scarce and many would-be farmers forced to fish or trap for a living.

It was inevitable that the search for still more territory would continue, and there were few in Iceland who did not hear with excitement of the sighting by the sailor Gunnbjorn Ulf-Krakasson of yet another, even bigger, island to the west. Like the earlier discovery of Iceland, this too was an accident, another instance of a ship carried beyond its target by a great storm. But in fact the land in question might have been dimly suggested from the top of Iceland's Snaefells Glacier, an iced-over volcano on the western coast of the island. What could have been seen is not the land itself, but a northern mirage, what Norwegians call an *is-blikk,* or ice-glimpse, a phenomenon that casts shimmering "pictures" across great distances. These may in part account for the repeated chance sightings at sea (see box, page 53).

Despite reports of Gunnbjorn's blurred sighting to the west sometime between 900 and 930, no expedition was mounted to investigate it until 978 — and that proved unsuccessful. However, in 981 or 982 Eric the Red, outlawed by his Icelandic peers and still barred from his native Norway, set out in search of Gunnbjorn's find.

"He put out to sea past Snaefells Glacier," says the *Greenlanders' Saga.* "He found the country he was seeking and made land near the glacier he named Mid Glacier; it is now known as Blaserk. From there he sailed south down the coast to find out if the country were habitable there." It was indeed habitable.

Eric spent three summers ducking in and out of harbors, tracking the western wilderness and naming the major landmarks after himself. The fourth summer he returned to Iceland, where he announced that he had discovered a country he called Greenland, "for he said that people would be much more tempted to go there if it had an attractive name."

It was a marketing coup worthy of the modern advertising age, and the following summer 25 ships filled with hopeful colonists set out with Eric on a return voyage to his island discovery. Only 14 reached their destination, but one more link had been added to a chain that now stretched almost across the Atlantic. When Eric and his followers established a settlement along the southwestern coast of Greenland, only the few hundred miles of Davis Strait lay between them and the North American continent. That this historic gap should be closed in Eric's lifetime seems inevitable to us today. But proof was not obtained until 1961, when, as schoolchildren are now taught, the remains of a Norse settlement were first unearthed near the village of L'Anse aux Meadows on the bay at the northeastern tip of Newfoundland.

The discovery was made by a Norwegian explorer, Helge Ingstad, and his archeologist wife, Anne Stine Ingstad, who had spent the better part of a decade tracing Leif Ericsson's route from Greenland to Vinland. That the Ingstads' mission succeeded was due to persistence and careful research, both historical and archeological. But as Helge Ingstad has made clear, their long search for Vinland was not merely inspired by the

sagas: it was quite literally directed by them. Even those scholars who were predisposed to view the sagas as rough historical documents assumed that they had no more than approximate geographical accuracy. Ingstad, however, recounts that he "read the sagas rather literally as to courses, landmarks, and sailing times. I believed that information about the sea and ships would be likely to survive uncorrupted in traditions of a seafaring people."

Contrary to the majority view, Ingstad proposed a solution to a second problem regarding Vinland's probable location. "Although the sagas," he writes, " . . . indicate that Vinland was a northern place, most scholars have believed that *vin* referred to wild grapes; thus they have placed Vinland rather far south on the Atlantic coast: near Boston, on Cape Cod, Martha's Vineyard or Long Island, among many sites. I saw it differently. I came to share with Swedish philologist Sven Søderberg the conviction that 'vin' in Vinland had nothing to do with grapes, but instead was used in the old Norse sense of 'grass' or 'grazing lands.' "

Though nearly alone with Søderberg in this interpretation — the firm consensus among most scholars is that the *vin* in Vinland meant "wine" — Ingstad clearly did himself a favor by adopting it. For by dismissing the problem of grapes, which are found no farther north in America than Passamaquoddy Bay, between New Brunswick and Maine, he was able to return once again to the sagas with complete confidence and finally deduce that "Vinland must most logically be looked for in northern Newfoundland."

For further support of his hunch, Ingstad looked to the Icelandic map drawn by Sigurdur Stefánsson in the late 1500's. There, directly opposite the British Isles, across an Atlantic that looks no larger than one of the Great Lakes, lies a northward-pointing peninsula labeled *Promontorium Winlandiae:* ("Promontory of Vinland"). To Ingstad, the clues in the saga, combined with this graphic hint, were as markers on a forest trail — unmistakable and irresistible.

The clues, of course, start in Greenland, and Ingstad had first to look toward the New World with the eyes of a 10th-century Icelandic merchant. One is tempted to call Bjarni Herjolfsson "Bjarni the Uncurious" for his resolute refusal to explore not just one but three separate landfalls he made while trying to reach Greenland. But discovery was not on Bjarni's mind, only a terrible need to find his father; his story, which is the subject of chapter two in the *Greenlanders' Saga,* is a story not of discovery but of filial devotion. In an accident of history that not only predates but greatly exceeds in irony Columbus's unexpected 15th-century landing in the West Indies, Bjarni Herjolfsson, the first European to sight North America, was also the first to turn back. But it was his voyage in the North Atlantic that showed the way for subsequent expeditions, and so it is that one must begin with the uncurious Bjarni Herjolfsson.

He "was a man of much promise," the *Greenlanders' Saga* says. "From early youth he had been eager to sail to foreign lands; he earned himself both wealth and a good reputation, and used to spend his winters alternately abroad and in Iceland with his father. He soon had a merchant ship of his own."

In the year 985 or 986, the saga records, while Bjarni was in Norway on business, "his father, Herjolf, sold up the farm and emigrated to Greenland with [Eric] the Red. . . ." When Bjarni arrived back in Iceland the following summer, this news so devastated him that he "refused to have his ship unloaded. His crew asked him what he had in mind; he replied that he intended to keep his custom of enjoying his father's hospitality over the winter — 'so I want to sail my ship to Greenland, if you are willing to come with me.'

"They all replied that they would do what he thought best. Then Bjarni said, 'This voyage of ours will be considered foolhardy, for not one of us has ever sailed the Greenland Sea.'

"However, they put to sea . . . and sailed for three days until land was lost to sight below the horizon. Then the fair wind failed and northerly winds and fog set in, and for many days they had no idea what their course was. After that they saw the sun again and were able to get their bearings; they hoisted sail and after a day's sailing they sighted land.

"They discussed amongst themselves what country this might be. Bjarni said . . . it could not be Greenland. The crew asked him if he wanted to land there or not; Bjarni replied, 'I think we should sail in close.'

"They did so, and soon they could see that the country was not mountainous, but was well wooded and with low hills. So they put to sea again, leaving the land on the port quarter; and after sailing for two days they sighted land once more.

"Bjarni's men asked him if he thought this was Greenland yet; he said he did not think this was Greenland, any more than the previous one — 'for there are said to be huge glaciers in Greenland.'

"They closed the land quickly and saw that it was flat and wooded. Then the wind failed and the crew all said they thought it advisable to land there, but Bjarni refused. They claimed they needed both firewood and water; but Bjarni said, 'You have no shortage of either.' He was criticized for this by his men.

"He ordered them to hoist sail, and they did so. They turned the prow out to sea and sailed before a south-west wind for three days before they sighted a third land. This one was high and mountainous, and topped by a glacier. Again they asked Bjarni if he wished to land there, but he replied, 'No, for this country seems to me to be worthless.'

"They did not lower sail this time, but followed the coastline and saw that it was an island. Once again they put the land astern and sailed out to sea before the same fair wind. But now it began to blow a gale, and Bjarni ordered his men to shorten sail and not to go harder than ship and rigging could stand. They sailed now for four days, until they sighted a fourth land.

"The men asked Bjarni if he thought this would be Greenland or not. 'This tallies most closely with what I have been told about Greenland,' replied Bjarni. 'And here we shall go in to land.'

"They did so, and made land as dusk was falling at a promontory which had a boat hauled up on it. This was where Bjarni's father, Herjolf, lived, and it has been called Herjolfsness for that reason ever since.

"Bjarni now gave up trading and stayed with his father, and carried on farming there after his father's death," the chapter concluded.

Enter Leif the Lucky

Three unfamiliar landfalls but not one landing! A poor showing for a Norseman, and one omitted in the *Eric's Saga* version of events. In that account, now generally agreed to be the less reliable of the two sagas, the chance discoverer of Vinland is Leif Ericsson, who, after "prolonged difficulties at sea," while en route from Norway to Greenland, "finally came upon lands whose existence he had never suspected. There were fields of wild wheat growing there, and vines, and among the trees there were maples." *Eric's Saga* has it

that, unlike Bjarni, Leif made a landing, and "took some samples of all these things."

In fact, Leif's contributions were substantial, but they resulted not from accident but from a deliberate voyage made some 15 years after Bjarni's, with the express purpose of exploring the lands Bjarni had failed to investigate. Word of Bjarni's sighting had circulated throughout the Norse-speaking world and by the year 1000 most Norsemen had heard of it. "There was now great talk of discovering new countries," the *Greenlanders' Saga* records. "Leif, the son of [Eric] the Red of Brattahlid, went to see Bjarni Herjolfsson and bought his ship from him. . . ." Leif persuaded his reluctant father to lead the expedition, insisting that Eric "would still command more luck than any of his kinsmen." But on the way to the ship, Eric's horse stumbled, and he was thrown. According to Norse superstition, such a fall on the eve of a journey was an extremely bad omen. He told Leif: " 'I am not meant to discover more countries than this one we now live in.' " While his father retired to Brattahlid, "Leif went aboard the ship with his crew of thirty-five. . . . The first landfall they made was the country that Bjarni had sighted last. They sailed up to the shore and cast anchor, then lowered a boat and landed. There was no grass to be seen, and the hinterland was covered with great glaciers. . . . It seemed to them a worthless country.

"Then Leif said, 'Now we have done better than Bjarni where this country is concerned — we at least have set foot on it. I shall give this country a name and call it *Helluland*,' ("Slab Land").

"They returned to their ship and put to sea, and sighted a second land. Once again they sailed right up to it and cast anchor, lowered a boat and went ashore. This country was flat and wooded, with white sandy beaches wherever they went; and the land sloped gently down to the sea.

"Leif said, 'This country shall be named after its natural resources: it shall be called *Markland*' ("Forest Land").

"They hurried back to their ship as quickly as possible and sailed away to sea in a north-east wind for two days until they sighted land again. They sailed towards it and came to an island which lay to the north of it." This was the land of the sweet-tasting dew, where they tarried but briefly, then sailed into a sound between the island and a headland to the north.

"They steered a westerly course round the headland. There were extensive shallows there and at low tide their ship was left high and dry, with the sea almost out of sight. But they were so impatient to land that they could not bear to wait for the rising tide to float the ship; they ran ashore to a place where a river flowed out of a lake. As soon as the tide had refloated the ship they took a boat and rowed out to it and brought it up the river into the lake, where they anchored it. They carried their hammocks ashore and put up booths (temporary shelters of stone and turf, covered with

The Viking Hoaxes

In 1898 Olaf Ohman discovered, entangled in the roots of a tree on his farm near Kensington, Minnesota, a 200-pound stone with an inscription detailing a 14th-century Viking expedition to America. Although the scholarly community has labeled the Kensington Stone a 19th-century forgery, no one had evidence until recently as to who perpetrated the hoax.

The first experts to examine the stone, which contains a series of runes (a form of writing used by early Scandinavians), unanimously declared it a fake. Linguistic specialists insisted that the inscription contained colloquial expressions that had developed in 19th-century Minnesota, and accusations of fraud were made against Ohman and his neighbors. Nevertheless, a number of scholars were convinced, including some at the Smithsonian Institution in Washington, D.C., which displayed the stone in 1948-49.

But even though the stone is a fraud, unanswered questions remain. Can we believe the children of Ohman's neighbor when they confessed in 1974 that their father had helped to chisel the runes? Why did some professional runologists accept the stone? And how could the Smithsonian have been so easily duped?

Yale University made a similar error in 1965 with the so-called Vinland Map. The map, purported to be a 15th-century chart of the Atlantic showing the Vinland of the sagas, was bound with a manuscript called *The Tartar Relation,* which was judged to date from around 1440. Both the map and the manuscript contained worm holes, but they did not match up.

The material was given to Yale University which subsequently, and perhaps too coincidentally, received a 15th-century copy of an earlier work called the *Speculum Historiale (Mirror of History),* which happened to have worm holes that matched some of those in the other two documents. Experts at Yale felt that the evidence made a strong case for the authenticity of the map.

Upon publication of *The Vinland Map and the Tartar Relation* in 1965, however, doubts set in. Three years later, under mounting criticism, Yale hired its own team of investigators and in 1974 was forced to admit that the Vinland Map was a fraud. Tests showed that the inks used in the two manuscripts were of medieval origin while the ink on the Vinland Map contained elements not developed before the 1920's. As with the Kensington Stone, no one knows who fabricated the Vinland Map — and unless someone steps forward with new information, we may never discover the solution.

A critic proposed that the precise outline of Greenland on the Vinland Map, above, suggests it was probably traced from an atlas.

The Kensington Stone once exhibited at the Smithsonian Institution is now housed in a Douglas County, Minnesota, museum.

canvas). Then they decided to winter there, and built some large houses."

If one sets sail as Leif did, west from Brattahlid at the southwest tip of Greenland, one soon comes to the frozen expanse of Baffin Island, a cold, stony place not quite a fourth the size of Greenland. A memorably inhospitable landfall, it was easily recognized by Leif as "the country that Bjarni had sighted last." When he saw this coast, Bjarni pronounced the territory "worthless"; 15 years later, Leif said the same, as have innumerable observers in the days since.

If one continues southeast, tracing Bjarni's path in reverse, in time one comes to the stands of trees that caused Leif to name the place *Markland* ("Forest-Land"). The topography is unmistakably that of Labrador, the easternmost bulge of contiguous Canada. Here are the *furdustrandir* ("Wonderstrands") of the saga, which served as a landmark for later voyagers. According to the American historian Samuel Eliot Morison, who subscribed to Ingstad's literal reading of the sagas, the Wonderstrands are without doubt the "thirty-mile-long stretch of beach on the Labrador coast, between latitudes 53°45′ and 54°09′ N, broken only by Cape Porcupine. Here are magnificent yellow sand beaches with a gentle gradient, longer than any that the Norsemen could ever have seen, and the more wondrous because they occur almost miraculously in the middle of a barren, rocky coast. Behind these Wonderstrands, a level plain — unique for southern Labrador — nourishes a fine stand of black spruce. . . ."

Continuing south, the modern sailor reaches a virtually unavoidable destination, as did Leif, in Ingstad's view: "When the Norsemen, traveling without compasses, coasted south along Labrador pushed by the strong Labrador Current, they would almost inevitably sight and hold their course toward northernmost Newfoundland. They could hardly avoid a landfall there." Morison concurs, and makes the point that the "island to the north of the mainland" in the saga has to be Belle Isle, which sits at the mouth of the Strait of Belle Isle, between Labrador and Newfoundland. The distance of 165 nautical miles from the Wonderstrands to the island is consistent, Morison says, with the two-day sailing period described in the *Greenlanders' Saga*.

And so Leif and his companions, with nothing more to guide them than Bjarni's 15-year-old memories, groped their way to the New World. Rarely out of sight of land, they hugged the cold coasts of North America until they stumbled on what to their sea-weary souls must have seemed an Eden. "In this country," the *Greenlanders' Saga* says, "night and day were of more even length than in either Greenland or Iceland: on the shortest day of the year, the sun was already up by 9, and did not set until after 3."

"There was no lack of salmon in the river or the lake," the *Greenlanders' Saga* records, "bigger salmon than they had ever seen. The country seemed to them so kind that no winter fodder would be needed for livestock: there was never any frost all winter and the grass hardly withered at all."

With great expectations, Leif's party built shelter for the winter and made plans to explore. It was during this initial season in Vinland, according to the *Greenlanders' Saga,* that they discovered the wild growing grape vines that inspired Leif's name for the country and thus fixed it as a place of Nordic yearning forever. But they left for home before learning that this "so kind" land was already inhabited, therefore misunderstanding altogether the chances for permanent Norse settlement. That lesson was learned by their successors.

The sagas tell many things of Leif Ericsson: that he was "tall and strong and very impressive in appearance"; that he fathered a son by a noblewoman "of unusual knowledge" (perhaps she was skilled in magic and witchcraft); that "there seemed to be something uncanny" about the child all his life; and that Leif converted his mother to Christianity but failed with old Eric. They do not tell why he never returned to Vinland. There were three more successful expeditions west, but Leif led none of them.

In place of Leif would go, in turn, three of his relatives: his brother, Thorvald; Leif's widowed sister-in-law, Gudrid, in an expedition led by her third husband, Thorfinn Karlsefni; and finally, his sister, Freydis, who led the last known Norse party to settle the New World.

Thorvald set off in the summer of 1004, with a crew of 30, having not only "prepared his expedition with his brother Leif's guidance" but taking his ship (the one Leif had bought from Bjarni) as well. " . . . there are no reports of their voyage until they reached Leif's Houses in Vinland," the *Greenlanders' Saga* says, suggesting both that the trip was uneventful and that Leif's route was easily retraced. Thorvald and his men spent the winter cozily in Leif's Houses, and in the spring a small group was sent forth to "sail west along the coast and explore that region. . . ."

Up Against the Natives

"They found the country there very attractive, with woods stretching almost down to the shore and white sandy beaches. There were numerous islands there, and extensive shallows," the saga tells. "They found no traces of human habitation or animals except on one westerly island, where they found a wooden [hay-] stack cover. That was the only man-made thing they found; and in the autumn they returned to Leif's Houses.

"Next summer Thorvald sailed east with his ship and then north along the coast. They ran into a fierce gale off a headland and were driven ashore; the keel was shattered and they had to stay there for a long time while they repaired the ship.

"Thorvald said to his companions, 'I want to erect the old keel here on the headland, and call the place *Kjalarness.'* "

Did Leif name North America "Wine-land" (Vinland) because wine could be made from fruit like the squashberries shown here — an abundant species in Newfoundland — or was he really talking about grapes found much farther south?

Farther east they came to a wooded promontory near the mouth of two fjords and went ashore. Thorvald thought it was a beautiful spot and said he would like to make his home there. Then, the saga relates with appropriate foreboding: "On their way back to the ship they noticed three humps on the sandy beach . . . . When they went closer they found that these were three skin-boats, with three men under each of them. Thorvald and his men divided forces and captured all of them except one, who escaped in his boat. They killed the other eight and returned to the headland. . . . Then they were overwhelmed by such a heavy drowsiness that they could not stay awake, and they all fell asleep — until they were awakened by a voice that shouted, 'Wake up, Thorvald, and all your men, if you want to stay alive! Get to your ship with all your company and get away as fast as you can!'

"A great swarm of skin-boats was then heading towards them down the fjord.

"Thorvald said, 'We shall set up breastworks on the gunwales and defend ourselves as best we can, but fight back as little as possible.'

"They did this. The Skraelings shot at them for a while, and then turned and fled as fast as they could.

"Thorvald asked his men if any of them were wounded; they all replied that they were unhurt.

" 'I have a wound in the armpit,' said Thorvald. 'An arrow flew up between the gunwale and my shield, under my arm — here it is. This will lead to my death'. . . .

"With that Thorvald died. . . . [His men] spent the winter there and gathered grapes and vines as cargo for the ship. In the spring they set off on the voyage to Greenland; they made land at Eiriksfjord, and had plenty of news to tell Leif."

The first recorded encounter between Europeans and New World natives, who may have been ancestors of the Algonquin Indians encountered by later European explorers of northeastern North America, is sadly prophetic of relations to come. No explanation is given in the sagas for the ultimate decision of Thorvald's party to slaughter the Skraelings on first meeting, but the Norsemen's name for the Indians tells the story. *Skraeling* means "savage," or "wretch." The only difference in the exchanges between the Norsemen and Skraelings recorded in the sagas and those that would occur 500 hundred years later between the Spanish and Portuguese and the Indians of Central and South America was the outcome. Even without firearms Thorvald's men were much better armed than the Skraelings. However, the threat of sporadic harassment and attack by Skraelings in far superior numbers was more than enough to prevent the Norsemen from establishing a permanent settlement.

Perhaps with that fact in mind, the next Norse party to attempt settlement was more than double the size of Thorvald's (according to the *Greenlanders' Saga; Eric's Saga* has it even larger — 160 men and women). It was led around the year 1010 by Thorfinn Karlsefni, "a man of considerable wealth," who had arrived in Greenland the year before and had married the estimable Gudrid, widow of Thorstein Ericsson, Eric the Red's third son and Leif's younger brother. Karlsefni's plan was the most ambitious to date: he intended to make a permanent settlement in Vinland if he could, and he and his companions loaded their ships with "livestock of all kinds," including a bull.

"Karlsefni asked Leif if he could have the houses in Vinland;" the *Greenlanders' Saga* says, but Leif said he would rather lend them, suggesting that he might be hoping to return to Vinland himself some day.

As with Thorvald's expedition, this third voyage to Vinland was apparently uneventful: Karlsefni's party "put to sea and arrived safe and sound at Leif's Houses and carried their hammocks ashore." They passed a quiet winter: in the following summer they had their first glimpse of the local Indians, "when a great number of them came out of the wood one day. The cattle

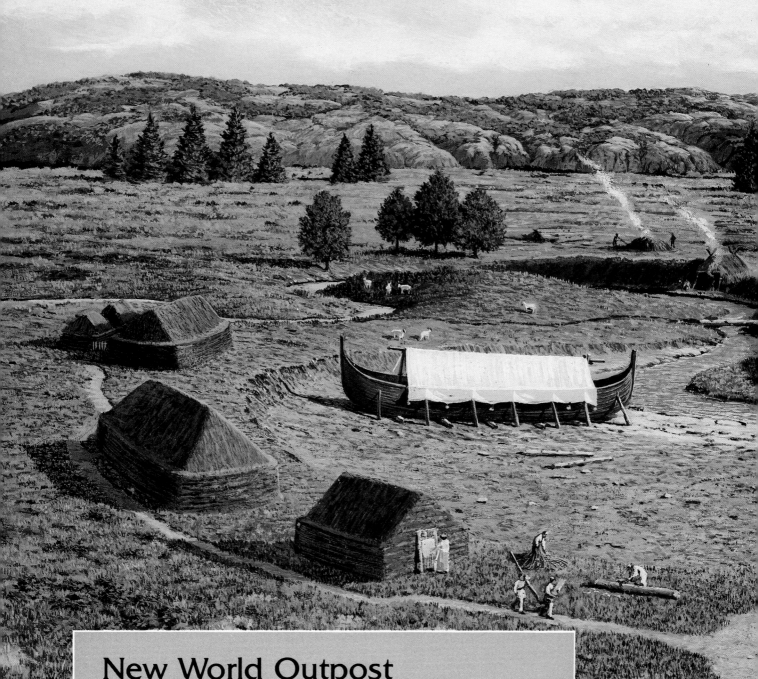

New World Outpost

It is midsummer early in the 11th century, and lingering ice has at last
melted from a shallow bay in northern Newfoundland. In a vain attempt to
establish a North American colony, Viking settlers are hastily erecting a
longhouse for their winter's stay — the smaller dwellings at left having
proved inadequate. The ocean-going *knarr* in which they arrived is beached
and covered for protection; smaller fishing craft are drawn up on shore.
Everyone is pressed into service: trimming logs to frame the building,
cutting sod for its thick, insulating walls, gathering saplings to support
the roof. Women weave and cook, as a party of men butcher a beached
whale. Goats and sheep brought along as provisions graze in the middle
distance, while on the far side of the stream, smoke rises above the
charcoal pit and the smithy where vital iron tools are being forged.

were grazing near by and the bull began to bellow and roar with great vehemence. This terrified the Skraelings and they fled, carrying their packs which contained furs and sables and pelts of all kinds. They made for Karlsefni's houses and tried to get inside, but Karlsefni had the doors barred against them. Neither side could understand the other's language."

A mutual inclination to trade overcame the language barrier; the Indians surrendered their richly stuffed packs for a taste of cow's milk, and "carried their purchases away in their bellies. . . ."

After this incident, Karlsefni ordered a palisade to be built around the camp, and when the Indians returned the following winter to trade again, they simply threw their packs over the top. By then, Gudrid and Karlsefni had produced a son, Snorri, the first European to be born in North America. The *Greenlanders' Saga* introduces a ghostly visitant to warn of trouble: Gudrid is sitting beside Snorri's cradle when a strange-looking woman suddenly appears and, in answer to Gudrid's question, says that her name is Gudrid as well. A moment later, there is "a great crash and the woman vanished, and in the same instant a Skraeling was killed by one of Karlsefni's men for trying to steal some weapons. The Skraelings fled as fast as they could, leaving their clothing and wares behind."

Karlsefni rightly reckoned that the Indians would return in force and so led most of his men out of the palisade to meet the enemy in a clearing. A fierce battle ensued. In *Eric's Saga*, the battle is described in some detail: " . . . a hail of missiles came flying over, for the Skraelings were using catapults. Karlsefni and Snorri saw them hoist a large sphere on a pole; it was dark blue in colour. It came flying in over the heads of Karlsefni's men and made an ugly din when it struck the ground. This terrified Karlsefni and his men so much that their only thought was to flee. . . ."

In *Eric's Saga*, Freydis, Eric's pregnant daughter, is present on this expedition, and it is she who saves the day. Unable to retreat with the men, "She snatched up the sword and prepared to defend herself. When the Skraelings came rushing towards her she pulled one of her breasts out of her bodice and slapped it with the sword. The Skraelings were terrified at the sight of this and fled back to their boats. . . ."

The battle nonetheless demonstrated that there could be no permanent settlement in Vinland while the Skraelings remained. In the *Greenlanders' Saga*, Karlsefni's party departs the following spring, carrying with them "much valuable produce, vines and grapes and pelts." Karlsefni and Gudrid eventually retire to a farm in Iceland. Following Karlsefni's death, the thrice-wid-

Cultures in Contact

When the first Scandinavians arrived in Greenland in 985 or 986, they found on both coasts, east and west, "human habitations, and the remains of skin boats, and stone artifacts from which it can be concluded that the people who had been there before were of the same race as those who inhabit Vinland, whom the Greenlanders call Skraelings." By the time these words had been written — in the 12th-century *Book of Icelanders* — Greenland had already witnessed hostile encounters between Vikings and nomadic Inuit. The watercolors reproduced above come from a collection painted during the 1860's by an Inuit engaged in writing down the oral traditions of his people. At left, natives get their first glimpse of the Europeans' presence. At right, in a skin boat disguised as an ice floe, they prepare to attack the settlers. But the Inuit lifeway was better adapted to the cold and harsh land than was that of the European colonists. After 500 years the last of the Greenland Vikings died out.

owed Gudrid becomes a nun, while their Vinland-born son, Snorri, raises a son and a daughter, each of whom was the progenitor of a bishop.

In *Eric's Saga,* Karlsefni's expedition is the final one, and Freydis's adventure is merely a part of it. In the *Greenlander's Saga,* however, Freydis mounts a final expedition the year after Karlsefni's.

As in most of the famous Icelandic sagas, the exploits recorded here reflect the daring of many individuals rather than one, and they repeat or embroider incidents that are told in other sagas.

Viking Ruins in Newfoundland

The basic purpose of the Vinland sagas is nevertheless simple: to tell of the westward sorties by sons and daughters of Iceland and Greenland. And it was material evidence of these sorties that Helge Ingstad sought and found in Newfoundland.

Having already explored the coasts of Rhode Island, Massachusetts, and Nova Scotia without result, Ingstad was invited aboard a hospital ship making calls at fishing villages in Newfoundland in the summer of 1960. At every little port he inquired of local fishermen for any hint of ruins that might prove to be Viking. "One day," he writes, "after many disappointments, I asked yet another fisherman my routine question. He scratched the back of his head and said: 'Well, not so long ago George Decker over at L'Anse aux Meadows was talking about some ruins there.' "

Shortly thereafter Ingstad walked with Decker through what the local man called "Lancey Meadow." "A few minutes' walk to the southwest," Ingstad writes, "brought us to Black Duck Brook, splashing through scrub willow and grass down to the shore. Cattle and sheep grazed on some of the most northerly good pastureland on Canada's Atlantic coast. An inviting place, peaceful and untouched.

"Along an old marine terrace about 12 feet above sea level, I detected a few overgrown outlines in the ground. They suggested remains of walls of very old dwellings.

"We hiked inland and found that the stream flowed from a lake. On our way back, we climbed a small hill west of the sites, and there I discovered the ruins of three very old rock cairns."

Looking out to sea, Ingstad was struck by the similarities between his surroundings and Leif's description in the *Greenlanders' Saga,* yet he knew that "a coincidence of landmarks and a few hints of ancient structures were not enough. Only excavation would give firm proof of an ancient Norse settlement."

Digging began the following year, led by Ingstad's wife, Anne Stine Ingstad. Almost at once, Ingstad saw his theory confirmed by his wife's discovery of a slate-lined ember pit measuring 8½ by 10 inches and demonstrably similar to the ember pits in Greenland.

The tiny hearth was but the first of many artifacts that the site eventually yielded to the Ingstads and that

This page from Eric's Saga *describes an encounter between Vikings and North American natives: "They were small and evil-looking, and their hair was coarse; they had large eyes and broad cheekbones." Although winners in this skirmish, the Vikings decided it was wiser to return home.*

were examined by other scholars reviewing their work. Successive summer searches produced evidence of a substantial Norse community: three "great houses" one with an interior measurement of 80 by 18 feet, with a large center room in the Norse style, as well as five smaller dwellings, some with their own hearths; a smithy, in which lay irregular pieces of slag, bog-iron, and a few fragments of iron; and nearby, a charcoal pit, containing fragments of charred wood. When radiocarbon testing was done on material taken from the smithy, readings of A.D. 860, give or take 90 years, and A.D. 1060, give or take 70 years, were obtained. Even more persuasive is the fact that neither the Inuit nor the American Indian groups known to have inhabited Newfoundland at various times knew how to smelt iron. The remnants found at L'Anse aux Meadows had to have been left by people familiar with the process, as the Norsemen were (and the Inuits were not).

In the fourth year of digging, Anne Stine Ingstad turned up a tiny artifact with major implications — a soapstone spindlewhorl of the kind used to twist raw wool into yarn. Just over 1¼ inches in diameter, this tool is a twin of spindlewhorls found in profusion at sites in Greenland, Iceland, and Norway, and confirms, as no other evidence at L'Anse aux Meadows does, that women were counted among the Norse settlers, a sign the colonists intended to stay.

In fact, Ingstad's claims for the site are cautious: Norse, definitely, and in this he receives ample support from independent scholars. But as to proof that this was Leif's camp, that these structures were Leif's Houses — there is none. So far, the strongest evidence that L'Anse aux Meadows is the site of Leif's camp referred to in the sagas is simply that no competing Norse sites have ever been uncovered in the region (nor do the sagas refer to any other settlements of substance in Vinland — although there are reports of lumbering expeditions to North America as late as 1347).

The problem so briskly dismissed by Ingstad, however, continues to trouble other investigators, for whom L'Anse aux Meadows is too northerly a site to be Vinland. A Vinland without grapes is to these scholars unthinkable, and critics of Ingstad's interpretation of the sagas can point with conviction not only to the philological consensus on the root of the word *Vinland* but to the way in which the great find of grapes is presented in the sagas. Lest there be any doubt that the saga writer knew what he was talking about when it came to grapes, responsibility for their discovery and identification is conspicuously laid to a non-Norse, the German named Tyrkir, who was Leif's foster father. A Norseman might never have seen grapes before, but Tyrkir certainly had, and it is he who wanders off, causing Leif to rebuke his men for carelessness. On returning, however, Tyrkir is in "excellent humour" as he reports his find.

"At first Tyrkir spoke for a long time in German, rolling his eyes in all directions and pulling faces, and no one could understand what he was saying. After a while he spoke in Icelandic.

" 'I did not go much farther than you,' he said. 'I have some news. I found vines and grapes.'

" 'Is that true, foster-father?' asked Leif.

" 'Of course it is true,' he replied. 'Where I was born there were plenty of vines and grapes.' "

It is of course possible that the Tyrkir episode was a plant, inserted to substantiate the claims made for Vinland (in the tradition of Eric the Red naming Greenland for what it was least), but however *that* question is resolved, there is no longer any doubt that Norse settlers made their way at least as far as Newfoundland.

Fade-out in the West

A thousand years later the story of Vinland seems tantalizing but bittersweet. A venture of daring and promise cut short and lost to history for centuries, it has few rivals as a tale of "what might have been."

The failure of the Norse enterprise, however, can hardly be thought tragic in and of itself. For one thing, the retreat of the would-be settlers spared America's indigenous peoples European cruelty for another 500 years. And for the settlers, hopeful as they were, Vinland was only an interlude, never a complete investment. Yet the collapse of the hope that was Vinland contributed in time to events that overtook the descendants of the sagas' several heroes, and those events must surely be called tragic. The underlying purpose of the Vinland adventure was never simple glory but rather survival. Even with a population of some 3,000 and the freedom to trade without restriction with Iceland and Europe, Greenland's resources were strained to the limit from her earliest days. For almost 300 years, however, from around 985 to 1261, Greenland survived as an independent nation: her small agricultural communities were nearly self-sufficient, while her valued exports — walrus ivory and white falcons for the hunt — purchased necessary additional goods. It was a hard economy always, and there was from the start an urgency about Greenland's glances westward. With no chance for an expansion to the west, Greenland was all too soon isolated from the east as well.

It is a difficult story to piece together, but the collective surmise of historians is that Greenland withered slowly throughout the 13th and 14th centuries, her contacts with Europe first reduced, then altogether severed. Greenland became dependent on the rare dock-

The Norwegian explorer Helge Ingstad, together with his wife, the archeologist Anne Stine Ingstad, made expeditions for almost a decade in search of a Viking site in North America. In 1961 they found such a site, outside the village of L'Anse aux Meadows, at the north end of Newfoundland.

The 11th-century spindlewhorl found in Newfoundland by Anne Ingstad (1964). Scandinavians used spindlewhorls to spin thread for weaving cloth.

Ruins of a church beside Eric the Red's original farmstead at Brattahlid in Greenland. Among the last Vikings in Greenland Christian observance dimmed to mere memory — according to a letter of 1492: "Once a year they exhibit the communion cloth used by their last bishop about a hundred years ago."

Another poignant reminder of the Viking colonization of inhospitable Greenland, this carved ivory head depicting a stern-faced Norseman was done by an unknown Inuit artist.

ings of Norwegian ships for all needed imports. Plentiful elephant-ivory from Africa undercut Greenland's profitable export, and the Black Death of 1347–51 reduced Norway's population by two thirds and curtailed contacts across the North Atlantic. Perhaps the cruelest blow of all was the one that the Greenlanders could do least about: a sudden drop in the summer temperature. This brought drifting ice that made sea voyages even more risky and reduced a growing season which was barely long enough to sustain the population in the first place.

"It is a sad picture," Samuel Eliot Morison writes in *The European Discovery of America: The Northern Voyages, A.D. 500-1600,* "the gradual snuffing out of this far-away colony so gallantly planted by Eric the Red. His last descendants, hardly able to find enough food to keep alive, staring their eyes out all through the short, bright summer for the ship from Norway that meant

their salvation. By September it becomes certain that she will not come that year. The long, dark winter closes in, and there is no more oil for lamps. Cold and hungry, the people live merely to survive until next summer when surely the ship will come; but it never does. At some time in the second half of the fifteenth century, the last Norse Greenlander died, 'unknell'd, uncoffin'd and unknown.'"

And so there came an end not just to the Vinland adventure but to the adventurers themselves. Greenland would be occupied by Europeans again — colonized in 1721 by the Kingdom of Norway and Denmark; since 1814 Danish territory — but it never had independence, nor did it figure as dramatically in world history as in those early years. That "so kind" land brought glory to other peoples altogether, and Greenland's brave settlers became supernumeraries rather than protagonists in the epic of New World history.

IN SEARCH
OF
EARLY MAN

HOW NEW IS THE NEW WORLD?

Europeans called it the New World, but they were late arrivals.
Most scientists agree that the first immigrants reached
the Americas from Asia via a vanished land bridge. Recent evidence
suggests they were in South America more than 30,000 years ago.

Since the late 1960's the scientific search for the first Americans has focused mainly on the far northwestern corner of Canada, in that remote and fabled territory called the Yukon. There, on July 12, 1966, at an extreme northeastern point along what was probably prehistoric man's overland route from Asia to the North American continent, paleontologist C. R. Harington of the National Museums of Canada and his field assistant, Peter Lord, were working their way along the Old Crow River in a flat-bottomed boat. They were watching the riverbank for fossilized animal bones, tusks, antlers, and teeth, either "weathered out" of the riverbank or washed out by spring meltwater and deposited, by the thousands, at the foot of its 100-foot-high bluffs.

A paleontologist's business is not usually human remains. But the Old Crow Basin is what Harington once called "a paleontologist's supermarket." Along with the Rancho La Brea tar pits in Los Angeles, it is one of the Western Hemisphere's richest deposits of Pleistocene, or Ice Age, animal fossils. Might not Ice Age man have passed this way as well? Harington had asked Lord, a native of the town of Old Crow, to be on the lookout for human remains. Landing at a spot that looked promising, Harington and Lord each began turning over bones, shells, wood, and ancient spruce cones. Harington was absorbed in cleaning off an animal's fossilized jawbone when Lord, grinning broadly, approached and said: "I guess this is what you are looking for!"

The bone — a caribou leg bone whose upper end had been pared down and notched — looked significantly different from its neighbors. Harington knew instantly that no accident of nature could have produced such a neat effect. No river erosion, no gnawing by an ancient four-footed predator, no random destruction by Ice Age rock or grinding glacier — only the hand of man could have made notches like this. Obviously it was some kind of tool. But what kind? (Harington later learned that Ojibwa Indians in Manitoba still make such "fleshers" from moose bones and use them to scrape the insides of animal hides.) And just as obviously it was old. Harington knew from its dark-brown stain that it had undergone many hun-

The Old Crow River meanders through some of the wildest country in the Americas. Archeologists, whose base camp is visible on the sandy point at center, come to this land of conifers and caribou to search for traces of the first Americans.

Twenty years after Harington's find (see opposite page), the 100-foot-high banks of the Old Crow River — a 150,000-year slice of life — are still rich with Ice Age fossils.

dreds, if not thousands, of years of weathering. He could scarcely contain his excitement.

If the bone was as old as he thought it might be, here finally was proof of Early Man in the New World near the eastern end of the former Bering land bridge — exactly where most prehistorians thought it should be.

In fact, if there was a mystery, it was why no one had found any evidence of Early Man's presence before. After all, the Old Crow Basin in northeastern Beringia (the area that comprises not only the former land bridge but the regions to the west of it in Siberia and to the east of it in Alaska and the Yukon) was a likely spot to find traces of early people. They could easily have reached it by following the Yukon River to its great bend and then following the Porcupine River. And there was another reason why the Old Crow Basin was a good bet. During the last great Ice Age, the final advance of which is known in North America as the Wisconsin period, there were glaciers fully two miles high around Beringia. To the east was the great Laurentide glacier, which stretched over half of North America from the Atlantic Ocean to Alberta; to the south were the Cordilleran glaciers, which reached from the Pacific Ocean over the Rockies. And there were glaciers in all of the high valleys of the nearby Alaskan ranges.

But for reasons having to do with continental aridity, most of Beringia was untouched by the glaciers. This one enchanted part of the far north became an ice-free refuge for all living creatures — including, no doubt, man. It provided, right in the middle of an ice age, a steppe-tundra environment so hospitable to living creatures that it has been compared to Africa's fabled Serengeti Plain. And, contrary to what we who live in temperate climates might think, human beings not only survived in "periglacial," or near-glacial, environments, they flourished there. Their ancestors had adapted to the cold thousands of years before, and arctic landscapes probably held little terror for them. As Alan Bryan, a leading Canadian prehistorian, says: "People who live in the north have no fear of the cold."

The whole region of Beringia would have attracted early immigrants, especially during the cold periods. No doubt there is some evidence in central Beringia, under 180 feet of Arctic water — too near the limit of free diving. Scouring the sea floor with remote-controlled sensing devices is costly and, to a scientist, unsatisfying. And until recently not much was known about Beringian sites on the Siberian side of the land bridge. This left Alaska and the Yukon as the most promising areas to look for evidence of Early Man in the New World.

In short, there was a lot riding on Harington's find, as he well knew. Many times he had watched the fireworks over archeological discoveries with the detachment of a paleontologist: "I find camel remains up there," he says wryly, " — *camel remains* — and nobody bats an eyelash. But then you mention man, and

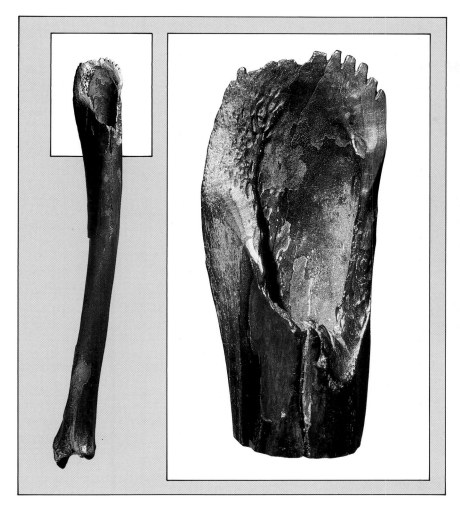

At far left, a replica of the 10-inch-long Old Crow caribou bone scraper, notched by early people for scraping the insides of animal hides. At near left, the worked portion — all that was left of the scraper after the original radiocarbon test. Above, a glimpse inside an Old Crow field laboratory, where artifacts are sorted, cleaned, and classified for future study.

it's as if an alarm goes off!" This time it was he who was talking about signs of human activity.

He showed the tibia to archeologist William N. Irving, who was also working in the Old Crow area. Irving, having spent a frustrating day uncovering old jack knives and broken harmonicas, was equally enthusiastic. Yet they were reluctant to sacrifice the precious find to radiocarbon analysis (see "Dating Methods," page 75), hoping to find other material to support the antiquity of the tool. But finally, after a few more seasons of searching had failed to produce anything quite as remarkable, the two scientists agreed in 1969 to submit the caribou bone to chemical analysis. The result was astounding. According to this first test, the scraper was about 27,000 years old. This was a real discovery. No relic of Early Man even half its age had ever been found in the New World — and for the next 16 years the notched caribou bone scraper was largely believed to be the oldest radiocarbon-dated human artifact in the New World.

The Old Crow find sent ripples throughout the archeological community. There was at the time a con-

sensus among prehistorians that the first Americans only arrived 12,000 or 13,000 years ago. Would all the textbooks have to be rewritten? Early Arrivalists — those prehistorians who claim to see evidence for man's presence in the New World earlier than 30,000 years, and perhaps as early as 250,000 years ago — nodded, as if to say, "What is so remarkable about a 27,000-year-old artifact?" Middle Arrivalists — those who believe people came to the New World sometime between 30,000 and 12,000 years ago — were pleased to have an artifact of such seeming antiquity that was so obviously the work of man. But the Late Arrivalists — those who say that all so-called evidence for man in the New World prior to Clovis Man (see "America's First Patent," page 84) about 11,600 years ago is dubious and not to be trusted — came up with a number of objections.

First, they questioned the radiocarbon date, which came from carbon obtained from the apatite, or inorganic portion of the bone (usually in dating bone, carbon from the organic, or collagen, portion of the bone is used). Even C. Vance Haynes, the man who first

71

experimented with bone apatite dating, now repudiates this dating method as subject to possible contamination from the surrounding soil or groundwater. And indeed, this ultimately proved to be the case. Using the particle accelerator radiocarbon dating method (see "Dating Methods," page 75), Canadian scientists in mid-1985 proposed that the scraper was a mere 1,350 years old — 25,650 years off the original date!

Some skeptics had maintained all along that while the caribou whose leg bone caused all the fuss may well have died 27,000 years ago, it was likely that the tool was modern. Couldn't an Indian within the past several hundred years have used an ancient bone as a scraper? But, defenders countered, why would an arctic hunter even try to make a serviceable tool out of a brittle old bone? Old bones have a way of disintegrating in your hands, and fresh caribou bone was easy to obtain.

However, even believers in the antiquity of the Old Crow site know that they are working at a great disadvantage in the Yukon. True, Old Crow was never ice covered. And true, the river's 100-foot-high bluffs provide prehistorians with rich Ice Age fossil exposures embedded in an all-preserving permafrost. But trouble comes in the spring and summer — and has for the past 10,000 years — when the languorous Old Crow River turns into a raging flood. The river undercuts the bluffs until a whole side of the frozen cliff melts and slumps, depositing its contents (often including priceless artifacts) down by the river's edge. The river then carries artifacts downstream, even farther from their original "context." Bones of recently bagged caribou and Ice Age fossils can end up right next to each other.

Meanwhile, erosion of the riverbanks continues, often bringing new fossils to the edge. For an archeologist the trick is to get to the riverbank after a new fossil bed has been exposed and before it is carried away.

Since there are no roads at all along Old Crow, it is impossible to keep tabs on all parts of the river. And though permafrost preserves, it also makes excavating without heavy equipment a nightmare. As can well be imagined, this is galling to anyone trying to make sense out of the prehistory of the Old Crow Basin. An archeologist may find something extraordinary lying on an Old Crow River sandbar. He may think that it was once handled by man — because it bears what appear to be butchering marks, for example, or because it is whittled to a point. He may even know it was man-made — as in the rare case of the caribou scraper. But likely as not, he'll never know exactly where or how it was used.

It is true that archeologists are accustomed to reconstructing whole lifeways on the basis of bits and pieces of human detritus — a discarded stone chopper, a single ivory bead, or an antler someone used a few times thousands of years ago as a hammer. As one archeologist put it, interpreting a piece of archeological evidence is "like taking a key and building a car around it."

But where the first Americans are concerned, prehistorians don't even have the key. They are divided on the most basic issues — *who* the earliest immigrants

Two inches high, this Alaskan dwarf willow probably resembles Ice Age willows; its spring-blooming catkins, or flowers, are as welcome to present-day moose as they no doubt were to

Pleistocene browsers. At right, on a lichen-encrusted rock, is an arctic tern which, to judge from its summer colors, has recently completed its astonishing migration from Antarctica.

At left, the Yukon River northwest of Dawson. This broad stream, which drains about 320,000 square miles in the Yukon and Alaska, may have served the New World's first immigrants as a pathway into the interior. Below, dwarf birch aflame in fall color. Birch shrubs have covered Arctic tundra since the end of the last Ice Age.

were, *where* they came from, *how* they got here, and *when* they arrived. And the truth of the matter is that the Old Crow scraper raised more questions than it answered.

As to *who* were the first people to arrive in the New World, the conventional assumption has always been that they were Asians. And this assumption seems to be holding.

The rather obvious physical similarity between American Indians and Asians — even today, so many hundreds, and perhaps hundreds of thousands, of generations after the immigration — has often been noted. Thomas Jefferson commented on it in his 1785 *Notes on the State of Virginia.*

Scientific corroboration for this idea comes from studies Arizona State University's Christy Turner

made of the teeth — the most durable part of the human body — of New World skeletons. Turner says that prehistoric American teeth closely resemble northeast Asian teeth and that they are unlike the teeth of any other people anywhere in the world.

The first Americans came from northeast Asia — so much we could have guessed. But what did they look like? And how did they get here?

The 18th-century exploration of the Bering Strait confirmed what earlier European writers had surmised — that the continents of Asia and North America nearly touch. In fact, only 56 miles separate them. We now know much more. Soundings have indicated that the Bering and Chukchi seas are not very deep and that the sea floor is uniformly flat. Studies of ancient shorelines, analyses of sea-floor core samples, and esti-

OVERLAND FROM ASIA

Early Man reached the New World from Asia — passing through Beringia, a now-vanished land bridge to North America that was as big as the continental United States. In pursuit of big game, these ancient hunters moved south, traveling an ice-free corridor between two major glaciers or perhaps hugging the shoreline; later arrivals trekked eastward across the top of the continent to Greenland. As the first Americans were coming, 27,000 or more years ago, other Asians traveled an incomplete land bridge to Australia, rafting deep water between continents.

KEY TO MAP

Route of Early Man

Emerged land at glacial maximum

Land

Glacier

Present continental outline

mates of the volume of ice formerly locked up in glaciers — all point unarguably to the existence of a land bridge. This was a land bridge that would, of course, emerge in cold periods when what scientists call "the water budget" was locked up in glaciers and sea levels fell; it would then disappear in warm periods when the glaciers retreated and sea levels rose, only to reemerge during the next cold spell.

The discovery of the land bridge was certainly a breakthrough for the study of New World prehistory. But in a sense it was too much of a good thing. Working backwards in time, prehistorians constructed elaborate timetables, or schedules, according to which early

people were said to have crossed the land bridge during a cold period. Then during a subsequent warm period, the waters rose over the land bridge and cut off their retreat — one prehistorian called this a one-way valve mechanism. In any case, once on the American side, immigrants were said to have made their way along the eastern slopes of the Rockies, between the Laurentide and the Cordilleran superglaciers, down an "ice-free corridor" — which supposedly existed when the two ice sheets separated — and thus out onto the American Great Plains. According to one timetable favored by Late Arrivalists, early people traveled this corridor during a warm part of the last Ice Age known as the Two

Creeks interval, ending about 11,800 years ago, making their first appearance at the Clovis, New Mexico, site 11,600 years ago.

It wasn't always easy to make the land-bridge-and-corridor timetables work. The land bridge depended on cold (when the climate was warm, it was flooded); the corridor depended on warmth (when the climate was cold, the two superglaciers coalesced and the corridor — if it ever existed — would have closed up). So textbooks would speak of the early immigrants as if "poised for entry" into the New World and presumed to be traveling on a "tight schedule." The amount of time it would take them to get to the bottom of South America — as if continent-crossing were a competitive sport — was scrupulously calculated.

What is more likely is that the first Americans moved slowly through Beringia, following herds of game animals. Perhaps they even made central Beringia their home for thousands of years. In fact, they would have been totally unaware that they were crossing from one continent to another. The Bering land bridge was 1,000 miles wide at its widest north-south point.

Furthermore, who says the first immigrants came dry-shod at all? They might have crossed on winter ice, which would have formed even during a relatively warm interglacial period. And as for the so-called ice-free corridor, some prehistorians ask why, if it really was a highway south for early people, some evidence of their passage hasn't turned up. For years archeologists have been looking in vain for such evidence.

Perhaps people went south, not by the easiest route, but by the hardest one. Knut Fladmark, an archeologist at Simon Fraser University in British Columbia, believes early people could have traveled south along the rugged Pacific northwest coast. Inlets may have been ice filled during the coldest periods, he says, but this would only have facilitated travel; and boats would have enabled them to skirt the most heavily glaciated areas. These resourceful people, whose ancestors had been living in cold climates for hundreds of thousands of years, may have simply kept to the coastal environment they knew. Food is plentiful along an ocean littoral, especially for people who know how to exploit it.

And so the arguments went, until some startling evidence from halfway around the world — Australia, of all places — added two brand new ideas to the discussion. During the last Ice Age, sea levels were lowered worldwide, not just in Beringia but everywhere, by an average of 325 feet. New Guinea, for example, was part of Australia, and Borneo and Java were part of the Asian mainland. But Australia has throughout the known evolution of mankind been separate from Asia. So people must have reached Australia by boat. The question was — when?

It was once believed that Early Man was not capable of the technological sophistication necessary to make boats or rafts or to negotiate even the shortest sea voy-

age. And in any case, man in Australia couldn't have any real antiquity. Australia was a continent full of marsupials but with no primate other than man. So man must have been a recent arrival — a few thousand years ago at the most.

But in 1968, prehistorians began turning up substantial evidence of human occupation of Australia between 25,000 and 30,000 years ago. Now the date has been pushed to 40,000, and educated guesses by some experts take us back as far as 100,000 years ago, or more. Collections of freshwater mussel shells, charred bones, and stone artifacts were found at a site along the shores

Dating Methods

Twentieth-century technological wizardry notwithstanding, scientists still have no single dating method that covers all human history. The most accurate method is one Leonardo da Vinci thought of five centuries ago — *dendrochronology,* or tree-ring dating. By matching the annual growth rings of living trees with the ring patterns of progressively older dead trees (such as roof beams from ancient houses), an overlapping and continuous chronology can be constructed — one stretching more than 8,000 years into the past.

The standard dating technique employed by archeologists, however, is *radiocarbon* (or carbon-14) dating. Carbon-14, a radioactive element absorbed by all living things through the food chain, begins to decay as soon as the organism dies. Since they know the rate of decay, scientists can test the age of any sample of once-living matter (such as wood, rope, bone, shell) by measuring the ratio of stable carbon-12, which does not decay, to whatever carbon-14 is left. The less carbon-14, the older the sample. A new radiocarbon dating method, which uses *particle accelerators,* is a notable improvement: its sample size is much smaller (1/1000 of what the old carbon-14 method required) thus sparing more of the relic being dated; it is faster; and one day it may date objects up to 100,000 years old, double the upper limit of traditional carbon-14 dating.

Each dating method has its drawbacks. *Potassium-argon* dating, another "atomic clock" method, is most useful in dating objects older than 250,000 years. *Thermoluminescence* is useful in dating pottery but gives limited information. A new dating method called *amino acid racemization* may help bridge the age gap between radiocarbon and potassium-argon, but its accuracy depends on having a climatic profile from the site. With *archeomagnetic* dating, objects can be dated according to how metals within them are magnetically oriented, but only if the object has never moved from its original position.

Since no single dating method can tell them everything they need to know, scientists for the time being must get their answers piecemeal.

of Lake Mungo, an extinct inland lake in a now semi-arid region of New South Wales in southern Australia. Since then, human remains — notably the skeleton of a young male — have been found at a level dated probably at 28,000 years ago. And the evidence from Lake Mungo continues to pile up. There can no longer be any doubt that early people reached and crossed a continent at a very early date — and they came by boat.

So the question became irresistible: if early people reached Australia by watercraft, why couldn't they get to the New World the same way? Why would they need the land bridge at all?

Alternate Routes

Prehistorians now had to consider some new scenarios. First of all, perhaps early peoples didn't arrive during a cold period when the land bridge was a nice wide highway. If they came by boat, they could have arrived on American shores virtually anytime — during warm periods as well as during cold ones. Second, now there were more routes they could have traveled. A logical approach to the Americas, suggests Sylvia Hallam, of the University of Western Australia, would have been via northern Japan, the Kurile Islands, the Kamchatka Peninsula, and the Aleutians.

So much for tight schedules. The early use of watercraft — and what that implied for the New World — was Australia's first surprise. But there was another one coming. Workers digging an irrigation canal at Kow Swamp, 150 miles south of Lake Mungo, had come upon the skeletal remains of some 40 aboriginal Australians. The bones were not that ancient — they have since been estimated to be between 9,000 and 15,000 years old. What caused all the fuss was that they belonged to a very mysterious people — a people whose prominent brow ridges and massive jawbones looked very old. And yet, a modern-looking, or "gracile," as archeologists put it, skeleton from Lake Mungo had been assigned an older age — 28,000 to 30,000 years. These Kow Swamp people, then, looked more primitive — but were much younger — than the Lake Mungo people, who looked more modern — but were much older. Apparently here were two very different racial stocks coexisting in one continent.

In any case, one thing was certain. Bones are not always as old (or as young) as they look. Criteria for judging the age of bones too old for traditional radiocarbon dating — criteria such as prominent brow ridges — can be very misleading.

There is a lesson for New World prehistorians here. Now when they dig up a modern-looking skull in association with ancient material in the New World, perhaps they will be slower to dismiss it as young just because it looks young. Perhaps modern people (such as the Lake Mungo people in Australia) have been in existence in the New World for much longer than previously thought. Perhaps we already have ancient skeletal material sitting on museum and university shelves.

This sandstorm-swept Australian landscape was a pleasant lake 30,000 years ago. Early people collected freshwater mussels and birds' eggs and hunted such local fauna as wallabies, rat kangaroos, and wombats. The partially excavated 28,000-year-old skeleton at right is Australia's oldest.

Human evolution in the New World may turn out to have followed a significantly different path from the one it followed in the Old World.

The Australian evidence led to much soul-searching as well as head-scratching. So much of what often passes as pure luck depends, scientists realize, on an archeologist's knowing what he's looking at. As the great 19th-century scientist Louis Pasteur put it: "Chance favors only the mind that is prepared." First comes recognition, Pasteur seems to be saying, and only afterwards comes discovery.

The same sort of serendipity-plus is at work where cultural artifacts are concerned. An archeologist who expects the earliest evidence of man in a New World site to be spear points is unlikely to make the "chance" discovery of anything earlier. Such an archeologist might look straight at an early artifact and not even see it.

It is not difficult to see why stone tools sometimes are virtually unrecognizable. Let's say an early American picks up a nicely rounded river pebble — one that is comfortable to hold in his hand — strikes it a couple of times against another stone to make a rough chopping edge, and then, after using it once to cut branches, discards it. The only evidence of his tool-using that is likely to withstand thousands of years of glaciers, frost, erosion, floods, fires, and radical swings in temperature is that one chopping edge. How is an archeologist going to be able to tell the difference between a genuine *artifact*, such as a tool with a man-made chopping edge, and a *geofact*, a stone looking much like the one described above but whose edge was made naturally — for example, when a flood tide carried it across another stone? In the absence of datable material, the question is

at the very heart of the matter of how *new* the *New World* really is.

In archeology, America is the Dark Continent, not Africa. No one has ever seriously considered the Americas as a possible place of origin for mankind, and few recognize even the possibility of pre-*Homo sapiens* in the New World. One might expect New World prehistorians to resent this situation, but not so. Actually, some observers point out that there is a sort of double standard at work, by which something that would be a perfectly acceptable stone chopper in the Old World is summarily rejected if it turns up in California. Which is exactly what happened to no less a luminary than the late British archeologist Louis B. Leakey in the case of the Calico Hills site in California's Mojave Desert.

The Calico site is highly controversial. Some believe there is good evidence there for a human presence as early as 200,000 years ago. Others say that the entire excavation has been a colossal waste of time and money. Largely because of the controversy, and because the famous Dr. Leakey was involved, it has become what must be one of the most intensively studied sites anywhere in the New World. Work began at Calico in 1964. It is still going on.

Ruth DeEtte Simpson, curator of archeology at the San Bernardino County Museum in Redlands, California, is the one who started it all. She thought she saw evidence near Calico of a stone industry much cruder than Clovis, and in 1963 she took Leakey, then a visiting professor at the University of California at Riverside, to the site. Leakey was mightily intrigued by what he thought he recognized as the kind of primitive stone tool that turned up all the time at his famous

Olduvai Gorge site in East Africa. In the following year, with funding from the National Geographic Society, he chose two spots and sank two major excavation pits (a third was sunk after Leakey died in 1972).

Human Workmanship?

Since 1964, over 11,000 specimens have been found — specimens which Simpson believes, and Leakey believed, are genuine tools. Skeptics do not see human workmanship in the stones, though they agree the site is old. They point out that the pits are dug into what geologists call an "alluvial fan," a sort of delta of river-deposited sediment built up over thousands of years. They point out further that alluvial fans in general tend to mix strata vertically as well as horizontally. That is, artifacts of different ages might appear in the same level. The Calico fan is particularly large; some have called it a "giant gravel crusher," implying that natural forces within the fan were more than enough to alter the stones the experts were calling artifacts. Proponents do not dispute that forces other than the human hand can knock a flake off a stone, but say they can tell the difference. They point out that the 11,000 specimens represent a small portion of the stone removed from the pits. They invite any and all to examine their stockpiled "nondiagnostic" stones — that is, nontools.

The stones in question cannot be dated by radiocarbon. For that, organic remains of some kind are needed. But this was also a problem, since the only organic remains were tusk fragments, probably from a mammoth, found at a depth of 151 inches in 1967, and these went off the radiocarbon scale, thus indicating — if the test was accurate — a minimum age of 40,000 years. This was already impressive. But by a different kind of test run more recently an even older date was obtained on the calcium carbonate coating that had formed around some of the stone specimens. And that test indicated an astounding age of 200,000 years.

By 1968 the excavators were down 279 inches (for a New World dig, this was a remarkable depth) and still finding what they claimed were man-made tools, when they hit pay dirt. A semicircular arrangement of 13 cobblestones was uncovered in Master Pit II. Most of the stones were touching, which seemed to indicate deliberate placement. Also, large and small cobbles seemed to alternate in a pattern of 3-2-3-2-3. And oval-shaped stones pointed out from the center like spokes of a wheel. Despite the lack of visible charcoal, it cer-

tainly looked like a hearth, and a preliminary test measuring the magnetic properties of one of the cobbles indicated that yes, a fire had indeed burned inside the circle at one time.

Here seemed to be evidence that the New World was indeed not new at all. This didn't surprise Leakey, who had expected it all along. Didn't the many different languages spoken by tribes from Alaska to Cape Horn, he asked, indicate a presence in the New World of more than just a few thousand years? Such diversity could not have developed overnight. And Leakey was accustomed, from his years in East Africa, to looking for evidence of human workmanship in the simplest kind of unifacial stone tool.

In California's Mojave Desert, just 50 miles from where the space shuttle landed at Edwards Air Force Base, Early Man may have walked some 200,000 years ago. Calico Project director Ruth Simpson (above with the late Louis B. Leakey) has supervised the excavation of three major pits, whose sun-shaded entrances are shown above right. At right is a view of Master Pit I, with its five-foot-square reference grid at ground level and a "witness column" left standing for future study.

So he must have been genuinely surprised by the resistance he encountered when the Calico results were announced. There was so much resistance that eventually the L. S. B. Leakey Foundation, the University of Pennsylvania Museum, and the San Bernardino County Museum called a conference in 1970 so that scholars from all over the world might come to the site and see the artifacts for themselves. The International Conference on the Calico Project, held in 1970, was the first of its kind — rarely does a single site generate so much controversy. The conference produced some converts, but many remained unconvinced. The Calico mystery has only deepened with time. A recent thermoluminescence test (see "Dating Methods," page 75) cast doubt on the Calico "hearth" — even Simpson now agrees it probably was not a hearth. But no mudslide, no stream action, no erosion, no tectonic stress could produce such an orderly semicircle. So what was it? We may very well never know.

Meanwhile, the Calico site has become a sort of outdoor archeological museum. Since it opened to the public, 150,000 people have come to see for themselves. The excavators left some artifacts — including the "hearth," now referred to simply as a "feature" — just as they were found. Other artifacts are being scrutinized under microscopes by "use-wear" experts to see whether they show such signs of man's handiwork as flaking, cutting, scraping, or high polish from rubbing. Simpson is hopeful — she says that out of 4,000 specimens in one study, 1,000 were pronounced tools, and of those, 10 to 15 percent showed unarguable signs of use-wear. Needless to say, not everyone agrees.

Calico is not the only contested Early Man site. Another is the so-called Woolley mammoth site (named not for the woolly mammoth but for geologist John Woolley who found it) on Santa Rosa Island, one of the Channel Islands off Los Angeles. Santa Rosa has long been known for its prehistoric population of "dwarf" mammoths — elephants that stood no more than six feet at the shoulder. And primitive stone tools had turned up, too, but never in clear association with the bones or with anything else that could date them. Then in 1976 Woolley came upon what looked like a hearth — a bowl-shaped area of reddened earth almost 10 feet in diameter. From it, he extracted bones, tools, and finally charcoal that yielded a radiocarbon date in excess of 40,000 years.

But was it an undisturbed hearth? Or was it a mishmash of, say, very old bones and much younger tools — that is, unrelated objects dumped in the same spot by who knows what process of erosion? Rainer Berger, head of the radiocarbon lab at UCLA, is convinced it is a good site. But others disagree. Some say the reddened area is just a burnt tree stump. And one geologist, Donald Johnson of the University of Illinois at Champaign–Urbana, says the whole site is a jumble of "reworked debris."

But a good Early Man site may yet turn up on Santa Rosa Island. For one thing, says Johnson, Santa Rosa's geologic record of the past 50,000 years is astonishingly complete. So the record of a human presence — if it is found at all — may well be found in an unimpeachable context. But why would early people have come to an island like Santa Rosa at all? The mammoths, strange as it may sound, apparently swam the four or five miles separating the island from the mainland in lowered-sea level times. Did early people follow them on rafts? Was it what Johnson calls "the Bali Ha'i syndrome" — whereby a coastal dweller, spotting a distant isle on the horizon, feels an urge to get there somehow and somehow finds the means to do so?

At other sites — notably one at Texas Street, also in California — claims are made of 100,000 years and more. But such sites are all, according to skeptics, flawed in one way or another. Either the geologic context is ambiguous, or radiocarbon dating is impossible for one reason or another, or the so-called stone industry in question is so crude as to be unrecognizable. What the truth is cannot be said.

If ancient stone tools are hard to identify, bone tools are worse. For the 20 years since Harington's discovery of the caribou scraper at Old Crow, prehistorians have been coming to suspect that early people made tools out of bone as much as, if not more than, out of stone. Though not as sharp as stone, bone was, very simply, more readily available. Hunters could use the bone of an animal they brought down to make the tools needed to bring down the next one. There are, in fact, so many bone artifacts coming out of Old Crow that one author referred to ongoing work there as the search for "Bone Age Man."

Reenacting Ancient Dramas

One of the best ways for scientists to understand how ancient people did things is to do it themselves. Experimentation is a vital cross-check on archeological theories. Nowadays, before an archeologist assumes anything about how early hunters fixed their stone points onto their spears he may try hafting some points himself. Dennis Stanford, an anthropologist at the Smithsonian Institution, tried using not only sinew as binding cord but also animal blood, which he believed might have been used as a sort of natural glue. He found it worked very well.

Stanford went further than this. He, Robson Bonnichsen of the University of Maine, and Richard Morlan of Ottawa's National Museum of Man decided to test their ideas as to how early hunters really butchered their game animals. Could they duplicate ancient butchering techniques? And could they prove a few things along the way — that those bones from Old Crow had been modified by early people, that scientists could "read" the marks on bones just as they had learned to "read" the marks on stones, and that early hunters could make good sharp bone tools out of the animals they butchered?

Thus, in 1978 when a 23-year-old female elephant named Ginsberg died of a blood clot in a Boston zoo, the Smithsonian Institution had the two-ton carcass sent to a Virginia site, where the research team proceeded to carve her up.

It may have seemed odd for three anthropologists in 20th-century America to be wallowing about in elephant blood. But then archeologists are in the business of reconstructing the past, and the scene in Virginia couldn't have been any more grisly than a real Ice Age hunting scene. And there were a few significant differences. The research team did something no Pleistocene mammoth hunter could have done — they brought along a computer and hooked wires up to their butchering tools so that each time they sliced, sawed, or pounded, their movements were recorded. They learned plenty. For instance, they noted that, for piercing the tough hide of an elephant in the butchering process, stone knives did better than bone knives. But they also observed something with their own eyes that they couldn't explain. With the help of an atlatl, antler spear points actually performed better than stone spear points. For one thing, they weren't as brittle as stone. But they seemed to travel through the air more easily than stone. What was it about the ballistics of bone and antler projectile points that gave them this edge over stone? No one as yet can say — more experimentation is needed. But the team made one thing absolutely clear — a toolmaker can use the same techniques on bone that he uses on stone. Out of Ginsberg's leg bones, they made tools that looked extraordinarily similar to some of the "altered bone" coming out of Old Crow. While this wasn't proof that the Old Crow artifacts were genuine, it was another piece of the puzzle. And when the butchering was finished and the butchering tools examined, the wear marks were unmistakable, and yet another piece of the puzzle fell into place. Ginsberg had certainly done her part!

Evidence from Siberia

Meanwhile despite the protestations of a few die-hard Late Arrivalists, the evidence seems to be piling up in the Middle Arrivalists' corner. For one thing, work done in three sites in the Aldan River valley in northeast Siberia by Soviet archeologist Yuri Mochanov is beginning to provide solid evidence of a human presence there beginning about 35,000 years ago. This makes a crossing to the New World of about 30,000 years ago all the more likely and would have been consistent with the original dating given to the caribou scraper from Old Crow. For another, the number of sites in North and South America with evidence for a human presence more than 12,000 or 13,000 years ago is steadily mounting.

One firm Middle Arrivalist is H. Marie Wormington of Colorado College. According to her, the strongest evidence for an entry date of about 30,000 years ago comes from sites near Valsequillo, an area south of the

central Mexican city of Puebla, where a radiocarbon test of a freshwater snail shell indicated it was about 22,000 years old (a human presence was established by a stone scraping tool found in the same level). After the initial excavations in the 1960's by archeologist Cynthia Irwin-Williams and her Mexican colleague Juan Armenta Camacho, there was a scuffle about the age of the sites. Several scientists — among them Harold Malde of the U.S. Geological Survey, who participated in all three seasons of archeological digging, and Virginia Steen-McIntyre, an associate of Malde's and a scientist whose speciality is dating volcanic ash deposits — published a paper stating their belief that they saw geologic evidence at one of the Valsequillo sites of a far greater age, namely 250,000 years. This is quite a hefty claim — in fact, the Malde/Steen-McIntyre date is probably the current record holder as far as serious estimates of New World man go. Most prehistorians find this very difficult to swallow, and continue to see Valsequillo not as the earliest of Early Arrival sites, but as one of the best of the Middle Arrival sites.

Another site that convinces all but a few New World prehistorians is Meadowcroft, a rock shelter on the north bank of a small tributary of the Ohio River not far from Pittsburgh in Pennsylvania's coal mining country. The rock shelter turned out to contain an al-

At a Virginia research station (left), archeologists reenact an Ice Age butchering scene. The carcass is that of an elephant that had died a natural death in a Boston zoo. Above, archeologist Dennis Stanford adjusts wires connecting his wood-handled stone knife to a computer that recorded the process.

most undisturbed series of 11 distinct layers — one of the longest occupational sequences in the Western Hemisphere. Beginning in 1973 the site was excavated — in Wormington's words, "superbly excavated" — by a team headed by James Adovasio of the University of Pittsburgh. The work was large-scale and small-scale. Not only did they cart away 230 cubic meters of soil, but with the kind of care you might expect in a coronary bypass operation they scraped "living floors" with razor blades. The archeologists determined that there had been a series of rockfalls in the cave's history. That is, on numerous occasions the overhanging ceiling had broken loose and crashed to the cave floor. In fact, rocks the size of a small house had fallen twice. Undismayed by these interruptions in the site's otherwise impeccable stratigraphy, they simply proceeded to locate the levels corresponding to the rockfalls, and then to map the roll marks on the cave floor. As Adovasio put it with some understatement: "That's careful digging."

Before they were through at Meadowcroft, workers extracted some 3.5 million objects from the rock shelter. There were bones of 116 different animal species and stone artifacts from a surprising number of quarries — only 10 percent of it was local in origin. From the next-to-lowest layer came over 400 stone artifacts,

bits of charcoal from a fire pit, and — best of all — a charred fragment of what looked like a basket made of bark. This was a one-of-a-kind discovery, and its radiocarbon date — in excess of 19,000 years — made it a candidate for being one of the oldest radiocarbon-dated human artifacts in the New World — second only to the date originally given to the caribou scraper. And if it is a basket, it may be the world's oldest.

Old Crow has been considered a Middle Arrival site. Nearby, about 40 miles south of the Old Crow Basin, atop a ridge of dolomite and limestone overlooking the Bluefish River, is another Middle Arrival site. Since 1978 Jacques Cinq-Mars, of Ottawa's National Museum of Man, with the help of a few other specialists and the occasional visitor, has been investigating several caves there. If Old Crow is off the beaten track, Bluefish is pure wilderness. There's nobody around but the voles — and, late in the season, caribou making their way toward winter quarters. A helicopter drops supplies once a week. Fresh food doesn't last long, even if you dig a hole and bury it in the near-permafrost, but one can make a passable lunch, says Cinq-Mars, out of kippers, sardines, soup, and cheese. Not much need for fuel — the summer sun never sets in the far north. A bit chilly even in summer, by August temperatures hover around freezing; when a bad front moves in, it drizzles as well. But all in all, he says, it's worth the trouble because he has been turning up something prehistorians may never find in the Old Crow Basin — nicely stratified sites with stone and bone artifacts bearing marks of human workmanship. Radiocarbon dates ranging from 10,000 to 18,000 years indicate that people occupied the cave during the most severe part of North America's last Ice Age. This places Bluefish Caves squarely in the Middle Arrival group of sites.

Early Man in South America

So far we have only mentioned North American sites. There is also a growing body of evidence for pre-Clovis man from South America. Sites currently taken very seriously by Middle Arrival people range from Taima-taima, a mastodon kill site in Venezuela (radiocarbon dated at about 13,000 years) to Pikimachay Cave in the Peruvian highlands (which is at least 14,000 and perhaps 25,000 years old), and all the way down to Patagonia, South America's southernmost region, where a rock shelter at Los Toldos was radiocarbon dated at 12,600 years.

One of the most extraordinary of all South American sites is Monte Verde, a "wet" site near the south central Chilean city of Puerto Montt, where not only mastodon bones and stone artifacts, but also 11 wooden house structures have turned up — at 12,000 to 14,000 years old, they are the oldest architectural structures yet found in the Americas. The extraordinary conditions of preservation are apparently due to the fact that a bog covered the site, sealing the wooden artifacts from the decay that normally sets in when wood is exposed to air. Excavation has been going on since 1976, led by Thomas Dillehay of the University of Kentucky, who says: "This is the first time in the Americas we have found a wood technology so complete and so well preserved." Monte Verde has also yielded three wooden mortars containing fragmentary seeds, fruits, and stalks of various edible plants. With the mortars were several grinding stones. All of this raised the possibility of settled village life, with permanent or semipermanent houses, as long as 12,000 or

14,000 years ago. It seemed unthinkable. And yet there was the evidence.

Then there is the evidence uncovered in the northeastern Brazilian state of Piauí, near São Raimundo Nonato, where 172 surveyed limestone rock shelters show evidence not only of continuous human occupation over many thousands of years but in several caves what may be the oldest rock art in the New World.

Brazilian archeologist Nième Guidon has been concentrating on one of these caves, Toca da Pedra Furada,

Skeleton Keys

If, as some prehistorians suggest, Early Man arrived in the New World tens of thousands of years ago, where are the skeletons to prove it? Although archeologists say that looking for human remains is like looking for a needle in a continent-sized haystack, it's not as if there aren't any bones around at all. In fact, as long as you don't insist on great antiquity, there are many. The Smithsonian alone has upwards of 30,000 skulls.

But it's old bones everyone is looking for. Among the candidates for First American are "Marmes Man" (actually the remains of at least five separate individuals) uncovered near a now-flooded rock shelter in southeastern Washington; "Midland Man" (actually the skull of a 30-year-old woman) from Texas; the "Taber Child" (a months-old infant, judging from its just-erupted baby teeth and its 1/4-inch-thick skull) from Alberta, Canada; "Tepexpan Man" from Mexico; and a collection of what one skeptic calls "fringy" skeletal material from California, including "Laguna Girl," "L.A. Man," "Del Mar Man," "Sunnyvale Man," and "Yuha Man." The prob-

lem is not lack of bones; it is how to date them.

With Yuha Man, four different dating methods yielded four different possible ages, ranging from 10,000 to 23,600 years. Moreover, burial cairns such as the one under which Yuha Man was found only date back perhaps 5,000 years. Being at the center of such a controversy was discomfiting enough. But a worse indignity was in store for Yuha Man — the green footlocker in which he was being kept in storage at southern California's Imperial Valley College vanished without a trace one night in the fall of 1980.

Vanishing bones are one obstacle to getting at the truth about Early Man in the New World. Out-and-out hoaxes, most notably the famous Cardiff Giant, are another. Over 10 feet tall and weighing almost 3,000 pounds, the stone figure had been carved and doused with acid to make it look old, then buried in the dead of night on an upstate New York farm. The perpetrator of the hoax, George Hull, wanted to show a particular preacher that the phrase in the Book of Genesis — "There were giants in the earth in those days" — was not to be understood literally. Hull's fondest hope — that the gypsum giant would eventually be unmasked — came true within months of its discovery in October 1869. There are, of course, honest errors. Something an eminent 19th-century scientist called "Nebraska Man" turned out to be the jaw and tooth of an extinct piglike creature called a peccary.

Yuha Man (above) was not long for this world. His bones surfaced in southern California in 1971 but were stolen nine years later. Del Mar Man (right) is still with us, but nobody can agree about his age. One dating technique says he is 70,000 years old, another a mere 8,000.

In northeastern Brazil an archeologist came upon a series of rock shelters whose walls were painted with these animated hunting scenes in still-unfaded natural colors. Preliminary radiocarbon dates of 17,000, 25,000, and 32,000 years would seem to make this rock art even older than the famous prehistoric European cave paintings at Lascaux, France, and Altamira, Spain.

where on the interior walls of the cave she has found paintings of spear-wielding men and their quarry. The natural pigment paintings are themselves undatable by radiocarbon. But stratigraphic evidence supports their antiquity: broken-off fragments of the paintings turn up in layers whose radiocarbon dates indicate ages of 17,000 and 25,000 years. In any case, this is certainly a very old human occupation site: excavations are continuing in deeper levels in this extraordinary cave, which apparently was occupied at least 5,000 years before the date originally proposed for the Old Crow scraper.

Were there really people living in a Brazilian cave — half a world away from the Bering land bridge — thousands of years before the earliest known occupation of North America? If so, then here was a wholly new ballgame. The same nagging questions that were originally asked about Old Crow — who these people were and where they came from — must now be asked about Brazil. There are no easy answers. All we know is that, contrary to what was once thought, man has quite a respectable antiquity in the New World.

And who knows what older undiscovered sites lie beneath our feet? The New World may well turn out not to be new at all.

The trouble is that early people didn't leave any tem-

ples behind for us to scrutinize. They were survivors, not empire-builders. Their achievement was simply that they were the first. They peopled the New World. And according to all the available evidence, they did it in the middle of an ice age. The coldest periods of that Ice Age created ice fields two miles high, which was bad enough. But the warm periods in between were worse; grass-rich tundra turned to sodden marshland. And the "environmental crash" that occurred toward the end of the Ice Age (if it was the end) about 12,000 years ago, brought about the extinction of many of the great ice age animals and must have been hardest of all. But they were resourceful people, because they survived this too. Would we do as well?

About the specific details of their lives, we can only guess. Perhaps one day New World archeologists will find an Early Man site with good stratigraphy, reliably dated skeletal material, and excellent conditions of preservation — that is, the key around which they can proceed to build the car. Until then, they can only keep looking. But they don't seem to mind. William Irving, for example, a confirmed Early Arrivalist at the University of Toronto, is not in the least dismayed by the challenge of having so much left to learn. He is just impatient to get on with the next digging season. Says Irving, "It's just *beginning* to get interesting."

AMERICA'S FIRST PATENT

A chance discovery by a black cowboy, early this century, led to proof of Ice Age man in the Americas. The elegant weapon crafted by these ancient hunters 11,000 years ago signaled a technological revolution.

In July 1926 Aleš Hrdlička, curator of physical anthropology of the Smithsonian's United States National Museum, confidently wrote that there was not in the Americas "a scrap of a bone or implement" that was truly ancient. "As to the antiquity of the Indian himself," he added, "that cannot be very great." Known for his vigorous stand against the existence of Ice Age man in the New World, Hrdlička was about to be proved decisively and dramatically wrong.

The story really begins in 1908. A middle-aged black cowboy named George McJunkin was inspecting damage done to fence posts by a recent and particularly violent flash flood that had almost destroyed the little town of Folsom in northeastern New Mexico. As he picked his way along the upper edge of a ravine known locally as the Wild Horse Arroyo on Crowfoot Ranch property, about eight miles from Folsom, McJunkin chanced to notice some bleached bones sticking out of the arroyo wall about 10 feet below ground level — apparently exposed by the recent floodwaters.

Now McJunkin was no ordinary cowboy. Born in Texas to slave parents, by 1900 he had become foreman of the Crowfoot Ranch. He was, among other things, a self-taught naturalist and rock collector with a powerful curiosity about ancient things. He knew the bones in the arroyo wall were too big to be cattle bones. Besides, what were they doing buried 10 feet down? He dismounted and, using a pair of barbed-wire clippers, dug out a few of the bones. Not guessing the far-reaching significance of what he held in his hands, he simply put the samples into his saddlebags and resumed his inspection of the fence posts.

Fortunately for science, McJunkin's interest persisted. After his first bone trophies crumbled, he obtained and shellacked a second set. He also told and retold his story. About four years after his discovery in the arroyo, he was in a blacksmith's shop in the neighboring town of Raton. The "bone pit" came up in conversation because the blacksmith — one Carl Schwachheim — shared McJunkin's interest in fossils.

The conversation bore no immediate fruit. But Schwachheim never forgot what McJunkin told him, and some 10 years later, in December 1922 (McJunkin had probably died the previous spring), Schwachheim

Designed to penetrate an Ice Age mammoth hide, the carefully crafted five-inch Clovis projectile point at right turned up in 1848 as a sacred object in an Idaho Indian's medicine bundle. The drawing shows the point attached to a spear shaft.

and four others took an automobile trip out to the Crowfoot Ranch. They found the bone pit to be everything McJunkin had said it was, and the group brought back "nearly a sack full" of samples. He and a local amateur taxidermist named Campbell spent the evening trying to identify the bones. By this time Schwachheim was too involved to let the matter drop, and he tried to interest museums in the site, eventually corresponding with Jesse D. Figgins, director of the Colorado Museum of Natural History in Denver.

Figgins, as it happened, was just the right man to hear the story of the bone pit. He had already learned of the possibility of Ice Age man at a site in Texas. But the Texas excavators, not realizing the significance of the three stone points they turned up in association with fossil bison bones, had not preserved the matrix — that is, the soil in which they were found. Without such proof of context, no archeologist could be sure the points were really as old as the bison bones. Although only a local museum official, Figgins was eager to cross shovels, as it were, with Hrdlička. He believed the evidence from Texas, and he was ready to say so publicly. But he needed proof.

Figgins hurried to the Wild Horse Arroyo site in New Mexico; and, after a second visit in the spring of 1926, he knew that a full-scale excavation was in order.

The 1927 Folsom find — stone point (see arrow), ribs of an extinct bison, and surrounding clay matrix — was shipped intact to the Denver Museum of Natural History. It was the first proof that Ice Age man had been in the Americas.

The 1926 excavations yielded broken pieces of a projectile point near bison vertebra — one piece was even preserved and sent, in its matrix, to the laboratory for cleaning. But the skeptics were not to be moved. After all, they hadn't actually seen the artifacts come out of the ground.

It was in August of the following year that the tide turned. A point almost touching the rib of an extinct bison (shown at left, below) was found. The man who uncovered it was none other than McJunkin's blacksmith friend Carl Schwachheim, who was now field assistant at the excavation. This time all work stopped before the dirt was even cleaned off the point. Figgins sent telegrams to leading American museums and universities inviting them to send archeologists to come and see this evidence of Ice Age man for themselves while it was still in the ground.

Convincing Evidence

The telegram to Barnum Brown, still on file at the American Museum of Natural History in New York, reads tersely: "Another arrowhead in position at Folsom can you personally examine find answer telegram." (It is an indication of how little was known about American prehistory that Figgins was calling the projectile points "arrowheads" — in fact, these stone points were rather too large to be arrowheads, and it is now believed that the bow and arrow did not appear in America until much later.) Brown and two other archeologists answered the call. What they saw at Folsom convinced them (as it did not, apparently, convince Aleš Hrdlička at the National Museum, who went to his grave without ever taking official notice of the 1927 Folsom find). Gradually, as word got around, and more people came, the Folsom find — which eventually yielded the bones of 23 separate extinct bison together with 19 Folsom stone projectile points in undoubted association — came to be recognized for its revolutionary significance. Later, radiocarbon dates confirmed it: man had been in the New World for at least 10,000 years — that is, since the end of the last Ice Age.

This raised all sorts of questions. Who were these people? How did they survive the rigors of an ice age climate? And where had they come from? But before any of them could be answered, fresh — and still older — evidence was found in 1932, first at a site called Dent near Denver, Colorado, and then at a site called Blackwater Draw near the town of Clovis, New Mexico, about 180 miles southeast of Folsom.

The Dent site points were large and rugged — quite different from the small, elegant Folsom points. But the excavators at Dent, not knowing any better, called them "Folsom points." Not until archeologists at the Blackwater Draw (Clovis) site came upon two layers, one on top of the other, did it become clear that there were two distinct cultures. The points in the Clovis layer, because they were underneath the Folsom layer, were clearly older, though by how much no one in the

After more than 50 years of excavations, Blackwater Draw is still yielding secrets. Above, James Hester of the University of Colorado inspects excavated mammoth bones. At right, a modern toolmaker, using a protective hide pad, tries duplicating an ancient skill to make a razor-sharp obsidian blade.

1930's could say. Radiocarbon dating later filled in the picture. Clovis people had occupied the Blackwater Draw site between 11,600 and 11,000 years ago. Folsom people, who may have been their descendants, are known to have occupied it from at least 10,500 to 10,000 years ago.

Underneath the Clovis layer at Blackwater Draw, there was only "sterile earth," as archeologists term the lack of human or animal remains. This meant that, until something indisputably older came along, Clovis man was the first American.

Since 1932 more than a dozen well-documented Clovis sites, all about 11,000 years old, have been found, most of them in the High Plains of New Mexico, Colorado, Wyoming, Oklahoma, the Texas panhandle, and southern Arizona. But hundreds of single fluted points have turned up throughout the New World, from Alaska to southern Chile. The "Eastern fluted point tradition," for example, appears at Clovis-type sites in the Eastern Woodlands of North America from Nova Scotia to Virginia. And at the very southern tip of South America, not far from the Strait of Magellan, there is a site called Fell's Cave with evidence that about 10,700 years ago people there were killing giant ground sloths with fluted projectile points not too different from Clovis points.

Clearly, Clovis people covered a lot of ground — and they apparently covered it with breathtaking swiftness. Could these early people have crossed the Bering land bridge about 12,000 years ago? (See "How New Is the New World?", page 68.) Did their descendants hunt at Blackwater Draw 400 years later, and, in less than 1,000 years, spread not only across the rest of North America but cover the more than 10,000 miles to the bottom of South America?

Who were these people? If they were descendants of Clovis people, and not of some other human group that had long inhabited the Americas, then the "Clovis Revolution," as it has been referred to, was a revolution indeed — a human revolution.

This is how C. Vance Haynes, a geoscientist at the University of Arizona, sees the Clovis phenomenon. According to a model he constructed in 1966, a single Clovis band numbering perhaps no more than 30 individuals — five families of six persons each (two grandparents, two parents, two children) — crossed the Bering land bridge from Siberia and moved south at a rate of about four miles a year. Given a population that increased by a factor of 1.2 in each 28-year generation, Clovis people could have populated the entire New World in 500 years.

The Haynes model assumes, of course, that people kept moving. Some prehistorians, however, feel this is unrealistic. They refer instead to a model of a much more gradual human expansion. One such model, created by the late arctic archeologist J. L. Giddings, Jr., proposed that the Arctic was a center of population rather than a way station. According to this model, America was populated by "people slowly filtering down from the arctic population," rather than by people in a hurry to move south.

Furthermore, the Haynes model assumes that these early people would not have encountered any resistance from already-settled human groups along the way. Whether or not this is true, we do not know. But it certainly presents a neat picture — Ice Age mammoth hunters emerging from an ice-free corridor along the eastern flanks of the Rockies onto the virgin American plains, a sort of big-game hunter's paradise full of mammoths, mastodons, wild camels and horses, caribou, and bison.

A Revolutionary Weapon

Another way of looking at the Clovis evidence is that the Clovis achievement was a technological revolution — perhaps America's first. Perhaps the Clovis projectile point turns up suddenly in sites about 11,000 years ago simply because just then someone — a member of a group whose ancestors might already have been in the New World for thousands of years — had a bright idea. The idea was so good, and the weapon thus fashioned so effective, that the idea, not the people, spread like wildfire across two continents.

What was so revolutionary about the Clovis weapon? Archeologists describe it as a *fluted,* usually *bifacial,* stone *projectile point.* It is called a *projectile point* because, fastened somehow (probably with sinew or gut lashing and possibly with some sort of natural glue) onto a beveled or split-wood shaft, it was probably propelled like a spear. The point is too large and too heavy to have been used as the stone tip of an arrow, though it might conceivably have been attached to a shorter wooden shaft and used as a knife or a lance to be thrust into the side of the prey. *Bifacial* means that it was worked, or chipped, on two sides. Finally, in what was the Clovis point's most distinctive feature, it was *fluted.* The fluting refers to the single flake that the stoneworker removed — presumably after the weapon was essentially shaped — from the base of the point.

It has been suggested that the fluted point worked on a principle similar to the "blood-gutter" on the modern bayonet — that is, it hastened the flow of blood from the wound. Most likely, though, the flute was a simple and ingenious way of making sure the stone point fitted snugly against the wooden spear shaft. A spear so hafted would have been a formidable weapon.

The Clovis point was also a first. There are no fluted points in the Old World. François Bordes, a French archeologist and lifelong student of prehistoric stoneworking techniques, is respectful of the ingenuity of the stoneworker who thought of the fluted point. It was he who called it "the first American patent."

But the fluted point, though extremely well made and the first of its kind, was still just a spear point. There is indirect evidence, however, that Clovis man had something else in his arsenal that made him an especially good hunter, and that was the spear-thrower, known in the New World by its Aztec name of atlatl. (It has gone by many names — Cro-Magnon men used it in France about 14,000 years ago; Eskimos used it until recently; and Australian aborigines, who call it the *woomera,* still use it.) The spear-thrower, which looked something like a giant crochet hook, consisted of a short launching stick of wood or bone about two feet long, with a barb or notch at one end, a loop or some other kind of handgrip at the other, and a weight in the middle for balance. The hunter seated the butt of his spear on the barb or in the notch, lifted the combined weapon to throwing position, and then

Big-Game Hunter's Paradise

Ice Age hunters, such as the one below, found in the New World a wealth of big-game animals the likes of which the world may never see again — not a congregation as in the idealized scene at right, but more likely one at a time, in caves, near waterholes, on the edges of the forests, or in great herds on the American plains. The best known of the Ice Age megafauna (so called because they were larger than their modern relatives) was the mammoth, whose very name is a synonym for "huge." The nine-foot-high woolly mammoth was adapted to life on cold northern plains, thanks to three inches of insulating fat, an undercoat of wool covered with long, shaggy hair, and small ears to reduce heat loss. It probably used its curving tusks (one pair was 16 feet from tip to tip) to sweep ice and snow off vegetation. The giant ground sloth, a 20-foot-long vegetarian aptly called a gravigrade, or creature "heavy of gait," was powerful enough to uproot small trees, but slow enough to fall prey to hunters, as long as they avoided its lethal claws. Other giant Ice Age creatures were the giant beaver, a bear-sized rodent; the mastodon, a woodlands browser; the armadillo–like Glyptodont, four feet long excluding the tail; the giant bison, with its seven-foot horn spread (a modern buffalo's is just over two feet); the giant short-faced bear, a powerful New World predator; the dire wolf, a dangerous hunter and scavenger; and, of course, horses and camels, which first evolved, and then died out, in the New World. The camel left a few distant relatives in South America (see page 100), and the horse came back with the Spanish conquistadors. These splendid animals, for reasons which are still poorly understood, all became extinct about 10,000 years ago.

snapped the atlatl in a forward arc. At the top of the arc, the spear disengaged and flew on to its target. Like a fly-casting rod, the atlatl acted as an extension of the hunter's arm.

The atlatl hunter could throw farther and with more power, which was no doubt all to the good. An infuriated mammoth at close range must have been a dangerous opponent. Furthermore, extra thrust was essential. As Vance Haynes, puts it, "A mammoth's hide was probably as tough as an eight-ply truck tire."

Armed with the fluted point and the atlatl, Clovis hunters were well equipped to kill the great, 13-foot-high mammoths that roamed the American plains. In fact, according to the "overkill theory" of University of Arizona geoscientist Paul Martin, Clovis hunters were responsible for hunting these enormous, tough-hided creatures right into extinction. Climatic upheaval

no doubt also played a part — this was after all the end of a major ice age. In some areas, grasslands turned to bogs; in others, drier weather altered whole ecosystems; tumultuous glacial meltwaters carved new river channels, thus marking new habitats; and the sea rose in central Beringia. The ice-free steppe-tundra habitat that had supported so much life during the Pleistocene sank under chilly arctic waters. As nature's supreme irony would have it, it may have been the warming trend that followed the Ice Age, and not the Ice Age itself, that spelled death for the great grazing herd animals of North America.

Martin, however, lays the blame squarely on Clovis hunters. He points out that mammoths were simply unused to being preyed upon. Weighing in at close to five tons, they were hardly fleet of foot. Clovis hunters could simply wait for the great thirsty mammoths to

Giant sloth

Camel

American mastodon

Woolly mammoth

Horse

Giant beaver

Short-faced bear

Glyptodont

Dire wolf

Giant bison

come to a favored waterhole where, knee-deep in a stream or marsh, the beasts would have been at a distinct disadvantage. And many Clovis sites are, in fact, located near ancient stream heads and lakes — the mammoth remains at Blackwater Draw were found in what had been the marshy drainage channel of a Pleistocene pond. Also, since the mammoth's gestation period was probably close to two years, and a cow usually had only one calf at a time, the species could not rapidly recover from excessive predation. They were, in short, despite their massive size and thick hides, extremely vulnerable creatures.

Whether or not Clovis hunters are to blame, the great mammoths were gone by the time Folsom people came along. And so Folsom hunters became specialists in taking the gregarious herd animal, the bison — either the large *bison antiquus* or the smaller *bison occidentalis,* both now extinct. Folsom hunters probably separated a few animals from the herd and drove them into a gully or box canyon, where they were easier to kill. Occasionally they engaged in mass kills, stampeding whole herds over the steep side of an arroyo. At the Olsen-Chubbuck site in southeastern Colorado, for instance, almost 200 bison skeletons were found in a bone bed that, at its thickest, was 12 feet wide and 7 feet deep. Thirteen of the skeletons were completely intact, meaning that the carcasses, being at the bottom of the gruesome pile, had not been touched. The hunters probably couldn't get to them. The ones they could reach, however, had been butchered with great efficiency. At this and other sites, the animals were apparently butchered on a sort of assembly line — skulls in one pile, leg bones in another, pelvic bones yet in another.

These early people didn't subsist entirely on mammoth or bison meat. At one Clovis site, for example, archeologists found evidence of hackberry seeds and nests of mud-daubers, or wasps, whose larvae Clovis people probably ate. And at both Clovis and Folsom sites, remains of other animals — mastodon, wild camel, wild horse, bear, tapir, saber-toothed cat, cave lion, giant ground sloth, dire wolf, as well as smaller animals such as vole, rabbit, turtle, and various kinds of birds — frequently turn up. This doesn't necessarily mean that these animals were part of early man's diet: the animals might simply have occupied the sites when people were not around. To find out exactly what early people ate, scientists examine fossil human excrement, specimens of which are known as coprolites. Microscopic bits of animal hair and bone resist digestion, as do plant seeds, and so offer useful information on diet. One coprolite expert says: "It's a capsule record of what passed through a person's digestive tract thousands of years ago."

In the several hundred or so years between Clovis and Folsom cultures, early man refined his tool kit. Highly specialized burins, or engraving tools — prob-

No advancing white settler ever actually witnessed a "buffalo jump" (pictured above). But because of sites such as Olsen-Chubbuck in Colorado (right), with its carefully excavated, stepped trench, archeologists can reconstruct the event, down to the direction the wind was blowing the day of the stampede.

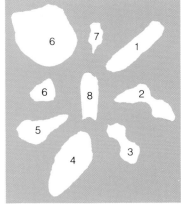

The composite Folsom tool kit at left consists of scrapers for cleaning hides; knives for cutting through thick bison bones; gravers for cutting out bone needles or strips of sinew (and possibly for tattooing as well); drills for boring holes in wood or bones; and spokeshaves (named for a similar tool used by wheelwrights) for rounding spear shafts. As for the flawless projectile point made of petrified wood (center), the Folsom toolmaker clearly chose his material as carefully as Michelangelo chose his marble.

1. Knife
2. Spokeshave
3. Graver/
   spokeshave
4. Knife
5. Knife/drill
6. Scraper
7. Graver
8. Projectile
   point

ably used by Folsom people to make other tools out of bone or wood — turn up frequently at Folsom sites. A grinding stone was found in one of the layers at Blackwater Draw. Vance Haynes believes it may have been used for grinding hematite (a reddish iron oxide) into powder that, mixed with clay, forms red ocher. At the Anzick site in Montana, red ocher was sprinkled ceremonially over a grave, and it may also have been used for body painting or tattooing. A few bone needles and small art objects have turned up at Folsom sites, but these only leave us wishing for more.

Archeologists must be content to examine the material culture of a vanished people. Other aspects of culture, such as conversation, are ephemeral — much more perishable than organic material — and are quite beyond our reach. What did they say to each other 10,000 years ago around the campfire at Blackwater Draw? We will never know.

What these people did leave behind for us to wonder about, and to admire, were their projectile points. The Clovis point, totally unknown in the Old World, ap-peared first in the Americas like a bit of very early Yankee ingenuity. But with the Folsom point, ingenuity became artistry. It was still a fluted bifacial projectile point. But it was streamlined — smaller, more uniform, razor-sharp, and skillfully retouched so it would not chafe against the lashing that held it in its wooden shaft. And most of all, the fluting had been perfected. Clovis people had worked stone mainly by percussion. Folsom stoneworkers used a technique known as pressure-flaking. By leaving small, wavy protuberances as guides, they applied controlled pressure to, rather than struck, just exactly the right spot on the stone. The result was a truly elegant weapon.

In the history of technology — as we know to our chagrin having exchanged marble for concrete, ceramics for plastic — new materials are not necessarily an improvement. Clovis and Folsom people had neither iron nor bronze to work with. But they were consummate craftsmen. There could be no improving what they had achieved in stone. America's first patent was not only efficient — it was also quite exquisite.

THE BIRTH OF FARMING

The moment man the hunter and gatherer became man the farmer was a great turning point for humanity. An American scientist's careful research lifts the heavy curtain of time to give us a look at how this happened.

Hunting societies never achieve a complex material culture of their own, for their hold on the environment is necessarily tenuous, their goals narrowly focused on survival, and the rewards of any day's effort rather short-lived. Agricultural societies, by contrast, are sedentary, their engagement with the land intense, their labors more constant, and their works frequently enduring. Having learned to cultivate some plants so that they will yield more food, more consistently, and having domesticated certain animals so that they are reliable providers of either food or labor, farmers are to a significant degree masters of their world. Such relative security inclines these men of the soil to accumulate the possessions, to build the structures, to evolve the specialized skills, and to make the long-term investments in posterity that become the foundation stones of civilization.

Identifying the origins of agriculture in any prehistoric society thus becomes one of the most interesting and significant aspects of archeology, with a host of complex questions that must be posed and ultimately answered. What, for example, led some people to make the gigantic leap from hunting to farming? Did the change come to them slowly and in many evolutionary stages or was it a technological revolution? Was

it born of one group, and then diffused by the process of cultural contact to many other peoples; or was it independently invented in many parts of the world under different sets of environmental and social circumstances? Like most other matters archeological, the whole truth of agriculture's beginnings, both in the Old World and the New, remains to be discovered — though certain "facts" are now generally accepted.

The cultivation of an indigenous grain contributes to the beginnings of virtually every civilization. According to all the available evidence, agriculture seems to have originated independently in several different parts of the world. One was Iraq's Zagros Mountains, where barley and wheat were first domesticated about 9,000 years ago. Another was China, where millet was first raised along the Yellow River about 5,500 years ago and where rice was grown on the southern coast slightly later. At the same time many animals were domesticated as suppliers of meat, milk, wool, or

A wild grass that became the staple crop of New World civilizations, corn is shown here as crafted by Inca-period artisans. Its gilded husks and silver cobs, now showing age, must have been dazzling when new, some 500 years ago.

muscle-power — goats, sheep, and cattle in the Near East, and pigs in the Far East.

In the New World, the transition from gathering to planting occurred at two locations within several hundred years of each other, one in certain parts of Mesoamerica (southern Mexico, Belize, Guatemala, and northern Honduras); and slightly earlier in the Andean areas of Ecuador, Peru, and western Bolivia. And to no one's surprise America's unique grass, *Zea mays* ("maize," or "corn"), was found to be the first major grain, if not necessarily the first crop, domesticated by people emerging from the food-gatherer stage. And it was corn, of course, that was the staple crop of nearly all the great pre-Columbian civilizations. Remarkably little, however, was accomplished in the way of domesticating animals (see box, page 100).

The precise circumstances that prompted men to make the irreversible move from foraging to farming in Mesoamerica and the Andean area remain a matter of lively debate and speculation, but one prehistorian who has devoted his career to studying the beginning of New World agriculture, Richard "Scotty" Mac-Neish of Boston University's Department of Archeology, believes he has some very good ideas.

To begin with, says MacNeish, certain "necessary conditions" had to exist before man the hunter could evolve into a primitive subsistence farmer. The first prerequisite he identifies is a regional landscape offering sufficient geographic and climatic diversity to support a variety of wild edibles that lend themselves to domestication and that could be the basis of a successful, surplus-producing food supply. Another necessary characteristic is plants in each life zone or microenvironment that ripened at different times so that the gatherers, by adopting a regular, scheduled pattern of migration, could exploit several of them in their respective seasons. This annual cycle of different subsistence activities for different ecospheres is often stimulated by great seasonal fluctuations, including a harsh dry season that spurs people to move on to wetter areas as well as to store goods to last until the rainy days arrive. Also crucial to agricultural birth is the potential for relatively easy travel within the region; in MacNeish's view ancient bands or family groups circulating in a given area needed the stimulation of contact with one another and the opportunity to exchange both material goods and ideas, in order to evolve the innovative technology of plant and animal husbandry.

As MacNeish notes, both the Tehuacán Valley of Mexico and the Ayacucho Valley of Peru were richly provided with these conditions. Central Mexico offered among its wealth of indigenous edibles seed-grown plants such as wild maize, mixta squashes, pumpkins, chili peppers, and runner beans. The Andean region had a number of indigenous "root" vegetables — that is, plants whose natural means of propagation is by growing new stock from fragments of the parent; these included white and sweet potatoes, mani-

oc, and peanuts. This region also had such important seed crops as lima and common beans.

MacNeish cites a pair of "developmental conditions" that had to coexist before men would give up their established patterns of hunting-gathering in favor of other, more strenuous, but more efficient methods of feeding themselves. The first was some climatic and environmental change that upset, perhaps very subtly, perhaps dramatically, people's established habits of subsistence. The dramatic changes in world rainfall and temperature patterns that occurred about 12,000 years ago toward the end of the Ice Age led to mass extinctions in the Western Hemisphere of such large animals as mammoths, mastodons, giant sloths, wild horses, and camels. Hunting became an increasingly unreliable source of daily food. But almost equally important in initiating agriculture, in MacNeish's view, the people so threatened had to have within their immediate experience an alternative means of subsistence if they were to survive the change. The alternative need not be highly developed, much used, nor even well regarded by the hunters at the start, but there had to be a basic awareness that it existed. New World Paleo-Indians, MacNeish asserts, were well adapted to their environment. They collected seeds, leaves, and stems, picked wild pods and fruits, and tracked small animals — rabbits, rats, birds, and turtles among them. In short, they were developing some rudimentary knowledge of what could and could not be eaten, and when, and what could be safely stored.

As for corn, neither MacNeish nor his colleagues can say with certainty exactly when it was first eaten regularly as a wild plant, much less exactly when it was domesticated. But they are convinced that in seeking those answers they are coming to know a great deal about the development of civilizations in the New World — and very possibly about the larger forces that promote human innovation in general.

Reconstructing Wild Corn

The first problem researchers have had to confront is knowing what to look for. Even where such cereal grains as wheat, barley, and rice have living wild varieties, we can only guess at the genetic pathway from ancient wild varieties to modern domesticated ones. But corn in all its myriad modern varieties has no known living wild relatives, and so it presents a special and unusual problem.

One point seems clear, however. Wild corn has to have looked and behaved in ways remarkably different from those of modern maize, for the plant we call corn today is physically incapable of regenerating itself without the active assistance of man. Modern corn's strength and its weakness lie in its unique grain-bearing "ear," a highly specialized flower cluster whose hundreds of seeds are compactly arranged along a rigid cob, the lot enclosed in tight-fitting, multi-layered husks. These husks prevent the seed kernels from dis-

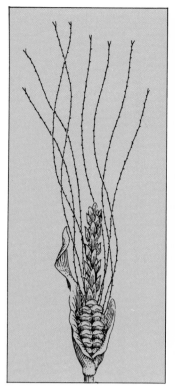

Of all the varieties of corn in the world today, not one is wild. To find out what wild corn looked like, scientists rely partly on archeological evidence and partly on genetic backcrossing between living wild grasses such as Tripsacum *(above cen-* *ter) and teosinte (above right). The reconstructed wild corn (above left) has inedible kernels; but unlike modern corn, which cannot reproduce without man's help, the wild corn must have been able to open at maturity to release its seeds.*

persing on their own either on the stalk or when the ear falls to the ground. In fact, only when the ear is shucked and the kernels are forcibly freed can the seeds go forth to start another season's growth. Wild corn, by definition, must have been able to reseed on its own, but by what mechanism, in what physical form?

The first substantial advance in tracking maize's missing ancestor was made in the 1940's when Herbert Dick, a graduate student in anthropology at Harvard University, was spending a summer's dig at an abandoned rock shelter known as Bat Cave in west central New Mexico's Catron County. The cave had been occupied from about 3000 to 1750 B.C. by people engaged in a simple form of agriculture.

As Dick and his associates worked their way slowly through layer after layer of occupation debris, they found a continuous series of corncobs — some of the popcorn variety with small, hard kernels and some pod corn, characterized by unique husk-like structures that enclose each kernel — at virtually every level. What made the discovery particularly exciting was the fact that, in terms of size, a distinct evolutionary pattern was revealed, with the largest cobs in the topmost strata and progressively smaller ones appearing as they dug farther down. Here, then, was evidence that corn had

somehow been manipulated genetically, from varieties that were less satisfactory in size and productivity to varieties that were large and yielding more food value. The possibility that still earlier, more primitive types might be found no longer seemed impossible. What was needed was a more systematic search.

It was about this time that MacNeish and botanist Paul C. Mangelsdorf of Harvard University began their collaboration. To the assignment Mangelsdorf brought a strong conviction that previous attempts at unraveling the origins of corn had been directed at the wrong plant family. *Zea mays* has two close relatives among the grasses that currently grow in Meso-america. One is teosinte (meaning "God's grass" in Nahuatl, the Aztec language), which grows as a weed in the cornfields of western Mexico, Guatemala, and Honduras and bears a noticeable resemblance to modern corn in terms of its stalk, leaves, and tassel shape, but has hard inedible kernels. The other native grass is *Tripsacum,* which has leaves and stalks like teosinte and corn but unlike teosinte has nutritious soft kernels, albeit small ones. Mangelsdorf's predecessors had tagged teosinte as corn's probable wild ancestor, noting that it continues to thrive in that part of Guatemala where descendants of the brilliant Maya civilization still live.

To these researchers there was neat logic in declaring the first New World civilization to be that of the Maya and to base it on the domestication of wild teosinte. But Mangelsdorf was skeptical. He thought teosinte was a relatively recent species of grass resulting from the natural crossbreeding of wild maize and *Tripsacum*. He set out to reconstruct what he believed might be a close approximation of ancestral corn.

Modern farmers select the most edible corn for propagation. Mangelsdorf selected the least, repeatedly backcrossing and working his way toward smaller, more primitive varieties whose tassels and stalks represented progressively more effective systems for germinating and releasing seeds. In time he developed a hybrid that was indeed smaller than any at Bat Cave and, most important, had no all-encompassing husk that would prevent the kernels from dispersing on their own. The reinvented wild corn had but two small husks that parted slightly at maturity to release the rows of kernels within. Its kernels were small and hard like those of popcorn; and its cobs were mounted atop the ear next to pollen-bearing tassels.

Now MacNeish, who had already spent a decade investigating various sites in Mexico for evidence of Paleo-Indian occupation, had something specific to look for. After careful consideration of all the information at hand, including climate, rainfall, topography, and geology — he decided to launch "The Great Corn Hunt" in the Tehuacán Valley about 150 miles south of Mexico City, where conditions were notably favorable for early occupation and for the preservation of fragile evidence of corn gathering and corn producing if such were to be found.

"The Great Corn Hunt"

The Valley of Tehuacán is an elevated semidesert region, approximately 70 miles long by 20 miles wide, straddling the border between the modern states of Oaxaca and Puebla and drained by the Salado River. Two mountain ranges frame the basin — the Sierra de Zapotitlán to the west and the Sierra de Zongolica to the east — putting the valley within an area that receives only 16 to 20 inches of rain per year, and that primarily in two summer months. Its climate and terrain have created four distinctly different vegetational zones of which only one — the valley floor — is naturally suitable for farming. The others, consisting of slope lands, have relatively poor soils and minimal moisture except for oasis-like springs. They support a variety of such animals as deer, peccary, rabbits, gophers, and rats, and such vegetation as cactus, maguey, and avocado. However, these poorer zones also offer dozens of commodious caves where, presumably, nomadic peoples could take shelter seasonally.

MacNeish began his investigation of Tehuacán in January 1960. He searched 38 sites before he was finally rewarded with pay dirt at Coxcatlán Cave, a long narrow rock shelter in one of the canyons along the south-

Archeologist Richard "Scotty" MacNeish (above, examining an ancient mano, *or grinding stone, for wear marks) believes corn was first domesticated within 100 miles of Mexico's Tehuacán Valley (above right). He searched 38 caves before finding 6,000-year-old corn in Coxcatlán Cave (right).*

eastern edge of the valley. Describing that momentous day in his field diary, he writes, "After a long, hot walk along the edge of the mountains, through thick stands of cactus and mesquite, we arrived at the rock shelter. Even from a distance it looked promising. The artifacts and refuse on the surface, the size of the shelter, and the quantity of vegetal material that lay beneath the goat dung covering the floor showed that this was a site to be tested.

"From January 21 to January 27 the three of us, Pablo, Hector [his Mexican assistants], and I, tested this cave. Behind a large rock roughly in the center of the shelter we dug a two-meter square to a depth of about two meters, using trowels. We took out everything, including the loose dirt, by bucket loads and put it through a mesh screen to be sure that we missed nothing. Slowly we peeled off the successive strata. . . .On January 27 after lunch, Pablo, working well down in the preceramic stratum, recovered a tiny corn-cob no more than an inch long. Only half believing, I took his place in the bottom of the pit. After a short period of troweling and cleaning away dirt with a paintbrush, I uncovered two more tiny cobs. We held in our hands possible ancestors to modern domesticated corn."

Examining the corn cobs at Harvard a month or two later, Mangelsdorf confirmed the supposition. Still lat-

er the cobs were dated to 3610 B.C., give or take 250 years. These were the oldest corncobs that had ever been unearthed.

MacNeish subsequently returned to lead a major three-year long investigation of the valley. To get some sense of the study's thoroughness, consider that 392 sites were surveyed for potential value, 30 test trenches were dug, and 12 sites — 5 of them open sites, 7 of them caves — were chosen for extensive excavation and examination. In what was, at the time, a somewhat novel approach MacNeish engaged 50 specialists in the project. To the task force came such experts as a plant pathologist who dissected 237 coprolites (fossil excrement), a paleontologist, a zoologist who studied 12,000 bone fragments, and paleobotanists who examined 100,000 plant samples — among them beans, squash, and corn. One botanist's job was to study what were thought at the time to be the two oldest cultivated cotton bolls in the entire world. The Tehuacán researchers collected and identified 750,000 lost, broken, discarded, and outworn fragments of life as lived in this highland valley over 10,000 long years.

When the work was done MacNeish had what amounts to a new model for considering not only the sequential growth of agriculture, most especially the domestication of corn in the Tehuacán Valley, but also, with modifications, the development of seed crop farming in every other part of the Americas — and perhaps the world. Not every Mesoamerican specialist shares MacNeish's certainty that corn was first domesticated within 100 miles of the Tehuacán Valley, but most specialists agree that it was first domesticated somewhere in Mesoamerica — and everyone agrees that MacNeish's work in the Tehuacán Valley was of incalculable value in understanding the rise of agriculture in the New World.

MacNeish sets forth his view of the early history of the valley in nine sequential chapters based upon evidence turned up in successive layers of excavations there. The beginnings of agriculture are described in the first four phases, opening with the Ajuereado phase, so named for the cave in which the earliest record of human occupation has been discovered. Stretching backwards at least 12,000 years, Ajuereado is estimated to end 9,000 years ago. As the Ice Age ended and mammoths and other large grass-eating herd animals such as horses and camels became extinct, Tehuacán's big-game hunters were driven to supplement their diets with the meat of deer, peccary, and birds, and to trap cottontail rabbits and other rodents. Indeed, for most hunters, big game was something they probably dreamed about but seldom encountered.

Though MacNeish calls this first phase "poorly defined" by surviving evidence, he and his team uncovered 20 Ajuereado sites and a few thousand artifacts. What he uncovered led him to the conclusion that while the Paleo-Indians of Tehuacán showed some generalized cultural connections with the Indians of

North America, they were, in an essential sense, operating independently within a distinctly Mesoamerican cultural sphere.

MacNeish also found it significant that amongst the Ajuereado sites uncovered there was not a single "kill site," suggesting that they were trapping only small game and that gathered food — prickly pear, the fruit of the wild avocado, mesquite pods, and setaria grass seeds — was beginning to play a substantial role in these people's diet. And, by the end of this period, they had learned to store seeds as security against lean times. The archeologist estimates that wild plants may have represented as much as a third of the calories consumed, taking as his guide the proportion of plant to bone remains.

As for the communal groups themselves, MacNeish proposes that they were thinly distributed in what he terms "microbands" composed of four to eight members of the same family. Their yearly wanderings took them from cave-based wet season camps to various locations on the valley floor in periods of extreme dryness. He postulates that the families were patrilineal, that is, dominated by male members, with wives being absorbed from other one-family bands whose paths might cross occasionally. The number of Tehuacanos living in the valley at any one time was small, perhaps no more than 20 as late as 7,000 years ago.

Changes in this pattern show up in the second, or El Riego, phase, dated by MacNeish between 9,000 and 7,000 years ago. MacNeish postulates that almost half the diet by this time was based upon gathered plant foods. Correspondingly an assortment of stone tools specific to plant gathering and preparation appear, including primitive mortars, pestles, and milling stones.

Notably, the tools were shaped and finished not by crude chipping techniques, but by grinding, a significant technological advance. He also found evidence that the Tehuacanos were given to trying new foods — the remains of chili peppers, amaranth ("pigweed"), and walnut squash were exhumed at the El Riego level. Because significant differences in the size of avocado pits appear, some of them far larger than any that have been dated earlier, MacNeish suggests cautiously that the Tehuacanos had already begun to take their first halting steps from simple plant gathering to plant tending and food production. The process, which would in the next few thousand years lead to dramatic changes in the character of a host of useful plants, including corn, is inferred from scant evidence, but MacNeish and others think it probably began quite by accident.

Here, for example, is a hypothetical model of how one of the El Riego bands of hunter-gatherers might have initiated the first stages of plant domestication. Imagine that a handful of Tehuacanos are making their annual circuit of the valley. It is summer — time to scout for wild squash. As luck will have it they come upon a collection of squash vines whose fruit is fatter, ripens earlier, and is far tastier than those of their

Some things — like the mano *and the* metate *— never change. For thousands of years Mexican women have been using these two basic stone implements to grind corn. The pre-Columbian pottery figure at right is from western Mexico.*

On the front of the Zapotec funerary urn from Mexico at left is a figure whose elaborately carved headdress is topped by stylized corn silks. Flanking the face of Cocijo (the rain god peering out at top) are ears of life-giving corn probably molded on real corncobs. Ancient potters used the corn motif so often and so realistically that they furnished Harvard botanist Paul Mangelsdorf with precise information on prehistoric corn.

Experts believe that the incomparable Moche potters of Peru's north coast also probably used actual ears of corn in making the vessel below. The rows of kernels appear in alternating pairs, a feature generally overlooked by potters and sculptors.

more ordinary neighbors. Another bonus: its dried seeds can be stored for eating during the dry season ahead. The gatherers, at this stage, know nothing of nature's tendency to vary through spontaneous mutation and hybridization. They may, in fact, ascribe the superior plants to some magic or some fact of divine intervention.

The Indians carry the squash back to camp where inevitably some of the seeds are scattered about in the process of preparing and eating dinner. Some find their way to a favorable clearing where they eventually germinate. When the hunter-gatherer band returns to camp the following season, they discover that a few noticeably more robust squashes are growing literally under their noses. Perhaps the mental connection between the selectively harvested squash of last year and the new growth is not made immediately, but the group may return to the site of last year's gathering to repeat their good fortune. In time — and we may be talking about scores of generations at this stage — the El Riego hunter-gatherers come to recognize a predictable pattern of cause and effect. The notion of deliberately helping the process along, of actually poking a small hole in the ground with a digging stick and planting a seed, dawns.

As circumstantial evidence that the gathering practices of the Tehuacanos changed during the El Riego phase, MacNeish cites the fact that their movements from one camp zone to another are now tied to the seasonal availability of key plants. He also finds indications that bands were beginning to join together into larger communal groups when food supplies were sufficient to support them. Macrobands of perhaps 16 to 30 people assembled on the valley bottom and alluvial slopes during the relatively lush spring and summer. However, they scattered into smaller parties once again during the drier, more difficult fall and winter seasons, when plant materials were in short supply and hunting-foraging offered, at best, a meager subsistence.

MacNeish also sees in the positioning of occupation sites the first indicators of tribal territoriality — as though groups were beginning to establish a degree of possessiveness over particular areas. Possibly there was also some weak degree of specialization of roles within the groups — such as part-time leaders, shamans, and the like. The deduction is based in part on evidence of comparatively elaborate burials — some bodies ceremonially bound, perhaps as part of a religious sacrifice, others richly furnished. He also infers from human remains that some form of population control had been adopted. At one burial site his team found two decapitated children, their heads switched. At another, apparently a family grave, the father had died a natural death but the mother and child had been killed by some violent means. Still other children, victims of unnatural

---

Domesticated Animals of the New World

New World people domesticated fewer animals than their Old World counterparts. Besides the dog (there is a radiocarbon date of 10,300 years on a canine skull from Idaho's Jaguar Cave), ancient Americans domesticated the muscovy duck, the turkey, a stingless honey bee, and the guinea pig — a gregarious little rodent that has been doted upon, as well as eaten, in the Andes for perhaps as long as 6,000 years.

More importantly perhaps, South American herdsmen domesticated two of the four New World camelids. The best known of these is the llama which, at 300–350 pounds, is the largest of the four. Although it can only manage a 100-pound load and therefore could never do the heavy draught work of Old World oxen, it is a superb pack animal, well adapted to subsist on the sparse vegetation of the Andes. The llama's cousin and fellow domesticate, the alpaca, is a dependable producer of high-quality wool, and the wool-exporting countries of South America are practicing selective breeding in an effort to improve the quality still further. The third camelid is the totally wild guanaco, which has been hunted for its meat and hide ever since the first people came to South America tens of thousands of years ago. Although its range has been severely restricted, it still exists in healthy numbers at the very tip of South America, where vast ranchlands, dense forests, and a fairly sparse human population help it survive. The fourth (and, at 100 pounds, the smallest) camelid is the lovely wild vicuña. Until 51 nations agreed in 1973 to ban international trade in its skins, the vicuña produced one of the world's finest and costliest wools; it brought a market price five times that of cashmere. But vicuñas resist domestication. They can be ranch-raised and will breed in captivity, but their genes are apparently so strong that attempts by man to produce a stable hybrid by crossing them with alpacas, for instance, appear to fail.

All four South American camelids can interbreed (and produce fertile offspring) and presumably have interbred in the past. Indeed, some experts are coming to believe that the alpaca's evolutionary parent is the vicuña: somehow, that is, nature succeeded where man failed.

Nothing common about these two common domesticated animals. Inca artisans rendered the alpaca's long coat in hammered silver; the llama in soldered silver. Their human companion was cast from solid silver.

Ceramic "food" from pre-Columbian potters — at right, a tripod vessel in the shape of a gourd with parrot legs, from western Mexico's Colima culture (A.D. 400–800), and below, a stirrup spout vessel in the shape of a warty squash (a real warty squash was most likely used to make the mold), from Peru's Moche culture (100 B.C.–A.D. 750).

deaths, were found in single graves. Was infanticide part of some religious ritual? Or did the fragility of the food supply make these harsh measures necessary when the male hunter of a family died? MacNeish says probably both explanations are true.

Developing out of El Riego was a third phase Mac-Neish calls Coxcatlán, radiocarbon dated from about 7,000 to 5,500 years ago. By this time, Tehuacanos were actively engaged in the cultivation of several plants. Continuing the hypothetical model of the El Riego planters, we can suppose that the Indians have noticed that plants grown in relative isolation are somehow more vigorous generally than those that must compete with others for space and moisture, so they take to weeding and watering their gardens. Perhaps they have also observed that the camp's refuse dump sprouts consistently larger plants, which leads them to experiment with enriching the soil of their garden plots with decayed vegetable matter. Perhaps, too, they were growing more than they could immediately eat and learned that the surplus could be stored not only to

provide "insurance" but also to save them the trouble of moving so often.

As botanists know, all this pampering turns out to have a marked effect on the plants genetically, that is to say, on their fundamental natures. A harsh rule of life in the wild — that only those plants that are toughest and most adaptable will survive — has been softened by the protective measures of man. Certain naturally occurring mutations that previously would have been snuffed out within the life cycle of a single plant are forgiven. Certain cross-pollinations between genetically different but still closely related varieties of the same plant may also take place as the result of plants being artificially transported from their place of origin to other locales. The genetically altered, somehow less hardy, misfit survives. The plant tenders naturally prefer those hybrids that vary in the direction of a new, still better, food plant, and they do their best to keep them while selectively killing those that are less satisfactory. At some point in this interactive process a generation of the protected variety becomes irreversibly "captive," or domesticated, meaning, strictly speaking, that it can no longer grow without the hand of man.

For the Tehuacanos the moment when their fate as farmers was sealed cannot be targeted precisely, but the beginnings of what one anthropologist has called "the tyranny of the overbred cultigen" must be traced to the Coxcatlán period. There could be no turning back to simple food gathering. About 14 percent of the fruits, nuts, roots, pods, and other edible plants consumed by the Indians were now under human care and on the way to becoming fully domesticated. Probably among them were black and white zapotes, a local fruit called chupandilla, chili peppers, amaranth, two varieties of squash, tepary beans, jack beans, and bottle gourds, the

Harvesting the Sea in Ancient Peru

Prehistorians seldom look twice at a culture that produced no fancy pottery and irrigated no fields. Yet at more than a dozen so-called preceramic sites along Peru's desert coast, people left cultural remains up to 45 feet deep without a single potsherd and without any evidence of plant domestication. What did these people of 4,000 to 5,000 years ago eat?

The answer, says Chicago Field Museum archeologist Michael Moseley, lies in the cold, upwelling, protein-rich waters of the Peruvian, or Humboldt, Current just off the coast. There, in one of the world's richest food chains, phytoplankton nourish vast schools of anchovies; anchovies feed bigger fish (sea bass, drumfish, tuna, mackerel, pompano, croakers); those fish feed a wealth of sea birds (pelicans, penguins, boobies, cormorants) and sea mammals (sea lions, seals, whales, porpoises). Man, of course, reaps the end harvest. Moseley points out that invading Spaniards encountered Peruvian natives on a balsa raft well out from shore — which certainly suggests a seaworthy culture, if not an economy based on fishing. Furthermore, in some seasons, early people could have clubbed sea lions nesting on the beach and scooped anchovies out of the surf.

Moseley's critics point out that the sea, though rich in protein and fat, is poor in carbohydrates. Moreover, they say, the sea is unreliable as a food base and cite, as evidence against Moseley's theory, the periodic devastations by the weather phenomenon known as El Niño (see page 126). Perhaps early people simply learned to shift their diet accordingly. The debate goes on, but meanwhile scientists are returning to Peru's preceramic sites to look for specific diet information. Among other things, they are beginning to use extremely fine-mesh dirt-sifting screens in order to catch the tiniest anchovy bones. As the data come in, we will get a better picture of how a "simple" fishing culture built a civilization.

Above and at left, fishing motifs on pottery from Peru's coastal Nazca culture (A.D. 100 – 800). Below, evidence from an adobe wall at Chan Chan, an ancient Peruvian city, that, to early fishermen, some fish seemed bigger than life.

last presumably used as containers for food and water. And, of course, the dwarf-eared, semidomesticated maize that turned up during MacNeish's first explorations of the valley.

Not all the plants were indigenous to Tehuacán. More than half of them appear to have been introduced as cultivated plants whose wild origins have been traced elsewhere in Mesoamerica, giving archeologists useful indicators of the cultural interchanges that had come to be a part of the Tehuacanos' milieu. Corn, for example, may have begun its evolutionary voyage toward captivity somewhere within a 100-mile radius of the valley rather than at Tehuacán itself.

As for their communal life cycle, the Coxcatlán-phase population is estimated to have swelled to perhaps 10 times its original number. Because Coxcatlán people were capable of producing a surplus crop, they probably stayed together in macrobands for longer periods of time each year, presuming that the cultivated gardens, located at spring-summer meeting grounds, gave them greater food surpluses of longer duration. Indeed the season for nomadic hunting in one-family bands by this time may have been limited to the dry winter months when the gardens were barren, the wild edibles few, and small game about the only regular food available.

If MacNeish is right about the importance of cultivated gardens at this phase, then he is probably correct in speculating that man was in turn being domesticated by the plants he had to tend. Once a communal group had staked out a particular area as a garden, a heightened sense of land "ownership" must inevitably have come into play. And as experience in gardening grew, the gardener became aware of the part played by various natural phenomena in the success of his enterprise — rainfall, day length, temperature, the times of planting and harvest — all of which generated rituals, ceremonies, mythic beliefs, and the shamans to oversee their favorable outcome.

As for craft industries, the Coxcatlán-phase people had upgraded their grain-grinding implements to create forerunners of the roller stone and slab device still used in parts of rural Mexico: the *mano* and *metate*. And they laboriously produced stone water vessels and bowls, rubbing stone against stone to shape them.

The Coxcatlán phase was followed by the fourth, or Abejas phase, dated 5,500 to 4,300 years ago. The chief distinguishing characteristic of these Tehuacano generations was their building of semipermanent villages, some of which seem to have been occupied virtually year round. Each spring they planted a bit more so that the surplus at summer harvesting would allow them to remain longer in the fall, until they would be able to stay through the winter. The houses, five to ten per village, were typically clustered on river terraces along the valley floor, where they could get maximum corn crop yields. Their number indicates that the population had grown substantially to 30 or even 40 times the

original settlers — due in no small part to the food reserves that did away with crisis periods.

By now the Tehuacanos had domesticated dogs. There are several archeologists who think that a few descendants of Asian wolves, already domesticated as dogs, had entered the Americas via the Bering land bridge with their masters in the first wave of settlers. But the frequency of remains discovered in Tehuacán suggests dogs were standard members of the community. The Abejas-phase people also used cotton to make nets and weave simple unpatterned fabrics. However, none of these changes can be said to constitute a "revolution" in technology; rather the changes were, as before, steady, progressive, all in all rather conservatively paced. Abejas tools, for example, were little better than those of the Coxcatlán phase, and wild plants and animals still supplied much of the Tehuacanos' food.

Increased population together with an increasingly intensive agricultural system led inevitably to changes in the political and social structure. Such had been the case in agriculturally ripe Egypt, in Sumer, and in the Indus River settlements; and certainly it happened in

Hawaii's Mysterious Cotton

The Hawaiian island chain is the world's most isolated: the nearest continental landfall is San Francisco, 2,400 miles away. Whatever people, animals, and plants got to these volcanic islands did so by conquering awesome distances. Yet when Captain Cook landed in 1778, Hawaiian cotton — a wild hybrid species with one set of chromosomes from New World cotton and another from Old World cotton — was already well established. How did it get to be a hybrid and how did it get to Hawaii?

The genetic makeup of Hawaiian cotton immediately made botanists wonder whether people had anything to do with the hybridization. But if Old World people and New World people each brought their respective cotton plants to Hawaii, and the hybridization occurred there, where are the two parent species? There are other species of cotton in Hawaii, but they are all traceable to postcontact times. Could the unique species have come, already hybridized, as part of the cultural baggage of the first Polynesians, who had arrived 13 centuries earlier? Not likely: its poor-quality fiber makes it virtually unusable. Did birds eat, carry, and excrete a few lucky cotton seeds on a Hawaiian beach? Probably not: all cotton seeds contain varying amounts of a toxic substance. Maybe a seed floated all the way from the Americas. A 500-mile ocean trip is not out of the question, thanks to the seed's protective kernel. But it is unlikely a seed could have survived a 2,400-mile voyage. So how did cotton get to Hawaii? The truth is we haven't a clue.

This 1,400- to 1,600-year-old Teotihuacán vessel, part turkey and part quetzal, was dubbed "the crazy duck" by its excavators. The red ceramic plumage, shells, and mica discs apparently were whimsical later additions to the pot.

the Tehuacán Valley. MacNeish's sequence continues through five other phases, during which the demand for food increased, irrigation made possible more productive use of the land, and Tehuacanos discovered ways to grow two and even three crops annually on a single plot of earth.

The Tehuacán Valley had come of age. More-intensive farming required greater labors, more efficiency, finer skills, and a high degree of organization to oversee the redistribution of the communities' wealth. Society began to sort itself into distinct levels of responsibility and divisions of labor, creating a small elite at the top, a middle rank of specialist-managers, and a broad lower base of farmers.

MacNeish is the first to say that his interpretation of Tehuacán Valley sites is not meant to be a universal model for the rise of agriculture in all parts of the Americas. But he does believe that some parts of his reconstruction can be used to explain the transition to farming elsewhere. In every region differences in climate, geography, scarcities or abundance of wild foods and game, the happenstance of cultural isolation or contact with other centers of human occupation, must all be factored into the picture if we are to understand how one group came to invent farming on its own, another to borrow it, and another to remain fixed in a more primitive stage of subsistence. But despite these differences, there may be some general trends that are common to all.

MacNeish's studies in the central highlands of Peru, a few years after those in Tehuacán, provide a case in point. There, at about the same time as their neighbors to the north in Mexico, hunter-gatherers evolved a set of survival skills that included animal husbandry and the domestication of both root and seed crops.

MacNeish chose for an analysis a promising area known as the Ayacucho Valley, which included high elevation (more than 9,000 feet above sea level), humid woodlands, thorn forests, and semidesert. He and his team see a picture of gradual progress toward civilization that began perhaps 25,000 years ago — a disputed figure — with Pleistocene hunters whose winter shelter was Pikimachay Cave within the forest zone. For thousands of years their living patterns continued essentially unchanged. Then sometime about 6,000 years ago, these early Peruvians began raising guinea pigs for food. And about that same time they may have expanded their husbandry efforts to herd llamas. By 5,100 years ago MacNeish finds them building corrals for their livestock in the region's alpine meadows.

MacNeish also finds evidence for the cultivation of white potatoes about this time. Some of the root crops, identical to those grown in the Andes today, had a high degree of frost resistance but a bitter taste. By a process of freeze-drying, perhaps as old as cultivation, they may have been converted — as they still are today — to the tasty, easily stored staple called *chuño*. Sweet potatoes, manioc, coca, peanuts, quinoa, lima beans, guava, South American varieties of squash, bottle gourds, common beans, cotton, and chili peppers were also developed either in the highland valleys or in neighboring lowlands.

MacNeish and his colleagues continue to examine the rise of food production and its attendant social changes, for there are still many pieces of the puzzle that defy easy placement. At the same time, a minority of prehistorians believes that agriculture was not invented in the Americas at all but introduced from the Old World. One theorist, Donald W. Lathrap, suggesting a date far earlier than any of MacNeish's sites have indicated, makes a most intriguing case for world agriculture having a single origin in Africa. He proposes that it was the lowly bottle gourd that literally contained the seeds of change. As he states it: "In almost every part of nuclear America where there has been a successful search for very early plant remains, the bottle gourd appears at the very bottom."

Lathrap traces the cultivated bottle gourd from sub-Saharan Africa 40,000 years ago to the tropical forests of western Africa then to fishing settlements along the coast where it became part of the equipage of primitive fishing nets. He proposes that successive waves of fishermen became castaways in dugout canoes and were carried by the prevailing currents across the South Atlantic. Landing on the eastern bulge of what is now Brazil 16,000 years ago or earlier, they brought with them not only bottle gourds, their seeds still dry and viable inside, but also fishing techniques, African cotton, boat building, tropical gardening technology, and other patterns of culture new to South America. Lathrap postulates further that his transplanted fishermen mixed with native Indian populations, introducing their skills and budding forth as new colonies up the

From the New World's cornucopia came not only corn but tomatoes, potatoes, sweet potatoes, avocados, pineapples, papayas, virtually every bean except the soybean, and several kinds of squashes including the pumpkin. Cortés found the Aztec ruler Moctezuma drinking a chocolate concoction made from powdered cacao beans, red peppers, and vanilla — all three gifts of the New World. Manioc, or cassava (whose root is the base for tapioca), also came from the Americas, as did green peppers, cranberries, guavas, maple syrup, peanuts, wild rice, and even chicle (the base for chewing gum). In fact, what is on sale today in a Cuzco market (above), except for such Old World imports as citrus and onions, is probably much the same as what was available there about 600 years ago. At left is the renowned Mexican muralist Diego Rivera's vision of an Aztec marketplace, painted in 1952.

Amazon River system, until eventually by 10,000 years ago their influence was felt all over the tropical river lowlands of Central and South America.

Lathrap's idea about the bottle gourd making its way from Africa to Brazil is only one "diffusionist" idea. There are others (see pages 10 to 31). Diffusionism has often invited highly imaginative connections and many prehistorians are wary of it. But the fact is that there are still some New World botanical mysteries — the mystery of where wild Hawaiian cotton came from is one example (see page 103) — that no one can explain except by some form of diffusionism.

Not all, however, is unresolved mystery. Thanks largely to Richard MacNeish's work in the Tehuacán Valley in Mexico, the slow change from gatherer to planter, and from hunter to herdsman, is well documented. What the famous Australian archeologist V.

Gordon Childe once called the "Neolithic revolution" we now understand was a much slower process — perhaps more properly called, as MacNeish suggests, the "Neolithic *evolution.*" But slow or not, the change it wrought in human lives was so great that it is beyond measuring. The cycle of crop planting and harvesting tied people to the land, and in that sense limited their freedom (though it must be said that hunters, dependent as they were on the movements of game animals, were not free-roaming either). But it created a surplus of food, and with food surpluses came larger populations, specialization of labor, and especially for those who were not tending the crops, time — time to dream, time to study the heavens, time to build, time to weave and sculpt and hammer gold. There was, suddenly, more than maize sprouting in the fields of the New World. There was civilization itself.

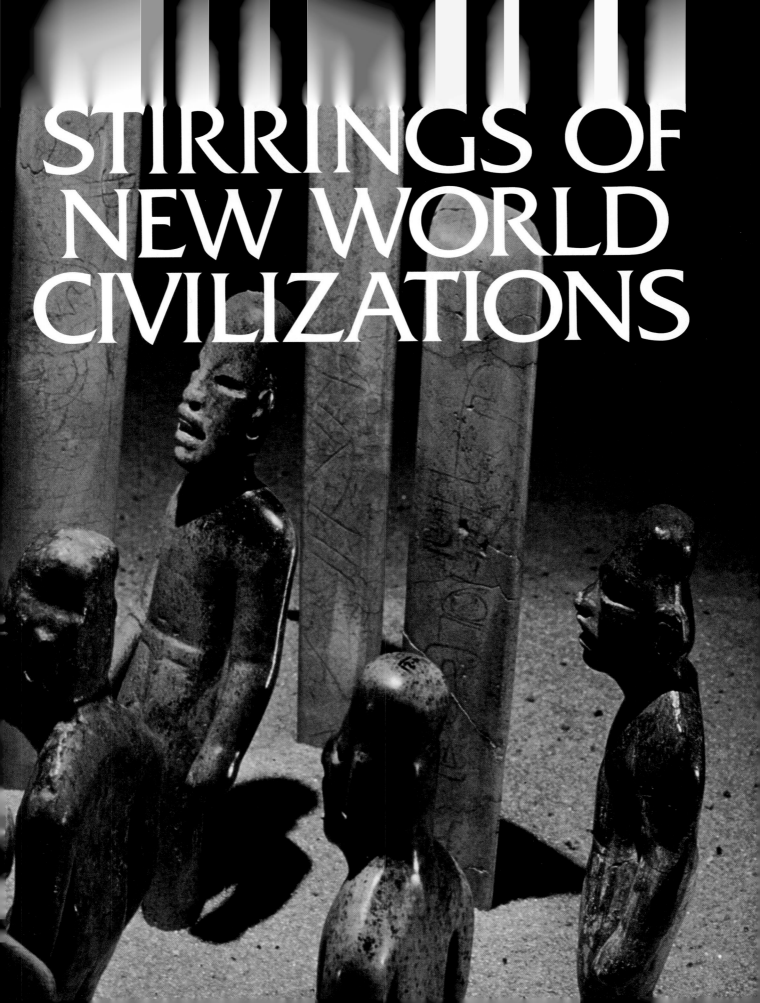

STIRRINGS OF
NEW WORLD
CIVILIZATIONS

THE PEOPLE OF POVERTY POINT

Close to 3,000 years ago enormous and unique earthworks were constructed in the Lower Mississippi Valley by a forgotten people. Strangely enough, their identifying hallmark is a small clay ball they made to use in cooking.

No one knows for sure how Poverty Point acquired its name, but it is said that in the 1840's and 1850's the settlers at this site on Bayou Macon in northeastern Louisiana suffered crop failures and outbreaks of fever, and were in dire distress. Coming to their rescue, the federal government sent supplies by boat to the settlement because there were no roads or railroads leading there, and after a time the landing became known as Poverty Point. The name stuck, and a century or so later it was applied to the culture that was centered there some 3,000 years ago.

It is a rather modest legacy that this obscure culture left behind: an assortment of flint blades and tools; flint dart points fashioned in many shapes and sizes, along with stone weights to send them hurtling toward their targets; and a hundred or so small clay figurines, all but a handful of them broken and headless. There are also shards of stone vessels, exquisite examples of lapidary work, fragments of pottery, and, outnumbering all these, a vast collection of small fired clay objects that were shaped by ancient hands, to be heated through for use in baking pits.

If that were all that remained to tell about the Poverty Point people who once lived in the Lower Mississippi Valley, there would be little to inspire interest. But

some 2 1/2 millennia after their decline, the most spectacular accomplishment of these little-known people remains: earthworks that spread out along the curving banks of Bayou Macon.

So vast are the Poverty Point earthworks that from ground level they can hardly be recognized as a manmade formation. But from the air, the eye can detect the outline of several long hummocks in a formal, semicircular configuration of enormous proportions. It is the incredible mark of a culture ahead of its time, a prehistoric people who were not yet engaged in agriculture but who probably cultivated gourds, squash, and native seed plants, and who were limited to the most elementary tools and weaponry. And yet they were capable of constructing what was possibly, around 1000 B.C., the most elaborate and massive complex of earthworks in the Americas.

Lapidary work was a thriving industry among the Poverty Point people, whose fondness for red jasper is displayed by these artifacts. Shown here are a necklace of tubular beads and bird-head pendants (top), a human effigy tablet and a bird head (center), and a gorget with delicately notched edges and an engraved design possibly representing serpents (bottom).

The natural questions to ask are who, how, when, and why. Were the people who built the Poverty Point mounds indigenous to Louisiana, or did they come from other places and at different times? Were they a link between the Olmec, their Mexican contemporaries (1200–300 B.C.) who also built earthern mounds, and the Adena Mound Builders, who occupied the Ohio Valley somewhat later? How could a primitive people have planned such an enormous and formally designed project and then carried it through to completion? Did it take generations, or even centuries, to build? Presumably only a sedentary — and socially stable — people could have been capable of such a work. But could they have been sedentary without farming? Did Poverty Point represent a cultural revolution, an advance from a band existence to an organized, class-structured society with laborers, overseers, and rulers? What inspired these people to build great earthworks? And finally, what happened to them?

So far there are no answers — only shrewd conjectures about the shadowy past of Poverty Point. In their researches archeologists are often frustrated by the paucity of artifacts; rarely is there an opportunity to investigate an American culture as old as Poverty Point and find sufficient clues for drawing a broad picture of life as it was then lived. Attempting to interpret the findings, archeologists have arrived at a number of conflicting views about the origin, social organization, and life of the Poverty Point people. Further excavations may clear the haze and solve the puzzles. But in the meantime the quest for answers has led to more questions about the rise of this culture on the North American continent long before the Christian Era began.

It is a popular notion that progress is made along a smooth and consistently upward path. Every step forward, whether scientific, technological, or even athletic, tends to be seen as leading to a further — and always grander — step. If man walks on the moon today, then tomorrow he is bound to reach a star. If one runner breaks the four-minute mile, surely another will soon break three and a half. And yet for most of man's history, progress has been uneven and happenstance, and strides in one area have been no guarantee of parallel advances in others. Repeatedly cultures have flowered, achieved great things of one sort or another, and then faded away, often for no discernible reason. It is in this context that the flowering and decline of the Poverty Point culture must be seen. It was capable of a monumental undertaking, and yet it passed on little to succeeding cultures, and left only its grand earthworks and some modest artifacts to stir our curiosity. The Poverty Point culture does not stun with an abundance of riches. It is in fact the unevenness of its achievements that catches our interest.

Enigma of the Ridges

The existence of the Poverty Point ridges and mounds was first noted in print by the Smithsonian Institution in its annual report for 1872. They remained essentially forgotten until 1913 when Clarence B. Moore, a wealthy Philadelphian interested in archeology, noticed the formation from his steamboat. His associates surveyed and studied the site and concluded that the unusual prominences had been raised by man, not nature. But it was not until 1952 — when aerial photographs taken by the U.S. Army Corps of Engineers revealed the geometric pattern formed by the ridges — that scholars began to suspect that something out of the ordinary was to be found there.

What at ground level appeared to local residents to be natural rises of earth were revealed to be the unmistakable remnants of a man-made enclave consisting of six concentric ridges, nested one inside the other, laid out in an open horseshoe facing Bayou Macon. Four aisles, or passageways, radiate outward from the interior of the formation, cutting through the series of ridges. The ridges, now somewhat eroded, are approximately 75 to 80 feet wide at the base, about 6 to 10 feet high, and about 125 feet apart from crest to crest. They

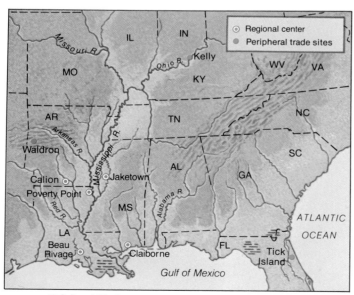

Of the 150 Poverty Point sites in the Lower Mississippi Valley, five have been designated regional centers; related artifacts found at more distant sites may indicate trade links.

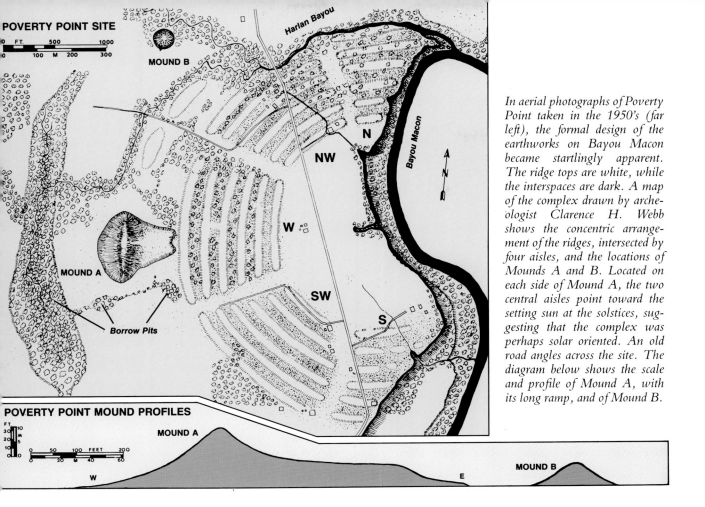

POVERTY POINT SITE

MOUND B

Harlan Bayou

Bayou Macon

N

NW

W

SW

S

MOUND A

Borrow Pits

In aerial photographs of Poverty Point taken in the 1950's (far left), the formal design of the earthworks on Bayou Macon became startlingly apparent. The ridge tops are white, while the interspaces are dark. A map of the complex drawn by archeologist Clarence H. Webb shows the concentric arrangement of the ridges, intersected by four aisles, and the locations of Mounds A and B. Located on each side of Mound A, the two central aisles point toward the setting sun at the solstices, suggesting that the complex was perhaps solar oriented. An old road angles across the site. The diagram below shows the scale and profile of Mound A, with its long ramp, and of Mound B.

POVERTY POINT MOUND PROFILES

MOUND A

MOUND B

W

E

span three-quarters of a mile from one side to the other, and have a total length of almost seven miles.

Centered behind, or west of, this horseshoelike formation is an enormous mound that sprawls out in an irregular T-shape. One scholar suggested that the mound (designated Mound A) is a bird effigy. If so, it would probably be one of the oldest known earthen representations of this motif in North America. Seventy feet high — equivalent to an eight-story apartment building — the mound stretches 680 feet from north to south (the presumed wingspread of the bird) and 690 feet from east to west. The eastern side of the mound falls away to a low earthen platform, or ramp, that suggests to some the tail feathers of a bird.

About two-fifths of a mile to the north is a smaller mound (Mound B) that rises to a height of 21.5 feet from a base 195 feet in diameter. Possibly it covered a crematorium, because bits of charred human bone have been found in one ash bed. Somewhat farther away are two additional mounds. The larger of these lies on a direct line with the center of the ridge formation and is approximately as large as Mound A.

The great size of the earthworks and their formal arrangement strongly suggest that the Poverty Point site was a major ceremonial center for a fairly large population. But who were the people and where did they live?

More than 150 smaller sites revealing cultural similarities to Poverty Point have been discovered along the waterways of Louisiana, Mississippi, and Arkansas, and there may be many others. As at Poverty Point, most of the settlements were on or near water — on embankments overlooking major rivers, on natural levees, at the junctions of rivers and lakes, and along the estuaries and marshes of the Gulf Coast. All the sites were located in congenial environments where land and nature combined to sustain life generously. Varying from less than a quarter of an acre to 150 acres in extent, they seem to have ranged from single-family dwellings to hamlets and regional centers that were sizable but secondary to Poverty Point itself. Some of the sites were apparently seasonal camps for hunting and other activities.

Also resembling Poverty Point in its location on Bayou Macon, many of these sites were constructed in a semicircular or semioval pattern with the open side facing the water and with one or more mounds located nearby. But their earthworks were not nearly so massive, nor did they have the special geometric arrangement of Poverty Point.

It seems clear that Poverty Point was an important center where people from outlying settlements convened to participate in social, political, and religious activities, and in trade. Possibly it was the center of a chiefdom, but scholars think it is doubtful that societies on the chiefdom level existed in North America 3,000 years ago. More likely, says archeologist James B.

Griffin, it was the center of a loosely integrated network of tribes. Culturally linked by the similarities in their settlement patterns and their artifacts, the various groups inhabiting the widely scattered sites have become known as the Poverty Point people. They traded widely, had somewhat similar magical and religious beliefs, and probably contributed to the ceremonial and religious activities at Poverty Point.

Although habitation at Poverty Point and in the Lower Mississippi Valley goes back about 8 to 10 thousand years, the Poverty Point culture seems to have emerged gradually, around 1500 B.C. Its florescence (about 1200 to 800 B.C.) was in the general time frame of Egypt's 21st Dynasty, following the reigns of Tutankhamen and Ramses I, while the years of its decline (around 500 B.C.) saw the rise of classical Greece. But Poverty Point bears no resemblance to those cultures of the Mediterranean. It had no writing, no true agriculture, and no architecture except for its earthworks. Its weapons were simple: the spear, the atlatl (a spear thrower), the dart, the knife, and possibly the bola, (a cord with stone-weighted ends, which was hurled to ensnare fowl and small game). Even the bow and arrow was unknown to these people.

More provocative is a comparison of the Poverty Point culture with that of another people about 1,000 miles to the south — their contemporaries, the Olmec (see "The Olmec Enigma," page 130). A few archeologists, trying to unravel the mystery of Poverty Point's origins, see a Mexican influence in its earthworks, its clay figurines, and perhaps its lapidary work.

Considering the massiveness of Poverty Point's ridges and mounds, one naturally assumes that they were built over many generations or even centuries, as were the pyramids of the Maya and some of the great cathedrals of Europe. It has been calculated that the entire earthworks contain 1 million cubic yards of earth. According to one estimate, it must have taken 35 to 40 million 50-pound baskets of soil to build the earthworks at Poverty Point.

Even so, archeologists James A. Ford and Clarence H. Webb decided after investigating the site that the earthworks were probably built in a single great effort over a relatively short period of time. (Ford, then a staff member at the American Museum of Natural History, had been the first to examine the aerial photographs of Poverty Point.) Not only was the project overwhelming from a physical point of view, but its construction had to follow a carefully worked out geometric design. The achievement could only be the result of "central planning and direction," the two colleagues reasoned. It was unlikely that the overall plan would have prevailed had Poverty Point grown in piecemeal fashion over a long time. Ford and Webb suggested that several thousand people, members of a "rather strictly organized" community, joined in the construction. The archeologists found it "difficult to visualize how in a loosely organized society this quantity of essentially non-productive labor could have been expended."

In support of their theory, Ford and Webb called attention to the hearths, cooking pits, and domestic artifacts found in excavations of the ridges — evidence that a town existed there while the construction was under way. Although Poverty Point was a ceremonial center, it also had thousands of inhabitants, the archeologists concluded, and so its construction was undoubtedly completed as quickly as possible to accommodate them. Could a religious motivation account for the drive these people must have had? Whatever spurred them on, their effort was well controlled.

A stand of trees almost obscures Mound A and its ramp, but the mound's significance is even more obscured by the passage of time. What inspired the Poverty Point people to carry some 10 million basketloads of earth for its construction?

In contrast to this view of a planned and rapidly constructed community, Griffin suggests that the Poverty Point site was a base for populations of varying size for many centuries. But the duration of its habitation by any one population is unknown. In his view, "a population of more than a few hundred at any one time would be phenomenal." Furthermore, says Griffin, there is no way of telling that the Poverty Point earthworks of, say, 500 B.C. resembled the earthworks of 1000 B.C. — there is nothing to indicate that they were built in one grand effort early in their history.

It is still far from clear who lived upon the ridges or what transpired there. Very little has been found to indicate the sort of housing that might have been erected. Nor are there any clues about the dwelling pattern of the supposed townspeople to indicate a class structure. Perhaps the Poverty Point site was a sacred ceremonial center occupied by a privileged elite or a priestly class. But so far the evidence is lacking, and the earthworks remain a mystery.

Another puzzle is how the Poverty Point people could have devoted their time and energy to the colossal enterprise unless they farmed to assure themselves a dependable food supply. For most hunting and gathering groups, the procurement of food allowed little time for anything else, and the winters were often periods of deprivation. But the food resources of these people were apparently sufficient to fill their larders and permit the diversion of millions of man-hours to construction work.

To be sure, they were fortunate in their benign environment. In the fertile valley area, with its flatlands nourished every year by flooding rivers, and its gentle climate (the region was probably somewhat cooler and drier in those times), nature's bounty was generous. The Indians drew fish from the rivers and lakes, hunted fowl and game in the marshy countryside, and gathered nuts, seeds, fruits, roots, and plants from the forests and grasslands. Dart points and fragments of shell and bone unearthed along with residues of food at some sites tell us that the people had a richly varied fare that included clams, turtle, alligator, bass, garfish, catfish, turkey, duck, goose, rabbit, deer, hickory nuts, acorns, walnuts, persimmons, wild grapes, and sunflower seeds.

At a few sites squash seeds have also been found, but the dating shows that the squash was from an earlier period than Poverty Point times. Also, it is not clear whether the seeds are proof of a domesticated crop or of a wild harvest. Squash was cultivated for its seeds and for use as containers in the southeastern United States as early as 3000 B.C., and possibly it was grown by the Poverty Point people.

Those who contend that the Poverty Point people grew crops point to the solar orientation of the great earthworks as substantiation, claiming that at the vernal and autumnal equinoxes certain features in their arrangement form a straight line with the rising sun.

Such an "earth calendar," they say, shows a farmer's interest in the seasons and his need to know when to plant. But while it is true that solar orientation reveals a knowledge of the seasons and the movement of the sun, it is not proof of agriculture. It is more likely, others contend, that the Poverty Point people simply associated the equinoxes with the growth of vegetation, fruiting, and other natural phenomena.

The little hand-modeled clay figurines found at Poverty Point sites have also been put forth as possible evidence of crop growing. The 1- to 2 1/2-inch-high figures of seated women make up most of the recovered representative art of the Poverty Point culture.

Only a few of the figurines are whole (most appear to have had their heads broken off), but the torsos are quite lifelike and several of them suggest pregnancy. The pregnant figures are interpreted by some to be fertility symbols intended to encourage the productivity of the earth. But archeologists who are authorities on Poverty Point say that the figurines simply indicate that the Indians associated plant growth with human fertility, and they doubt that they were symbols of anything beyond human reproduction.

A few scholars have also proposed that the figurines resemble the solid clay figurines of the Olmec in various ways — especially in the seated posture, the representations of pregnancy, the coiffure clefts, and the slits for eyes and mouths. On the other hand, the Olmec clay figurines show a high degree of artistry, while those modeled by the Poverty Point people are extremely crude. And there is nothing truly unique about figurines of pregnant women — they have been made by prehistoric people all over the world. And so the significance of the clay figures and the possibility of an Olmec connection remain unresolved, as do so many other questions regarding Poverty Point.

Cooking Balls

Although we know little about the Poverty Point people and their extraordinary center on Bayou Macon, we do know a great deal about their cooking habits. The profusion of homely objects found at all the sites shows a similar approach to the basic business of daily home life: the preparation of food.

The most typical of all the artifacts is — surprisingly enough — a small baked clay ball, only one to two inches in diameter and two to three ounces in weight. The odd-looking balls, most often molded in melon, oblong, cylindrical, spiral, and biconical shapes, were used in cooking. Thousands of them have been unearthed so far. Indeed, so ubiquitous are these tiny finds that they are the hallmark of Poverty Point culture and are simply called Poverty Point objects. Their discovery in widely scattered sites has helped to identify the settlements culturally.

The practice of cooking with clay balls did not originate with the Poverty Point people. Other prehistoric peoples had used heated stones to cook with, dropping them into a container to bring food to a boil, or piling them around food on a hearth. But in alluvial and coastal areas where there is little rock — from South Carolina to Louisiana — clay balls were often used instead. The Poverty Point people used them not only more intensively than others, but also more innovatively, for a new style of cooking: pit-oven baking. Distinguishing the Poverty Point objects from the clay cooking balls of other groups are the additional finger molding they show and the use of fluting, grooves, and punctations for ornamentation.

Although no depictions have been found of a division of labor by sex, it seems clear that cooking was woman's work, as in most societies. And the making of the clay balls was one of her culinary activities. That her children occasionally helped with this task is evidenced by some of the finger imprints on the hand-squeezed objects: they are far too small to have been made by adults. Apparently each housewife had her own preferences for design and shape, because most of the balls found in any one pit are similar in type.

At site after site, researchers have uncovered earth ovens characteristically filled with the clay objects and sometimes with a residue of ash or possibly charred vegetation. The pits vary in size, ranging from 12 to 24 inches in diameter and 9 to 20 inches in depth. Experi-

menting with the technique of pit-oven cookery, field-workers learned that the clay balls, like pottery vessels, had to be air-dried before they were fired, and that they could be used about 10 times before they cracked apart. They also found that by wrapping fish, meat, and potatoes in wet leaves and then placing the wrapped food on a bed of hot coals in the bottom of the pit and covering it with a layer of hot clay balls, an entire meal could be cooked efficiently in about two hours, much the way it is done at a clambake. The Indians probably layered their food with vegetation, which would cause it to steam as well as bake.

The Poverty Point people may have depended on pit-oven cookery because, strangely enough, until 1000 to 500 B.C. they had no cooking pots. In view of their extensive use of clay for making cooking balls, it seems remarkable that they did not do more with the material. Tribes in South Carolina and Florida were making pottery as early as 2500 B.C., but the skill was introduced in the Mississippi Valley only around 1200 B.C. or later, probably through trade contacts. Shards of the earliest Poverty Point pottery show that most of it was tempered with fiber (probably shredded palmetto) and made in a very simple and primitive way. They turned out very little of it, and there is no evidence of pottery cooking vessels. But they were well supplied with

Only a few of the solid clay figurines discovered at Poverty Point sites are intact. Most of them are tiny, hand-modeled torsos of seated females, rounded off at the thighs, and typically only about 1 to 2 1/2 inches in height. Several broken-off heads have also been unearthed. The charming figurine above is of special interest because of its coiffure with a split, or part, down the center: a few scholars have noted a similarity to the coiffure clefts displayed by some clay figurines from the Olmec culture.

114

Found by the thousands, these strange, variously shaped clay balls are the primary identifying artifact of the Poverty Point culture. Scholars were at first baffled by the ubiquitous objects but are now in agreement that they were used in cooking.

bowls and platters of steatite (brought from Appalachia) and sandstone. Some pieces had polished interiors, and two were handsomely embossed with eagle and animal designs. Impressions of simple plaiting found on clay cooking balls show that baskets, or perhaps cane mats, were sometimes used as food containers for pit cooking (as well as for transporting soil for their earthworks).

The Poverty Point people must have had a special feeling for stone, because they traveled afar to obtain it; their stonework shows impressive workmanship and care for ornamentation. Myriads of stone tools have been found at many sites, and although most were fashioned of local chert and quartzite, others were made of off-white chert imported from the Ozark Mountains in Arkansas, Missouri, and Oklahoma, of Arkansas novaculite, and of flint brought from Illinois, Indiana, and Ohio. Patiently chipping and flaking the stone, they made a variety of small tools with chisellike edges for cutting, scraping, and sawing. They also turned out sharp drill points, perforators, and needles. At the Poverty Point site alone, nearly 30,000 of these microflint tools — some only one to two inches long — have been found. Among the larger implements are reamers for enlarging holes, stone hoes for loosening soil to be carried to mound sites, and milling and grinding stones for food preparation.

In addition, they manufactured a wide variety of projectile points, ranging from slender leaflike points for their darts to stout, widely triangular shapes, and fashioned heavy blades for knives and spears. A number of other stone objects have yet to be identified. Especially intriguing are the plummets, which archeologists believe are bola weights, although they might be weights for fishnets. (The bola would have been useful to the Indians living along the Mississippi flyway for migratory fowl.) The plummets, most often made of hematite in graceful teardrop or oval shapes, are often decorated with beautifully executed stylized designs representing serpents, owls, and human figures.

But it is in lapidary work that the Poverty Point people excelled. Pendants, buttons, beads, and small tablets are worked in an array of such colored or translucent stones as red jasper, amethyst, feldspar, red and green talc, galena, quartz, and limonite. Most of these stones were obtained by a far-flung trade. Among the pendants are a number of bird effigies — red jasper owls and parakeets, and bird heads worked in polished jasper and black and brown stones. There are also representations of a human face, a turtle, claws, and rattles, and stubby but carefully made tubular pipes that might have been used ceremonially or medicinally.

In these various pieces some archeologists find resemblances to Olmec carvings. Others, finding no cultural tie-in, emphasize that in primitive portrayals of humans, birds, turtles, and snakes, some resemblance to each of these would be expected, and that the resemblance goes no further. Certainly the Poverty Point people, following the trails and traveling the waterways in dugout canoes, had many trading contacts with other societies in the eastern and midwestern United States. Could they have crossed paths with the Olmec some 1,000 miles to the south? So far no Poverty Point artifacts have been found across the Gulf of Mexico; nor has any Olmec material been found at Poverty Point. The gap is considerable.

As mysterious as the origin of the Poverty Point culture, with its mound-building proclivity and other special traits, is its gradual decline. By 500 B.C. it had virtually disappeared. No cataclysmic environmental changes had occurred, and there is no evidence of an invading warlike people. Possibly its decline was caused by some internal disruption of a political or religious nature. But in all probability the dissolution of the culture was the outcome of a changing technology and altered patterns of behavior. Gradually the people adopted the manufacture of pottery and experimented with new methods of cooking. With cookpots they could stew their food, and so they no longer needed to make clay cooking balls. With pottery containers they could also store food for lean times. Less creative, they didn't make stone ornaments or microflint tools, and long-distance trade for stones became unimportant. Gradually also they may have abandoned the regional centers and dispersed to smaller settlements, and massive mound building came to a halt. Losing all the distinguishing traits of the Poverty Point people, their descendants adopted the simpler life-style of a much earlier period. Centuries would pass before another culture rose to the heights of Poverty Point in the southeastern United States. But never again in the Lower Mississippi Valley — or anywhere else in the world — would people build such unique earthworks.

ANCIENT SHRINE OF THE ANDES

In the millennium before Christ, pilgrims came
to a sanctuary high in the Andes for religious rites,
sacrifices, and possibly to hear an oracle.
After six centuries the cult died out. No one knows why.

Around the time that the remarkable Nebuchadnez-zar was building the famous Hanging Gardens of Babylon, some six centuries before the birth of Jesus, something quite magnificent and mysterious was flowering in the north-central highlands of Peru.

It was the first great Andean civilization, but it had no armies. Its monumental structures were the product of sophisticated engineering and architectural techniques — and yet its artisans never used the wheel. Somehow, a unique and rather complicated culture spread rapidly over thousands of square miles, even though its advocates were illiterate, and thus unable to send written messages or to keep records. Nonetheless, the artistic and religious domination of this culture remained unchallenged for more than half a millennium, probably from 850 to 200 B.C., although most of these influences were destined to fade away.

In fact, the Chavín culture and its puzzling religious cult were not even identified until the 1920's, when the great Peruvian archeologist, Julio C. Tello, began to investigate an important ceremonial center, Chavín de Huantar. This rich site, half-buried in a remote, sparsely populated area, lies more than 10,000 feet above sea level in the narrow valley of the River Mosna, a tributary of the Marañón, which farther downstream joins the Ucayali to form the mighty Amazon River.

Although its days of glory were long past and its temple had fallen into disrepair, Chavín de Huantar remained a center for sorcery and divination as late as a century after the 16th-century Spanish Conquest. Except for the occasional romantic observer, like the Spanish missionary Fray Antonio Vázquez de Espinosa, the world at large remained totally unaware of the significance of these remote Andean ruins. Passing through early in the 17th century, this Carmelite priest wrote, "Near this village of Chavín there is a large building of huge stone blocks very well wrought . . . one of the most famous of the heathen sanctuaries, like Rome or Jerusalem with us; the Indians used to come and make their offerings and sacrifices, for the Devil pronounced many oracles for them here, and so they repaired here from all over the kingdom. There are large subterranean halls and apartments. . . ."

Is this the insight of scholarship or the talebearing of

A row of stone heads once studded the exterior walls of Chavín's temples. Guardians of the sacred precincts, these heads, sculpted to portray a half-human, half-beast image, may have been intended to overawe the humble peasant pilgrim.

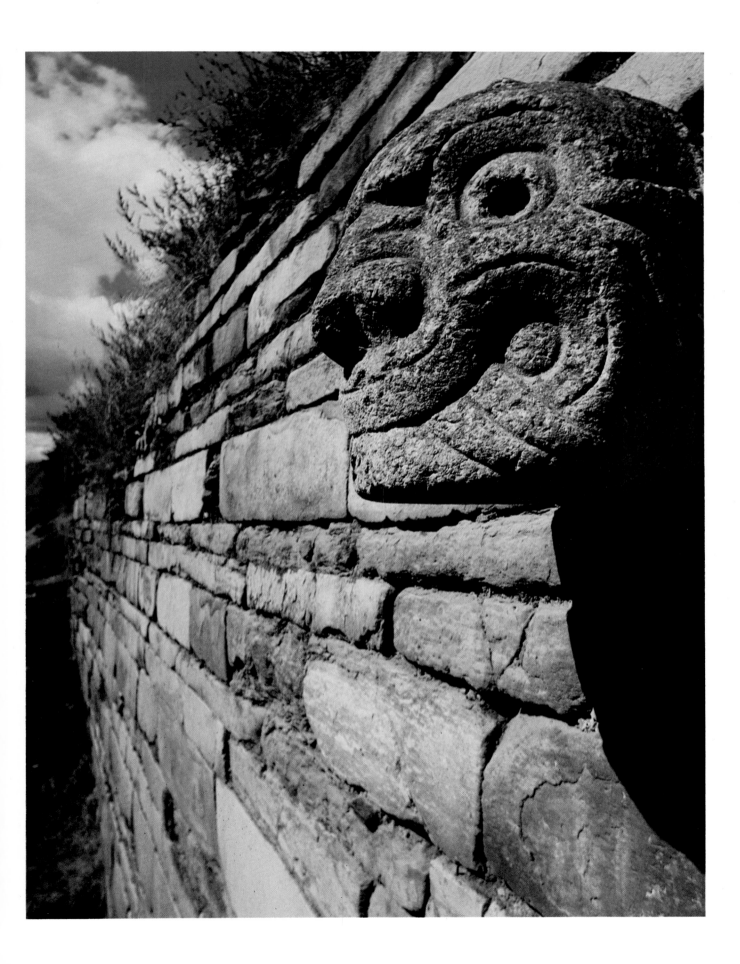

a gullible tourist? No one was to ask, or care. The traveler's account was to languish in obscurity for the next 300 years, when Fray Antonio's manuscript was unexpectedly discovered in 1930 in the Vatican archives. The discovery came too late, at any rate, to find out how the author acquired his background information. Other written references to the "sanctuary" or its possible rites are no more informative than his.

On the other hand, archeological discoveries of the past few decades have increased our knowledge of this unusual culture at an astounding rate. Continuing discoveries, and a close examination of the remains, have resulted in constant reassessment of theories about Chavín, its origins, and its beliefs.

Well-intentioned scholars vie furiously with one another in pursuit of the elusive answers to many basic questions: Where did the Chavín people (or peoples) come from? What is the meaning behind their exotic, and rather frightening, religious art? How, without warfare, did the culture gain such ascendancy over so many farflung villages? What held this culture together, since there is virtually no evidence of political unity?

Some things are known, and they are astonishing. For much of the first millennium B.C. Chavín ideas held sway over most of what is modern-day Peru. From the fertile valleys of the Andean range to the bone–dry desert wastes of the Pacific coast, Chavinoid motifs proliferated in both public and domestic art. Throughout this enormous area, great forces of com-

munal labor were organized to construct Chavín-style temple complexes and other public work projects. Some of these monumental centers, both along the coast and in the highlands, reached their own cultural peaks before the rise of Chavín de Huantar, perhaps centuries before, and their architectural achievements would be refined at the later site.

The Awesome Gods of Chavín

The most obvious thread binding together these widely scattered Chavinoid centers was an eerie cult of the supernatural. On public statuary, images of half-human, half-animal creatures proliferate; the jaguar and the cayman — a relative of the alligator — mingle with human forms, writhing snakes, and such birds of prey as the eagle and the hawk. The gods of Chavín are more awe-inspiring than comforting. Presumably, these nightmarish creatures had to be ritually placated by sacrifice, since the litter found at various ceremonial sites includes the remains of foodstuffs, as well as the bones of such domestic animals as the guinea pig and the llama — and the skulls of human beings.

Bizarre and unappealing as this pantheon might look to us, the popularity of the cult is unmistakable. It virtually swept across north-central Peru, and towards the end of its dominion had spread hundreds of miles to southern Peru, perhaps carried there by Chavín priests. Unlike other religions in history, it apparently encountered little or no opposition. It existed side by side with local beliefs and religious practices.

Because there is no evidence of fortifications or extensive weaponry, it seems unlikely that the strange new religion was imposed by a conquering army. For reasons we may never come to understand, the Chavín cult was an all-encompassing cross-cultural success. Something in the religion itself compelled belief among an agricultural people dependent on the vagaries of climate and weather. Its ritual fascinated the early Peruvians. It held together a civilization, if not an empire, with a shared view of the cosmos.

Certain guesses about its nature can be hazarded. The many animal figures were probably symbolic of deities of the water and sky. Near sacred shrines, or *huacas,* archeologists suggest, *coca,* a mildly narcotic leaf, was ritually chewed and the hallucinogenic drug mescaline was used to induce a state of exaltation. To this day, the Quechua tribes of the Peruvian highlands believe that animallike gods roam the highest peaks of the Andes. They are particularly in awe of a catlike spirit, the *Ccoa,* said to be the bringer of hail and lightning and destroyer of crops.

It is probable that these deities were invoked to ap-

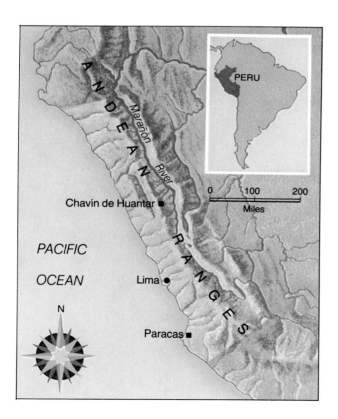

During Chavín's six centuries of cultural dominance, its religion held sway throughout 1,000 miles of Andean highlands and coastal desert. It was the first of the great Peruvian cultures whose ideas spread beyond narrow local boundaries.

Snarling feline mouths, crossed fangs, flowing serpentine lines, and abstract decorative designs were hallmarks of Chavín's widespread religious art. The original inspiration for this art is typified by the stone mortar in the shape of a puma (above, left), which comes from Chavín de Huantar itself.

The ceramic stirrup spout jug (top, left) and the golden breast ornament (top, right) were found in the Lambayeque Valley, which lies some 300 miles northwest of Chavín. The painted and incised flask (above, right) mingles all elements of Chavín's distinctive art. It too was found in the north.

pear in the flesh, in a sense. Priests of the mystery might have clothed themselves in animal skins and prayed for the god to take possession of them. The half-human mythological beings carved on temple walls may represent pictorially the spiritual experience of a mystical ceremony. The god would become incarnate in the chanting, supplicating body of the officiating priest. This illusion, no doubt, would be strengthened, for both priest and other worshipers, by the use of hallucinogens.

Possibly these rites were restricted to a very few special initiates or to a relatively small and obviously powerful priestly caste. The rooms of Chavinoid temples are usually quite small, windowless, and thick-walled. When the god did make himself known to his followers, he would be a shadowy presence in dimly lit, disorienting galleries of the temple. Surely, the primary religious experience of the cult could not easily be put into words. It must have been a search for religious ecstasy, an attempt to lose oneself in an ineffable mystical moment. In addition, there were rites of purifica-

tion and penance that apparently made use of the invigorating, cleansing effects of hot pepper.

Chavín's distinctive, unnerving art may have been intended to recall for the knowing believer the religious experience of such strange rites, since the highly stylized forms and conventions defy all other rational explanation so far.

With numbing regularity, certain features reappear endlessly: oval, round, and even rectangular eyes, upward-looking pupils, animal hide markings in the form of crosses or quatrefoils. Other characteristics seem to have some metaphorical meaning. Eyebrows or hair, for example, may be portrayed as writhing snakes. A kind of optical illusion is created with statuary faces that, viewed upside down, reveal other faces. And in "reversability of perspective," features are arranged so that a viewer, by changing his angle of vision, can see different figures in the same sculpture.

And so it goes, a clever repetition of elements that animates the overall design, conveying to these compelling images of Chavín's deities a feeling of dynamic power and the sense of supernatural forces in motion.

Is there a key, so that each curious detail has some literal translation? Or is the Chavín style more comprehensive, an echo of the ideology behind the cult? Without written evidence, without analogies in other civilizations, the archeologist to date has little more than intuition to help him address such questions.

But elements of the art were fervently reinterpreted in centers hundreds of miles away from Chavín de Huantar. Long-distance travel by foot was no obstacle, of course. Throughout Peruvian history the Indians have casually sprinted from the sea coast to the 13,000-foot-high *Altiplano,* from one rocky precipitous valley to the next daunting gorge. And textiles found in contemporaneous graves, inspired by Chavinoid wall designs, are further evidence of the pervasive influence of this distinctive art style.

Use of these flat patterns may be related to another characteristic of Chavín art. Rarely is a figure modeled in the round. Almost always, the work is executed in low relief on a two-dimensional surface, perhaps fur-

ther emphasizing stylization over any semblance of naturalistic depiction. The result, in the phrase of one scholar, is "managed realism."

Architectural characteristics, too, seem to have been transmitted with little variation throughout the area of Chavinoid influence. Temple complexes were usually U-shaped, fronting a sunken courtyard. The monumental buildings were rectangular and layered, causing the sacred platforms to be vertically distinguished from their surroundings.

The so-called Castillo at Chavín de Huantar is the most famous of Chavinoid structures, an almost 45-foot-tall, virtually windowless, solid-looking mass that is, surprisingly, honeycombed with narrow galleries and odd compartments at various levels. The striking outside walls are built of alternating rows of large and small stone blocks set in clay mortar. Interior walls, which were plastered and painted in the past, are made of small rocks and clay. The whole complex faces toward the east.

Destroyed by the catastrophic landslides that period-

In the galleries of Chavín's oldest temple stands the Smiling God (left), a stone shaft that is the oldest ceremonial object in the Americas still in its original setting. The Staff God (center) is an incised figure, half-human, half-feline, with a staff *clasped in each clawed hand. Serpents sprout from its rectangular head, surmounted by an elaborate headdress. The Tello Obelisk (right) is an exuberant rendering of cult symbolism, ranging from animal tusks to seashells and birds.*

Ice- and snow-covered peaks tower above the ancient ceremonial site at Chavín de Huantar. This neighboring valley, the Callejón de Huaylas, is about two days' walk from Chavín, and its people probably helped to build the temple complex.

ically afflict Peru or looted by antique hunters were hundreds of Chavín sculptures that once adorned the temple complex. Some were ornaments, some structural components, while others are interpreted today as religious idols. Of the latter, there are three important surviving Chavín examples — a half-human, half-feline deity called the Smiling God or the Cruel God; another cat-human deity known as the Staff God, because of the staffs it holds in each hand; and an obelisk known as the Tello Obelisk, for the pioneering Peruvian archeologist, Julio C. Tello (see opposite).

It seems that the Staff God was replaced at some point by the Smiling God, which still stands in a central gallery facing eastward toward the entrance. It would have been a terrifying cult figure, exhibiting the intricately writhing surfaces to be expected of this art style. There is, moreover, some evidence that Chavín de Huantar might have been, like Delphi in Greece, the home of an oracle. A groove running from the statue's raised hand to its nose may once have led to the room directly above. Conceivably, the "oracle" could lie in the upper chamber and boom his reply down through the statue to the appropriately impressed supplicant. Other oracular devices have been found elsewhere in Peru, a country so unchanging for centuries that analogies are almost always useful.

Oracle or ceremonial center or both, Chavín de Huantar's very existence provokes some difficult questions. Fertile as the valley is, it nevertheless could not have supported a large population, perhaps no more than 2,000, on agriculture alone. In other words, Chavín de Huantar might have been a holy city, a kind of

Vatican, fed in part by the small farming villages nearby. Additional sustenance must have come in the form of offerings from the pilgrims who would visit from faraway villages. On the other hand, a small permanent population could not possibly have built the ceremonial complex. The facing stones do not occur naturally in the area; they were quarried elsewhere and dragged to the highland site. Even with outside help, any major project would have required the efforts of thousands of men working over long periods of time. In fact, some form of construction, restoration, or renovation went on continuously at the site for at least five centuries.

Could the ruler-priests of Chavín de Huantar call upon such hordes from all over the region under the religious center's influence? Was work on the temple a kind of personal sacrifice to the powerful Chavín cult? Since there is no clear evidence of forced labor or military coercion, it seems likely that followers of the cult were in fact fulfilling a religious obligation.

Again, analogy with other Andean cultures, even a current one, might give an answer. Bolivia's Copacabana attracts annual pilgrimages from the Andean Indian population, and yearly religious festivals take place throughout Latin America. Probably, adherents of the cult assembled in much the same way at Chavín de Huantar, bringing offerings and building materials. There could have been some communal labor projects at this time, for the heaviest tasks, but the bulk of the construction was probably the responsibility of the moderate-sized permanent population. With the efficient planning that is characteristic of all Andean civilizations, the ruler-priests undoubtedly insured that

Chavín de Huantar

A strategic position — at the confluence of two rivers in a verdant Andean valley and athwart trade routes linking mountain villages with coastal settlements — brought wealth and power to the ancient Peruvian cult center. Herding their llamas, often destined to be sacrificed, pilgrims come from afar with food, clay vessels, and shells to offer to their gods. The original temple, at the far corner in this view of the completed complex, was a simple structure begun around 850 B.C.; but throughout the ensuing six centuries it was extended to the left and out to the river. Priests conduct their rituals in the sunken courtyard at front flanked by two buildings that serve as viewing platforms for the faithful. Around 200 B.C. Chavín de Huantar, for reasons still unknown, lost its preeminence as a religious center and disappeared from history.

enough material was delivered to keep the temple workers occupied the rest of the year.

Not that life in Chavín de Huantar would have been necessarily work dominated or otherwise oppressive. There was an abundant diversity of food, since the cult center was a true crossroads: protein-rich fish from the Pacific, a variety of vegetables and root crops from the farming villages of the coastal valleys, exotic fish and fruits from the Amazon basin. This crossroads aspect, in fact, may explain why the site was chosen for the chief ceremonial complex of the age. It was centrally located, both vertically and horizontally. Perhaps ancient politics was at work in the selection of the site, and the center was the best compromise possible between the claims of earlier Chavinoid towns.

In any event, the inhabitants were probably considered fortunate. They would have had access to luxury goods produced by the increasingly sophisticated Peruvian villages and towns. Along the southern coast, the weavers of Paracas, for example, were beginning to

Fifteen centuries before the Christian Era, gold was being worked in Peru. By Chavín times, artisans were skilled enough to fashion delicate objects like this breast ornament, which ranks among the oldest gold jewelery in the Americas.

produce exquisitely fine fabrics. Any enhancement of design or other advances in fashion would have found their way to Chavín de Huantar. And people nearby developed the metalwork in gold and silver, including delicate jewelry for the upper class, which would later so ignite the greed of the Spaniards.

But if Chavín de Huantar was a focal point, or even a catalyst for so many Andean cultures, did its fame also attract attention from more distant centers of civilization? And did some of these cultures, much better documented historically, antedate the Chavín achievements, even transmit influences that helped establish the unique Chavinoid character?

Peruvian studies have come a long way from the days when one scholar could seriously argue that Andean culture had been transplanted whole from ancient Egypt. Or when another observer said that Tiahuanaco, about 12,000 feet up in the Bolivian highlands, must have been destroyed by a giant tidal wave.

Influences from the Outside World

Recent finds, however, suggest that Chavinoid contacts with the outside world may have been extensive, as implausible as this seems at first blush. Is it sheer coincidence that the art of the Shang period in China has several characteristics in common with Chavinoid art? Each makes use of eyebrows drawn as snakes, of horned cats lacking lower jaws, of bands of scales on the tails of feline monsters.

There are other strange similarities. In both cultures, before the time of Jesus, "toy" dogs were bred. Each civilization raised dogs especially for the temple, for sacrifice, and for food. A type of anthracite mirror has been found that is associated primarily with Chavín and with a province of China; very specific, traditional decorative motifs appear in both places. As a consequence of these apparent correspondences, some scholars are willing to speculate that Chinese traders crossed the Pacific with some ease. Had they made a landfall along Peru's north coast, they might have had an immediate impact, if only of novelty, on a less advanced, but enthusiastically receptive, indigenous culture.

A much shorter imaginative leap is necessary to accept the possibility that the Chavín culture owes some of its traits to earlier societies of present-day Ecuador. From there, it has been suggested, cultural traits spread south to Peru and north to Mexico, there to inspire the Olmec civilization, whose rise and fall roughly coincides with the curve of Chavinoid cultural domination (see "The Olmec Enigma," page 130). There is a striking similarity in the monstrous creature — half-human, half-animal — that haunts the ruins of Chavín and Olmec alike. Their votive sculptures are executed in a curiously related style, in which soft, flowing curves are set off by sharp, straight lines, and elements from man and beast are fused into a whole.

Whatever the origin of Chavín, the intriguing questions may still be: What was its appeal? Did the culture

A fondness for drink has characterized rural life in Peru since Chavín times. From the later Moche culture, which flourished from the 1st to the 8th century A.D., comes this pottery flask of two women holding up an inebriated man.

fill a spiritual vacuum? Did it arise in response to some great sweeping social change in the Andean regions? Did it unify society after one of the physical catastrophes that periodically assault the region — an earthquake, an avalanche, a flood?

We don't know. From our own cultural perspective, it is difficult to guess. The distinctive aspects of Andean life are so exotic, though they intrigue rather than repel, that we find ourselves puzzled.

How did these early societies become so tightly organized? From everything known, it seems clear that all the major Andean cultures established a strong central power as a unifying force. But Chavín appears to have been the exception, although the later Inca concept of *mit'a*, or work tax, probably was enforced at some level. An Inca farmer, for instance, had to donate a certain amount of his time to working lands retained by the emperor; an artisan made ceramics or objects of gold and silver for ritual or state use. So far as we know, no one found the system unfair. No one rebelled against its demands.

The Incas so refined the concept that light, unessential tasks were assigned to the handicapped, so that they would feel they were contributing to the life of the community. In one famous example of *reductio ad absurdum*, the arrogant Incas imposed a ludicrous *mit'a* on the Uros Indians, a minor and despised tribe. Each year, the Uros were required to turn over a tribute of reeds filled with dead lice, as if this were the only work they could capably handle. The Incas, like the Romans with whom they are often compared, believed firmly in the letter of the law.

But there is no evidence that this later Andean tradi-

125

tion, with its implications of the individual's relationship to the powerful (and perhaps all-powerful) state, was flourishing when Chavinoid influence was at its peak. Even if Chavín de Huantar was not the political capital of a centralized government, it is difficult to imagine that individualism and personal expression counted for much. Whether it was cheerful cooperation or unreflective acceptance of the status quo, the common man in Chavinoid times lived a life that was characteristically communal.

And, as in the Andes today, the year in Chavinoid villages must have sparkled with community feasts and family celebrations. We know that temperance has never been considered a prime Andean virtue. *Chicha*, a sickly-sweet fermented drink, has been a mainstay of Peruvian life from the beginning. Even such a routine maintenance task as the cleaning of an irrigation canal was pretext enough for a *chicha*-drinking party. Coca, from which cocaine is extracted today, was chewed not just in holy rites but, when it could be afforded, as a stimulant to offset the harsh climate and as a drug of pleasure. Folk music, hauntingly piped through simple reed instruments, must have been just as poignant then as it is today in the highlands, when the sound of a shepherd's flute wafting through the valleys seems to sum up all the loneliness and mystery of the great jagged mountains. The group dancing of Chavinoid celebrations was undoubtedly as zestful and exuberant as today's, and perhaps as brilliantly costumed. Even the religious pilgrimages undertaken by zealous Indians

The Unpredictable Current: El Niño

El Niño, "The Christ Child" — the very nickname shows the ironic humor with which Peruvians must approach life in one of the world's most contradictory environments — beautiful, often fertile, and just as often unpredictably harsh. For El Niño, so named because this current often strikes without warning around Christmas, creates a cataclysmic weather system that brings widespread death, not the Christian promise of eternal life.

It has always been so. At intervals of from four to seven years and in widely varying strengths, this startling reversal of weather patterns can set off a disastrous chain of events — decimation of wildlife, destruction of settled villages, deformation of the landscape. What might look like a coastal event has consequences at every elevation of the Andean cordillera.

El Niño cuts at the heart of Peru's amazing natural resources, the Peruvian, or Humboldt, Current, destroying the food chain that depends upon that nutrition-rich flow. In normal years, the deep, cold current churns up from southerly waters bringing to the surface such nutrients as nitrates and phosphates, often in a swath several hundred miles wide. Plankton feed upon these minerals and thrive, the first step in a process that will produce huge schools of food fish, including anchovies, which today are used solely for fish meal or fish oil in agriculture and industry.

But the current not only fosters this superabundance; it also sweeps the schools of *anchoveta* near the desert shore. It was thus that these tiny fish made available a measure of the protein necessary for civilization to begin putting down roots along the coast of South America. The fish appeared in great numbers, were accessible from shore, and in the arid desert climate could be dried, ground, and stored for future use. By lashing together bundles of the dried *totora* reed into a rudimentary raft, an Indian fisherman could paddle out past the line of breakers and hover near the schooling anchovies. He probably lay prone upon the craft, rather like a surfer of today's Pacific waters. In fact, a similar small boat, the *caballito,* or "little horse," is still used by inhabitants of Peru's southern coast.

Long before the rise of Chavín, cotton was grown in the coastal valleys, and there is evidence from early graves that a fishing people twined it into netting, which was kept afloat with gourds. Thus equipped, fishermen merely reached down and took their fill of this maritime paradise's harvest.

This is no idle fantasy about an idyllic past. The same conditions exist today. The waters off the coast of northern Peru have supplied at least one-fifth of the world's food fish since 1970, and scientists are in agreement that the basic environmental conditions of the area have not altered significantly in millennia.

But this situation can be wrecked by at least two unpre-

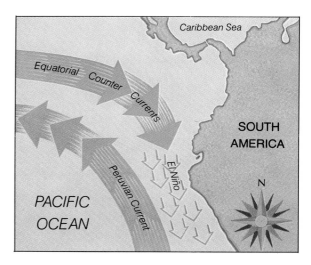

Disaster strikes coastal life when the warm equatorial current of the Pacific Ocean moves too far south and prevents the cool, nourishing Peruvian Current from rising to the water's surface.

from other regions may have served a double purpose. While they brought people together to share in the ritual of sacrifice and to exchange exotic goods with the Chavín priesthood, these gatherings may also have offered the opportunity of marketing the participants' native produce and handicrafts.

Other typically Andean beliefs did not yet exist when Chavín de Huantar was at its peak, however, and perhaps their absence helps explain the appeal of the cult and its attendant civilization.

It is at present not known if the worship of one's ancestors had become the pervasive force it was to be. There was not yet a cult of the past. Even more odd, in a part of the world where people would one day trot out the mummified remains of their progenitors for gay public festivals, there seems mysteriously to have been no particular emphasis on burial practices at Chavín de Huantar, although other Chavinoid centers have yielded rich burial remains.

A few obviously wealthy individuals have been found buried with their most prized possessions. Perhaps infant burial was practiced with special rites. Some excavations have led to speculation that men and women were interred with differing ceremonies. But the most significant circumstance is the notable absence of concern with the dead and, perhaps, with the question of an afterlife.

If the Chavín cult really was a mystical religion, with a stress on the liberation of the spirit from the body, it might be that the physical act of burial was considered dictable factors: man, and El Niño. The former, until quite recently, did not have the ability to cause serious damage. There were too few people to upset the balance. Thanks to economic overreaching, however, the waters were being picked clean in the 1960's. Only careful planning and restraint on the part of the giant commercial fisheries will husband this resource for future generations. Fortunately, the Food and Agricultural Organization of the United Nations and the Peruvian government are deeply concerned about the problem; and conservation efforts may give the fish a second chance.

Catastrophic Consequences

El Niño, however, has probably existed as long as the Peruvian Current and its marvelous cornucopia. The local consequences of a strong Niño are staggering. Simply put, the phenomenon begins when the trade winds that prevail off the Peruvian coast begin, unaccountably, to relax. Warm surface waters that are ordinarily blown off toward the west remain in place, actually burying the colder current. Without the seasonal flow of nutrients, the fish starve. In one stunning blow, the annual marine harvest will have been wiped out. The mass of dead bodies littering the ocean floor decomposes, producing such enormous quantities of bad-smelling hydrogen sulfide that ships' hulls and seaside homes are soon blackened. This ghastly attendant of death is called *el pintor,* the painter.

That is not all. Air blowing across the unusually warm waters heads toward the arid coast and then unleashes torrents of rain. Crops can be washed away; irrigation systems destroyed. Villages disappear beneath the flow of water, mud, and debris; and people and livestock are buried beneath mudslides.

Yet some scholars believe that El Niño also atones for its devastation. In a phenomenon dubbed the "El Niño florescence," these same disruptive rains cause the arid desert to bloom and warm-water fish to replace the cold-water anchovies. Such unexpected bounty could have provided the population with temporary sustenance and even prosperity in the unreliable Peruvian environment.

El Niño returned in force in 1982–83 and was widely reported by the world's press and broadcasters. It brought with it floods, mudslides, and critical disruptions of the fish supply. Man is still in thrall to this powerful, seemingly whimsical, phenomenon.

There is one advance, however. Through a cooperative worldwide effort of metereologists and other scientists, it is slowly becoming possible to predict the emergence of El Niño and thus be alerted to its long-range consequences. The operative factors begin to make themselves known in Indonesia, thousands of miles and about several months away from the eventual disaster in South America. Even so, the extent of the damage is unpredictable. Sometimes El Niño is little more than an inconvenience; on rare occasions, it can bury a civilization, bringing back the bare desert stillness that Herman Melville described as "emphatic uninhabitablenèss" when he stopped in Peru.

The weather factor, therefore, remains only one among the many imperfectly known, but perhaps decisive elements in our efforts to illuminate the shadowy mysteries of the Peruvian past.

How many cultures are lost to us, their principal artifacts and records covered over by the cruel vagaries of Andean weather? How often have we made the wrong assumptions about an important development, a migration, or a religious movement, because we cannot know that the natural world turned topsy-turvy for a people who were overpowered by forces beyond their science and comprehension?

Weighing the slender evidence now available, we may be wildly misreading such little-known cultures as the obviously complex society that looked to Chavín de Huantar as its fountainhead of art and ideas. We see a portion of its beauty; we can begin to admire its achievements. But we may be a long way from coming to recognize what actually motivated a people who knew the sea that nourished them could also bring disaster that would destroy civilization as they knew it.

unimportant. Why be distressed about the condition of earthly remains if the spirit has ascended to the sky in the company of the ruling deities? It would follow, then, that the characteristic Andean preoccupation with mummification and other burial rituals would become meaningful after the failure or exhaustion of the cult. Chronologically, at least, that is how events stand.

Yet another characteristic feature of later Andean culture has not been apparent in explorations of Chavín sites — the deification of the living ruler. At its most extreme, this tendency was to make the 16th-century Inca ruler so fearsome to his subjects that only those of highest rank could look at him directly; from others, he was hidden by a screen. All of the emperor's clothing

A hollow pottery figure in the shape of a flute player belongs to a late period when Chavín's art was more naturalistic. The head and paws of a jaguar pelt serve as the musician's headdress.

Stirrup spout jars, like this one from northern Peru, are often discovered in burial sites. The well-defined jaguar head and the round pelt markings testify to its religious significance.

and leftover food was stored away and then ritually burned once a year so that no one could harbor ambitions to own what had once been his.

Nothing discovered so far would suggest that any temporal ruler of the Chavín era was considered divine. Deity, it seems clear, lay in the spirits of the universe alone. They could manifest themselves in human form, perhaps, and the ruler-priest might have the gift of making contact with them. But there was no worship of men by their fellows during the ascendancy of the cult. It was only after the Chavín religion had faded away, the evidence seems to indicate, that Andean societies began to revere a ruler and his family as descendants of the gods. We know that in the case of at least one later culture, the Chimú, members of the nobility considered themselves a race apart, literally descended from gods who had visited earth. Even more astonishing, they seem to have been successful in convincing their subjects of this belief.

Despite all we do not know about daily life in Chavín times, about the fears and hopes of its people, we do know that it was an era of stability. Did the predominant cult offer a cosmology that answered the crucial questions men have pondered throughout history? Was life unusually easy in those times?

Peace in a Bountiful Land

Archeologists believe that the period may have seen a major transition from isolated village life to the semblance of a cultural web. In other words, small and secure towns, though growing, were not yet a threat to one another; there may have been no need to compete for resources. These early communities might slowly have learned the benefits of peaceful trade with their neighbors, without leaping to the more "advanced" notion of acquisition by military conquest.

It seems likely that food was plentiful everywhere, not just in a cultural center like Chavín de Huantar. Along the coast, sea life was usually abundant, and irrigation of the coastal valleys made possible the harvesting of two and sometimes three crops of native vegetables annually. In the highlands, as in the area around Chavín de Huantar itself, rougher conditions allowed only one growing season, but many different staples could be grown. For variety in the diet, there was wild game or the meat of such domesticated animals as the guinea pig, still an Andean delicacy.

The Chavín period, then, may have been an unusually peaceful, complacent one. It may have been a remarkably tolerant era as well, open to such intriguing new concepts as the Chavinoid cult. It may also have been a time when the generally frequent natural disasters of Peru did not occur. Chavinoid beliefs may not have been put to a severe test, as a way of explaining or dealing with the catastrophes that so often disrupt Andean society. But when the test finally came, perhaps in the form of some especially horrendous natural disaster, the religion might have lost its hold.

A fragment of woven wool, perhaps as much as 25 centuries old, was found in Paracas in southern Peru. The characteristic feline portrait suggests that Chavín's influence may have been carried south by missionaries proselytizing its faith.

That is one possible explanation for the mysterious collapse of Chavín de Huantar about 200 B.C.

We do not have a precise date for the loss by Chavín de Huantar of its religious primacy or know how, much less why, this happened. If the religious beliefs were somehow discredited or found wanting, perhaps the people stopped coming to the holy sites. Gradually, without attentive repair or maintenance, the monumental structures would have begun to decay. Perhaps instead, an earthquake or flash flood struck the Mosna Valley, undermining the principal buildings so badly that repair seemed foolhardy. It would not be unprecedented for believers to read such a disaster as an omen and resort to other centers for worship.

What seems unarguable is that a "sack" did not occur, either at the hands of disenchanted believers or conquering strangers. Temple walls were not defaced, religious images were not smashed, the land was not scorched bare. Local villagers moved into the religious center but allowed its temples to fall into ruin. Chavín de Huantar lost its cultural eminence, but it did not become a ghost town. The practical, hard-working Peruvians continued to farm the nearby fields and herd their llamas on the high ground.

Although it still remained a pilgrimage center for people of the Andes during the next 700 years, Chavín de Huantar fell under the dominion of a succession of other cultures. All these people disappeared from history almost as silently as they arrived — their departures showed no signs of major violence.

Coincidentally, perhaps, the Olmec disappeared, just as unaccountably, at about the same time as the Chavín collapse.

There would never again be a vibrant cultural center in the valley of the Mosna River. The Chavín gods and their transcendent appeal gave way to more literal, often bloodier, religious beliefs and practices.

But the wild-eyed images of the half-human, half-feline deities would not be completely forgotten. Widely dispersed in both time and place, the occasional ceramic image, the discarded bit of pottery nostalgically recalls the once-supreme ideology of Chavín. In a poor man's grave in the desert coastal regions, in the atypical frieze of a public building high in the Bolivian Andes, there is proof again and again that the mystical message of the Chavín cult was not entirely lost. It would echo down through Peruvian history, surviving today only as a faint recollection of an ancient mystery.

What is there in the Andean soul that responded so profoundly to the fantastic, serpentine carvings of Chavín de Huantar? Hundreds of lost villages and towns lie forgotten still beneath the ever-shifting soil of the Peruvian landscape. We may someday learn that the answer has been preserved in one of them, waiting for the archeologist's spade to resurrect the meaning of these age-old gods.

THE OLMEC ENIGMA

In the 1920's archeologists began to refer to a previously unknown Mexican civilization as Olmec, a term derived from the Aztec meaning "dweller in the land of rubber." We will never know the real name of these innovative people.

The best way to experience the brilliance of the ancient Olmec civilization — which began to unfold around 1200 B.C. along the Gulf Coast of southern Mexico and which some 900 years later came to an inexplicable end — is to study the remarkable art these dynamic people left behind them. Indeed, Olmec art furnished the earliest intimations that a forgotten civilization lay buried in southern Mexico.

Since it first came to light in the middle of the 19th century, Olmec art has exerted an unusual fascination over those who have studied it. "I have been struck," observed Matthew W. Stirling, the pioneer Olmec archeologist, "by the number of individuals who after becoming involved with a single fine specimen of Olmec art, spent the rest of their careers as Olmec enthusiasts." What was true of others, was also true of Stirling. In 1918, while still a student in California, he came across a photograph of a jade mask that so intrigued him that two years later he made a trip to Germany to see the original. "The bait that hooked me into a career of Olmec research," explained Stirling, "was a small blue jade mask in the Berlin Museum."

Beginning in 1938 and for the rest of his life, Stirling explored and interpreted the ancient civilization of the Olmec. His achievements in opening the door to the splendors of the Olmec world are comparable to the contributions made by Heinrich Schliemann in discovering Troy and by Arthur Evans in reconstructing ancient Knossos.

Unlike other great pre-Columbian cultures, the Olmec was unknown to the conquistadors. When Stirling began his researches, there was even great doubt whether an Olmec civilization had ever existed. It was the Maya who were looked upon as the great civilizers in Mesoamerica. Yet the masks, statuettes, and figurines of jade and serpentine relinquished by the jungles in Veracruz and Tabasco in southern Mexico, which gradually found their way into the hands of art collectors and museum curators, gave rise to numerous theories and speculations. Olmec art did not fit into any culture then known. Had there been another civilization in Mesoamerica? A vanished people? "Some of the most mysterious and exciting sculptures of Middle America," wrote the Mexican artist Miguel Covarru-

The figure in serpentine at right, bearing traces of cinnabar, may be a real-life portrait of an Olmec ruler. Two faint lines on his right cheek, now barely visible even under close scrutiny, give him the name "The Lord of the Double Scroll."

bias, "certainly belonging among the masterpieces of world art, lie scattered in the jungle and swamps of the southern Gulf Coast. . . .its aesthetic ideology is in the spirit of the early cultures: simplicity and sensual realism of form, vigorous and original conceptions."

Perhaps the most intriguing and exotic of all the objects that led at last to the discovery of the Olmec were the huge stone heads unearthed in the states of Veracruz and Tabasco. In 1862 a farmer in Veracruz stumbled on the first of the gigantic heads, which he mistook at first for an overturned kettle because of its smooth surface. Disappointed that it was not a treasure trove, he explored no further. Some years later the head came to the attention of a Mexican archeologist, José Melgar y Serrano, who in 1869 reported on it in a scientific journal. As the first published account of any Olmec find from that area of Mexico, this was a landmark step, although the conclusions Melgar drew were questionable. "As a work of art," he wrote, "it is without exaggeration a magnificent sculpture . . . but what astonished me was the Ethiopic type represented. I reflect that there had undoubtedly been Negroes in this country. . . ." Melgar's report stirred little interest at the time. However, the discovery of a second, similar head several decades later began to focus archeological attention on this neglected area of Mexico.

In 1925 Frans Blom, a Danish-born scientist, and Oliver La Farge, an American writer, set out on an exploration of Mexico, which took them to La Venta in Tabasco. There, at a vast, overgrown ceremonial center, they came upon "the most amazing monument of them all — a huge bell-shaped boulder. At first it puzzled us very much, but after a little digging, to our amazement, we saw that what we had in front of us was the upper part of a *colossal head*."

Tracing Olmec Roots

In 1938 Matthew Stirling embarked on his first exploration of southern Mexico, which was then still, archeologically, relatively uncharted country; a hinterland, he called it. It was a land laced by meandering, sluggish rivers — the most important one, the Coatzacoalcos with its many tributaries — and lagoons bordered by mangrove forests. Small settlements of Indian farmers were scattered here and there, usually connected by water transportation. The air was hot and humid, and the annual rainfall sometimes reached 100 inches. With the exception of the Tuxtla Mountains, averaging only 1,600 feet in altitude, this was a lowland, coastal landscape, whose river levees were flooded each year to a depth of 21 feet. That the first great pre-Columbian society should have arisen in this seemingly inhospitable environment is perplexing. But as the anthropologist and Olmec scholar Michael Coe pointed out in 1981, Olmec civilization, like that of Egypt, is "the gift of the river." Both the Nile and the many rivers of southern Mexico leave behind a deep, rich soil after each year's flooding, conferring an invaluable asset on

an agricultural people. Here was land that did not have to be cleared before planting and then left to lie fallow after two seasons' use. What had appeared at first glance to be an environment hostile to settlement and the growth of a stable society was shown, on examination, to be as if ordained by nature to become a cradle of civilization.

Gradually, beginning in the 1940's, the legacy of the Olmec civilization and its achievements have emerged. Within a 6,000 - to 7,000 - square-mile area — smaller than the state of Vermont — there are at least four major ceremonial centers that have been excavated; uncounted smaller ones and hundreds of earthen mounds have yet to be explored. Archeologically, the Olmec Heartland — as this area has come to be called — is still barely touched. The four major sites that have been explored are San Lorenzo, the earliest center with dates ranging from 1200 to around 900 B.C.; Laguna de los Cerros and La Venta, which both date from around 1000 to 600 B.C.; and Tres Zapotes, a transitional site with imprecise dating. Tres Zapotes bridges the time between the end of the Olmec civilization, around 300 B.C., and the Veracruz culture, which followed.

In the early 1940's, when Matthew Stirling first published the results of his excavations at Tres Zapotes and at La Venta — where he had found works of art ranging from huge stone monuments to fragile clay images — he called forth one of the most savagely unforgiving debates in all archeological history. "The mysterious producers of this class of art," reported Stirling, "have been called the 'Olmecs', a people whose origin is as yet very little known. Present archeological evidence indicates that their culture, which in many respects reached a high level, is very early and may well be the basic civilization out of which developed such high art centers as those of the Maya. . . ." On one side the Mayanists were convinced that all Mesoamerican civilizations originated with the Maya. They attacked Stirling's theory and denied the very existence of the ancient Olmec or would at most concede that they were a minor, late, and decadent branch of the Maya. Arguing against them were Mexican archeologists such as Alfonso Caso, who had reconstructed the ruins of Monte Albán, and Miguel Covarrubias, joined by a small band of Amerian scholars. The fact that some pieces had been found — a stele (known as Stele C) in Tres Zapotes and a small jade statuette in the shape of a duck — with hieroglyphic writing and a date that preceded Maya civilization was dismissed by the Mayanists. The dates and glyphs might have been carved later, ran the argument. Not until the mid-1950's when radiocarbon dating of La Venta artifacts provided irrefutable proof of Olmec antiquity and importance was the existence of their civilization widely accepted. Recognition as the mother culture of Mesoamerica came late to the Olmec.

Of all the Olmec ceremonial centers, none exceeds La Venta in impressiveness; it has been called "the glo-

Exploring the site of Tres Zapotes in 1939, Matthew Stirling, above, uncovered an Olmec colossal head. It measures 6 feet high and 18 feet around and weighs over 10 tons. The following year, at La Venta, Stirling discovered four more helmeted heads. The Olmec wore close-fitting headgear probably as protection against their enemies' war clubs.

ry of the ancient Olmec." It stands on an isolated, sandy island, two miles square, which rises some 40 feet above the surrounding swampland and the tidal Tonalá River. The ceremonial precincts lie roughly in the center of the island and are made up of a sunken plaza and pyramids, including one whose shape is unique in all the New World. Rising some 103 feet above the rectangular site, it dominates the other structures and may have originally looked like a fluted volcanic cone. It was artificially built of 3.5 million cubic feet of clay. Some scholars have suggested that the people of La Venta sprang from the volcanic Tuxtla Mountains and that this pyramid commemorates their ancestral origins. Whatever the inspiration may have been, the pyramid exemplifies the sheer monumentality of Olmec construction and the unlimited man-hours of back-breaking labor that went into it.

What is true of their building is equally true of their sculpture. The large pieces are characterized by an imposing massiveness. At La Venta, Stirling found four colossal heads, each weighing as much as 20 tons, and a giant stele that weighed 50 tons and stood 14 feet tall. Seven altars, one of which measured 11½ feet in length and more than 5 feet in height, were also unearthed; rectangular in shape and carved with figures and scenes, these stupendous blocks of stone look like altars but may actually have been thrones for Olmec rulers.

Since no stone suitable for carving exists in the swamplands around La Venta, it had to be transported from the Tuxtla Mountains, which lie 56 miles west of the site. How did the Olmec with the primitive technology of the Stone Age move the huge blocks and boulders of basalt, the igneous dark-gray to black stone that was used in the sculpture? Or were the stones carved in their place of origin in the mountains? As yet no workshop debris has been found at the mountain sites. No matter whether the carving was done at La Venta — or at San Lorenzo or Tres Zapotes — or in the mountains, the stone still had to be moved. It was an amazing undertaking. "The logistics of transporting these stones," writes Michael Coe "comprise one of the greatest puzzles of New World archeology, and there have been many attempts to solve the problem." At San Lorenzo, for instance, it took 50 workers to lift a head upright using poles and ropes, "small efforts compared to the magnitude of the tasks faced by the Olmec. We imagine that many hundred, perhaps up to a thousand, Olmec laborers were harnessed to this gigantic moving operation."

Scholars have surmised that the boulders and slabs were rolled on logs or dragged on wooden sleds to the nearest river, a tributary of the Coatzacoalcos, a distance of some 25 miles from the source of the basalt. At the river's edge, the workers hoisted the stones onto a wooden raft and floated them down to the mouth of the river. If the stone was destined for La Venta, it had to travel along the Gulf shore to the mouth of the Tonalá and lastly upriver some 12 miles to the site.

Neither brute strength nor limitless patience alone could make such prodigious tasks possible. They also called for a well-run social machine, an obedient work force, and a strong guiding hand from the seat of power. Anthropologists agree that Olmec society was, in fact, authoritarian and highly stratified. It seems likely that the major centers were governed by dynasties with absolute power to enforce obedience and discipline. Like the Maya who followed them, the society below the rulers was divided into administrators, engineers, foremen, and straw bosses — with a large, subservient peasantry at the base. The gifted sculptors and artists to whom we owe our awareness of this brilliant civilization probably constituted a social entity unto themselves. Philip Drucker, one of the excavators of La Venta, has theorized that as such a society grows larger "the social structure becomes more rigid, especially in the area of class distinction. Ceremonialism becomes more complex and spectacular, drawing vast crowds of offering-laden pilgrims."

How did such a society develop from the simple, egalitarian life of a small farming village? The probable explanation lies in the bounty of the soil in the Olmec Heartland. Gradually these rich lands along a river bank came into the possession of one family and their kin, giving them a margin of wealth denied to other villagers. With wealth came power that over generations could elevate one family to a position of overall authority. This social transformation, which began between 1300 and 1200 B.C., before Olmec civilization came into being, led finally to the establishment of authoritarian rule.

Three thousand years after the Olmec lived, their colossal heads give us some idea of what these ancient rulers looked like. Among scholars, it is now almost universally accepted that the colossal heads — so far there are 13 in all from three different sites — are portraits of actual rulers. But there are a few who still treasure theories that the colossal heads represent alien invaders, whether Africans, as Melgar believed, or Polynesians blown ashore on Mexico's west coast.

At first glance all the heads resemble one another, but on closer examination differences emerge; some faces are rounder than others, some are jowlier, some noses are narrower, and the outlines of mouths vary. Every head wears a close-fitting helmet with an insignia or adornment on the front. No two are alike, and they may represent dynastic glyphs, the equivalent of a

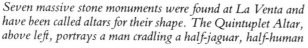

Seven massive stone monuments were found at La Venta and have been called altars for their shape. The Quintuplet Altar, above left, portrays a man cradling a half-jaguar, half-human child, a theme that is repeated four more times in bas-relief (above, right) on the sides of the altar. Whether these scenes have a religious or a dynastic meaning remains a mystery.

royal coat of arms. Even today, the heads exert a sense of authority, power, and brute force.

It would be a mistake to interpret Olmec civilization as based solely on physical strength. Evidence has come down over the centuries that suggests surprising technical skills.

For example, it is possible that the Olmec at San Lorenzo were using a magnetic lodestone compass before 1000 B.C. — 1,000 years before the Chinese are credited with discovering it. In 1967 Coe found a magnet at San Lorenzo carved in the form of a grooved oblong bar. To test his supposition that it might be part of a compass, he cut a piece from a cork mat and floated it in water with the compass on top. The bar consistently aligned itself slightly west of magnetic north. When the bar was turned over, the alignment was slightly east of magnetic north. Other, more sophisticated experiments conducted six years later indicated that the Olmec probably manufactured and used a simple compass.

The Olmec were also especially skillful in working iron ores. Their most startling achievements were highly polished, concave iron mirrors, which, Olmec sculpture tells us, were worn as pendants, probably by the elite, to symbolize their power and authority. Remains of the mirrors have been found at La Venta and at San Lorenzo, but the technology used to achieve the high polish and the perfection of the curvature still amazes scientists. Studies under a microscope reveal no traces that abrasives were used, and yet, as one scholar put it: "Their polish is so extraordinary that it reaches the limit of possible perfection."

Among their other talents, the Olmec were master engineers. Excavations at La Venta and San Lorenzo have turned up a complex drainage system, whose exact purpose is still unknown. At San Lorenzo, excavators have found a main drainage line measuring 558 feet, with subsidiary lines of 98 feet. The drains are made of 30 tons of basalt, all brought from the Tuxtla Mountains more than 35 miles distant. Each block of stone was hollowed out and fitted with a stone cover. The whole main line runs at a gentle 2 percent grade from east to west. The man-made ponds that dot San Lorenzo were possibly connected to this system. Were these pools sacred and therefore worthy of such elaborate drainage? Could they have been part of a holy ritual for pilgrims?

Many of the rites and rituals of the Olmec are lost in the past, but recent research has disclosed that the pantheon of their gods was much more complex than was

Known as the "Little Grandmother," a bucktoothed kneeling stone figure from La Venta, above, holds a rectangular vessel. The monkey at left, also from La Venta, was uncovered in 1956 but without a face, which has since been fancifully reconstructed.

135

A strong, expressive realism pervades Olmec art. The sculptor of the famous basalt statue, The Wrestler, at left has translated his grasp of the structure of the male body into kinetic form. The acrobat or dancer, above, his body reddened with cinnabar, moves with convincing vitality. And the naked baby of hollow ceramic at top left — a favorite Olmec theme — is portrayed in a pose characteristic of infancy.

once thought. Olmec religion had at first seemed obvious to the archeologists; wherever they looked they saw evidence that a cult of the jaguar pervaded the Olmec world. His image appeared on stone altars and steles; it was carved in jade and serpentine and painted on the rocky walls of caves. Half-man, half-beast, he was pictured with a snarling mouth, an upturned nose, flame-shaped eyebrows, and at times a receding lower jaw. At least two carvings, and perhaps three, which appear to depict a jaguar in sexual intercourse with a woman, have been interpreted by some archeologists as portraying an Olmec origin myth. However, the latest research, undertaken by David Joralemon, shows that the Olmec worshiped 10 major gods — a jaguar god among them — all of whom appeared later in different guises throughout Mesoamerica. One of these gods, who played a large role in the Aztec pantheon, was the rain god, frequently represented as an infant by the Olmec. "The association of a human infant with rain," Michael Coe writes, "recalls the annual sacrifice of little children to the god Tlaloc among the Aztec . . . the more they cried, the more auspicious the sacrifice . . . the tears of the hapless children called down the tears of the heavenly cumulus clouds."

Human sacrifice may have been practiced by the Olmec as part of religious ritual. Two pieces of monumental stone sculpture support this possibility. At the top of one, there is a hole about eight inches in diameter and five inches deep that was unquestionably a receptacle for liquid. Matthew Stirling, who found a similar cavity on top of a monument at Tres Zapotes, described it as "a sacrificial stone, as it would be of the correct dimensions for this purpose, and the basinlike bowl at the top would serve for collecting blood." Further evidence of sacrifice are cannibalized human bones found among the debris at San Lorenzo; they are mainly adult bones, presumably, those of captives.

Prodigious offerings to the gods, not of human flesh and blood but of stone, have also been unearthed at La Venta. In a courtyard north of the fluted pyramid and enclosed by basalt columns each more than 6 feet high, the Olmec laid huge mosaic pavements, which measured 14½ by 19½ feet. The work for these ritual offerings was begun by digging deep pits along La Venta's central line, which forms the north-south axis of the island (with a deviation of eight degrees west of true north). Meticulously laid out in the shape of a jaguar mask, each pavement consisted of some 485 blocks of green serpentine set in colored clays. These vivid offerings were then covered over with more clay, to remain hidden until Stirling brought them to light some 25 centuries later. What was their purpose? There is as yet — and likely never will be — an answer, but as Michael Coe has observed, the Olmec "obviously believed in the principle of conspicuous waste when it came to expending labor and materials."

Another, even more intriguing offering found at La Venta, in 1955, was a scene that is so alive that it could be from real life (see pages 106–107). Figures of jade and serpentine, measuring from 6 to 10 inches high, stand grouped around a leader to whom they appear to be listening attentively. They are dressed in loincloths, and their heads, deformed by binding at birth, are close shaven — probably with an obsidian razor. For their shape and their smoothness, Mexican archeologists call these heads — which also appear among Olmec ceramics — *cabezas de aguacate,* "avocado heads." Another curious fact about this offering was the evidence that at some later date a shaft had been dug down through the layers of colored clay to inspect the offering. Why? To make sure it had not been stolen? Everything about this unique Mesoamerican treasure baffles the experts. "We can only wonder," say the archeologists who found it.

The ancient Olmec made great use of colored clay and colored sand in building their ceremonial centers. "A visit to La Venta in its heyday must have been a truly psychedelic experience," comments archeologist Richard Diehl. Clays of red, pink, purple, blue, and yellow, and sands of white, orange, or brown were used in geometric patterns to achieve a vivid effect. The colors, which were natural, were kept carefully separated in their use, and the result must have resembled a modern geometric painting, although nothing remains today on the surface of the ground to recall this colorful exuberance of the past.

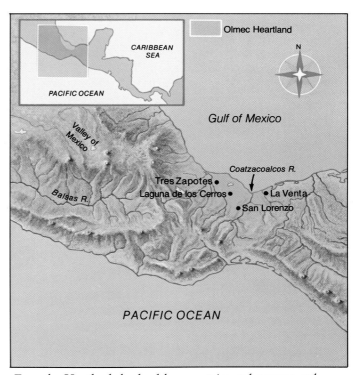

From the Heartland, bordered by mountains and swamps and crossed by rivers, the Olmec traveled far and wide in quest of jade; in so doing they left a cultural imprint on Mesoamerica.

Much has been made of the grotesque in Olmec art. Olmec sculptors were attracted to pathological human figures as subject matter. It is as though the artists felt an obsessive fascination with deformities. Dwarfs, hunchbacks, sufferers from Down's Syndrome, and the overweight were all depicted with great artistry and care in stone and clay. Did the Olmec look with wonder at a fellow human being born with a deformity? In their eyes it was a manifestation of the will of the gods and conferred a magic and sacredness upon the ill-formed and misshapen. And the families of even those Olmec born without deformities deliberately reshaped their new-born babies' heads by tying a board in an oblique position against the forehead. This custom, also practiced by the Maya, may have been a mark of the elite to set them apart from the peasantry; and examples of it are pervasive in Olmec art.

Above all else, these ancient people prized jade. From jade, ranging from a beautiful translucent bluish color to blue-grays and dark greens, Olmec artists carved thousands upon thousands of exquisite figures and ornaments, most of them offerings to the gods. "The Olmec," writes the Mexican archeologist Ignacio Bernal, "were not only the first and the finest sculptors of Mexico; they were also the first to work jade and indubitably were the greatest. . . ." Of the several different minerals known by the generic name jade, jadeite is the most valuable, but the Olmec also cherished other translucent stones such as quartz and amethyst. Carving the delicate figurines with the tools available must have been a long and tedious process. First, the natural block was examined and scraped to assess its quality. In order to shape the stone, unwanted parts had to be removed by tapping and sawing, using thin slabs of stone or clay fragments as tools. The main contours of a figure were then delineated by means of bores. As a last step, the artist rubbed and polished his creation to achieve the deep brilliance that has made Olmec jades such highly esteemed works of art.

The number of jade pieces produced by La Venta artists is staggering. In 1941 Matthew Stirling came upon a cache of jade offerings that required "a half hour to take out . . . 782 specimens in all!" And another cache offering at a small site on the Rio Pesquero, a tributary of the Tonalá, yielded up dozens of life-size jade masks and thousands of ceremonial axes of jade and serpentine — many of them since vanished. Why did the Olmec bury such large quantities of their highly valued jade? Their donations may have carried with them the same kind of social prestige that a rich man today garners by donating a new museum wing. Or again, the worth of jade may have been increased by taking it out of circulation.

The acquisition of jade carried the Olmec far beyond the boundaries of their country, for nowhere within the confines of the Olmec Heartland was any jade to be found. The demand for jade — and also for other hard stones — drove the Olmec into the southwest of Mex-

ico and perhaps as far to the south as modern-day El Salvador, nearly 500 air miles from the Heartland. Olmec trade routes snaked across Mesoamerica, following along river beds and cutting through mountain passes. Michael Coe has named this far-flung network the Jade Route. Along it, in the volcanic Mexican highlands and following the Pacific coast, the imprint of Olmec civilization is still visible. In rock carvings and in cave paintings, at burial sites and on sculpted monuments, the intervening millennia have not obliterated traces of the Olmec presence.

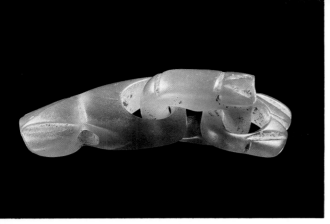

The highly polished jade figure at far left may have been deliberately damaged during a ritual mutilation rite of the Olmec. The articulated crustacean at top left, only two inches long, was carved from a single piece of jade, testimony to the skill of its creator. The part-jaguar, part-man jade figure at bottom left represents the rain god. It came to light in 1909 during the building of a dam, and was one of the earliest clues that led to the discovery of the Olmec civilization.

ly red, with touches of ocher and a bluish-green, the painter depicted a human figure dressed in a bird costume and seated upon a throne decorated with the head of a dragon. An owl, a standing man with a jaguar, and a serpent monster with protruding tongue are all elements of these paintings, whose meaning has yet to be definitively interpreted.

Not far from the paintings of the Oxtotitlan Cave are others buried more than three-quarters of a mile inside a cave near Juxtlahuaca. These were not identified stylistically as Olmec paintings until 1966. Once again, they portray a person of importance clothed in red and a serpent with green feathers. Was this an Olmec shrine? "If one could only conjure up the scene of its dedication — a great procession of Olmec royalty," writes Coe, "lit by the flare of pine torches, and probably accompanied by chanting and drumming."

Wherever the Olmec went in Mesoamerica they brought their civilizing influence with them. In the highlands of the Valley of Mexico they transformed a village world, which produced simple pottery, into a society characterized by sophisticated craftsmanship and imaginative variety and the production of exuberant clay effigy sculpture: hourglass vases and pots in the form of shells, fish, birds, armadillos, and strange, half-beast, half-man creatures. Clay figurines, similar to those found at San Lorenzo, show women with tiny waists and wide hips; those of men have painted faces and bodies, headdresses, and jewelry.

The magnificent art of the Olmec, by which today we can trace their march across Mexico, is only the visible sign of the civilization's role in the history of Mesoamerica. What else they bequeathed to the Indian cultures that followed is often intangible but no less real. Both the Olmec and the Classic Maya 1,000 years later enshrined and portrayed their rulers as specific individuals of power and authority. The religious symbolism of the Olmec was passed on not only to the Maya but to other, later cultures such as Teotihuacán and Aztec. The macabre rite of bloodletting, in which the worshipers pierced themselves in homage to the gods, was practiced by the Olmec and the Maya alike. Sharp instruments of jade and stingray spines have turned up in both regions.

It seems probable that a game much like soccer was invented by the Olmec of San Lorenzo; the remains of an earthen ball court and clay figurines of ball players have been found there. There is even evidence of what

Among the most striking works are the rock paintings at Oxtotitlan near Chilpancingo, which lies a few hours' drive to the southeast of Mexico City and almost 200 miles due west of the Olmec Heartland. There, at the mouth of two grottoes and weathered by centuries of exposure, Olmec paintings dated from 900 to 700 B.C. are still still discernible. One, measuring 12½ feet wide and a little over 8 feet high, can be seen more than 10 feet above the bottom of the cliff. How the artist reached that height is one of the puzzling questions about the rock painting. Using predominant-

must surely be the original American football; fragments of a possible large rubber ball were dug up in 1967, and when a flame was held to them they gave off the acrid smell of burning rubber.

The roots of the calendar and of Maya hieroglyphic writing can also be traced back to the Olmec. In a rudimentary form, they used abstract identifying symbols; a U sign, perhaps signifying the moon, and the *kin* symbol for the sun are common to the Olmec and the Maya. All these first steps were carried further by Olmec-influenced cultures on the Pacific Coast and transmitted by them to the Classic Maya. Some experts believe that a bar and dot numbering system was already in use by the Olmec as early as 400 B.C. While this use cannot be confirmed, it is true that Stele C — from Tres Zapotes — bears the Long Count date 32 B.C., which comes close on the heels of the last remnants of Olmec influence.

Around 900 B.C. the Olmec civilization at San Lorenzo came to an abrupt end. In contrast, La Venta, which continued to carry the culture forward for some 300 years, slowly ceased to be a center of power and influence. Coe described La Venta's decline: "All construction comes to a halt, no more tombs are built and stocked, no more offerings are made beneath its multicolored floors. Its rulers and people are gone."

But there was more. In death as in life the Olmec did things on a grand scale. Their demise at San Lorenzo was characterized by violence and destruction — bizarre acts that appear to have come from overwhelming hatred and rage. Monuments were battered and broken into fragments. The heads of anthropomorphic statues were knocked off. Bas-relief stones were shattered, some weighing as much as 50 tons. Altars, equally massive, were cracked. And the multi-ton colossal heads — too gigantic actually to break — were pitted and grooved. Then everything was buried, often face down. The physical labor and engineering skill that went into this mass destruction and mutilation must have been staggering.

When archeologists first tried to explain such wholesale destruction, they interpreted it as the work of outsiders, conquerors who destroyed Olmec monuments. But, in the late 1960's during Coe's excavations at San

The Fine Art of Faking

No one has yet had the temerity to counterfeit a colossal Olmec head, but when it comes to smaller pieces of Olmec art — and to almost every other work of pre-Columbian artisans from Peruvian gold objects to the pottery of the Southwest United States — fakers have outdone themselves. Their occupation is by no means a recent one. It began almost as soon as the first European landed in the Americas. Early forgers supplied Spanish conquistadors with Aztec crystal skulls to take home as mementoes. Since then, the profitable enterprise of faking has foisted many a spurious clay vessel or bogus stone sculpture on private collectors and museums. And for the past 30 years, the counterfeiting of pre-Columbian art has flourished as never before. For one thing, the supply of this art — as with all ancient art — is finite. For another, laws about its export from countries of origin are being enforced more stringently. Concurrently, pre-Columbian art has become fashionable and its market value has increased dramatically. All these conditions are ideal for the propogation of frauds.

There are master forgers, who produce adept and skillful copies, and there are others — mere shoemakers — who slap together a piece that is only intended to fool the passing tourist. Master forgers go to great lengths to endow their work with the aura of authenticity. For clay objects, they grind ancient sherds to temper their modern paste; for wood fakes, they obtain lintels from a Maya site; and for an Olmec jade figure, they have been known to acquire genuine but unadorned ceremonial axes and then to carve them. Finding the right quality of jade to imitate the unmottled, translucent jade favored by the ancient Olmec has proved so difficult that determined fakers have traveled to China to find it.

Today a really first-class forger educates himself in the iconography and style of the period he copies. Many work with an open art book before them. The increasing number of excellent art books, often portraying an object from all sides, makes the forger's work easier. No longer is it possible to identify a fake by the faulty treatment of the sides and back.

Detecting quality fakes of pre-Columbian art is no simple undertaking. It is made even more difficult by the looting of grave and other sites, which still goes on throughout the Americas. As a result, a great deal of art arrives at the market place with no verifiable history. As counterfeiting has increased, more and more specialists have learned to winnow the true from the false. Technologies, like radiocarbon dating and thermoluminescence, are of limited help if the forger has used ancient materials. Blatant mistakes of iconography have grown rarer and many sophisticated fakers now emulate the ancients and use hand tools. Machine-made marks are a dead give-away as is evidence of the use of sandblasting or acid to create a 2,000-year-old patina. Yet in the end, the exposure of a superior forgery is not only a matter of knowledge gained by intense study but also of intuition. One specialist who has spent as many as 80 hours examining a genuine object with a microscope and also handling it, says that when a fake comes into his hands, it feels wrong. The exposure of a fake, then, is often a matter of such total absorption in pre-Columbian art that the expert acquires a fingertip virtuosity and a sense of the correct style, and the aura of authenticity so sought after by a forger vanishes under his scrutiny.

Lorenzo, he uncovered unusual evidence. He found that the basalt monuments had first been mutilated "and then laid out in long lines on ridges around the peripheries of the site. . . ." At La Venta, too, it was discovered that the mutilated sculptures had been buried in a pattern of clusters. Why would an invading force go to such trouble? These discoveries opened up the possibility that the Olmec themselves were responsible for the destruction.

In the early 1980's the idea that there was a symbolic meaning to the mutilation of Olmec monuments was put forward. Drawing a parallel between Olmec religious beliefs and those of today's Canelos Quichua Indians, who live in the tropical forests of South America, the archeologist David C. Grove has speculated that the destruction of monuments was carried out by the Olmec themselves at the death of a ruler. The Canelos Quichua, Grove points out, believe that a supernatural power, derived from the underworld, resides in the possessions of a chief or a priest: his wooden stool, his ax, the hut in which he lives. While a man is alive, he is in command of this dangerous power, but once he dies, there is no one to control it. To guard their society against this threat, the Canelos Quichua destroy and bury the dead man's possessions. Did the Olmec subscribe to the same belief 2,000 years ago? The analogy, Grove believes, is not farfetched. It would also explain the curious fact that the greatest destruction was visited upon the altars. If an altar was indeed a throne — and thus the seat of power of a ruler — it would have been the chief repository of his supernatural underworld power and the most frightening of his possessions. By destroying and burying thrones, supernatural forces were successfully quelled and controlled.

Yet another theory, which has recently been espoused, turns to the early Maya for its corroboration. At Cerros in Belize, a center dated from 350 B.C. to the 1st century A.D., excavators found traces of the defacement of monuments. The evidence shows that bonfires were lit at the base of pyramids, that pottery was deliberately hurled at walls and destroyed, and that steles were broken and buried. Archeologists call these outbreaks "termination rituals" and believe that they occurred at the death of a ruler or with the rise of a new, charismatic leader, who urged his people to erase their past. Could this have been the case at San Lorenzo? Although there is evidence at La Venta that these rites were followed there too, it is at San Lorenzo that the intensity of the destruction takes on an apocalyptic character. Like so much else about the ancient Olmec, the true explanation of the destruction may lie forever beyond the horizon of our knowledge.

By the time the Spaniards arrived in Mexico in 1519, almost two millennia had gone by since the closing centuries of Olmec civilization. Yet, succeeding generations of Mesoamerican Indians had, perhaps, not forgotten "the ancient ones." An Indian legend, recorded by the Spanish priest Bernardino de Sahagún, tells of a

Although a feeling of massiveness emanates from this mask from the Templo Mayor, it is only 4 inches high and 3½ inches wide. Two holes indicate that it was a pendant.

people of the distant past who lived in a land called Tamoanchán, which has been placed just south of Veracruz. There "they devised . . . the count of the years, the book of dreams." From these people, the legend runs, sprang the civilization of Teotihuacán in the Valley of Mexico with its monumental pyramids dedicated to the sun and the moon.

But the Olmec may have been more than just a shadowy folk memory to those who came later, for they left behind them a legacy of exquisite works of art. On a November day in 1978, during the excavation of the Templo Mayor, the great Aztec double pyramid in the heart of modern-day Mexico City, a perfect miniature green stone mask came to light (above). The power and simplicity of its style proclaimed it to be Olmec. Treasured as an heirloom by the Aztec, they had deemed it worthy to be part of a ritual offering to their gods. Across the centuries, the mask spoke to the Aztec of their predecessors recalling the greatness to which they owed so much of their own civilization.

PYRAMID MAKERS AND MOUND BUILDERS

THE MAGNIFICENT MAYA

Who were the people that built towering temples and dizzying stepped pyramids in the jungles of Mesoamerica? "Savages never reared these structures, savages never carved these stones," concluded the 19th-century traveler John L. Stephens.

When Europeans first landed on the shores of Mexico's Yucatán Peninsula early in the 16th century, the great Maya centers were already faded relics — timeworn, overgrown, and abandoned. And yet they still possessed a haunting beauty, enveloping all who came near in a flood of amazement. For there, deep within the dense tropical forests or clustered on the barren limestone tip of the peninsula, rose not one or two monuments, or even one or two settlements, but vast architectural complexes studded with palaces and pyramids, each structure and each setting a triumph of grace and power.

The awe-inspiring remains of the 60 or so Maya "cities" were simply the most visible and enduring evidence of a civilization spectacular in its learning and achievement. In addition to being master engineers and architects, the Maya were sophisticated mathematicians, accomplished astronomers, and meticulous historians, who refined a complex hieroglyphic system of writing for recording their past. In their art and architecture, they achieved a style that is intricate and as technically dazzling as it is visually impressive.

The true dimensions of Maya civilization, however, were lost upon most Spaniards, who, in their haste to conquer and convert, failed to comprehend what lay before them. Not until the 19th century did the extent and grandeur of Maya culture begin to be fully explored and publicized, awakening a quickly captivated world to the fact that a high civilization on the order of ancient Egypt had flourished for nearly 1,000 years in the New World.

To appreciate the accomplishments of the Maya (as well as the difficulties faced by those trying to render the Maya world coherent long after the fact), one must first understand their geography. The territory the Maya inhabited, some 125,000 square miles, encompasses the present-day countries of western Honduras, El Salvador, Guatemala, and Belize, and the Mexican states of Tabasco and Chiapas to the west as well as the entire Yucatán Peninsula, which is bordered by the Gulf and Caribbean coasts. Though the tip of the Yucatán is barren and dry, as one moves farther south and inland one is met by a towering rain forest rising out of strangling tropical growth, oppressively hot and hu-

A limestone lintel from Yaxchilán, Mexico, shows two elaborately clothed nobles, who are rendered here with the exaggerated profile typical of Maya portraiture. This detail from a painted bas-relief dates from A.D. 600 – 900.

platforms that surrounded the centers served as foundations for homes of humbler Maya families.

Of the actual houses, built of thatch and wood, nothing remains except an occasional posthole, but these suffice to tell experts that extended families lived in clusters of houses surrounding an open courtyard. The platforms, ranging in height from one to three feet, served to keep insect life at bay and also helped to ventilate the houses. The courtyard was the center of family life; here the women ground maize and artisans worked with feathers, wove and dyed fabrics, and molded pottery. Off in a corner or in the center, there often stood a shrine, which also served as a burial place for a venerated forebear. The height and area of a platform evidently varied according to social standing. Those of the upper classes were higher and larger and in some instances have left remains of stone benches and inscribed tablets. The peasant farmer's house barely cleared the ground and was probably no more than a simple thatched hovel.

Like the rest of their Mesoamerican contemporaries, the Maya were farmers, having cultivated maize, their principal crop, for 2,000 or 3,000 years prior to the Classic era. The Maya also grew beans, sweet potatoes, manioc, squash, cotton, and cacao. Both these last crops were highly valued in Maya society, cacao beans being not unlike cash.

The monumental aspect of the Maya city-states depended heavily on the efficiency of the average farmer, who had to feed himself and his lords before he was free to leave his plot and help build pyramids and other monumental structures. Until recent years, it was assumed that this implied high level of efficiency was achieved through the most rudimentary form of slash-and-burn agriculture. According to this system of farming, the land is first cleared and the brush is left on the ground to dry for a few months. Just before the start of the rainy season, the tangle of trees and undergrowth is set on fire. The resulting nutrient-enriched soil is then planted for only one or two seasons before it is surrendered to the forest. This practice is an extravagant consumer of land, for the abandoned fields must lie fallow for a period of four to seven years before they can be cleared again by slash-and-burn methods. Al-

161

though it was assumed that the Maya grew root crops among the maize of their *milpas,* the name given these jungle patches, and eked out their diet with beans, there was still no adequate answer to the problem of how the 3 million or more Maya were fed.

Only in the 1960's, through intensive and painstaking research, did the way the ancient Maya peasant used his land come to light. In some areas elaborate terraces were uncovered, while in other swampy, lowland regions aerial photography and ground investigations revealed the existence of networks of ancient drainage canals. These were dug in a grid pattern, leaving rectangular areas of well-drained soil for cultivation. Crushed limestone was spread over these fields, and it was covered by rich bottom soil, renewed with each clearing of the canals. The result was raised fields, expanses of exceptionally fertile land with the added advantage that the canals could be used for water transportation by canoe. A millennium later, long past the time the canals were first dug, the conquistador Bernal Díaz del Castillo noted in his account of Cortés's march through the lowlands of Yucatán that the natives went everywhere by canoe.

From planting to cooking, maize dominated the lives of men and women. Crops were sown in succession throughout the rainy season, May to August, and har-

The Unvanquished Maya

Neither the sword of the Spaniard nor the gun of the Mexican soldier in later centuries was able to conquer and subdue the Maya nation. Of all the native peoples of Mesoamerica, none matched the Maya in boldness of spirit and ruthless, skillful warfare. It took the conquistador Francisco de Montejo 20 years, from 1526 to 1546, to gain control of the Yucatán Peninsula, and even then his conquest encompassed only the northwest corner of the Maya domain. Those Maya who were under Spanish rule lived in virtual slavery, and the next 250 years were punctuated by small but fierce revolts.

A mere 80 miles from the capital, Mérida, lay the frontier; beyond this line, stretching along the Caribbean coast, the territory remained in the hands of the Maya, unconquered and nearly untouched by the Western world for centuries. In the 1840's, while the governing class of the Yucatán was embroiled in political strife, these Maya seized their chance. On January 15, 1847, they attacked Valladolid just inside Mexican territory, slaughtering the local population. Clearly it was the overture to war. Within 15 months, the Maya had gained control of four-fifths of the Yucatán — yet they turned home at this pivotal moment to plant their maize. But the Caste War — as it came to be called —was far from over; frontier attacks, burnings, and lootings went on for years. Army after army marched against the Maya only to be decimated along jungle trails. When 1,000 Yucatecan soldiers were killed in battle in 1855, the Mexican government decided that the subjugation of the Maya would never be achieved.

Behind their frontier, the Maya tended their *milpas,* practiced a part-pagan, part-Christian religion, and lived as their ancestors had. They set up their own outlaw state with one overall leader and many smaller chieftains, and raided for arms and slaves.

Gradually, the 20th century intruded on this anomalous, independent state. The last uprising took place in 1910. As the Maya were irrevocably drawn into a wider economy, their isolation from the outside world came to an end. Today, there are some 2 million Maya still speaking their language and still proud to be Maya.

162

vested during the dry season, November through late May. Farmers worked without the aid of machines or the wheel, and with no draught animals to help haul heavy loads. To women fell the time-consuming work of rendering the maize edible. After the corn was dried in the sun, the kernels were scraped from the cob, soaked in lime water to soften the skins, and ground into a paste. The grinding was done on a *metate,* a slightly hollowed flat stone, with a *mano,* a stone implement resembling a rolling pin. The paste was then kneaded and made into tortillas or tamales. To make tortillas the women pinched off a small piece of dough and fashioned it by hand into a flat circle, which they baked on clay. Tamales, made from the same dough with a little more moisture left in it, consisted of pieces of dough which were wrapped in corn husks and baked; these were carried to the field for lunch.

Avocados, guavas, and melons were plentiful throughout the lowlands, but sources of protein were scarce. The only animals the Maya kept were the domesticated dog and the wild turkey. They also collected honey from the stingless honey bee, native to Yucatán. Although peasants hunted for game, mainly deer, and fished, the most regular source of protein for the majority was the kidney bean. However, we do not know how plentiful a crop it was in Classic times, and

The clear notes of the musical scale sound once again, as a young Maya boy (above) blows on a bird-shaped pottery whistle that had lain silent in a child's tomb for some 3,000 years. The traditional Maya love of finery has not been lost over the ages. Men come to a carnival feast (left) attired in vivid red coats and beribboned hats, reminiscent of the pageantry of their ancestors. Despite today's reliance on store-bought clothing, Maya women (right) still carry on the time-consuming task of weaving richly patterned cloth on a hand loom that has changed little over the centuries.

163

among the many theories proposed to explain the decline of the Maya is poor nutrition, specifically, protein deficiency. Comparison of Maya remains from early and late Classic periods demonstrates a gradually declining level of nutrition over the years, a tendency that very likely led to increased vulnerability to disease. In fact, analyses of skeletons have revealed the presence of scurvy and other diseases resulting from malnutrition. The lower classes ate progressively worse toward the end of the Classic era.

Just how strained Maya resources were during the height of their power is not known with certainty. The little information we have is guesswork, based on population estimates and incomplete extrapolations of agricultural yield. The degree to which social factors influenced food distribution is also a mystery.

As with any people who stand out sharply against the blurred background of their lesser contemporaries, it is easy to think of the Maya as having existed in isolation. In fact, they were a people in constant contact with other cultures, their near and distant neighbors of Mesoamerica. From the earliest times, the Maya were known as traders, and their success in establishing both foreign and domestic markets greatly speeded and consolidated their cultural development. Indeed, some scholars speculate that the impulse of the Maya to build ceremonial sites sprang as much from their interest in creating stable trading centers as from religious centers, and certainly trade within the Maya region was intense. Each area had its distinctive goods to export, payment generally being made in cacao beans. The whole business was dominated by powerful merchants, who arranged for necessary land or river transport for their goods. From the lowlands came rubber, tobacco, vegetable dyes, honey, polychrome pottery, and animal skins. From coastal areas came salt, dried fish, pearls, and shells, and from the highlands in the south, jade, cinnabar, and obsidian, and rare quetzal feathers, to enumerate but a partial list.

A crucial item of exchange was salt, even during times of Spanish domination. With only scanty supplies in the central lowlands and in the highlands, this daily essential had to be brought in great quantities from the Yucatán flats. It is not known how much salt was actually produced during ancient times, but estimates of Yucatán's capacity made in 1917, when the techniques used to claim salt had changed little over 1,000 years, put production at a potential 60,000 tons per year, sufficient for a population of 20 million, or 17 million more than the estimated lowland population at the height of the Classic era.

The Collapse of Maya Civilization

But if trade nourished and sustained the Maya world for 1,000 years or more, in the view of some scholars, it may also have contributed to its collapse. Some scholars have suggested that the increasing scarcity of commodities led to destructive competition among city-states and eventually interrupted trade routes. In time the result was shortages of essential goods and consequent economic and cultural retrenchment, which hastened their downfall.

What caused the sudden abandonment of the great Maya city-states in the lowlands, the destruction of steles and temples, the cessation of learning, the collapse of the ruling dynasties? In center after center, the breaking point seems so pronounced that some early theorists proposed an earthquake or a plague to explain the suddenness of the change. A temple that was nearing completion was left unfinished, almost as if the workmen had been called away to other tasks, while the last recorded dates on steles at various sites suggest a dominolike tumbling: Piedras Negras, A.D. 795; Copán, 800; Tikal, 869; Tonina, 909.

Here and there, steles were purposely smashed, buildings partly destroyed, and yet no center was literally leveled, as one might expect if these changes were the result of full-scale warfare. The evidence points rather to an abandonment; although the centers were still used, no effort was made to maintain them. The question remains: Why? Was it willful or unavoidable? Were the people destroyed — by disease, economic failure, or intruders — or did they themselves constitute the purgative force, sweeping their lives free after centuries of oppression?

Certainly the Maya of the Classic times were not literally overrun by invading armies; but certain outside influences made themselves felt long before the general collapse of the city-states. The really great alien "intrusion," to use J. Eric S. Thompson's phrase, did not take place until after the wider collapse of the Maya centers, when a splinter group of the Toltec, a warlike people from central Mexico, moved into the Yucatán in the 10th century. Following this invasion a hybrid culture evolved that continued many of the Classic Maya themes and yet displayed a cruder, less refined aspect toward which the Classic Maya could never have been sympathetic.

In the absence of any clear proof, proponents of no single argument have succeeded in winning their case. Disease may have swept the Maya in successive decades of the 9th century, but there is no evidence that it did. If trade was interrupted, it certainly would have worked a hardship on the general economy and in time on the people who lived by it. In dealing with primitive farming systems, the question of shortfall inevitably arises, and the parallel demands of growing crops and building monuments may simply have become too great; in the last century before the collapse, in fact, monument building reached a fevered peak, and it may well be that a long-delayed crisis point was reached. Comparably, although there is no hard evidence of natural catastrophe, such as earthquake or prolonged drought, such an event could account for a complete break in the social fabric; the timing of lesser disasters may have helped bring down an already tottering soci-

The ravages of time provide a poignant reminder of the splendor that characterized Maya civilization. Crumbling roof combs of the House of Doves at Uxmal (below) stand tall amidst the overgrown landscape, while jungle growth slowly dismantles a corbelled arch (right).

ety. All these factors notwithstanding, in the opinion of Thompson, the Maya civilization of the 9th century was on the verge of collapse from within, vulnerable to that most cataclysmic and final interruption to life: revolution. The ingredients were surely plentiful in Maya society: the widening gulf of gross inequity between the masses and the elite, who had run this top-heavy world and whose directives had held it together.

As Thompson theorizes: "In city after city the ruling group was driven out or, more probably, massacred by the dependent peasants, and power then passed to peasant leaders and small-town witch doctors." With the passing of the elite, many of the secrets of Maya learning disappeared. By the time the Spaniards arrived, the glory days were over even in the Yucatán, and the cities of the Maya stood shrouded in mystery.

CLUES TO A FORGOTTEN PAST

Scattered across the eastern half of the United States
are amazing earthworks built long ago by little-known peoples.
Only gradually are scholars learning about the strange
ceremonial practices of the mysterious Mound Builders.

On a September day in 1883 Frederic Ward Putnam, curator of Harvard University's Peabody Museum, scrambled up the steep slope edging the waters of Brush Creek in Adams County, Ohio, and pushed his way through the bushes to follow the winding folds of a great earthen serpent that sprawled for nearly a quarter of a mile above the bend of the stream. The writhing form, with its tail tightly coiled and its distended jaw fastened on an egg-shaped object, cast its spell on him.

"The most singular sensation of awe and admiration overwhelmed me . . . ," Putnam later wrote, "for here before me was the mysterious work of an unknown people, whose seemingly most sacred place we had invaded. Was this a symbol of the old serpent faith, here on the western continent, which from the earliest time in the religions of the East held so many peoples enthralled, and formed so important a factor in the development of succeeding religions?

"Reclining on one of the huge folds of this gigantic serpent, as the last rays of the sun, glancing from the distant hilltops, cast their long shadows over the valley, I mused on the probabilities of the past; and there seemed to come to me a picture as of a distant time, of a people with strange customs, and with it came the

demand for an interpretation of this mystery. The unknown must become known!"

A century has passed since Putnam's visit, but the great Serpent Mound has yielded few secrets, and perhaps it never will: its symbolism and ritual function remain as mysterious as ever.

The famous mound is just one of thousands upon thousands of strange prehistoric earthworks of various shapes and sizes that are scattered across the eastern half of the United States, from the Great Lakes south to the Gulf Coast and Florida, and from the Appalachian and Allegheny mountains to the lands just west of the Mississippi River. Dotting the Ohio and Upper Mississippi valleys are mounds and hillocks rising anywhere from 6 to 70 feet or more, great geometrically shaped ramparts enclosing acres of land, and broad walled avenues. Farther south are mounds that are not only much more massive than the northern ones but pyramidal in form, with steep, well-graded slopes and flat tops

A glistening, stylized serpent cut from thin, transparent mica with flint tools attests to the artistry and skill of Mound Builder craftsmen. Found in Ohio, the sinuous one-foot-wide Hopewell piece may have been worn for certain rituals.

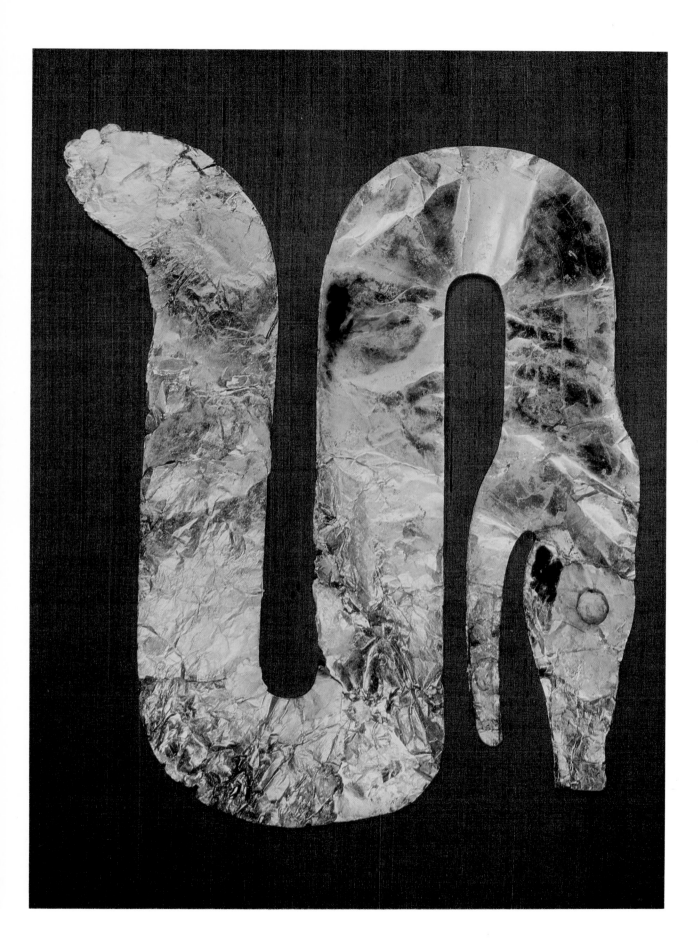

The largest such effigy in the world, Ohio's Serpent Mound measures nearly ¼ of a mile from tip to tip. Its body has an average width of 20 feet and is 4 to 5 feet high; the gape of the jaws is 75 feet. The effigy is attributed to the Adena because Adena artifacts were found in a conical burial mound nearby. Below is a diagram made by Squier and Davis in 1846.

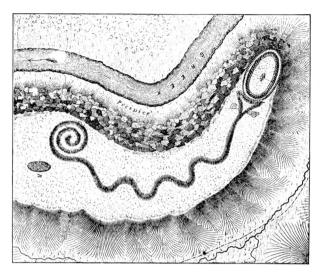

reached by ramps. And from Ohio westward to Wisconsin and Iowa are found hundreds of long, low ridges that trace the flowing outlines of great birds, tortoises, serpents, beasts, and humans. So enormous are these effigy mounds, as they are called, that many can be seen in their entirety only from above.

As explorers and settlers pushed into the interior in the late 1700's and early 1800's, numerous reports trickled back to the seaboard states about the mystifying earthen structures they came upon. In the 1780's, for instance, settlers reaching the site of Marietta, Ohio — on the bluff at the confluence of the Muskingum and Ohio rivers — found a large complex that included a rampart 25 to 36 feet wide at the base and 4 to 10 feet high; two walled-in squares (the larger of which contained 40 acres and four platform mounds); and a nearly circular earthwork enclosing a great mound 30 feet high. There was also a passage to the river bank 680 feet long and 150 feet wide, flanked for its full length by 8- to 10-foot-high embankments. It seemed likely to the newcomers that the passage had been a ceremonial avenue, and so they named it the *Sacra Via,* after the Sacred Way of imperial Rome.

One of the cofounders of Marietta, the Reverend Manasseh Cutler of Ipswich, Massachusetts, was particularly fascinated by the earthworks. Noting that many of the trees growing atop the Marietta mounds were of considerable size, and that some had grown up out of rotted stumps, he began counting the growth rings in the trees being cleared away. He found one mound tree with 463 rings and concluded that the

earthworks dated at least as far back as the early 1300's; obviously the builders of these structures were an ancient people, not the Indians presently living there.

The people of Marietta took a deeper interest in their historical environment than did many pioneer groups. Resolutions were passed to preserve the two great enclosures and the *Sacra Via* and to incorporate the tallest mound in the future cemetery.

As the number of reports about earthworks grew, so did curiosity. The apparent antiquity of the structures, the planning and labor they required, and the fact that the local Indians knew nothing about them led to fanciful speculations about the identity of the Mound Builders, as they were called. The Atlanteans, the Phoenicians, the Ten Lost Tribes of Israel, the Nephites, the Welsh, and the Vikings all had their champions.

But the most popular theory was that the mystery people were members of a vanished, superior race. It was a convenient rationale for land-hungry settlers. If the Indians had displaced the Mound Builders, it was argued, there was nothing inherent in their "right" to these fertile lands and hunting grounds. To displace them in turn was not a matter of injustice but rather a case of doing to them what they had done to others.

A leading proponent of the lost-race theory was Caleb Atwater, the postmaster of Circleville, Ohio. (The town was named for the circular earthworks on the site.) The scholarly Atwater had methodically investigated a good many ancient ruins in southern Ohio. Even as he worked, he noted sadly that the plow and the town builders were steadily demolishing the earthen structures. In 1820 he completed a weighty article that incorporated his own findings and the studies of others on the earthworks in the midwestern states. The paper, published in the new journal of the American Antiquarian Society, was one of the first detailed surveys of the mounds in that region, and was to become an important record for archeologists.

Atwater the theorist was not so solid as Atwater the scientist. It was his contention that the mounds "owe their origin to a people far more civilized than our Indians," and the evidence, in his view, pointed to the people of India. "The temples, altars, and sacred places of the Hindoos, were always situated on the bank of some stream of water," he wrote. "The same observation applies to the temples, altars and sacred places of those who erected our tumuli." Who knows, he asked, "but that the Muskingum, the Scioto, the Miami, the Ohio, the Cumberland, and the Mississippi, were once deemed as sacred, and their banks as thickly settled, and as well cultivated, as are now the Indus, the Ganges, and the Burrampooter?" This ancient civilization, he said, had been carried from Asia across the Bering Strait into Alaska and had spread slowly eastward to the Ohio Valley.

What had happened to this vanished people? Atwater was confident he had the answer to that as well: like many others, he believed the Mound Builders had left the Ohio Valley at least 1,000 years before and slowly migrated southward, honing their skills as they went along. Their eventual stopping place was Mexico, where they built the monumental stone structures found by Cortés. Atwater's migration theory was to be perpetuated for generations to come.

Americans were carried away by a wave of romanticisms about the Mound Builders. Such well-known figures as General William Henry Harrison (who became president in 1841) and the New England poet William Cullen Bryant rhapsodized about a society whose people congregated in large cities and lived in imposing style until they were assailed by barbarian hordes. Perhaps the most enchanting proposal of all,

169

put forward in the early 1900's, was that Ohio had been the Garden of Eden and that the Serpent Mound remained as a symbol of Eve's wickedness.

Not everyone endorsed such notions, however. Even back in the 1700's there were a few who thought the mounds were built by the American Indians. One of these people was Thomas Jefferson, who wondered whether the mounds were the mass graves of fallen warriors or were general sepulchers for village populations. Around 1780 he decided to excavate one of the mounds near Monticello, his home in central Virginia. After making a perpendicular cut in the mound, Jefferson examined the exposed strata and found bundles of human remains — males, females, children, and infants. He estimated that the mound contained a thousand skeletons interred over a period of time and noted that the remains showed no signs of a violent death.

Many years passed before a major effort was made to learn about the Mound Builders. In 1842 the American Ethnological Society was founded by Albert Gallatin, with the help of Henry Schoolcraft, to support research in American prehistory. Both Gallatin, who had served Jefferson and Madison as secretary of the treasury, and

Schoolcraft, a well-known ethnologist, were impatient with super-race theorists and all their romantic excesses and eager to sponsor a thorough study of the earthworks to obtain the facts. But it was the fortuitous acquaintance of two residents of Chillicothe, Ohio, that led to such an undertaking. They were Ephraim George Squier, the editor of the *Scioto Gazette*, and Dr. E.H. Davis, a physician who had grown up in Ohio and had been investigating mounds on his own for some time. Setting about their task in 1845, they opened and systematically examined no fewer than 200 mounds, surveyed 100 earthworks, and drew admirable topographical plans and sketches of them. Reviewing earlier writings on the Mound Builders and utilizing the research of others on more distant ruins, they turned out a comprehensive report, which the newly founded Smithsonian Institution in Washington agreed to publish. In 1848 their work appeared, a large volume titled *Ancient Monuments of the Mississippi Valley*, handsomely illustrated with more than 40 finely drawn plans of earthworks and 207 wood engravings. (The Mississippi Valley was defined to include the basins of the Ohio and other tributaries.)

As a summary of existing knowledge and as a record of the Ohio earthworks at that time, the report by Squier and Davis remains to this day an invaluable reference for archeologists. But it did little to clear up the mystery of who the Mound Builders were. For the two men concluded that they were a race apart with a superior knowledge that included the mathematical ability to measure angles. As an example of this ability they pointed to the massive complex at Newark, Ohio, with its precisely laid out geometric figures. Regarding the fate of the lost race, Squier and Davis agreed with Caleb Atwater that the Mound Builders had departed southward at some distant time.

Puzzled by some of the southern mounds, which were not only more complex than the northern ones but contained pottery and other grave goods of exceptional artistry, Squier and Davis suggested, as had Atwater, that the works in the South represented the advances achieved by the Mound Builders during their slow migration toward Mexico. But they also admitted the possibility that the southern and northern mounds had been raised by two different peoples who were contemporaries of each other.

In 1881 Congress appropriated funds to the newly founded Bureau of Ethnology of the Smithsonian Institution for an investigation to determine the identity of the Mound Builders. Cyrus Thomas, an entomologist, was invited to head the research. For more than a decade Thomas's small group of field workers crisscrossed much of the eastern half of the United States, surveying and excavating some 2,000 sites and preserving and cataloging thousands of artifacts. Rather than concentrating on a few places, they cast their net as widely as possible, for the earthworks were rapidly being destroyed by rural and urban development and by looters selling artifacts to collectors and museums.

Thomas's conclusion was an unqualified yes: the mounds were indeed the work of the North American Indians. Furthermore, he stated, they had not migrated north from Mexico; nor, conversely, had the Ohio Mound Builders moved southward. They were not, in fact, a single people at all. In his long final report, published by the Smithsonian Institution in 1894, Thomas explained that the builders of the mounds, acting across separate and broad spectrums of time, included a number of tribes or peoples who bore about the same relationship to one another as did the Indian tribes when first encountered by the Europeans. Thomas and the concurring archeological community finally disposed of the central myth of a vanished race.

In their ongoing efforts to pin down the identity of the Mound Builders, archeologists focused on mounds and burial grounds in their search for clues because the prehistoric Indians of the Eastern Woodlands had traditionally interred their dead with the things they valued most. Their graves, containing ornaments, tools, and other artifacts, constituted almost the only source of information about their social and economic patterns and their concepts of life and death.

Two years or so before the Thomas study was published, a major find was made on a farm belonging to a Captain M.C. Hopewell in southern Ohio. The earthworks there, close by the Scioto River in Ross County, included more than 30 mounds, the largest of which rose 23 feet in the midst of a rectangular enclosure of 110 acres. Excavating the great mound, the researchers uncovered about 150 burials accompanied by distinctive and superbly crafted grave goods. It is a tradition in archeology to name a culture for the place where its artifacts are first found. Thus farmer Hopewell became immortalized. (As Robert Silverberg has pointed out, in his popular account of the Mound Builders, had

This rather fanciful scene, showing Dr. Montroville Dickeson excavating a mound in Louisiana countryside strewn with tumuli, is a detail from "Panorama of the Monumental Grandeur of the Mississippi Valley," painted by John J. Egan in 1850. Dickeson commissioned the work and toured the nation with it. While he lectured, the 348-foot-long muslin painting was unrolled, awing rapt spectators for a 25¢ admission.

171

scholarship moved at a faster pace, the Hopewell culture might have been known to us "as the Clark or Ashley or Evans Culture," after one of the previous owners of the property.)

An equally important discovery followed in 1901 on a country estate named Adena, also in Ross County. There a burial mound yielded log tombs containing skeletons and quantities of grave goods. The finds were sufficiently different from the artifacts yielded by the Hopewell site that they were credited to another culture, which was designated the Adena.

At the same time it was becoming increasingly apparent that many of the mounds and artifacts found in the central and lower Mississippi Valley had been left by yet another, more complex culture.

After spending years studying, classifying, and segregating their finds according to their characteristics and presumed functions, archeologists gradually fitted together innumerable bits of information, like the pieces of a baffling jigsaw puzzle. As they did so, a picture began to form of three distinct mound-building Indian cultures that came to be known as the Adena, the Hopewell, and the Mississippian. The earliest of these, the Adena, had its dawn about 500 years before the time of Christ and continued in some areas until about A.D. 200. The Hopewell, overlapping, flourished from about 100 B.C. to A.D. 350. The last, the remarkable Mississippian culture, emerged around A.D. 800 and was in its twilight when the first Europeans set foot on American soil in the early 1500's.

The recognition of three different cultures was only the first step in the ongoing effort to learn about the Mound Builders, their origins, and their relationships to one another. Especially mystifying have been the Adena and the Hopewell, who occupied much of the same territory in Ohio and overlapped in time.

The Innovative Adena

Ever since Caleb Atwater in his article of 1820 characterized the Mound Builders as "short and thick," archeologists and physical anthropologists have been preoccupied with their stature and cranial measurements. Even as recently as the 1950's, a few archeologists were still persuaded that the Adena were a powerfully built and exceptionally tall people, some approaching seven feet, with large, round, flattened heads, in contrast to the "indigenous" Indians, whom they described as typically slender and long-headed. The implication that the Adena were intruders prompted a variety of tenacious migration theories proposing either a northern or a southern (possibly Mexican) origin for the Adena. Complicating the study of skeletal remains were the destructive burial practices of the Indians and poor excavation and preservation techniques.

Aided by the improved methods available in the 1970's for measuring and analyzing skeletal remains, archeologists and physical anthropologists have relinquished some of their long-held beliefs, and old ideas about a race of round-headed giants have been discarded. It is now generally accepted that the Adena were of average height and build and that any inherited physical variations were within the normal range of variations found within a population. It is recognized that the incidents of flattened skulls among the Adena were the result of deliberate cranial deformation, from the custom of strapping infants to cradleboards. It is also now believed that the Adena were an indigenous people and that their culture developed locally.

Indians had been living in the temperate woodlands of the Ohio Valley for thousands of years, migrating short distances with the seasons to procure food and traveling the rivers and streams in dugouts and bark canoes to trade. They were not a single people with a single language and identical customs and beliefs. Rather, they were composed of numbers of bands who intermingled, exchanged goods and ideas, and picked up new ways of doing things, but also kept customs of their own. Gradually they sharpened their skills in dealing with their environment and most likely began to practice a limited horticulture, cultivating pumpkins, squash, gourds, and a few other seed-producing plants. Becoming economically more stable, they settled in small communities and found time for activities other than procuring food. About 500 B.C. the people known to us as the Adena began to entomb their dead in conical earthen mounds.

The next few centuries saw the florescence of a culture notable for its innovations. While other Woodland Indians lived in caves or rock shelters, evidence suggests that most of the Adena constructed round houses that were unique and sometimes large enough for 40 people. Resembling inverted baskets, they seem to have been made by weaving cane or slender branches around a circle of paired posts set in the ground at an angle so that the walls slanted outward from the base. A thatched, steeply pitched roof projected well out beyond the walls to form wide, protective eaves. In the center there was usually a communal hearth where the women cooked. Their kitchen equipment included pottery vessels (made by coiling ropes of clay and occasionally decorated with incised geometric designs), wooden bowls and paddles, gourd containers, and spoons fashioned from turtle carapaces. Food was probably stored in pits dug in the clay floor.

Women's duties doubtless included weaving cloth and making sandals by plaiting grass and plant fibers, tending the garden, and gathering nuts, seeds, and edible plants and fruits, often with the help of the children. Home from a hunting or fishing expedition, the men made flaking and cutting tools from antler tips and beaver incisors and fashioned spearheads, projectile points, and knives from flint. They also created ornaments out of such rare and exotic materials as copper from the Lake Superior area and marine shells from the distant Atlantic and Florida coasts, which they obtained through far-reaching trade contacts.

The Adena,
circa 500 B.C. — A.D. 200

The heartland of the Adena culture was the Ohio Valley, with sites found in the five states named on the map at right. The abstract sandstone engraving from Ohio at far right is actually a highly stylized bird of prey in a split image with paired representations of the head, wings, feet, and tail. A common motif, the raptorial bird may have been associated with burial: bodies were sometimes placed outdoors, where birds of prey would strip the bones of flesh before final interment.

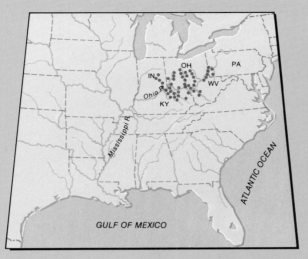

The Hopewell,
circa 100 B.C. — A.D. 350

Ideas and practices of the Hopewell culture, which reached its apogee in the Adena heartland, were widely adopted in the eastern half of the United States, as indicated on the map. The four-footed ceramic pot was unearthed at Mound City near Chillicothe, Ohio. Its ornamentation was carefully worked out by a Hopewell potter with an obvious eye for design. A conventionalized spoon-billed duck is centered on a panelled background, thus combining smooth and textured surfaces.

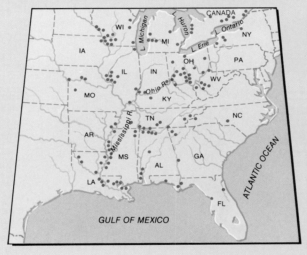

The Mississippian,
circa A.D. 800–1500

Mississippian characteristics spread from the central Mississippi Valley west to Oklahoma and Texas and southeast to Florida; some 100 sites appear on the map. Found at the Spiro site in Oklahoma, the deer mask at far right was most likely worn by a shaman in a ceremonial dance to ensure good hunting. Originally the face was painted, and the earlobes, like the mouth and eyes, possibly had shell inlays. The 11½-inch-tall mask was carved from a single block of cedar.

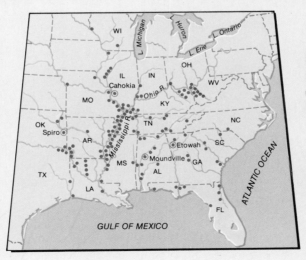

173

What set the Adena apart most noticeably, however, was not their living arrangements but their elaboration of older burial customs honoring the dead. Sometimes the deceased was first placed in the open air — in a tree or on a scaffold — and left until the skeleton was denuded of flesh; then the bones were interred in a grave. But the usual practice was to lay the corpse in a clay-lined pit or basin or a log tomb in the floor of a house. The remains of several persons were often put in the

This 8-inch-tall pipestone effigy, with deftly chiseled features and ear ornaments, is actually a tubular ceremonial pipe made 2,000 years ago by an Adena sculptor. The figure, perhaps of a dwarf, was found in 1901 on the Adena estate in Ohio.

same pit over a period of time before the shelter was burned down and covered over with earth.

Occasionally the dead were accompanied by an assortment of useful and treasured objects of exotic materials and distinctive design and workmanship — bracelets and beads of hammered copper, tubular stone pipes, shell beads, wolf masks, gorgets, and ornaments cut from sheets of glassy mica, which perhaps doubled as mirrors. There were also polished stone tablets of a size that could comfortably be held in the hand. Some were intricately engraved with such motifs as the raptorial bird (bird of prey) and the eye-in-hand symbol, which must have been related to the Indians' concepts of death and the soul. Scholars have suggested that these curious and painstakingly worked tablets were used for the preparation of ceremonial paints, such as the red ochre with which the dead were sometimes adorned. Or they may have been stamps used for tattooing or printing textiles.

As time went by, some of the Adena became more stabilized economically; among them authority was probably vested in a few individuals, and social position became a matter of growing importance. Deceased male adults of high rank were given preferential burial treatment. They were laid out in large log crypts with caches of exotic materials and elaborate grave goods that included effigy figures and unusual stone effigy pipes. Such items may have been put in the grave because they were thought to have magical powers. But they may also have been the deceased's prized possessions, which were considered his (or hers) to enjoy in the life beyond. Women as often as men were buried with grave goods, and frequently such items were put in the graves of children.

With a succession of burials over a period of time, perhaps 50 to 100 years, the mounds grew larger and higher. Sometimes several small mounds were incorporated into one large mound. Eventually Adena societies began to spend even more time on ceremonial activities and undertook the construction of great circular enclosures around some of their mounds, as at Marietta, or in close proximity to them. Numerous "sacred circles," as they are known, have been found in Adena territory. Obviously they represented a widely shared idea, but their meaning remains unknown.

From its heartland in southern Ohio, Adena influence spread west into southeastern Indiana, south into the bluegrass country of Kentucky, and as far east as Delaware, Maryland, and New York. It has been estimated that the total number of Adena mound sites in this region might be anywhere from 300 to 500. The trend-setting Adena can be credited with a number of "firsts," having introduced into the Ohio Valley not only burial mounds but also the concept of burial mound ceremonialism, the construction of circular earthen enclosures, the log tomb, and pottery making.

By the 1st century A.D. the Adena culture was on the wane — not because of decadence or some unknown

America's First Coppersmiths

Perhaps as early as 3000 B.C. the so-called Old Copper culture flourished along the shores of Lake Superior. Of these people themselves we know very little, but because of their artifacts they are credited with being the first known metalworking culture in the Americas. Yet, puzzlingly, their technological breakthrough seemed to go nowhere.

This remarkable advance in metallurgy was an instance of the exploitation of the environment. The Indians found nearly pure copper in surface nuggets in rock along the Lake Superior shore and on the lake's Isle Royale. By trial and error they learned how to extract it for their use — chipping the nugget-bearing rock loose with stone implements and heating it on a hearth until the rock cracked and the nugget could be extracted. Discovering the malleability of the copper, the Indians began to work it into the desired shapes by pounding it with stone hammers. They even discovered the process of annealing, heating and then cooling the metal to give it added strength.

The Old Copper people produced a wide range of weapons, tools, and ornaments (shown at right), including spear points (some of them socketed for the shaft), knives, axes, awls, chisels, fishhooks, beads, bracelets, and possibly finger rings. Some of their implements were ground with abrasive materials such as sandstone. Although they were hunters and fishermen, they seem to have made the Lake Superior region with its copper deposits their home base for more than 2,000 years, using dugout canoes (and perhaps birchbark ones as well) to reach the deposits on Isle Royale.

This early technology apparently failed to bring about any fundamental change in the lives of the Old Copper people beyond, perhaps, easing some of their tasks. Nor did it lead them to the founding of a higher civilization. By about 1000 B.C., in fact, the Old Copper culture had died out. The people didn't move away, but their cultural patterns changed and they began to make fewer and smaller tools. Whether some environmental factors were involved is unclear.

The Old Copper culture left its traces in widespread trading contacts with other peoples in North America. Its artifacts have been found over a wide area reaching from the Plains states to New York and south into the Ohio Valley. A millennium would pass before copper working was revived by the Adena and raised to an art by the Hopewell of the Ohio Valley.

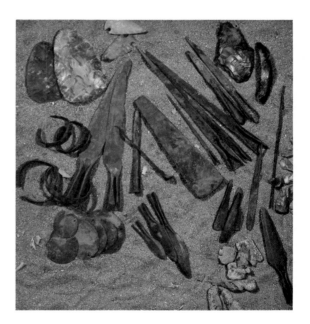

---

catastrophe but because, as the anthropologist Dean Snow put it, "Adena went out of fashion." The higher style of the Hopewell culture had caught on.

The Extravagant Hopewell

Although a variant of Hopewell, termed the Havana culture, is thought to have developed first in the Illinois Valley, it was in Ohio, in the heartland of the Adena, that the Hopewell culture blossomed. The Ohio Hopewell style was an accentuation of the Adena. Everything about it was "bigger and better" than anything known before — grander earthworks, a heightened taste for exotic imports and luxury goods, and more lavish funerary offerings. Its flamboyance proved to be contagious and through trade activities and the accompanying interchange of ideas, aspects of the Ohio Hopewell culture were adopted by local peoples scattered throughout the eastern half of the United States, except in central and eastern Kentucky where Adena traditions continued. None of these regional variants, however, matched the richness of the classical style that developed in the Ohio Valley.

Extravagant builders, the Ohio Hopewell constructed enormous earthworks that combined circles, squares, and octagons. Some of their enclosures were more than a quarter of a mile in diameter and contained as many as 20 to 30 or more conical burial mounds. Their building activity was especially intensive in the Scioto River-Paint Creek area where, in a 14-mile stretch near Chillicothe, Squier and Davis found earthworks located at an average of every 2 miles. Among these were the archeologically important Hopewell, Seip, and Mound City complexes. About 60 miles northeast of Chillicothe, as the crow flies, is the

Without the remarkably accurate map of the Newark ceremonial center, drawn by Squier and Davis in the 1840's, we would have little idea of its scale and complexity. Much of it has since been obliterated. Still remaining are the great circle and connecting octagon highlighted on the map and clearly visible in the aerial view above. What transpired in Hopewell times in these formally arranged enclosures where golfers stroll today? Archeologists are searching for clues.

ceremonial center of Newark, which once covered 4 square miles and contained an elaborate complex of circular, square, and octagonal enclosures connected by wide, walled avenues.

How and why the Hopewell built their enormous geometric earthworks may never be understood. In 1978 James A. Marshall, a civil engineer who has spent years studying the prehistoric structures, claimed that they were built according to scaled plans, using the same unit of measure (187 feet) that was employed at Teotihuacán in Mexico, and that the earthworks concentrated in the Scioto River floodplains were in alignment with one another. Marshall suggested that "small

groups of American Indian geometers must have made the trip from Mexico to Ohio as early as 400 B.C." The reaction of archeologists and anthropologists has been one of skepticism. According to James A. Brown of Northwestern University, in a paper published in 1982 on his own intensive investigation of the Mound City complex, the best evidence shows that the "mounds are irregularly arranged" and "their orientations make no overall pattern."

In their investigatons of the Ohio Hopewell earthworks archeologists have been perplexed by the dearth of habitation sites. Were these complexes "vacant ceremonial centers"? Did the burial mounds and their rich contents bespeak a "Cult of the Dead"? And who were the "honored dead"? Were they the same people who made the grave goods?

In the early 1960's radiocarbon dating seemed to archeologist Olaf H. Prufer to indicate that individual Hopewell mounds, unlike the Adena mounds, had been built over relatively short periods of time — too short to account for the considerable number of bodies they contained. In his view this suggested that retainers were sacrificed and buried "along with the important individual for whom the mound was primarily intended." Prufer began to believe that the Ohio Hopewell earthworks were ceremonial centers occupied only on ritual occasions, and found it reasonable to think the local population lived in "scattered hamlets" rather than close by the mounds. On the basis of his subsequent fieldwork in the bottomlands of southern Ohio and discovery of tiny habitation sites, Prufer also proposed that in some places, at least, the ancient farmers were Adena while the craftsmen were Hopewell people "engaged in the production of grave goods for the Hopewell cult." The cult, he believed, had been introduced from points west of Ohio by "a privileged minority who in some way had come to dominate some of Ohio's Adena people. . . ."

Speculations about a dominating cult group have been largely dismissed in recent years, and it is now thought that the local population and the "honored dead" were one and the same. But archeologists and anthropologists still debate whether the earthworks were occupied or were simply ceremonial centers, and whether they were built over a short or long period of time. James B. Griffin, widely recognized as an authority on the Mound Builders, is convinced that the Hopewell lived "cheek-by-jowl" with their earthworks, in permanent villages that are slowly coming to light. He points out that no major Hopewell mound has been adequately dated, but maintains that the large ones were built in several stages and that the dead interred in them represent an extended period of time. Some mounds contain several hundred burials apparently amassed over centuries.

Accumulating evidence indicates that the Hopewell lived in kin-related groups of 50 to 100 persons in large, sturdy houses which they built in the formal shapes of rounded squares, ovals, and rectangles. They tended small gardens in which they grew seed-producing plants, squash, and perhaps a little corn, but like their contemporaries, the Hopewell depended upon the plant and animal life of the countryside for their subsistence. Their domestic life was also probably similar to that of other Woodland Indians. As with the Adena, it is their mortuary practices that distinguish them.

Beneath the Hopewell mounds Squier and Davis had found large house structures with arrangements that they took to be "sacrificial altars." For a long time it was supposed that the submound structures were originally the domiciles of individuals of high rank and that

the houses were used later for the cremation and burial of the deceased occupants, after which they were covered over with earth. Recently it has been determined that these structures were actually charnel houses. They were as large and well built as a dwelling, with formal shapes, packed floors, and doorways in the opposite ends. The charnel houses were large because they had to provide space not only for interments but for all the activities involved in preparing the bodies for burial. These preparations might include the application of body paint or, frequently, dissection and reduction in a clay crematory basin, such as the one Squier had mistaken for a sacrificial altar. Then the remains were laid out on the floor, perhaps on a mat, and surrounded with tokens of wealth, which were carefully arranged to make an impressive display to visitors entering the charnel house. A charnel house could accommodate a

A Newark burial mound yielded this lively twin frog effigy cut from a sheet of hammered copper. The Ohio Hopewell fashioned numerous ornaments from Lake Superior copper.

number of burials, so in time it became a "gallery" of the dead. Eventually the charnel house would be covered with earth and a new one built adjacent to it.

In some places the Hopewell people stored the dead in crypts, large "boxes" sunk in the ground some distance from the village. These were lined with logs or rocks and usually roofed over to keep out scavengers. Some communities used both facilities, apparently in accordance with the rank of the deceased.

The higher the deceased person's status, the more elaborate was the burial. Not only did the richness of the mortuary offerings indicate status, but variations in the mortuary features of the charnel houses (and in the size of the mounds) also seem to have been related to rank. Many of the major mound sites have been repeatedly explored, and each time archeologists have gained new insights about Hopewell social organization. Excavations on the Hopewell farm in the early 1890's had yielded copper effigies of fish, birds, and serpent heads, copper breastplates, copper beads, 67 copper axes (including one ceremonial axe that weighed 38 pounds), ornaments of mica and slate, spool-shaped ear ornaments, flint knives, cloth, a ceremonial antler headdress carved of wood and sheathed with copper, and a human bone with an engraving of a man wearing an antler headdress. It is thought that the headdress and

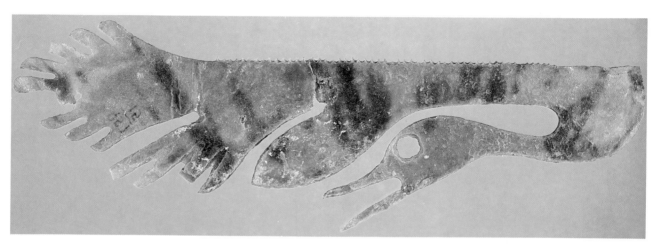

These riveting pieces, with their free-flowing lines, naturalism, and exquisite delicacy, help to place the Ohio Hopewell craftsmen among the great artisans of the Americas. Included are a trumpeter-swan comb fashioned from tortoise shell (above); a bird claw cut from mica (right); and a stone effigy pipe mounted by a peregrine falcon (below). The smoker placed aromatic leaves in a hole in the falcon's back, and then, with the effigy facing him, drew smoke through a hole in the platform.

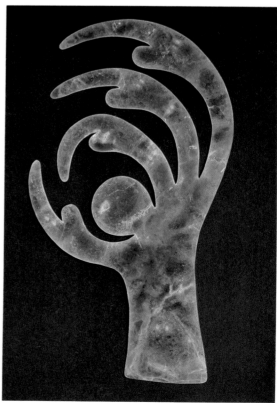

the engraving were intended to represent a shaman both in life and in death.

In later excavations on the Hopewell farm, archeologist Henry Shetrone found a charred skeleton accompanied by mica and pearl ornaments and several hundred pounds of obsidian. Shetrone concluded that the person interred had been a master obsidian knapper and that the obsidian was his personal property. In the central mound on the farm Shetrone uncovered the grave of a young man and woman who lay side by side. Both were adorned with necklaces of grizzly-bear teeth, copper ear ornaments, copper breastplates, and unusual copper nose pieces. Encircling the skeleton of the woman were thousands of pearl beads and copper-clad buttons of wood and stone. Probably she had been interred in a magnificent pearl-beaded mantle, the fabric of which had disintegrated. Altogether tens of thousands of freshwater pearls and shell beads have been recovered at the Hopewell site, the largest quantity from any site in the New World.

The most dazzling discovery was made at the great Seip Mound. There Shetrone found an interior vault, built of logs and timbers, in which the skeletons of four adults lay in repose side by side, while at their heads were the remains of two infants. Accompanying the burials was a profusion of copper, mica, silver, and tortoise-shell ornaments and thousands of pearls. Whether or not this was the tomb of a "royal family," it was clear that the occupants were of high standing, Shetrone observed.

Newspapers carrying the story of the Seip find referred to it as the "great pearl burial." Reports of caches of pearls taken from the mounds had long made sensational news, and the claim was made in *The Book of The Pearl,* published in 1908, that "In the age of the mound-builders there were as many pearls in the possession of a single tribe of Indians as existed in any European court." Reporters and readers apparently overlooked the fact that the pearls, taken from freshwater mussels, were of comparatively poor quality and of little value in the world market.

One of the most elaborate burials found was the "Great Mica Grave," uncovered at Mound City in 1922. The grave was an earthen basin surfaced with large sheets of mica. Upon the mica four cremations had been placed along with a copper headdress, a mica mirror, and other grave goods, including more than 25 pounds of galena crystals. (Galena was used to make a sparkling white body paint.) A layer of earth was mounded over the grave, which was then plated with more of the valuable mica.

In some Hopewell burials archeologists have found carefully scraped and polished human skulls. While obviously ceremonial in purpose, these so-called trophy skulls offer few clues as to whether they were retainers or relatives or even enemies of the honored dead.

The elaborate charnel house burials suggest a sizable community of some social complexity and economic

A Hopewell mother serenely nurses her infant. Remarkably detailed for its size, the 3½-inch-high painted ceramic figurine is one of six found together in Calhoun County, Illinois.

stability, with many residents who felt an obligation to the dead and who had the time and wherewithal to support the prolonged and costly rites of burial. But in the view of archeologists, Hopewell society was not highly organized, nor did it have an inherited aristocracy. Status was achieved, and the prominent people were the headmen and priests, the outstanding warriors, hunters, and traders, and the master craftsmen.

Possibly some of the fine ornamental objects for which the Hopewell are noted were made specifically as grave goods. In the 1970's and early 1980's several structures were found within the Seip and Mound City earthworks with debris that contained tools, scraps of raw materials, and fragments of artifacts, but no trace of either domestic or burial activity. Instead, they seem to be the sites of specialized workshops where a number of skilled artisans were employed, perhaps in making ceremonial grave goods.

The importance the Hopewell people attached to ceremonial goods fashioned of exotic materials required an extensive trade. Especially prized were obsidian from the Yellowstone area of Wyoming, shells from the Gulf and South Florida coasts, galena from the Missouri Ozarks and the Upper Mississippi Valley, copper from the Lake Superior area, mica from North Carolina, and chalcedony from the Knife River area in North Dakota. The Hopewell may have undertaken long-distance travel to obtain supplies. But some raw materials — and finished goods as well — most likely moved across the land over old trade routes and were passed along from one group to another through a network of regional and local exchange centers. It is unlikely that the Hopewell developed distribution centers, because this would have required stockpiling goods, great coordination, and careful scheduling. Little is known about their trading activities, but they seem to have imported more than they exported. One can imagine that in a trade transaction the "gift" of a choice Hopewell-made platform effigy pipe was reciprocated with quantities of raw materials.

By A.D. 300 or 400 Hopewell influences had affected local cultures from eastern Iowa to Ontario and western New York and from Michigan to the Gulf states and Florida. But in the 4th and 5th centuries the winds of change again swept through the Eastern Woodlands, and the Hopewell culture began to wane. Some have suggested that its decline was due to a climatic change, disease, or an era of violence and unrest. But such theories lack supporting evidence. In the view of Griffin and others, the demise of the Hopewell culture can only be observed as a marked decline in the production of rich Hopewell-style goods and a falling-off of interregional contact and exchange. Burial practices became simpler, and eventually the ceremonial centers were abandoned. The reasons for these changes are not understood.

The Remarkable Mississippians

In succeeding centuries agriculture gradually became important, and by the 9th century corn was widely cultivated. Well-made hoes replaced digging sticks, and the bow and arrow was adopted. With farming came more stability, concentrations of population in larger villages, regulatory systems to maintain order and direct activities, and a strong interest in societal land ownership. And with the bow and arrow, hunting and raiding became more effective. Social priorities gradually changed, and out of the remnants of the southern Hopewell culture new patterns formed. Around the beginning of the 9th century the most extraordinary of the prehistoric cultures in eastern North America began to emerge — the Mississippian.

Archeologists still find it hard to define "Mississippian," a catch-all term for behavioral patterns and beliefs shared by widely scattered societies. Originally the term Middle Mississippi was used to designate tempered ceramics. Later the term Mississippian was adopted to include other cultural traits, the most prominent of which were the construction of platform

mounds around a central plaza, the practice of flood-plain agriculture, and community organization with social rank and some specialization in craft work.

In the course of the next 700 years Mississippian traditions appeared in the central and lower Mississippi, lower Ohio, and Red River valleys and throughout much of the southeast. By the time this vibrant culture crested, between 1200 and 1500, there were thousands of Mississippian sites and hundreds of major towns, a few of which became very large centers.

Some of the towns and villages were still going strong in the 16th and early 17th centuries, and several were visited by Hernando de Soto and his party during their explorations of the southeast in 1539–47. In their recollections of the expedition (gathered and published by Garcilaso de la Vega in 1605), De Soto's men spoke of Indian villages dominated by man-made hills: "Then on the top of these places they construct flat surfaces which are capable of holding the ten, twelve, fifteen or twenty dwellings of the lord and his family and the people of his service, who vary according to the power and grandeur of his state. In those areas at the foot of this hill, . . . they construct a plaza, around which first the noblest and most important personages and then the common people build their homes." Dimming memories, and the impulse to make a good story better, doubtless led them to exaggerate the number of dwellings these earthen platform mounds could support, but their eyewitness account gives us a glimpse of this once-remarkable civilization.

One of the first, and the largest, of the big Mississippian centers was Cahokia, a complex that once covered nearly six square miles of fertile plain a few miles north of East St. Louis, Illinois. The development bordered a now-extinct meander channel of the Mississippi River, not many miles from the confluences of the Mississippi with the Missouri and Illinois rivers to the north and the Kaskaskia, Meramec, and Ohio rivers to the south. Cahokia, like St. Louis centuries later, was at the crossroads of the mid-continent, strategically located for trade and exchange. Its waterfront must have been a bustling place where large dugout canoes laden with raw materials from afar docked and then shipped out with such desired trade items as marine shells, pottery, and sturdy flint hoes.

In earlier times, a simple Woodland people were settled in this rich, broad bottomland, an environment of prairie and floodplain cypress forests that yielded an abundance of fish, waterfowl, beasts, berries, shoots, tubers, and greens. They lived in crude shelters, hunted and gathered food, and cultivated starchy seed-bearing plants. Eventually new ideas infiltrated the region and old traditions disappeared.

The period from 900 to 1250 witnessed the construction of some 100 mounds at Cahokia and the growth of a large central town with satellite communities that spread out over an area of about 125 square miles. At the height of its prosperity and influence, from about

A favorite game in Mississippian times was chunkey, a contest of skill in which a player (depicted at left in a stone pipe from Oklahoma) sent a hand-ground stone disk rolling down a court, while competitors hurled poles at the point where they thought the stone would stop. The one who came closest to the mark scored. Spectators gambled enthusiastically on the outcome. The chunkey stone shown above is from Georgia's Etowah site.

1050 to 1250, Greater Cahokia included a "central city," 10 or so outlying villages, 50 or more farming communities, and hunting and fishing camps. The largest of its "suburbs" was a community with 26 mounds of its own, located in the downtown area of present-day St. Louis. Some archeologists have estimated that at its peak Cahokia had a population of 40,000; others, however, including Griffin, doubt that the population exceeded 5,000 to 8,000 at any one time. Even with the more modest estimate, Cahokia looms as the largest prehistoric center north of Mexico.

The centerpiece of Cahokia is Monks Mound, which was built in at least 14 stages over a period of some 300 years, culminating between 1200 and 1300. The most colossal, completely earthen prehistoric monument in the New World, it covers about 15 acres of land and rises in four terraces to a height of 100 feet above the flatlands. The mound contains approximately 22 million cubic feet of earth, all of it carried by people in basketloads of 50 or 60 pounds, for the Indians had no horses or beasts of burden. As Cyrus Thomas noted in 1894 after studying the mounds, "we can scarcely bring ourselves to believe it was built without some other means of collecting and conveying material than that possessed by the Indians."

In 1809 a colony of French Trappist monks established a farm on the lowest level, on the south side of

the mound. After four years they abandoned the site, because of malaria, leaving nothing but a name to mark their presence there. Little did they dream that six centuries earlier Indian leaders in magnificent regalia greeted the rising sun from the top of Monks Mound and called for its blessings upon the land, or that the fields were formerly green with corn.

In Cahokian times Monks Mound dominated a great plaza, or town square, 30 to 40 acres in extent. On the uppermost level of the mound the Cahokians had erected a commodious stockaded building (104 feet long by 48 1/2 feet wide), which probably served as a temple and council house and the ruler's residence. On the lower levels there probably were administrative buildings and perhaps several residences.

Bordering the great plaza were lesser mounds approximately arranged in two rows. To the north, east, south, and west were other plazas, also surrounded by mounds. These lesser mounds included both the platform and conical types and a few low, rectangular ones with ridge tops.

Along the plazas and avenues there were also clusters of one-family dwellings that were probably occupied by prominent people with households of four to five members. The houses, mostly rectangular in shape, were built of closely placed upright poles interlaced with reeds and cane, and had steeply pitched roofs of

Mound Metropolis

As an autumn sun sinks behind "Woodhenge," a ruler and his advisers gather atop Cahokia's massive Monks Mound to announce that the crops are ready for harvest. Three and a half centuries of herculean effort had been required to erect the vast complex — the terraced main mound containing some 22 million cubic feet of earth, transferred one basketful at a time from borrow pits that survive as lakes. The great plaza spreading below Monks Mound serves as an arena for such community activities as games and ritual processions. Bordering the plaza are lesser platform mounds that house the elite — high places in the flat prairie being an assertion of power. A stockade with screened gateways protects the central city. Beyond the walls to the right trade canoes ply a meander channel of the Mississippi River.

In 1927, 234 skeletons were uncovered in an 800-year-old Mississippian cemetery at the Dickson site near Lewistown, Illinois. The remains, which are preserved exactly as they were found, are housed at the Dickson Mounds Museum. Archeologists speculate that the skeletons are those of a local population who had adopted Mississippian ways.

thatch. A good finishing coat of mud plaster inside and out helped insulate the house. Interior walls were sometimes hung with matting or painted with earth-red, black, or grey-blue pigments. Although houses usually had centrally located fireplaces for warmth, women probably did most of their cooking outdoors or in adjacent sheds. A domestic litter of baskets, gourds, ropes of beads, tools, weapons, and pottery, sleeping platforms strewn with hand-woven blankets and fur robes, and the aroma of a simmering venison stew must have combined to create a pleasing atmosphere. The residences of the elite probably differed only in being larger and a little more elaborate.

According to interpretation based on historic accounts of the Natchez, the cultural heirs of the Mississippians, the chief ruler was an absolute monarch who held the power of life and death over his subjects and whose slightest whim was obeyed. Ensconced on Monks Mound, the White House of Cahokia, he was probably regarded as sacrosanct, and his military advisers and other officials were undoubtedly required to follow the rules of protocol in order to see him. Possibly he delegated his younger brothers or other male relatives as chiefs of the outlying villages and appointed supervisors to oversee construction projects and keep track of farm production and the manufacture of goods. He also would have presided over games, civic functions, special festivities, and religious ceremonies, with the assistance of the priests.

Commoners, including those occupied at various times as traders, farmers, fishermen, hunters, and food gatherers, are thought to have lived in the outlying villages and communities. Cahokia's artisans were many, although they may not have been full-time specialists. Among the craftsmen were potters; textile makers; leather workers; flint knappers, who turned out hoes, arrowheads, and knives; men skilled in ground-stone work, who made axes and chunkey stones; stone engravers and sculptors, who fashioned effigy pipes and statues; shell workers employed in making beads and microdrills; and metalworkers, who created copper ornaments. Whether they had quotas to meet is unknown, but even so they must have been a busy lot to meet the requirements of commerce and the demands of the elite.

A great stockade enclosed the central city and was rebuilt several times over the centuries as the timbers rotted away. Each time the project entailed cutting and carrying thousands of stout logs, inserting them in deep trenches, and then plastering them with clay mixed with grass. The stockade was well engineered, with screened gateways to prevent head-on assaults and bastions placed at intervals of 70 feet, from which archers could defend the entire wall. Who were the potential assailants? Possibly they were from neighboring societies, but it is also possible that Cahokia's elite were troubled from time to time by turmoil and dissatisfaction among elements in their own society. The stockade may also have served to screen ceremonies and dances. But its existence suggests that external pressure affected Cahokian society and perhaps finally upset the social-political structure that existed during Cahokia's heyday and precipitated its decline.

Little is known about Cahokian religious beliefs, but as with various early agricultural societies, they were probably closely related to nature. Many Cahokian ceremonies must have been tied to observances of the solstices and equinoxes and related seasonal changes that affected the planting and harvesting of crops.

Excavations have revealed that there had once been a succession of four large circular arrangements of wooden posts a half mile from Monks Mound, which may have been horizon calendars for solar observations. One circle, 410 feet in diameter, was so precisely laid out — with a total of 48 evenly spaced posts about its perimeter and an "observation post" close to the center — that it has been suggested the Cahokians used a peg-and-rope compass. Certain posts have been found to align with the sunrise at the solstices and equinoxes. Was this the observatory of an astronomer-priest, who calculated planting seasons and moon phases? Archeologist Warren L. Wittry, who has made a special study of the circles, has dubbed the circle "Woodhenge" because of its similarity in form and possibly in function

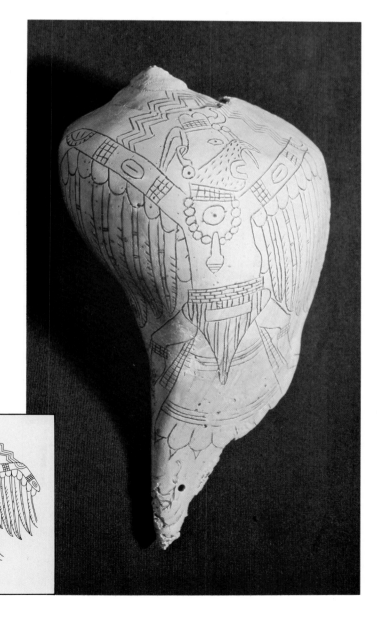

The rendering at near right shows in full the delicate engraving on a conch shell from the Spiro site in Oklahoma. A dancer ritually impersonates a raptorial bird; he wears a mantle embroidered with the feather markings of the bird's wings and a skirt resembling tail feathers. The association of birds of prey with warfare suggests to some scholars the prominence of a military faction at Spiro.

185

to Stonehenge in England. But the unknown heights of the posts, the interference of bluffs on the horizon 2,000 feet to the east, and ignorance about the Cahokian concept of sunrise (whether it was the first appearance of the sun's upper rays or the clearance above the horizon of the lower rays) make it a matter of conjecture. If these were indeed horizon calendars, they would be the only known examples of this device in the eastern United States from prehistoric times. Perhaps, as Griffin suggests, the sun circles served a variety of social and religious functions.

The large number of mounds at Cahokia probably signifies the existence of a stratified society over a period of centuries. Certainly Mound 72 provided startling evidence of an elite class and attendant ritual. It was an unprepossessing mound, a loaf-shaped earthwork only six to eight feet high, but its placement on a north-south axis with Monks Mound, a half mile away, intrigued researchers. Excavating it, they found the skeleton of a man in his early forties, laid out on a blanket of 20,000 conch-shell beads. He was surrounded by sacrificed retainers and quantities of grave goods that included rolls of copper, 2 bushels of mica, and 800 choice arrowheads of different styles and materials. Nearby were several burial pits containing the remains of many persons, but no grave goods. In one of these pits were 53 young women. In another grave were four males, lying side by side with their arms overlapped, but missing their heads and hands.

Mound 72 is thought to contain the graves of two chiefs. A hundred feet away from the first was another major grave where 455 fine flint arrowheads were found in a neat pile, about 700 bone arrowheads, and 36,063 shell beads. Altogether, 300 burials have been found in Mound 72, more than half of them sacrificed young women between the ages of 15 and 25. Possibly they were the wives, concubines, and servants of the two deceased rulers.

Around 1250 or 1300 Cahokia began to decline, for reasons even more puzzling than its rise to prominence. Possibly there were internal political and social problems and unrest. Maybe the great center overexploited its resources. Or perhaps its relatively dense population suffered from lack of sanitation and attendant diseases. Its population slowly dwindled, and by 1500 Cahokia was practically a ghost town.

Other Great Centers

Of the many Mississippian towns that continued to flourish after the decline of Cahokia, the most renowned are Moundville, Etowah, and Spiro.

Moundville, the second largest center after Cahokia, has been called "The Big Apple of 14th Century North America" because its influence was felt far and wide. Located on a plateau by the Black Warrior River near Tuscaloosa, Alabama, the palisaded area covered about 300 acres with 20 platform mounds (the largest of which rises almost 60 feet) and a 7 1/2-acre plaza.

There were also four ponds (perhaps originally borrow pits from which earth was taken for mound construction) stocked with fish, special areas for craft work and ceremonies, a game court, and a sweat lodge, which was used for purification, especially by warriors returning from battle. Among the residences of the elite was a seven-room house.

The settlement, which dates back to about A.D. 1050, was one of many along the river. In the early 14th century Moundville's ruling faction maneuvered itself into a position of unchallenged power in a territory of about 240 square miles, controlling trade, the distribution of food, matters of war and peace, and the lives of about 10,000 people. A number of smaller villages and hamlets along the Black Warrior River may have shipped food, raw materials, and other goods to Moundville's society and supplied labor upon demand.

About 3,000 burials have been unearthed at Moundville, only 100 of which (including men, women, and children) were associated with exotic grave goods. Among the other burials, men (perhaps artisans) were found with their tools and children with their toys. One woman was found with a corncob in her mouth. The fine goods produced by Moundville artisans, especially their ceremonial weapons and pottery vessels, were prized not only by local residents but also by other Mississippian peoples with whom they traded.

Etowah, on the banks of the Etowah River near Cartersville, Georgia, was settled about A.D. 1000 and continued as an active center for five centuries. A deep moat encircled the village, reaching from riverbank to riverbank and enclosing 52 acres; inside the moat was a palisade with bastions, making the village almost invulnerable. On the highest mound (63 feet) a clay ramp with steps led to a 1 1/2-acre platform top and a temple that may also have been the ruler's residence. There, at the summer solstice, the priest-ruler and his associates could turn to the east and watch the sun rise through a sharp notch in the Allatoona range.

A smaller platform mound was a mortuary structure where more than 500 society leaders were interred, buried in elaborate costumes and accompanied by special grave goods, among them the much admired marble mortuary figures of a man and a woman. The sequential burials over a long span of time have revealed marked changes in the diet, dress, trade, and social and religious practices of the people of Etowah.

Perhaps the most puzzling of the Mississippian centers is Spiro, located along the Arkansas River in eastern Oklahoma. The site, first substantially occupied around A.D. 900, spreads over an area of 80 acres and has 9 mounds. One of these is the great Craig Mound, which is composed of four conjoined conical mounds, the largest of which covers the remains of a charnel house. In the early 1930's Craig Mound was practically hollowed out by looters, and its yield was of such unparalleled richness — with magnificent stone effigy figures, wooden mortuary figurines, copper breast-

The modern world hardly intrudes at Moundville, which borders the Black Warrior River. From the top of its great mound (capped by a reconstruction of a temple) one can envision the town as it must have been, with houses atop the lesser mounds, people occupied in everyday pursuits, dogs barking, children playing, guards posted along the palisade, and the air pungent with woodsmoke. The carved diorite bowl below, with a crested wood duck on the rim, is from Moundville. Arresting in its elegant simplicity, it is an outstanding example of early North American art.

plates, masks, and headdresses, and intricately engraved shell cups — that newspapers advertised it as a new King Tut's tomb.

Archeologists attempting to salvage what remained found a great mortuary for the elite. The most prestigious burials were on cedar pole litters that were heaped with their personal possessions; some litters would have required at least four men to carry them. An unusual discovery was that skulls, teeth, hands, and long bones of the deceased were cared for separately. Among the grave goods were engraved shells, some of which depicted skulls and human body parts, and embossed copper objects showing costumed impersonators of such war-related symbols as the falcon and the antlered serpent. Because of the strange finds and the particular symbolism of the Spiro mortuary art, it has been suggested that somewhere between A.D. 1200 and 1350 Spiro became the major ceremonial center for clan groups who devoted an unusual amount of time and respect to mortuary ceremonial functions for their elite.

Sometime around 1400, well before the arrival of the Europeans, these great centers and others began to decline, as Cahokia had. The Mound Builders did not disappear. But their structured, centralized societies, which in some areas had almost reached the status of chiefdoms, broke down. The centers were gradually abandoned, and most of the Mississippian peoples returned to a simpler way of life. What had happened is a mystery still to be solved. But their decline was hastened after 1500 by the spread of European diseases and the establishment of trading post economies.

The great earthworks of the Adena, the Hopewell, and the Mississippians remain, haunting monuments of vital, complex cultures we may never fully comprehend. In a very real sense the Mound Builders took their secrets with them to the grave.

ANCIENT ARTISANS AND MASTER BUILDERS

A LEGACY OF BEAUTY

In 1520 the city of Brussels played host to the world's first display of American art. It was the treasure of Moctezuma, gifts from the Aztec emperor that Cortés had recently sent home to his sovereign, Charles V. Among the curious visitors was the German artist Albrecht Dürer. To him these works of gold, silver, and featherwork were "more beautiful to behold than things of which miracles are made." To this diary entry he added: "And I have seen nothing in all my livelong days which so filled my heart with joy as these things." He was simply astounded by "the subtle genius" of the New World artisans.

For Dürer, who was normally reticent and matter-of-fact in his writing, such language was uncommonly effusive. He was clearly fascinated by the sudden apparition of these objects, as strange-looking to him as if they had originated on another planet. At the same time, the expressive power of Aztec art, along with its richness and its superb workmanship, surely excited the artist in him — just as these qualities exhilarate art lovers today.

The art created by the ancient Americans is not only the most beautiful and perhaps most lasting of their accomplishments, it is also among their most awesome achievements. These gifted peoples excelled at every medium they turned their hands to. They produced an infinite variety of exquisite textiles, many of which were superior to those of contemporary Old World manufacture. The intricacy and delicacy of much of their work in gold, which often requires a magnifying glass to appreciate fully, dazzled and impressed Europeans of the day. The craft of featherwork they developed into a high art that is unique to them.

Most amazingly, with more than 2,000 years of artistic experience behind them, the tools they used remained simple, but their techniques were highly sophisticated. They created round, thin-walled pottery without the benefit of the potter's wheel. They had simple tools of copper but none of iron. Yet these technical handicaps seem only to have spurred them on to achieve the ultimate limits of manual skill. With nothing but stone chisels, wooden drills, and abrasive sands, they were able with deceptive ease to carve granite, basalt, and even jade into intricate shapes, finishing off surfaces with a high polish, in ways that have won the admiration of modern sculptors.

In their spacious cities and ceremonial centers the peoples of pre-Conquest America were surrounded by objects of beauty. Monumental sculptures of deities and heroes in wood and stone, terracotta and stucco, enhanced sacred precincts. Throughout the Americas the walls of sanctuaries were bright with murals celebrating the beneficence of the gods or the legendary feats of warlike princes. Ceremonial equipment such as masks, sacrificial knives, and ritual ceramic vessels provided another outlet for the artist, as did objects of personal adornment, the sartorial language of status so important to the ancient American elite. Here we find the elaborate ornaments of gold, silver, shell, jade, and other precious stones that so excited the lust of the Spaniards, as well as the extravagant featherwork and textiles that still amaze us with the richness of their color and technique. Art was also employed in equipping the dead, an industry in itself since many of the loveliest pre-Columbian works seem to have been created expressly for funerary purposes — such as the sumptuous Paracas mummy wrapping that appears on the previous two pages and much of what follows in this picture portfolio.

The demands for materials from which to create these works of art supported a brisk and diverse trade throughout the Western Hemisphere. Since Mexico had little natural gold, the Mixtec goldsmiths there had to obtain it from the south. The Peruvians obtained their turquoise, with which they encrusted their golden vessels, from Bolivia. The peoples of Panama, located between the two major core areas of ancient American civilization, traded with the Maya in one direction and with the Ecuadorians in the other. And in 1526, while seeking to reach the Inca Empire of Peru by sea, the Spaniards met a raft sailing north along the Pacific coast with a cargo of Peruvian pottery and metalware, bound no doubt for a trading center in Central America or Mexico.

Despite their apparent love of beauty, the meaning and function of art for the ancient Americans differed profoundly from ours. For them, virtually every object and image embodied a symbolic meaning related to the divine sphere. This supernatural reference extended even to the simplest-looking jade pendant, or feline pattern woven into a length of cloth, or puppy modeled in clay. Nor did the use of humble materials such as cloth or clay signify that a work of art was any less precious in their eyes than if it had been made of jade or gold. Our distinction between "arts" and "crafts" would have been incomprehensible to the ancient Americans, to whom all materials were equally expressive of religious truth.

This tiny silver Inca doll, costumed in textiles and feathers, was found next to the mummified body of a royal child left to die as a sacrificial victim in the cold, thin air of the Chilean Andes.

Yet the continual reference to the supernatural — the purpose of which was to explicate the divine sphere and thereby magically to influence it — often makes pre-Columbian art difficult to interpret. The ancient Egyptians produced a Book of the Dead, which explains the different meanings of their funerary images. The ancient Americans left us no such guide; and we may therefore never fully know what their art might be able to tell us across the gulf of centuries.

A different kind of barrier until recently was that pre-Columbian art, especially figural art, did not conform to European standards of esthetic beauty. It was

one thing to admire its technical virtuosity. It was quite another to accept it as art. To the 17th-century Spanish historian Juan de Torquemada, the fantastic demons so conspicuous in the imagery of the conquered Indians were "the hideous reflection of their own souls," and it was his Christian duty to eradicate them. In fact, the destruction continued for centuries after the Conquest. As late as the 1850's, beautiful pieces of pre-Columbian gold were routinely melted down for bullion at the Bank of England in London, at the rate of several thousand pounds' worth every year. In Panama until quite recently similar pieces were sold to dentists for gold fillings. Of the detailed inventories of the vast treasures shipped to Europe over generations, only a few objects have survived.

It has taken more than 400 years for the world to perceive pre-Columbian art the way Albrecht Dürer saw it. The great watershed was reached early in our own century when revolutionary ideas in European art, pioneered by such artists as Gauguin and Picasso, made people aware for the first time of the expressive power and artistic validity of forms of art that had until then been considered ugly and barbarous. The discovery of the beauty of African, Oceanic, and other "primitive" arts paved the way for an appreciation of pre-Columbian. As the remarkable subtlety and sophistication of this art became more clear, examples started appearing in chic art galleries rather than just in the musty showcases of natural history museums alongside shrunken heads and dugout canoes. From a lowly status as curios they advanced to elegant *objets,* eagerly sought by discriminating connoisseurs, ready to pay astronomical prices.

Pre-Columbian art has at last gained its rightful place in the record of man's creative spirit. Yet the change has heightened the problem of looting. Grave robbers ravage unexplored burial sites, scattering archeological evidence to the winds, wantonly destroying innumerable objects in order to seize the one that will fetch a high price on the inflated art market. For all that, the number of authenticated works steadily grows, as does the reputation of the host of anonymous artists of ancient America. A sampling of their spectacular work in different media is presented on the following pages.

High Artistry in Gold

"Sweat of the Sun," the Inca called it. And indeed, for the ancient Americans generally, gold was of divine origin, suited only for ritual use and personal adornment of the elite. Even the Spaniards occasionally recognized the beauty of what they were destroying. "I do not marvel at gold . . . ." wrote Spanish chronicler Peter Martyr. "But I am astonished to see workmanship excel substance."

How long ago the Indians learned their art remains a mystery, since goldsmithing's earliest known appearance in America more than 2,000 years before the Conquest finds craftsmen, equipped with rude tools, already fashioning gold sheet ornaments with astonishing skill. Later some also learned the art of casting by the lost-wax method, a technique widely known in the Old World. In this process the image is first modeled in wax and enveloped in a clay and charcoal mold. The mold is fired, the melted wax runs out, and molten gold is poured in, to create a perfect replica of the lost-wax original. The Renaissance goldsmith Benvenuto Cellini is said to have admitted bafflement over a flexible little fish from America, part silver, part gold. The fish is long gone, but the few pieces that survive reflect a lost splendor of the goldsmith's art.

A ruler and attendants on a raft, below, are executed in the lively style of the Muisca of Colombia. The scene may represent a ceremony in which each new ruler, stripped and powdered with gold, cast offerings and then dove into a sacred lake. Rumors of this ritual gave rise to the Spaniards' dream of El Dorado, the Gilded One. At right is a cast gold ring by Mexico's supreme craftsmen, the Mixtec.

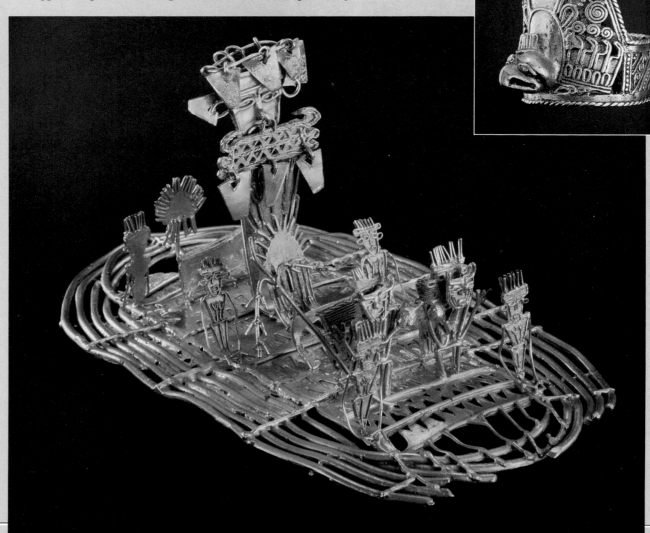

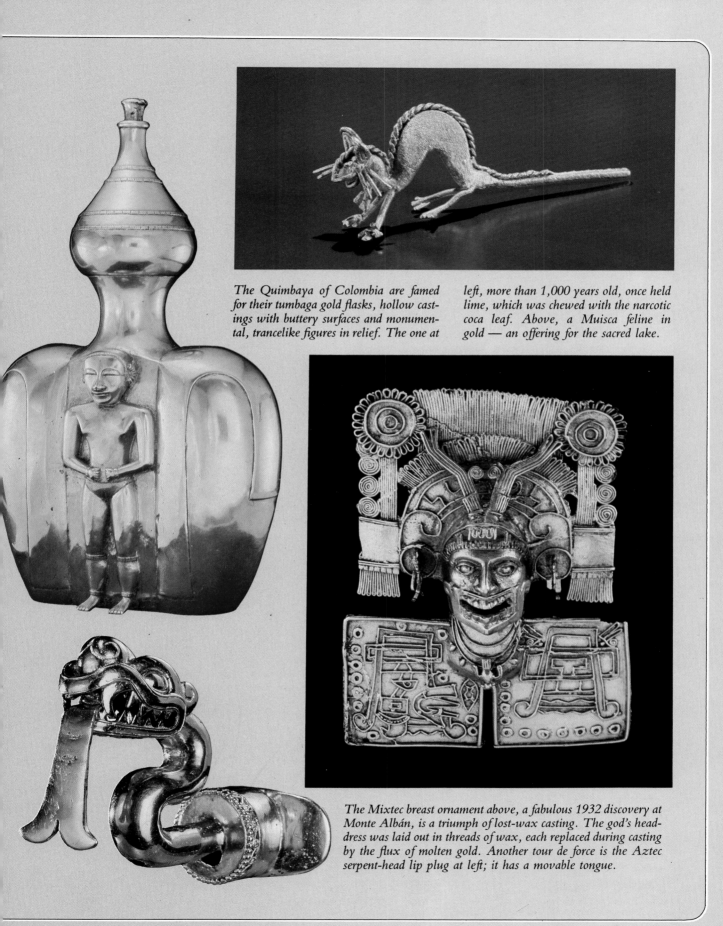

The Quimbaya of Colombia are famed for their tumbaga gold flasks, hollow castings with buttery surfaces and monumental, trancelike figures in relief. The one at left, more than 1,000 years old, once held lime, which was chewed with the narcotic coca leaf. Above, a Muisca feline in gold — an offering for the sacred lake.

The Mixtec breast ornament above, a fabulous 1932 discovery at Monte Albán, is a triumph of lost-wax casting. The god's headdress was laid out in threads of wax, each replaced during casting by the flux of molten gold. Another tour de force is the Aztec serpent-head lip plug at left; it has a movable tongue.

193

A Knowing Way with Alloys and Precious Stones

Archeologists believe that pre-Colombian goldworking got its start in Peru and spread north to Mexico, where it culminated in the exquisite jewelry of the Mixtec shortly before the Conquest. Each region along the way evolved a distinctive specialty. Among the Peruvians, who favored broad expanses of gold, the tradition of sheet metalwork continued, enhanced by cool accents of inlaid turquoise. Other craftsmen mixed gold with copper to create the alloy tumbaga, which has a lower melting point. They made it look like gold by removing the surface copper with acid, leaving a film of pure gold. In Ecuador, metalsmiths even learned to work platinum, whose high melting point was beyond the range of their simple furnaces. They did this by powdering gold and blending it with grains of platinum — a technique called sintering, which was mastered by Europeans only in the 19th century.

Turquoise inlay enriched much of the gold work of the pre-Inca civilizations of northern Peru. Three magnificent examples on this page include a bird-shaped ritual vessel (top), an embossed beaker with the image of a god (above), and a figurine of a similar design (right) with an openwork headdress that forms the handle of a ceremonial knife.

The Lambayeque burial mask above, 19½ inches wide, is of embossed sheet gold. The nose is a separate piece, attached with gold staples, as are the danglers over mouth and ears. The mask covered the face of a mummy and was painted red, the sacred funerary color in ancient America. The spectacular gold and silver nose ornament below, adorned with fox heads and shells of gold, was made in Peru before A.D 300. It is 8½ inches wide and was held in place by the clip at center.

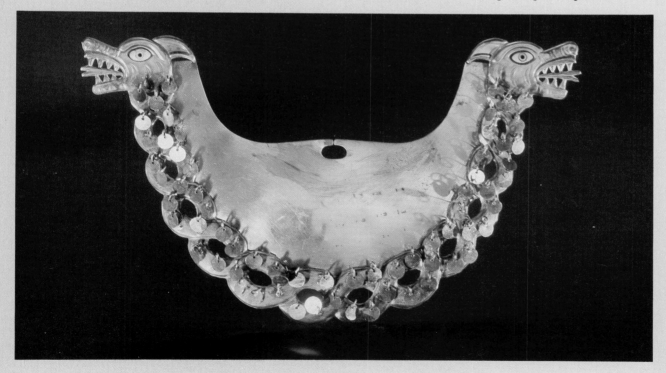

Jade: Sacred, Powerful, More Valued than Gold

Much as they appreciated gold, the substance prized above all others in pre-Columbian Mesoamerica was jade. With its subtle and varied ocean hues, ranging from deep blue-green to translucent emerald, jade was sacred, held to possess life-giving powers. It was also a status symbol, especially among the Olmec and later the Maya, who festooned their elaborate costumes with jade beads and even inlaid their teeth with jade.

Jade is an extremely hard stone, yet the ancient craftsmen handled the refractory material with deceptive ease, using only simple hand tools. To saw slices off the jade boulders they discovered in the mountains, they used flat pieces of wood or rawhide coated with quartz sand or other abrasives. To groove surfaces with curved lines, as on the serpent-head plaque below, they first drilled a series of shallow, close-set holes with fine, hand-twirled wooden drills dipped in abrasive, then rubbed down the ridges in between. To cut circular patterns or bore a hole clear through, they used various sizes of bamboo drills. The effort required immense labor as well as skill, but it resulted in some of the most exquisite creations of the lapidary's art.

Olmec craftsmen 3,000 years ago were creating powerful images of jade. The ceremonial ax head at right is a characteristic combination of the features of a jaguar and a crying baby.

The long-beaked bird pendant at left, not quite three inches high, was made in Costa Rica more than 1,000 years ago. The bird is more than it seems: it has human hands clasped on its breast and is perched on a tiny human skull. The Maya plaque above, carved with the emblem of the feathered serpent, is among the many treasures dredged early this century from Chichén Itzá's sacred well of sacrifice.

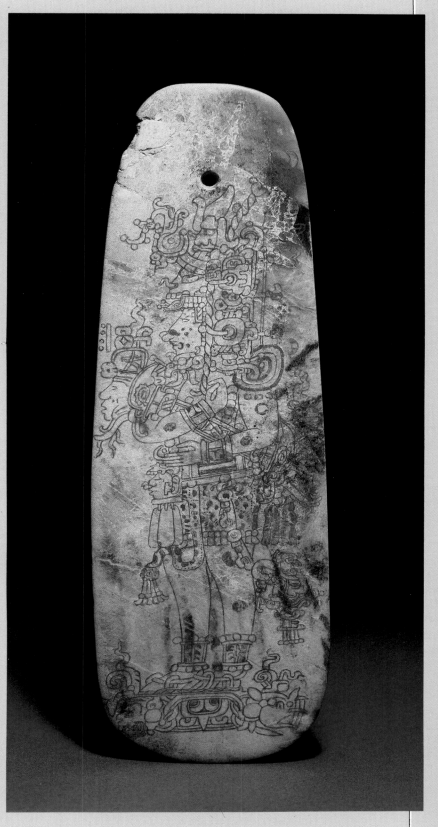

The jade sculpture on this page shows the range and versatility of the Maya's skilled gem cutters. The remarkable head at top is so lifelike that it could well be the portrait of an actual person. The grandee, above, strikes a pose often met with in Maya art; the plaque's irregular shape suggests that it is a fragment of a larger piece. The celt, or ceremonial ax, at right was incised with a tubular drill coated with jade sand to create the elegant figure of a Maya ruler. The red color is a later addition.

The Genius of Peru's Weavers

Ancient Andean textiles became world-famous after a sensational discovery in 1925 on Peru's arid Paracas Peninsula. A 2,000-year-old burial ground yielded 429 mummies, some wrapped in layers of cotton interspersed with fabulously embroidered cloth. The brilliant colors of the shrouds were perfectly preserved in tombs insulated from the desert sun. Minutely stitched in complex patterns, each must have taken years to produce — only to be hidden away in a grave.

Virtuoso spinners, dyers, and weavers, ancient Peruvian craftsmen practiced every kind of fabric construction known today; indeed, some of their techniques are too time-consuming to be used now, including the making of "double" and "triple" cloths and a unique method of interlocking tapestry construction for a more even surface. Tapestry weaving was a specialty; they used up to 500 threads per inch as against 85 in the best Renaissance work. No wonder the Spaniards mistook the finer Inca cottons for silk and recruited Indian weavers to create banners and church hangings.

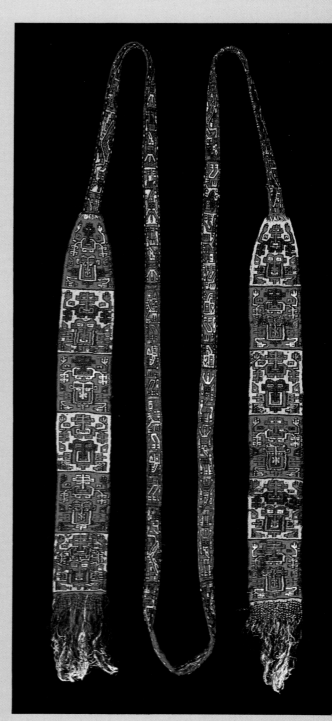

The border (left) of a cotton mantle from Paracas, embroidered with alpaca wool, shows stylized images of monkeys and tiny human and animal motifs. The richly colored headband, above, is from Nazca, farther south on Peru's coast. It is a piece of "triple cloth," a challenge for weavers.

A cat inside a cat inside a cat — or is it a bird deity? Such ambiguous creatures are typical in Paracas embroideries. So is the uncertainty as to the figure's meaning. Equally puzzling is the whimsical fruit tree made of cloth, below, with a human figure in its branches. It comes from a tomb in Chancay farther up the coast. A four-pointed Wari hat (below right), from central Peru, is a fine specimen of tapestry and dates from before A.D. 1000.

Magnificent Creations of Fragile Featherwork

The magnificent headdress of irridescent green shown below and the shield opposite may be the only survivors from that sumptuous treasure that Cortés sent to Spain's sovereign. The headdress, made of the tail feathers of the rare, greatly coveted quetzal bird (see sketch opposite), is a stunning specimen of Aztec featherwork. Such creations were strictly for the elite and achieved a high level of refinement.

In battle array, chieftains cut splendid figures in their multi-hued featherwork suits. Hangings, resplendent with images of birds, flowers, and insects, glowed on the walls of Moctezuma's palace. In that instance the feathers came from royal aviaries, where 300 attendants took care of a vast collection of birds whose bright plumage was converted into featherwork — so the Spaniards reported — by Moctezuma's wives and concubines. Because of its fragility, very little of this art has survived. That the royal headdress did so is a small miracle. For generations after the Conquest, it belonged to the dukes of Tyrol, whose children are said to have worn it at costume parties. Only in the past century did it find a safe haven in a Vienna museum.

Four feet high, the plumes of Moctezuma's headdress are woven into cloth and are set off by a brilliant blue fringe of cotinga feathers and by bands of tiny gold plaques. The headdress once sported a golden bird's head mounted in the center.

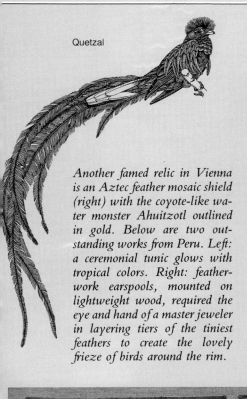

Quetzal

Another famed relic in Vienna is an Aztec feather mosaic shield (right) with the coyote-like water monster Ahuitzotl outlined in gold. Below are two outstanding works from Peru. Left: a ceremonial tunic glows with tropical colors. Right: featherwork earspools, mounted on lightweight wood, required the eye and hand of a master jeweler in layering tiers of the tiniest feathers to create the lovely frieze of birds around the rim.

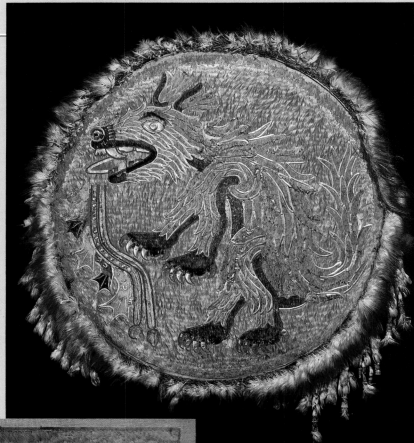

Rare Masterpieces in Perishable Wood

When we think of early American sculpture, we seldom think of wood, since little remains of the art works made in this perishable medium. Yet wood was widely used wherever there were forests. Finely carved wooden lintels were often incorporated into stone temples, and wooden images of gods and men adorned cities and sanctuaries.

Wood carving was probably a flourishing tradition for many centuries before artists plucked up their courage to attack solid stone with their simple tools. The shape of certain pre-Colombian stone structures seems to point to a heritage from wood. One authority on the Olmec surmises that their stone work developed out of wood carving, adding that it is possible the Olmec would have fashioned wooden steles akin to the totem poles of the Pacific Northwest coast. Indeed, wooden objects provide the few artistic links between the high civilization of Mesoamerica and the less complex societies of the Southeast. Today only a handful of masterpieces survives to recall a lost art.

The carved, painted board at left, from the south Peruvian coast, has human figures on top and birds down one side. Such ornate boards have been found next to mummies in Inca-period tombs. The regal Maya figure above, 22 inches high and made of tough sapote wood, is more than 1,000 years old.

The life-size Maya funeral mask at right, showing traces of original paint, once covered the face of a buried ruler. An idealized portrait, the mask is also meant to reflect the dignitary's divine attributes. As in all such funeral masks, the eyes are sealed.

An unusual North American artifact, this expressive hardwood panther from Key Marco, Florida, was found preserved underwater, the product of a culture dating back at least 1,000 years. The Aztec drum at right, in the image of an owl's head, is slotted to produce different notes when struck with rubber-tipped sticks.

Mosaic: A Miniaturist's Art

For the ancient Greeks and Romans, mosaics were designed to be spread across such large surfaces as walls and floors. For the early Americans, by contrast, mosaic was a way of decorating small portable objects such as masks, mirrors, pendants, and ear ornaments.

Mosaic was a miniaturist's art, a jeweler's art; and the materials used were accordingly rare and precious — turquoise, jadeite, obsidian, malachite, lignite, pyrite, garnet, beryl, lapis lazuli, mother-of-pearl, and seashells in a rainbow of colors. Each tiny chip was painstakingly shaped to fit alongside its neighbors and glued to backing that was usually of wood. Here again the ancient artisans dramatically display their familiar qualities of limitless patience combined with unwavering standards of craftsmanship. Mosaic was a Mesoamerican specialty, and the Mixtecs were the most accomplished mosaicists of all. One Mixtec ceremonial shield, less than a foot in diameter, is estimated to contain more than 14,000 chips, each separately cut and fitted. Unfortunately, only a few of these fragile, jewellike works have survived, mostly by virtue of having been sent home by the Spaniards as souvenirs.

The image at left of a man's head inside a wild boar's jaws was perhaps meant to convey the ferocity of Mexico's warlike Toltec. The intricate mother-of-pearl inlay is less than six inches high. The heavily restored mirror-back above dislays an elegant design in turquoise, pyrite, and mother-of-pearl. Dated about A.D. 1000, it comes from Peru.

The sinuous double-headed serpent at left was made by Mexico's renowned Mixtec craftsmen a century or so before the Conquest. A mosaic in turquoise and shell laid over hollow wood, the breast ornament is 17 inches wide.

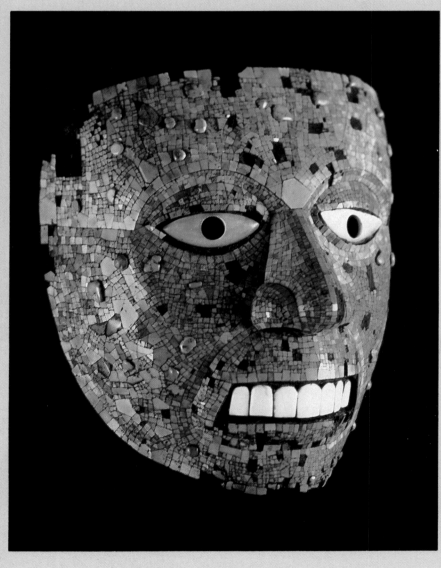

The mosaic burial mask at left was fitted together out of hundreds of tiny pieces of turquoise by Mixtec craftsmen for their Aztec employers. Eyes and teeth are of shell. The crouching-man knife handle, above, is also Mixtec work. Such ceremonial knives may have been used in human sacrifices.

Recording the Past in Picture Books

Among the most remarkable works in the legacy of the ancient Mesoamericans are the codices — books of deerskin or bark paper, made to open and close like folding screens. At one time there were hundreds of these rich displays of hieroglyphs and minutely detailed pictures; only 16 traditional codices survive, a few in fragmentary form. Some codices, notably those produced by Mixtec artists, are picture histories of ancestral rulers. Other codices are less easily defined. They may describe the geography of a region, establishing the territorial claims of the ruling class; depict mythological events; or set forth the calendars of religious ceremonies. Most likely the codices were made for the use of priests and rulers. Clearly, they are instructional, because everything in them has been subordinated to the aim of recording and conveying information. This is one source of their charm. Aztec scribes continued to make codices after the Conquest, and these, with Spanish captions alongside the native symbols, have become source books of ancient Mesoamerican history.

The detail from an Aztec codex at right shows the patron god of merchants with his attribute — a cross (representing a crossroads, where he will offer protection); the footprints, of course, symbolize travel. Behind him comes a merchant, carrying his precious cargo of quetzal birds to market.

The facsimile of a post-Conquest Mixtec codex below is opened to display four of its 52 pages, designed to be read from right to left. The page at far right shows how the world's original chaos was put into sacred order, thus setting the stage for civilized life. Divine spirits are depicted performing the necessary rituals in front of dwellings and mountain peaks (one of which sports the face of the rain god). The other pages catalogue actual Mixtec place-names — towns, hills, rivers, etc. — which may have just gained their identities through supernatural dispensation. On the left-hand page, column two, at top, the blue trough with a female standing in it represents a specific river. Farther down, the two quartered circles stand for two actual market places.

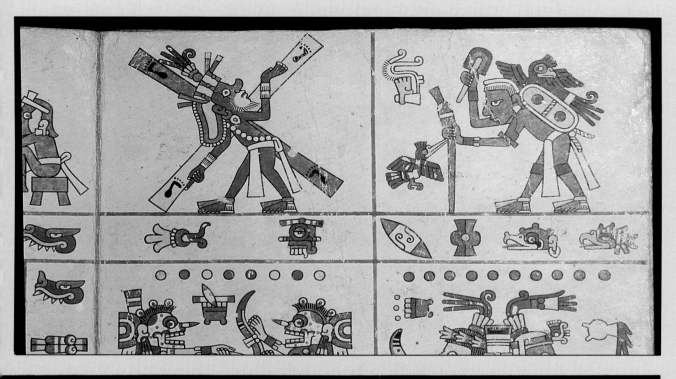

Drama in Glowing Colors by Unknown Masters

European art lovers in the 1880's were overwhelmed by their first glimpse of Nazca slip-painted pottery. The Nazca pots, their lustrous surfaces glowing with many different colors (right), helped bring about a new appreciation of pre-Columbian art. Maya painting has had perhaps an equal impact. Even on an object as unpretentious as the clay jar below, the lively rhythm of the figures, their easy naturalness, and the bravura rendering of costumes and glyphs reveal a stunning sophistication on the part of Maya painters 10 centuries ago. The biggest revelation has been the great Maya murals. The one opposite, discovered at Cacaxtla in 1975, may record an actual event: a violent battle scene, with elaborately accoutred warriors locked in furious combat. Cacaxtla is in the Mexican highlands, far from Maya territory, and the style, although predominantly Maya, is blended with influences from other cultures. Even so, the richness of the composition, the grandeur of the individual figures, and, not least, the magnificence of the color place these murals among the world masterpieces of ancient art.

A luminous Nazca effigy jar (right) displays the south-Peruvian ability to produce vibrant color. The two-foot-high vessel portrays the god of water; at center is an otter with streams of water issuing from its mouth. Trophy heads decorate the base.

A deer carried home after a hunt is depicted on the Maya cylindrical vase at left; the procession of hunters circling the vase is shown in the "roll-out" photograph above. What seem to be such daily life scenes as warriors in combat, ballplayers in action, and priests at ceremonial rites are actually renderings of Maya mythology.

In the recently discovered Cacaxtla murals, three details of which are shown on this page, warriors in jaguar costume — perhaps representing a highland tribe — fight against warriors in eagle costume, possibly lowland invaders. At top, an imposing eagle warrior stands guard, his taloned feet on a feathered serpent. Above, a jaguar defender turns to the attack to help win the final victory. At right, a border features realistic marine creatures, a typical highland motif.

Sculptors in Clay: Bridging the Centuries

Some of the greatest artists of the ancient Americas worked in clay. The challenge of firing hollow clay figures, sometimes life-size, without cracking them in the kiln called for technical skill of a high order. The finished works are amazingly vital and expressive, whether rigid, stylized images from western Mexico (below) or realistic portraits from Peru (far right). Vast quantities of clay sculpture were produced in every period, and since clay is durable and the Spaniards had no interest in the objects themselves, a great number have survived. They are the staple of many modern collections. But what purposes did these clay sculptures serve? Some, particularly the larger figures, stood in temples as cult images. The rest, for the most part, were evidently made to serve as tomb offerings to participate in the deceased's rite of passage into the afterlife. Yet through their very attention to detail, the ancient sculptors inadvertently provided us with a picture of the way people then looked and even how they lived. Beyond art, these works are social documentaries, all the more valuable in the absence of written literature to preserve their world for posterity.

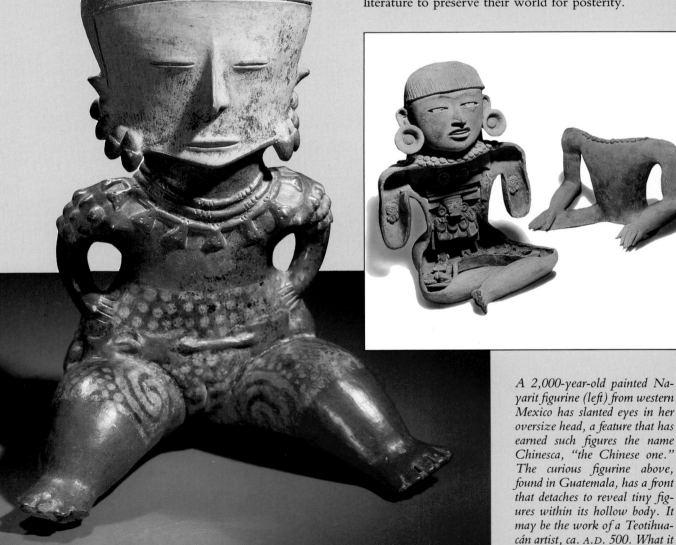

A 2,000-year-old painted Nayarit figurine (left) from western Mexico has slanted eyes in her oversize head, a feature that has earned such figures the name Chinesca, "the Chinese one." The curious figurine above, found in Guatemala, has a front that detaches to reveal tiny figures within its hollow body. It may be the work of a Teotihuacán artist, ca. A.D. 500. What it represents is a total mystery.

A Peruvian ritual vessel, left, heavily restored, shows a seated god or chieftain being served by women and shaded by a canopy held high by retainers. It is dated prior to A.D. 800. A formidable lady (below left) from Veracruz (7th century A.D.) gives useful clues to women's costumes in ancient Mexico. The handsome stirrup spout jug from Peru below, perhaps 1,500 years old, is one of the famous Moche portrait-head vessels, which are thought to picture actual individuals.

Sculptors in Stone: Creating a Pantheon

Stone sculpture brings us close to the religious world of the ancient Americans. Figures like those shown here did not just portray deities; they were imbued with a divine power of their own. The Spaniards, understanding this only too well, destroyed or buried every statue they laid hands on. Even then, they were never certain that the old idols had lost their potency. As late as 1823, when the authorities allowed the gigantic earth-goddess Coatlicue (far right) to be exhumed to make a plaster cast, they quickly reburied her so as not to arouse the peasants. Today the excitement is more apt to be esthetic rather than religious. The gifted craftsmen often chose the hardest stone to work with; yet their creations are all the more forceful because of the restrictions imposed by simple tools. "Mexican sculpture," said the modern sculptor Henry Moore, "seems to me to be true and right. Its 'stoniness,' by which I mean its truth to material, its tremendous power without loss of sensitiveness . . . make it unsurpassed in my opinion by any other period of stone sculpture."

An Aztec water goddess (left) in basalt adopts the same kneeling posture that Mexican Indian women long did in the churches of their new religion. From Guatemala's highlands comes an acrobatic little figure (above) balancing a hemispherical object on the soles of his feet. The same object appears in other small carvings of the region. Most likely, archeologists believe, it represents a mushroom cap, and the image is a ritual object of an hallucinogenic cult.

The sensitively carved head at top left, possibly the Maya maize god, was once attached to a temple at Copán, Honduras. The appealing little dog lifting its muzzle to the moon (left) is not what it seems. It is the Aztec's mythical doglike water creature sculpted in volcanic stone. The horrific figure of the earth goddess Coatlicue (above), 8½ feet tall, once stood in a temple in the Aztec capital, Tenochtitlán. She has two rattlesnake heads where her human head should be and a necklace of human hearts and chopped-off hands with a skull for a centerpiece.

A TESTAMENT IN STONE

We lived in the ruined palace of their kings; we went up to their desolate temples and fallen altars . . . ." So recalled John Lloyd Stephens, an American lawyer who plunged into the Mesoamerican forest in 1839 to begin exploring the great Maya ceremonial centers that so caught the imagination of his age. Uxmal, Copán, Chichén Itzá, Palenque — though glimpsed by the occasional curious traveler over the centuries, they had all been neglected; time and the luxuriant growth of the subtropics had entombed their colossal structures. But succeeding years were to see increasingly fervent probes into the pre-Columbian past, ranging from the scholarly to the larcenous. Discovery, rediscovery, and disinterment of ancient centers accelerated in virtually all parts of the Americas, where remnants of stone monuments yielded increasingly impressive testimony to the skills of vanished master builders.

Throughout the highland valleys and subtropical lowlands of Mexico and Central America, more and more centers of the Toltec, Mixtec, and Maya were located and researched. In Ecuador, Colombia, and Peru, a chance sighting could lead to discovery of a forgotten site high in the Andean cordilleras; an exploratory dig or a flood could expose evidence of a town, or even a previously unknown culture, remarkably hidden by rain forests. Like their counterparts in the cultures to the north, the Moche, Chimú, and Inca peoples of Peru apparently devoted a great deal of their time to construction and renewal of the public buildings that graced their cities and ceremonial centers.

This is an ancient world, festooned with ruins in stone — some so grand as to foster folk legends that they were built by supernatural beings, others so delicately carved and pierced with openwork that they appear to float in their environment. Not far from present-day Mexico City, the massive structures of Teotihuacán still attract tourists and scholars. An awesome religious complex, it dates back to the 1st century before the Christian era and was built by a people whose power and wealth were enshrined in legend by later generations of pre-Columbians. Tiahuanaco, its monumental stones indicative of a great and powerful culture, lies silent on the Bolivian *Altiplano* near Lake Titicaca. Confronted with these wonders, even the least imaginative of observers cannot help pausing to reflect and ask questions. What precisely were the religious concepts that motivated the construction of the huge temples and pyramids? Were these structures a source of pride for the commoner who helped quarry or haul the great slabs? Or were they symbols of authoritarian oppression? Did certain carved figures which may strike us as frightening or grotesque have that affect upon the men and women who apparently worshiped before them?

Only slowly are archeologists finding the answers to some of these questions; others will probably never be answered, because a key intellectual clue to an alien culture, the written record, exists only in difficult-to-decipher fragments for some pre-Columbian civilizations, not at all for others. This situation is in vexing contrast to our experience with ancient cultures in the Old World. So many tablets remain from Sumer that translators will be busy for decades, but the Inca, most powerful of ancient American empires, had no form of writing, nor did any other known South American culture. Although Maya hieroglyphs still exist in great number on steles and buildings, hundreds of written codices were destroyed during the Spanish Conquest. In recent years many glyphs have been translated but a great deal of scholarly detective work still needs to be done. The temptation is great, therefore, to invest an ancient pre-Columbian monument with meaning from our own perspective. The Governor's Palace at Uxmal, for example, strikes the contemporary critic as elegant in style, its long low facade an exercise in symmetry. Experts agree that the ruins of Palenque, at least from our point of view, are the most graceful of Maya survivals, employing a style that is less "ponderous," say, than that of the boldly soaring but heavy Temple of the Giant Jaguar at Tikal. Such judgments are harmless, so long as we remember that we have no indication that the architects of pre-Columbian America thought in such terms.

All we definitely know is that what we see, even physically, is not what a contemporary saw. Quite apart from the essential element of bustling crowds or hushed ritual groupings, most of the surviving stonework that pleases our taste for purity of line or truth to the material was, in fact, painted in bright colors or sheathed in gold, hung with extravagant tapestries, or roofed with elaborately plaited grass. The stone buildings of the Americas were obviously erected to last, and they were not, in their day, brooding, silent remnants standing stark against the timeless sky. Perhaps the best way to understand the stonework of pre-Columbian America is simply to look at the technique, for it is in every instance a tribute to ingenuity, resourcefulness, dedicated labor, and, most of all, patience. It was also fundamentally different from Western building tradition, since the 2,000 years of extensive building from approximately 500 B.C. to A.D. 1500 did not see the invention of the true arch nor, as is well known, the utilization of the wheel.

Nonetheless, as you will see on the following pages, pre-Columbian builders and craftsmen solved the practical problems of working in stone and used it for many purposes. The Inca, for example, had water and drainage systems that surpassed anything in medieval and Renaissance Europe, and their stone-walled agricultur-

An intricately carved stone doorway frames a view of the Temple of the Warriors at Chichén Itzá, Yucatán. Once roofed over, the columns at the base may have enclosed a council room.

al terraces were breadbaskets of sustenance and conquest. It was the skilled workmen in stone, too, who played a crucial role in what we would call the propaganda of the ruling aristocracy. The sculptured friezes of Maya structures show the ruling castes in their properly ordained place, sacrificing to the gods or dealing with prisoners of war. Inscriptions on steles, large freestanding stone slabs, glorify specific rulers by listing their dates and deeds. The faithful rendering of abstract geometric patterns, though the literal reference of the design is unknown to us, seems to be emblematic of cultural identity and political power. The state was triumphantly incarnate in stone.

Stone made possible the construction of permanent markers and observation platforms for celestial sightings — important for the study of the heavens to chart events in both the natural and supernatural worlds, closely bound together in the ancient Americas. The alliance between ancient astronomer and architect was close in other ways. For reasons not yet understood, for example, many Mesoamerican ceremonial centers are aligned in the direction of 15 to 20 degrees east of true north; other centers seem to be purposely aligned in some other direction. Moctezuma, the Aztec emperor, reportedly ordered an entire building dismantled because it was not in alignment with sunrise at the equinoxes. Clearly, it was prudent for masters of stone to confer in advance with astronomers.

Finally, the story of stonework in ancient America is again, as we have seen often throughout this volume, a story of cooperative effort. The work may have been grim or festive; we do not know. But it was always rigorously organized. We certainly see that a truly unimaginable number of man-hours went into the construction of the famed ancient centers. "In the midst of desolation and ruin we looked back to the past," wrote Stephens, "cleared away the gloomy forest, and fancied every building perfect . . . ." Upon the imposing armatures of civilization bequeathed to us by the ambitious architects of the ancient Americas, we may try to flesh out an imagined vision, but the message of the stones is perhaps the same as it was millennia ago: power, unity, obeisance to the spiritual.

Awesome Effort and a Shared Belief

In the high civilizations of ancient America, from Mexico to Peru, the state organized its citizenry for the building of massive pyramids, temples, and palaces. The sheer tonnage of earth removed, of rock transported and carved, of bricks dried in the sun never fails to astound the observer. In Mexico alone there may be as many as 100,000 pyramids still waiting to be uncovered. The number of ceremonial centers shrouded by forest in other parts of Mesoamerica or inundated by the desert sands in Peru must surely be large. Volume is as astonishing as number. Mexico's Cholula pyramid is the largest in the world. At Tikal, Guatemala, the tallest pyramid of the New World rises to 229 feet. To produce such impressive monuments required not only innumerable man-hours but a shared community belief, and almost all of the great structures of pre-Columbian times served a religious or political purpose. The pyramids were built as bases for temples, a possible attempt to make a connection between men on earth and the spirits of the unseen world. Perhaps to reinforce that idea, the great complexes seem to have been built with spatial relationships that have religious significance. These monuments did not stand unchanging, frozen once built; on the contrary, building seems to have been cyclical, succeeding generations adding their mark — often enclosing, or superimposing their own structures on, the works of their predecessors.

Monumental construction blends with vibrant detail in Mesoamerican architecture. At right, the Pyramid of the Sun at Teotihuacán, Mexico, required nearly a million tons of adobe for its 243-foot height, making it larger in volume than Egypt's Great Pyramid at Giza. The facade of the site's contemporaneous Temple of Quetzalcoatl (far right) is decorated with alternating serpent heads and images of a goggle-eyed rain deity. Below, careful planning shows in the Zapotec religious center at Monte Albán, which occupies a spectacular hilltop site painstakingly leveled some 2,000 years ago.

An Unexpected Variety in Decoration

Wildly phantasmagoric deities . . . convincingly naturalistic creatures of the forest . . . precisely repeated angular forms — the decorative stone sculpture of pre-Columbian cultures has finally come to be appreciated in all its unexpected variety, thanks to continuing excavation and expert restoration. Certain styles of ornamentation are readily identifiable by period and civilization; others show a myriad of influences.

The word "decorative" has a particular meaning in this context; whatever the fundamental esthetic appeal of a stone mosaic facade or a wall covered with realistically writhing serpents, the true function was likely to convey some message about the majesty and prestige of the state and its religion. The terrifying, vengeful statues of Aztec gods were surely meant to impress the pilgrim, the captive, or the ordinary citizen with the implacable power of their mighty empire. The strange carvings at Chavín, combining the purely imaginary with the exotic, conveyed a mystical meaning for the believer. Typically, the Inca produced relatively little decorative stonework, as if content to let the grandeur of their huge structures speak for itself. A 20th-century observer lacks the key to understanding the message of most pre-Columbian carving. Indeed, only a fragment remains, but this remnant documents a surprising flexibility within a unified style.

At left, the rich variety of Late Classic Maya style is expressed on the facade of the Nunnery Quadrangle at Uxmal, Yucatán, as boldly carved serpents undulate against repeated geometric forms. At nearby Sayil, above, a roughly contemporary carving shows a fantastic mask over a row of half columns.

The famous "mosaics" at Mitla, a Mixtec city, above, are actually chiseled stone plaques very precisely fitted to produce endless variations of the favored Mixtec stepped-key design.

Below, 20,000 dressed stones form the stunning mosaic frieze of the 322-foot-long Governor's Palace at Uxmal. Unfamiliar with the true arch, the Maya used a corbeled arch (center).

Massive Stoneworks Engineered with Precision

Supreme in Peru for less than a century, the Inca, sometimes called the Romans of the New World, nevertheless built monuments in stone that have rarely been surpassed for awe-inspiring bulk and precision of workmanship. The obvious question is still only partially answered: How did they do it with only simple tools, no wheels, and no draft animals?

A key to the answer lies in the organization of public labor for state projects. Recent evidence shows that Inca rulers carefully scheduled work parties, rotating workmen so that none would be overtired and all would share in the pride of building state monuments. Another clue: Inca patience and ingenuity. Stones were worked with stone hammers, a tediously slow process that included abrading the stone with a mixture of sand and water to create a smooth surface. To move the stones, many of them unbelievably heavy, large gangs of workmen must have pulled them slowly over surfaces that were artificially flattened or inclined, easing the journey with log rollers. Where interior building surfaces were rough, they were sometimes covered with a stucco wash for smoothness. Exterior walls were either squared off or laid in "courses," or rows, or were composed of polygonal blocks, which were worked until they fit neatly together in a jigsaw-like pattern, unique in world architecture.

The megalithic style of Inca masonry at Cuzco's great fortress of Sacsahuamán is shown at left below and, in detail, at right. Using stones as heavy as 200 tons and as tall as 16½ feet, its 15th-century builders made joins so tight that a knife cannot be forced between them. The enormous walls, up to 1,500 feet long, have withstood severe Andean earthquakes unscathed, but many of the buildings within the fortified area were destroyed by Spanish conquerors to eliminate a native defensive position and obtain building materials.

Below, the sturdy polygonal lower walls of Hatun Rumiyoc, a vanished Inca palace in Cuzco, feature a famous example of Inca craftsmanship: the 12-cornered stone in the right foreground. Typically, the wall inclines slightly inward, adding esthetic appeal as well as structural stability. The sharp contrast between precise fit and roughly textured surface was perhaps intended to emphasize the natural sculptural qualities of the individual stones.

Conquering the Mountains

Most Inca stonework, despite the romantic patina of age and legend through which we see it, was practical in nature. The lovely curved lines of agricultural terracing, for example, responded to the tremendous need for food of a state based on conquest. Huge stores of maize and other crops fed an army on the move or were warehoused against the frequent crop failures endemic to high-altitude farming. Built of rough fieldstone, the terraces sometimes inclined up hills as steeply banked as 60 degrees and alleviated the two chief problems of agriculture in an area with a harsh dry season — thin soil and inadequate moisture. These artificial fields were constructed by carrying topsoil and gravel, by hand, from the richer bottom lands to create a level environment suitable for growing maize, a crop essential for the making of *chicha*, a corn beer used in Inca rituals and feasts. To protect this precious crop against drought these terraces were often linked to elaborate canal systems.

The most famous slopes of terraces, at Pisac, near Cuzco, clearly produced more food than local villagers would need; surpluses must have gone to the national granaries. With their irrigation channels and economical use of land, the terraces were functional constructions, yet we can agree with the 19th-century observer who wrote, "No visitor can see them without being amazed at the skill, patience, and power to which they bear . . . a silent but impressive testimony."

Stone-walled farming terraces, known as andenes, *efficiently produced crops for the Inca state. Many of these intricately engineered fields, like those at 11,000-foot-high Pisac (left), are four or more centuries old and are still in use today.*

Machu Picchu, above, excites wonderment because of its dramatic, barely accessible Andean location and the absence of any reference to it in early Spanish accounts. Only rediscovered in 1911 and since reclaimed from forest overgrowth, its baths, drains, fountains, and administrative buildings attest to an exceptional building effort. It was probably a small but elaborate Inca town, seasonally used by the Cuzco elite but occupied yearlong by their retainers and local farmers.

Highways that Bound an Empire

The sprawling Inca empire was ruled with exemplary efficiency in part because of a superb highway system that included intermittently paved roads up to 24 feet wide, tunnels, bridges, and stepped pathways cut into living rock. The principal highland road, atop the spine of the Andes, ran 3,450 miles from the Colombia-Ecuador border to central Chile. Lateral roads linked it to the coastal highway, about 1,000 miles shorter. When necessary, the roads were raised upon causeways across marshy land — once for 8 miles. The thousands of bridges included pontoons, stone constructions using the corbeled arch, and rope bridges.

This extraordinary communications network was almost exclusively for official use: military movements, transport of supplies, and messages brought by relay runners. These young men, stationed in pairs along the highway about every 2 miles, conveyed their messages at an estimated speed of about 150 miles a day. Occa-

sionally, the luxury of fresh fish from the sea would be borne the 300 miles to Cuzco. Spaced along the road were resthouses with food and other supplies for those traveling on official business. Ironically, the very roadways that made it possible for the Inca to control their vast empire, rapidly moving an army to quell a rebellion, were the avenue of the empire's downfall, giving the Spanish conquistadors under Pizarro direct access to the heart of the kingdom.

Surviving stretches of the Inca highway network, at right and below, show the characteristic adherence to a straight line whenever the terrain permitted. The rocky paths in high mountain areas were quite adequate for a civilization that depended on human and animal transport rather than wheeled vehicles and are occasionally still in use in parts of Peru.

Literally breathtaking rope bridges like this one spanning the canyon of the turbulent Apurímac River were crucial in the Inca road system. Today's villagers rebuild it annually, using 22,000 feet of rope spun from grass.

Exploiting Water Resources

Water is vital to the growth and survival of civilizations. Many theories attribute the collapse of some ancient American civilizations to this powerful force; drought and flood have been advanced as reasons for the sudden disappearance of a city from the archeological record. Perhaps rightly so, for preoccupation with water as both a life-giving and a destructive force inspired many of the most remarkable and ingenious engineering feats of the pre-Columbian period. Each region had different problems. The porous limestone of the Yucatán, for example, does not hold water; it was necessary to settle near *cenotes,* or natural wells.

Swampy areas were reclaimed by both Aztec and Maya farmers, who heaped up islands in patchwork patterns in the marshes. Along the river edges of the arid Peruvian coast, successive civilizations constructed intricate canal systems for irrigation, drinking, and sanitation. Aqueducts that brought fresh water to the Inca in Cuzco still stand. On the coast, however, terrible failures occurred when the canal systems were disrupted by natural disasters, so the management and maintenance of this resource was crucial to survival. The collective effort needed to control water was no doubt the primary organizational concern in ancient America.

Mesoamerican skill in exploiting the available water supply took many forms. The aerial photo at right shows tracery remaining from irrigation canals and raised platform fields in marshland near Veracruz. Below right, a 19th-century lithograph portrays a 400-foot-deep natural well in the Yucatán. At left, the "floating gardens" near Mexico City are only remnants of vast agricultural islands built by the Aztec. Willows planted at the corners of a plot prevent erosion, and mud dug from the canal enriches soil.

The Celestial Vision of Ancient Americans

Ancient Americans lived close to the heavens. The night skies, without artifical light, were brilliantly clear. We know from surviving codices that wise men sat patiently, watching and calibrating the movements of the chief celestial objects and constellations. Their observations, made with the naked eye, and their calculations, made by horizon sighting with simple crossed–stick devices, were astonishingly accurate. The Maya, for example, who could successfully predict solar eclipses, determined the seasonal year to an equivalent of 365.2420 days; contemporary science calculates it as 365.2422 days. Such precision required years of collecting data and relatively sophisticated mathematics. Why this concentration upon the stars? The sightings, used to time planting and harvesting, were also incorporated into a formal rigid religious system. Consequently, calendars kept time but also glorified the deities. Even the great Moctezuma was required to offer incense to important stars "after dusk, at about 3 A.M., and immediately before dawn." Most astronomical records from pre-Columbian times have been destroyed or lost, but evidence being compiled by the new discipline of archeoastronomy indicates that man strove hard to live his life in harmony with the stars.

The Gateway of the Sun at Tiahuanaco, Bolivia, above, is one of the most puzzling relics of an unknown but obviously important pre-Columbian people. Winged figures and a staff god are carved on this single block of andesite in patterns suggestive of a calendar.

The Caracol, left, a Maya-Toltec building at Chichén Itzá, affords a view of the flat Yucatán countryside that would have facilitated horizon sighting and probably served as an observatory. Its windows may have been aligned with certain celestial events.

The famed calendar stone at right, almost 12 feet in diameter, represents the cyclical nature of Aztec cosmology. A mutilated deity (center) is surrounded by symbols for the four previous world ages and for the present age, whose sign is "Motion" or "Earthquake."

LOST
CITIES

A HIDDEN TOMB DISCOVERED

Deep within the pyramid that supports Palenque's Temple of the Inscriptions, an archeologist found the secret stairway to a royal Maya crypt. It rivals the tombs of Egypt's Pharaohs.

Among the 60 or so major Maya ruins known in Central America, none has held a greater fascination for travelers and archeologists than the hilltop ceremonial center known as Palenque. For Manuel Gamio, a leading Mexican archeologist in the early decades of this century, the ruins were nothing less than "an obsession"; and John Lloyd Stephens, a 19th-century American explorer, described the place as "unique, extraordinary, and mournfully beautiful." Brought to light more than two centuries ago, Palenque was the first site to make apparent the true measure of Maya social and artistic brilliance.

Palenque, or rather the ancient ruins that bear the name Palenque, for its true name is unknown, stands in southern Mexico, in the modern-day state of Chiapas, on what was the western frontier of the Maya domain. It is situated atop the first rampart of the rugged Sierra de Chiapas uplands, which are a transitional zone leading to the mountain chain that forms the backbone of Mexico and Central America.

Directly behind the complex of buildings, to the south, hills rise 820 feet to enclose much of the area in the lush green embrace of tropical forest. On either side, narrow passes lead back into interior valleys that are blessed with soils well suited to farming. Spreading out below Palenque to the north is a rich, swampy floodplain, covered by intermittent tropical forests and savannahs, underlain by a massive shelf of high-quality limestone that stretches some 50 miles to the Gulf of Mexico and the Yucatán. A narrow corridor of passable terrain skirts the base of the Sierra de Chiapas to put Palenque in a favorable position for overland trade and commerce, and a system of rivers, including the Usumacinta River, gives the center access by canoe to other Maya centers in the lowlands.

Living conditions at Palenque present many challenges, not the least of which is the abundant annual rainfall of more than 100 inches. There are two seasons here — a hot, rainy, tropical period that runs from May to December and a somewhat drier, windier one that accounts for the remaining months. In the rainy season Palenque is drenched for a part of each day, and even when the sun shines the high humidity keeps the atmosphere dank and steamy. At the same time, tem-

A life-size mosaic death mask is believed to reflect the somber countenance of Lord Pacal, Palenque's ruler from A.D. 615 – 683. Made from more than 200 pieces of jade with shell and obsidian eyes, the mask was discovered in his tomb in 1952.

peratures hover around an average of 83 degrees. In the drier months the *nortes,* cold gales that sweep down from the north and the Gulf of Mexico, periodically rattle trees and buildings with their force. "This climate," wrote one 18th-century traveler, "drains a man's strength, and kills women during their first child-bearing. The oxen lose flesh, cows their milk, and the fowl cease to lay eggs."

In such a climate insects and other pests flourish. Stephens found the *garrapatas,* or ticks, so numerous that it was all he could do to brush them off by the handful. Mosquitoes were "beyond all endurance"; although he devised ingenious defenses against them and covered every part of his body even in suffocating heat, he could not protect himself from constant assault. Dreadful pests called *niguas* burrowed into the flesh causing excruciating pain and infections, and black flies "left marks like the punctures of a hundred pins." In between times, scorpions, snakes, and bats threatened the comfort and safety of the 19th-century visitor — and possibly of the ancient Maya before him.

First Settlers

Presumably, it was the combination of favorable farming land, accessibility by land and water routes, and defensibility of the site that attracted Palenque's original settlers to this location, but precisely when they came or who they were is largely conjecture. One seemingly substantial clue comes from linguistic analysis: the study of various regional Maya languages and the reconstruction of what may have been the original ancestral Maya tongue. Employing techniques similar to those used to trace back to the common roots of the German, Dutch, and English languages, Norman A. McQuown, professor emeritus of anthropology and linguistics at the University of Chicago, has discerned a group speaking what has come to be identified as the distinct Cholan language. This group, he has proposed, broke away from their Maya homeland in the highlands of western Guatemala sometime between 1000 and 500 B.C. to find its way northwest to the Chiapas highlands. A version of Cholan, known as Chol, is still spoken in those highlands.

Current archeological evidence indicates that the first settlement at Palenque occurred sometime prior to A.D. 200, but for the next few centuries until well into the Classic era the center remained nothing more than a minor site. Then, sometime around 600, an ambitious building program was set in motion — evidence that the people of Palenque had set their sights on grander things. Magnificent temples, ceremonial courts, and palace complexes; sublimely decorated tablets and staircases; and extraordinary *cresterias,* or roof combs, came to symbolize the wealth and brilliance of what is believed to have been one of the four principal regional centers of the Maya realm in Classic times. The center grew to occupy some six square miles and to serve a population of perhaps 20,000, about half that of Tikal,

the most populous Maya center.. The initial burst of growth coincided with the coming to maturity of Lord Shield Pacal, Palenque's longest-living, and by all accounts greatest, dynastic ruler.

Thanks to the local practice of recording dynastic history in detail on tablets set on walls of new buildings rather than in the more abbreviated notation on steles, an innovation apparently begun in Pacal's time, archeologists have been able to discover more of the political, cultural, and architectural development of Palenque than of any other Maya site. According to Linda Schele and Peter Mathews, specialists who have devoted years of intense study to deciphering the inscriptions at Palenque, Pacal was born in A.D. 603, acceded to power in 615 at the age of 12, and reigned successfully until his death in 683, nearly seven decades later.

His most important building was the magnificent Temple of the Inscriptions, but other structures are credited to his reign. They include the Temple of the Count and the Temple Olvidado, both completed sometime before 648 and possibly dedicated to Pacal's mother and father, and a substantial part of Palenque's administrative center, the so-called Palace. Notably, the architecture of these buildings and those built by Pacal's descendants exhibited an innovative technique for the support of walls. A variation on the corbel-vault structural system, it allowed for thinner load-bearing walls, wider and more numerous doorways, and the enclosing of a greater volume of interior space. There is no direct evidence that Pacal originated the unique style that has come to be identified with Palenque, but his personal and political power are evident in the grand landscaping that preceded the building of each of his temples: virtually every one of them stands upon a hillock shaped by man to greater or lesser degree. The Palace complex, for example, rises from an artificial mound 300 feet long, 240 feet wide, and 30 feet high.

Pacal was succeeded by his son Lord Chan-Bahlum ("Snake-Jaguar"), who was 48 when he came to power and 66 when he died in 701. Chan-Bahlum, who is portrayed as having six toes on each foot, perhaps to the Maya a sign of divinity, built the temples of the Cross, the Foliated Cross, the Sun, and Temple XIV.

Chan-Bahlum was succeeded by his younger brother Kan-Xul. The new ruler devoted his energies to the enlargement and embellishment of the Palace complex, probably including the unique four-story tower that may have served as an astronomical observatory or a defensive structure. A stone tablet at Toniná depicts the humbled Palenque ruler as a captive, suggesting what might have happened to Kan-Xul. Late in his life he must have led an unsuccessful battle against a southern neighbor. After serving Palenque for perhaps 18 years — the dynastic records are somewhat clouded — he was succeeded briefly by another brother, Xoc, who lived but a year and a half.

Records are imprecise at this point and little is known of the next several decades at Palenque. Then,

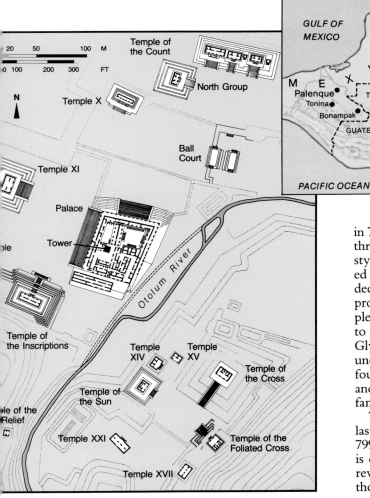

The hauntingly beautiful city of Palenque rises majestically out of a lush, tropical forest in the Chiapas highlands in the western quadrant of the Maya territory (see map, near left). This sprawling center (see plan, far left) was designed with great attention to natural land forms — the pyramids echoing the mountains behind. The Temple of the Inscriptions (above, left) and the Palace (above, right) are considered to be among the most important Maya architectural achievements thus far discovered by archeologists.

in 764 Lord Kuk, great grandson of Pacal, assumed the throne, to reign for at least one *katun,* as the Maya styled 20-year periods. Kuk, whose name is represented by the symbol of the quetzal bird, presided over a declining Palenque; he inaugurated few new building projects save some minor additions to the Palace complex before his death. His most significant contribution to Maya history is the now famous "Tablet of the 96 Glyphs." More than 1,000 years later this tablet was uncovered at the base of the tower, and archeologists found the most complete genealogical record of Kuk's ancestors reaching back well before Pacal's time to the family's mythical roots.

The glory years, however, were all in the past. The last dated event in Maya Palenque was the accession in 799 of a ruler known as 6 Cimi Pacal. This title, which is derived from the birth date of the new ruler and a revered ancestor, reveals a new naming pattern and is thought to show foreign contact, but the nature of the

Renowned British Mayanist Alfred P. Maudslay took the photograph above of the Palace tower in 1891. Probably built by Kan-Xul, Pacal's second son, about A.D. 721, it may have served as an observatory for viewing the winter solstice. The four-story tower today (right), which was meticulously restored in the 1950's, is unique in Maya architecture.

cultural influence is not known. In any event, no new construction was begun after 800, and by 820 Palenque's ruling lords had abandoned the center. Inexorably, the jungle began to repossess the land and the buildings in their faded grandeur.

In all likelihood, descendants of the Palenque Maya visited the site for decades after, just as local peasant populations visited other evacuated Maya city-states. J. Eric S. Thompson, a modern archeologist who devoted his career to Maya studies, believed that ceremonials and market days may have taken place at these collapsing centers long after the last nobility had disappeared. But as the wealth and organization to maintain the buildings no longer existed, they were simply allowed to deteriorate. In time Palenque was lost even to the local descendants of the ancient Maya, so that when Hernán Cortés passed within 30 miles of the place, none of the Indians interrogated about the region was able to tell him of Palenque's existence.

Meanwhile, life went on among the Chol Maya, who apparently continued to live in scattered settlements as subsistence farmers. At some unknown date a tiny village took shape on the lowlands about five miles from the old ruins. What the Indians may have called

their pueblo is not recorded by the Spaniards, who came later. The newcomers renamed it Santo Domingo del Palenque ("of the stockade") and erected a small church there about 1573. The name could also be a corruption of the name of the Maya demigod Xbalanque, a hero in Maya mythology. For almost 200 years Spanish priests and officials came and went without taking note of the ancient city above them. Around 1740 one Antonio de Solis was dispatched as curate to Santo Domingo del Palenque; then, ever so slowly, things began to happen.

The saga of discovery begins when Solis set about to create some new, more fertile farm land around the settlement. While exploring a ledge above the village, the Spaniard stumbled upon a pile of "stone houses" hidden from sight by the entangling jungle. One of Solis's nephews was so intrigued by the find that he was still talking about it when he went to study in Ciudad Real de Chiapas some years later. A fellow student, Ramón Ordóñez y Aguiar, heard the story and resolved to look into it. His opportunity came in 1773 when, as canon of the Cathedral of Ciudad Real, he was able to finance an expedition, led by his brother, to investigate the tale of Palenque's splendors.

The brother's report must have been evocative indeed, for the canon forthwith composed a *Memoria* to Don José Estachería, governor of Guatemala (of which Palenque and the state of Chiapas were then a part), urging him to look into the matter. The canon suggested that there might be great treasures buried among the ruins. After a delay of some 10 years, perhaps because of political troubles at home, the governor instructed the mayor of Santo Domingo del Palenque, José Antonio Calderón, to visit the site and report back. Calderón, who spent three days amidst the ruins in 1784, submitted an inventory of 215 "houses" plus a few rudimentary sketches. He offered the opinion that they had been built by the Romans, for had not Plutarch himself written that the "noblest of the Romans" wore sandals with half-moon motifs — precisely the decoration that appeared on reliefs at Palenque.

Dissatisfied with Calderón's conclusion, Estachería then sent the architect Antonio Bernasconi to investigate. In 1785 Bernasconi issued a lengthy report including the judgment that though there was a "somewhat Gothic" quality to the whole place, he could not associate the architecture with "any of those orders known to me, neither ancient nor modern." He did not, of course, think that ancestors of the Indians then living in the region had done the work. The document was eventually forwarded to Spain's Charles III, who was sufficiently intrigued to order that excavations begin.

Estachería now called upon Don Antonio del Río, a swashbuckling artillery captain with a great deal of energy but little in the way of antiquarian sensibilities to recommend him. Del Río arrived at his destination in early May of 1787, just as the rainy season was starting, and sought Calderón's help in hiring a team of Indian laborers. Calderón was able to muster 79 Chol-speaking Maya, 48 axes, and a few odd billhooks or brushcutters, and with Del Río at the head, the small army of despoilers took ancient Palenque by storm.

After two days of cutting, clearing, and brush burning, they finally gained access to the Palace complex. Then Del Río set upon the buildings with seven crowbars and three pickaxes. "By dint of perseverance," the captain later boasted, "I effected all that was necessary to be done, so that ultimately there remained neither a window nor a doorway blocked up; a partition that was not thrown down, nor a room, corridor, court, tower, nor subterranean passage in which excavations from two or three varas [approximately 5½ to 8 feet] were not effected."

As evidence of his thoroughness, the captain pried loose several sections of wall reliefs and dug up ceremonial offerings from three temples and sent them to Spain. By now Spain, like all Europe, had fallen under the spell of Romanticism, and while the crown always hoped to add treasure to its coffers, the notion of lost empires exercised a strong grip on the popular imagination. Del Río's finds eventually ended up in Spain's newly established Gabinete de Historia Natural, the

first Mexican art works to be so displayed in Europe.

The artillery captain's trophies were accompanied by a detailed report to Charles III. As unsophisticated as Del Río was, he was not impervious to the mysterious beauty of Palenque, and he advanced the opinion that "some one among the nations (Phoenicians, Greeks, Romans and others), pressed their conquests as far as this country, in which it is known they stayed no longer than the time it took for these Indian people to rework their inventions and crudely imitate such of their arts as they were prepared to teach them." Del Río thus allowed that Palenque was probably built by New World "barbarians" but with skills they had acquired from more-advanced Old World instructors.

Before anyone could act on Del Río's report, the king died. His successor, Charles IV, ordered that a complete survey of all of New Spain's antiquities be undertaken, and in 1805 Guillermo Dupaix, a retired officer of dragoons, began a three-year swing around Mexico in the company of the engineer-draughtsman Luciano Castañeda. Dupaix had the misfortune to travel at a time when Mexico was in the throes of a struggle that led to its eventual liberation from Spain, and he met with frequent hostility from both Indians and Spanish officials. On one occasion he was set upon by 30 Indians, who disarmed him and tied him up. As Dupaix recalled, "each of them vied with the others in pulling the ropes tight on each side of me, as though they meant to quarter me, and then they carried me, hoisted in the air, as if in triumph or apotheosis." An Indian elder interceded, and Dupaix was released unharmed. At Ciudad Real he met the aged Canon Ordóñez y Aguiar, who reportedly gave him some specimens of Palenque artistry. But before he could resume his journey to the Maya center, Dupaix was arrested by the Spanish authorities in the mistaken belief that he was really a Frenchman (Spain looked on France as its enemy after 100,000 Frenchmen had invaded Spain in March 1808). After enduring considerable hardship in jail, he was set free.

Early Theories About Palenque's Past

Dupaix, having traveled for three years among Mexico's ruins, was able to cast an experienced eye on Palenque's buildings, and he made careful observations of stonework, stucco, construction methods, and hieroglyphic style. For example, he recorded the presence of an ancient masonry bridge over the tiny Otolum River, which flows through the site. But his best guess as to the origins of Palenque was that refugees from the fabled island of Atlantis were responsible.

Rumors, wild guesses, and misinformation continued to bring adventurers and amateur antiquarians to Palenque in ever-growing numbers over the next few decades. One self-proclaimed authority assured his readers that Palenque was originally an Egyptian colony; another that the builders were members of the Lost Tribes of Israel; still another argued that the first inhabitants must have been Chinese of the T'ang Dynasty.

Undoubtedly one of the most picturesque characters to stake a claim to some knowledge of the place was an adventurer named Jean Frédéric Waldeck, writing under the questionable title of Count Waldeck. Waldeck, who claimed to be descended from a German noble family, had moved to France in his youth, ostensibly to study painting under the great Neoclassicists Jacques Louis David and Pierre Paul Prud'hon. Then in 1798 he had joined Napoleon's ill-fated Egyptian campaign, apparently as one of the corps of antiquarians and artists charged with surveying the ancient temples and other works standing along the Nile. Seized with the magic of exploration, Waldeck eventually went to Guatemala in 1821, then spent some years in London, where he was engaged by a British antiquarian to make lithographs of Del Río's original sketches of Palenque.

By Waldeck's account, "from the moment I saw the pen-and-ink sketches of that work . . . I nourished the secret desire to see the ruins of Palenque for myself and draw the originals." Eventually, Waldeck returned to the New World, where he found jobs managing a silver mine and working as a combination scene painter and bass singer in a traveling comic opera company. He gained the confidence of Mexican President Anastasio Bustamante, who gave him a permit and a small stipend to visit the ruins. In May 1832 the 66-year-old Waldeck set up housekeeping with a local girl in a thatch-roofed hut near the Temple of the Cross.

The count stayed for nearly two years, his idyll coming to an abrupt end when the Bustamante regime was overthrown. Summarily deported, the artist-antiquarian returned to France, where he published first an account of his Yucatán travels titled *Voyage pittoresque et archéologique* and subsequently, at the questionable age of 100, a more detailed description of Palenque.

Waldeck's *Voyage* probably appeared too late to influence the next historically important visitors to Palenque — John Lloyd Stephens and Frederick Catherwood — for they set out only a few months after the book first appeared in France. But the earlier reports of Del Río and some of the others, published in English in the 1820's, were more than enough to pique their interest. Stephens was then a 34-year-old New York lawyer-journalist with a considerable amount of experience in exploring Old World ruins. To finance the trip, the politically well-connected Stephens had himself appointed to President Martin Van Buren's special mission to the Central American Federation. His stated duties were to locate and make diplomatic contact with the officers of that shaky government, but from the start it seems to have been understood by all that the assignment was little more than a way to gain a measure of diplomatic immunity for the difficult trip. With utmost good sense, Stephens invited Catherwood along to record whatever he should find. Catherwood, six years Stephens's elder, was an English architect, professionally acquainted with such antiquities as Baalbeck, Jerusalem, and the ruins of ancient Egypt.

The "diplomats" arrived by ship at Belize, British Honduras, on October 30, 1839, and shortly began the arduous adventure that was to take them to what Stephens later described as "the crumbling remains of forty-four ancient cities . . . with but few exceptions, all were lost, buried, and unknown, never before visited by a stranger, and some of them, perhaps, never looked upon by the eyes of a white man."

After some five months of circuitous travel through Honduras and Guatemala, they came to the Mexican highlands above Palenque. To their dismay, they arrived in the rainy season, which made travel even more difficult than it had been. The road they followed was nothing more than a footpath threaded through dense jungle. At many places en route they had to dismount from their mules to pass under low-hanging branches or to negotiate steep and narrow stretches along the tops of 1,000-foot ravines. On one particularly frightening section of the trail, they resorted to being carried in slings borne by the more sure-footed native bearers in their party, but relying on Indians trembling with

New Maya Mystery

Situated in the Guatemalan tropical forest about 80 miles from Tikal, the most impressive Classic Maya center dating from the 7th and 8th centuries A.D., lies the latest piece in the challenging puzzle of Maya history — El Mirador, or "The Lookout."

This newly found city, much of which still remains unexplored, is dominated by three large pyramids: Danta, Monos, and Tigre, the last of which rises 183 feet above the canopy of trees. The magnificent 18-story Tigre surpasses Tikal's pyramids in size and is visible from miles around.

El Mirador was first discovered in the 1920's, probably by a group of botanists who went into the region, but it wasn't until the 1970's that archeologists began digging at the site. What they found seemed to contradict all notions of Maya history, for here was a pre-Classic city with huge pyramids, stone temples, causeways, and dwellings built specially for the Maya elite. What was surprising was the degree of sophistication that marked the architecture and the art. Recently archeologists unearthed a pottery shard dating from the 1st or 2nd century B.C. inscribed with the Maya symbol for "lord." All this seems to indicate that an advanced Maya civilization existed far earlier than archeologists and historians had dreamed — perhaps as much as five centuries before the traditional date ascribed to the start of the Maya golden age. As exploration continues and more and more information surfaces, El Mirador may cause historians to rewrite the Maya chronology.

Lord Pacal is depicted with his mother, Lady Zac-Kuk, on a stone tablet commemorating his accession to the throne. Seated on a jaguar throne, Pacal is shown accepting a headdress from his mother, who probably served as regent until his majority.

fatigue and fear proved even more unsettling than walking on their own feet. At length, Stephens and Catherwood descended to an open plain, where lay the village of Santo Domingo del Palenque. It consisted, wrote Stephens, "of one grass-grown street, unbroken even by a mulepath, with a few straggling white houses on each side. . . . It was the most dead-and-alive place I ever saw."

The explorers were initially met with indifference verging on hostility. None of the villagers cared to sell them supplies, and few even admitted to knowing of the ruins' existence. The visitors had a discouraging time hiring locals to help clear the site, but on the second day they located a colorful character who was not only familiar with the site but had some previous experience as a guide. He even affected a formal costume when performing the role. An earlier visitor to Palenque had described him as "dressed in a sort of uniform with a pair of fringe epaulettes and overalls of tanned leather with innumerable little buttons down the sides, and his horse was caparisoned in black leather trappings that gave it the appearance of a Rhinoceros."

With the guide's help the two men wound their way

upwards for an arduous 2½ hours until finally, as Stephens recalled the moment, "we spurred up a sharp ascent of fragments, so steep that the mules could barely climb it, to a terrace so covered . . . with trees, that it was impossible to make out the form. . . .Our Indians cried out 'el Palacio' . . . and through openings in the trees we saw the front of a large building richly ornamented with stuccoed figures on the pilasters, curious and elegant. . . .the first glance indemnified us for our toil. . . .We were in a building erected by the aboriginal inhabitants . . . before the Europeans knew of the existence of this continent . . . ."

The white men slung their hammocks within the Palace complex, dank and musty as it was, and then attempted to gain some sense of the extent of the ruins. "The people of Palenque say that [the buildings] cover a space of sixty miles; . . .[but] I am obliged to say that the Indians . . . know nothing of the ruins personally." As for the explorers ever finding out the true extent of ancient Palenque, Stephens deemed it a practical impossibility. "The whole country for miles around is covered by a dense forest . . . impenetrable in any direction except by cutting a way with a machete. . . . without a guide, we might have gone within a hundred feet of all the buildings without discovering one of them."

For the next few weeks Stephens was busy locating, clearing, and measuring the cluster of structures within the central area of the ruins. Catherwood, sometimes using a camera lucida, an optical device that projects images of objects before it onto paper, began tracing and sketching scores of reliefs, facades, *cresterias,* and other curiosities. Stephens could not get it out of his mind that they were intruding upon "the remains of a cultivated, polished, and peculiar people, who had passed through all the stages incident to the rise and fall of nations; reached their golden age, and perished. . . . In the romance of the world's history nothing ever impressed me more forcibly than the spectacle of this once great and lovely city, overturned, desolate, and lost." Stephens observed, as would generations thereafter, that it was only the roots of trees and the tangle of vines that was holding the city together.

The men found the overall working conditions at the Palenque ruins more oppressive than any they had experienced before. The incessant rains turned all their clothing, food, and artists' supplies damp and mildewed. Their weapons were rusting. Both were striken with a variety of illnesses ranging from insect bites to rheumatism. And their sleep was made so fitful by predatory insects that they were constantly on the verge of physical exhaustion. The two made plans to leave by the end of the month.

Meanwhile, Stephens was smitten with the romantic notion of buying the ruins in order to have free rein to excavate. He spoke vaguely of a plan to "fit up the palace and repeople the old city" on some future expedition. The purchase price was nominal inasmuch as no one in the village saw any worth in the place, but in order to become a landowner under Mexican law Stephens had first to marry a "daughter of the country."

A bachelor, Stephens gave serious thought to changing his status, but he found courting within the confines of modern Palenque society "embarrassing and complicated." Except for a 14-year-old girl, the only Palenque women unmarried and available were a pair of sisters, good-looking, amiable, and about 40. Stephens explained his predicament later: "With either of these ladies would come possession of the house; . . . but the difficulty was that there were two of them, both equally interesting and equally interested." The would-be landowner decided he could not make a choice, and when the fourth of June arrived, Stephens and Catherwood left without buying anything.

As it turned out, neither man ever went back to Palenque, but their observations, set forth two years later in Stephens's engaging *Incidents of Travel in Central America, Chiapas and Yucatán,* had an unsettling effect on archeological thinking of the time. Stephens was the first man of reputation to declare unequivocally that the ruins of Central America were the remnants of a wholly indigenous Maya civilization and the first to suggest that the people who built them were the ancestors of Indians living there. He went so far as to say that further exploration of the Central American interior might disclose "that mysterious city [where] unconquered, unvisited, and unsought aboriginal inhabitants" continued to live as their forefathers had. He challenged the archeological community to bring the same spirit of inquiry to the mysteries of the New World as they had given so unstintingly to the Old.

No such "mysterious city" was ever found, but Stephens's challenge was taken up by a succession of adventurers and archeologists who, bit by bit, brought

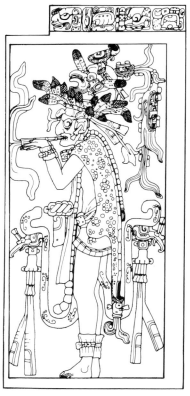

The panel at right, from a flanking relief in the Temple of the Cross, portrays God L, familiarly known as El Fumador ("The Smoker"). In her drawing above, Palenque expert Linda Schele captures the finely chiseled details. The figure, adorned with ornate feather headpiece and long jaguar cape, is shown smoking a cigar. The temple was built by Chan-Bahlum, Pacal's successor, in A.D. 684.

ancient Palenque back from the dead. By the turn of the century Santo Domingo del Palenque and its ruins had become sufficiently accessible by road that the town had need of a combination "Inspector of Archeological Monuments" and hotelkeeper to handle visitors. By the 1920's the techniques of modern archeology — precisely measured excavations, scientific correlation of artifacts, the deciphering of hieroglyphic materials — had begun to unlock some of Palenque's secrets. By the 1930's efforts were also underway to slow the deterioration of the ancient city's principal temples and courtyards.

A critical breakthrough in all these efforts came in 1949 when Alberto Ruz Lhullier, Director of Mexico's National Institute of Anthropology and History, undertook the excavation of the floor within the Temple of the Inscriptions in the belief that an earlier building might be discovered beneath it. He chose this particular temple because it was the tallest in the compound and therefore most likely to be standing on an earlier mound, because its copious hieroglyphic inscriptions suggested that the structure was of exceptional importance to the people of Palenque, and because its floor was still intact, owing to the unusual stone slabs that had been used to cover it.

Hidden Treasures

As he looked for a likely place to begin, Ruz chose the inner chamber of the temple. His eyes lit upon one slab that was slightly different from the others for it had a double row of holes drilled along its two long sides. These he took to be finger grips, and when the slab was lifted he found what appeared to be the capstone of a Classic Maya vault, a sure sign that there was something underneath. After several more days of delicate excavations he came to a step, then another and another, revealing a secret staircase leading downward into the heart of the pyramid. But progress was extremely slow because the staircase had been purposefully sealed up with an avalanche of rocks and clay.

It took four field seasons to clear the way. Ruz described the scene as it unfolded, "After a flight of 45 steps, we reached a landing with a U-turn. There followed another flight, of 2l steps, leading to a corridor, whose level is more or less the same as that on which the pyramid was built — i.e., some 22 metres [72 feet] under the temple flooring. In the vaulting of the landing two narrow galleries open out and allow air and a little light to enter from a near-by courtyard." It was obvious that before the building was raised level by level, the connecting staircase and the sarcophagus at the base had been completely worked into the plans.

"Above one of the first steps we reached we found a box-shaped construction of masonry containing a modest offering: two ear-plugs of jade placed on a river stone painted red. On reaching the end of the flight we found another box of offerings, backing on to a wall which blocked the passage. This time it was a richer offering: three pottery dishes, two shells full of cinnabar, seven jade beads, a pair of circular ear-plugs also of jade . . . and a beautiful tear-shaped pearl, with its *lustre* pretty well preserved."

The richness of the offerings told Ruz that he was coming close to something important. On July 13, 1952, he and his team uncovered a triangular slab, about six feet high, set vertically as if it were a door. At the base of the slab were the skeletons of six youths, evidently human sacrifices dedicated to the dead ruler at the time the door was sealed. Two days later the excavators were able to move the stone sufficiently to allow Ruz to slide in. "It was a moment of indescribable emotion for me when I slipped behind the stone and found myself in an enormous crypt which seemed to have been cut out of the rock — or rather, out of the ice, thanks to the curtain of stalactites and the chalcite veiling deposited on the walls by the infiltration of rain-water during the centuries. This increased the marvelous quality of the spectacle and gave it a fairy-tale aspect."

The crypt, which measured 30 feet long, was occupied almost entirely by what Ruz presumed to be a ceremonial altar, a colossal block of limestone 12 1/2 feet long and weighing some five tons; it rested on six great blocks of chiseled stone. The wall reliefs depicted ancestors; the hieroglyphs carved on the edges of the sarcophgus lid recorded dynastic dates in the 7th century A.D. Wanting to know if the base of the supposed altar was solid or not, Ruz bored horizontally at two of the corners.

"It was not long before one of the drills reached a hollow space," the archeologist related. "I introduced a wire through the narrow aperture and, on withdrawing it, I saw that some particles of red paint were adhering to it.

"The presence of this colouring matter inside the monolith was of supreme importance. . . . This colour was associated in the Mayan . . . cosmogony with the East, but also it is nearly always found in tombs, on the walls or on objects accompanying the dead person or on his bones. The presence of red in tombs came, therefore, to indicate resurrection and a hope of immortality. . . . Our supposed ceremonial altar must therefore be an extraordinary sepulchre." Before this momentous discovery it had been reasonably assumed that no Mesoamerican pyramid had ever been constructed for the sole purpose of being a burial monument. Clearly, Palenque was some kind of exception to Maya tradition.

Ruz then faced another challenge — how to lift the massive stone in order to peer inside. In the next feverish hours, he and his men fashioned huge pry bars from tree trunks, carried them to the pyramid, lowered them down the steep stairs, slid them through the narrow opening to the crypt, and, with the addition of railroad jacks, began the painstaking procedure of prying up the stone, inch by inch. Once the stone had been raised a few inches Ruz could see the outlines of a cavity cut within the limestone block, but its contents were covered with a finely polished cover. After several more days of work, the stone block was raised high enough that the excavators were able to remove the lid. Beneath they found a human skeleton, the face covered by a mosaic mask of jade (shown on page 233), the body festooned with pounds of jade necklaces, pendants, bracelets, and rings. Two jade objects, one a representation of the sun god, were placed alongside.

In the years since Ruz's stunning discovery, archeologists have learned a great deal about Palenque through careful studies of the inscriptions and iconographic reliefs found in this unique tomb. It now seems all but certain that the pyramid was built during the lifetime of Lord Shield Pacal, king of Palenque from A.D. 615-683, and that it is he whose remains were buried in its underground vault. But at the time, Ruz was uncertain as to the skeleton's identity beyond the fact that it belonged to a male personage of high rank.

Several points struck the archeologist as sufficiently uncharacteristic of what was known about Palenque to suggest that the figure might be that of a foreigner who somehow came to rule over Palenque. For example, Ruz found his stature impressive, "greater than that of the average Maya of today," and he was puzzled that the man so honored did not have his teeth filed or encrusted with pyrites or jade, as was typical with Maya leaders. Lord Shield Pacal was apparently born of the union of a Palenque princess, Lady Zac-Kuk ("Resplendent Quetzal") and her consort, Kan-Bahlum-Mo' ("Precious Jaguar-Macaw"), also of royal birth but not from Palenque. Thus, Pacal, was named for his maternal uncle.

Pacal became king of Palenque when he was barely 12, following a period in which his mother had apparently ruled in her own right. Presumably she continued to serve the city-state as a kind of regent until Pacal had matured sufficiently to assume the reins of king in fact as well as symbol. Inasmuch as Palenque artists had a stylistic tradition that was notably naturalistic, the portraits of Lady Zac-Kuk and her son Pacal are taken by Mayanists to be fairly true to life.

Pacal's mother, for example, is shown in numerous bas-reliefs to have had the clinical syndrome known as acromegaly, the progressive enlargement of bones and soft tissue resulting from an overactive pituitary gland. Merle Greene Robertson, an American archeologist who has spent several decades studying Palenque, notes that portraits representing her in later years show an abnormally enlarged jaw, puffy eyes, a prominent brow ridge, and "spadelike" hands. Though she was not the first female ruler of Palenque — Pacal's grandmother, Lady Kan-Ik ("Maize Wind"), reigned from A.D. 583-604 — Zac-Kuk is recognized for her distinct hair style, in having an area at the back of her head shaved in the manner of royal males. It has been speculated that she adopted this eccentricity as yet one more

Resting atop a huge pyramid, the Temple of the Inscriptions (above), which dates from the 7th century, is another example of the unique architectural style at Palenque. Through a narrow corridor, at the bottom of a hidden staircase, a Mexican archeologist discovered the probable tomb of Pacal, some 70 feet below the chamber. In a replica (right) at Mexico's National Institute of Anthropology and History, the tomb's cinnabar-tinged interior glows brightly as it must have long ago.

means to legitimize her family's right to rule, possibly at the time that she presided over a ceremony in which the six-year-old Pacal was recognized officially as the heir apparent. This event, recorded in the tomb reliefs, has been compared to the British investiture of the Prince of Wales. All these clues seem to indicate a sudden upsurge in the formalized symbols of authority in Palenque, which in turn suggests that Palenque was in the process of becoming a more important, more powerful center within the Maya domain.

Portraits of Lord Shield Pacal are also revealing. Robertson and others have identified a number of depictions of the ruler at different stages in his life: it appears that Pacal bore congenital defects in both his feet, the left being "split-toed" and the right club-footed. His face was well formed, almost delicate, with a "sensitive pointed chin and thin lips," not at all like his mother's. His figure was apparently consistent with his head, slender and graceful.

As the iconography on the tomb shows graphically, Pacal's subjects obviously revered him as a living deity, a communicant not only with earthly concerns and mortals but with the gods of eternity. In perhaps the most telling relief, that inscribed on the five-ton limestone

lid of his sarcophagus, he is shown beginning his descent from the world of the living to the world of the dead — the underworld — where, in the Maya cosmogony, rebirth must begin. Pacal is represented as falling with the setting sun into the skeletal jaws of the monster of the underworld in a reenactment of the death of each day. From the jaws of the monster emerge two symbols of Palenque kinship, God K (as he is known in the jargon of Mayanists, who have lettered the gods from A to P) and the jester god. Behind Pacal's figure the sacred ceiba tree, which symbolizes rebirth, is shown as a stylized cruciform rising from the mouth of an earth monster.

The allegory is marvelously echoed in the very construction of the Temple of the Inscriptions. By one of those acts of astronomical accuracy for which the Maya would become famous, the building is so designed and oriented that persons standing atop the Palace Tower on the day of the winter solstice see the setting sun appear to sink into Pacal's tomb, as if entering the western gateway to the underworld; it was a truly spectacular way of affirming once again Pacal's identification with the gods. Another architectural feature is the curious hollow stone duct that runs from the exteri-

or of the structure downward along the temple stairs, across the slab to the sarcophagus, and through an opening into the tomb itself. The duct, which archeologists have named a "psychoduct," served as a kind of speaking tube by which the spirit of Pacal could communicate with Palenque's chief priests and his blood kin even after the man himself had passed into divinity.

In summarizing the importance of the great Palenque tomb in understanding the Maya mind, Ruz has declared that "the monumental quality of this crypt, built by thousands of hands . . . and enriched with magnificent reliefs . . . the rich jade finery of the buried personage; all this expensive toil and this magnificence suggest to us the existence in Palenque of a theocratic system similar to that of Egypt, in which the all-powerful priest-king was considered during life or after death to be a real god." After Pacal's death it was standard practice for each successor to assert his descent from Pacal and Pacal's ancestors, the line being extended farther back in time to include the Maya deities themselves. No one, however, seems to have matched the great leader's ability to rule, his longevity, or his impact upon Palenque's history, and in less than 200 years his descendants ceased even trying.

243

CHILDREN OF LIGHT

In the sun-baked world of New Mexico's Chaco Canyon, an ancient
people known to later Indians as "Enemy Ancestors" launched a
remarkable building campaign to enlarge their stone pueblo.
A few decades later they abandoned it for reasons unknown.

About 900 years ago the sun rose on a town that
was unique in the pageant of Southwestern civilizations. Along the banks of an insignificant
stream, in the heart of a shallow, semiarid depression
known as Chaco Canyon, a dynamism gripped the
local people and propelled them into an incredible burst
of architectural activity. By the standards of their time,
they built huge, skillfully engineered, and well-con-
structed edifices. In the context of their marginal environment, the population they chose to concentrate and
support in a confined area was remarkable. Among all
the builders-in-stone of the Southwest, the inhabitants
of Chaco surged forward first, and most spectacularly,
into the realm of community development. The task
was accomplished with extraordinary craftsmanship
and style. They were a people who recognized the
immense powers of Nature, and were subject to its
whims, but refused to bow before its inevitability.
In a world that could be demanding and harsh, they
brought beauty and grace to their lives. Part of a prehistoric culture born in the Southwest known as Anasazi, they developed it to its brightest expression: they
were the people of Chaco, the children of light.

The stream along which they settled, Chaco Wash,
is born on the western slope of the Continental Divide
and meanders across northwest New Mexico to join
the San Juan River near Shiprock. As a body of water it
is unimpressive — even nonexistent between summer
thunderstorms — but along 10 or 12 miles of its course
lies a valley that possessed a strange magnetism for the
Anasazi. Although it is called Chaco Canyon, it is really only a broad depression, from one-half to three-
quarters of a mile wide, with perhaps 800 feet of elevation between its highest mesa and the deepest cut of the
wash. In the midst of the San Juan Basin, the region is
virtually barren of trees and dominated by rocks and
brush. A first impression is that it would take a fast-
stepping cow to find a meal in this country. But if the
traveler pauses along the rimrock and lets his eyes ad-
just to the earth tones that dominate the spectrum, the
forms of some remarkable structures begin to emerge
from the landscape.

Pueblo Bonito, the great attraction of Chaco Culture National Historical Park, is a huge stone edifice

*During Pueblo Bonito's golden age, around the time of the
Norman conquest of England, a thousand or so Anasazi lived
here, in an apartment complex probably much more pleasant
than the hovels of most Anglo-Saxon serfs of the time.*

244

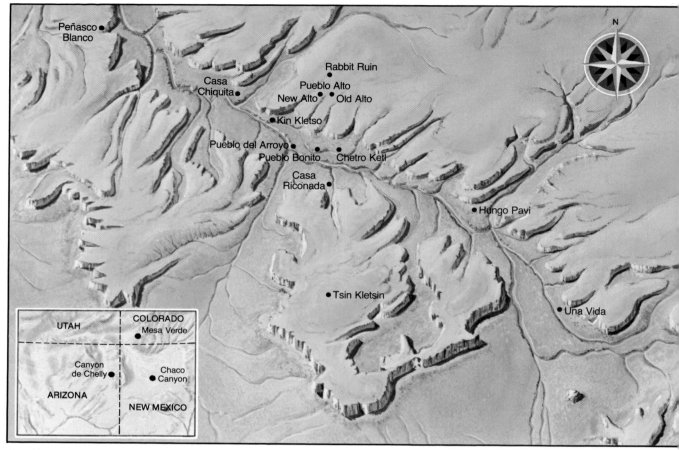

In addition to the massive ruins of Pueblo Bonito, there are 12 other Anasazi ruins along 6 miles of New Mexico's Chaco Canyon, ranging from Casa Rinconada's impressive canyon kiva to the mesa dwellings of New Alto. In the present "Four Corners" area of the United States are two related sites — Mesa Verde, Colorado, and Canyon de Chelly, Arizona.

that covers nearly three acres, and reaches four or five stories high in places. It is a D-shaped building, a single story high and flat along most of its 520-foot face, rising like steps to four or five stories as it curves back toward the bluff and mesa behind. Dominating the center of the lower level are two large plazas punctuated by the open, staring holes of ceremonial kivas stripped of their roofs by time. Empty, devoid of the people who gave it life and animation, Pueblo Bonito is a moving experience even for a jaded, 20th-century technocrat. Its very mass freezes the viewer, and then the intricacies of design and construction begin to unreel the imagination. People seem to appear on plazas and in doorways, stooped to everyday tasks, and the perspective is suddenly overwhelming. People lacking the wheel, the block-and-tackle, or even draft animals managed to build such a structure and survive in large numbers on this unprepossessing land.

In addition to Pueblo Bonito, there are other large sites — Chetro Ketl, Pueblo Alto, Casa Rinconada, Kin Kletso — and literally hundreds of lesser ones that range in size from small villages to housing for a single family. And scattered throughout the San Juan Basin are some 70 "outliers" — centers that feature public architecture in the Bonito style — all connected to Chaco Canyon by prehistoric roadways. As will be seen, the relationship between Pueblo Bonito and the outliers, and even other population centers 50 or 100 miles away, is not clearly understood. How this complex society functioned still defies firm definition. Perhaps it is somehow fitting that the people who created such magnificence in a hostile environment should confound our attempts to reduce their lives to mundane equations.

We don't even know what they called themselves, for they left no written records. The Navajo who invaded this land called them Anasazi, "Enemy Ancestors," and the name stuck. Pueblo Bonito, meaning "beautiful village," came from the language of the next wave of conquerors, but they took small note of towns not made of gold. In 1849 Lt. James Simpson, a topographic engineer who was exploring and surveying the

Southwest for the U.S. Geological Survey, came upon the ruins and made remarkably meticulous drawings and descriptions. His Indian guide obligingly provided names for the various ruins, which explains in part the curious admixture of Spanish and Athapascan place names that are scattered across the valley. From 1896, when the first systematic excavations were made at Pueblo Bonito, to today, when scholars are still sorting through the raw data accumulated during recent years of fieldwork, the Anasazi ghosts of Pueblo Bonito and Chaco Canyon have steadfastly resisted analysis.

These Anasazi were a complex people, who, more than any of their brethren in other parts of the Southwest, created a multifaceted society that produced a wide range of accomplishments. In addition to developing large, planned towns, the Chacoans fashioned distinctive pottery and jewelry, practiced irrigation and contour farming, traded with Mexico, built great roadways running for scores of miles, and conducted solar observations. And yet around 1150, not long after reaching their brightest cultural florescence, these same people abandoned all they had built in what seems to have been a mass exodus. All that remained was the dessicated husk of their beautiful village, left to blend into the seared earth from which it had risen.

The roots of the Anasazi are sunk deep in the prehistory of the Southwest, reaching back more than 7,000 years into a mistily understood Desert Culture. The people of this culture were nomadic hunters and gatherers, living in the open and following the fickle supply of meat and wild plants that the land provided. They left scant evidence of their passage upon the land and produced little that endured, so their story is hard to trace, but by about 5000 B.C. they had apparently developed the *mano* and *metate* for grinding edible seeds; increased their dependence on the gathering of plants, seeds, and roots; and slowed the pace of their migration enough to use caves for intervals longer than overnight stops. Around 1000 B.C. the course of their development was redirected by the introduction of corn from Mexico. The need to tend and protect their crops made them more sedentary, and permanent or semipermanent residence gave them the opportunity to develop textiles and basketry. In time, the convenience of a few possessions began to outweigh the need to travel fast and light.

Out of this gradual deceleration of nomadism in the Southwest emerged three distinct, though related, cultures: the Hohokam, the Mogollon, and the Anasazi. The Hohokam developed in the lowland deserts of Arizona, utilizing irrigation perhaps as early as A.D. 100 to 300 to ensure the success of their crops. By A.D. 500 the Hohokam people had settled in substantial communities and had begun building irrigation projects remarkable in their complexity and capacity. The influence of Mexico was strong among the Hohokam, in both trade and culture. Copper bells, shells from the Gulf of California, and rubber from the Mexican lowlands all found their way into the world of the Hohokam. The rubber, molded into a ball, was probably associated with a game that was played on a rather elaborate court excavated into the desert sand. The game may have been similar to one played in 14th-century Mexico, a combination of soccer (no hands allowed) and basketball (pass the ball through a hoop).

The direct borrowing of ideas by Southwestern cultures is difficult to prove, but certainly the Mexican influence is evident in agriculture and pottery. Mexican trade items such as parrots and copper made their way into the Southwest as well, and presumably cultural innovations trailed along. But the Mexicans were not conquistadors and the impact of their culture upon Southwestern peoples was only peripheral. The influence upon the Hohokam was strong, but farther east and north it was less marked.

The Mogollon were mountain people, relying less on irrigation and more on rainfall to ensure their crops. They were more avid hunters than the Hohokam, having a greater resource of game available. And they were

This ceramic jar, dating from A.D. 800-950, shows how a man of the times might have dressed. Wrapped in a blanket of typical design, he wears sandals, bracelets, and a beaded necklace. He may have worn turquoise pendants in his pierced ears.

247

quick learners: they not only acquired the technique of pottery making about A.D. 200 to 300, but they may have been the first to adopt the bow and arrow. They were also among the earliest North Americans to build permanent houses, albeit working in wood and earth. Their culture continued to develop, and around A.D. 1000, a group of Mogollon living along the Mimbres River in New Mexico began to produce handsome pottery distinctively painted in black on white.

In the plateau country to the north and east of the Mogollon, the Anasazi culture slowly began to flower. Eventually it transcended both the Hohokam and Mogollon cultures in some ways and left a more enduring mark upon the land. For a while, however, there was little to distinguish the Anasazi except their outstanding skill in basketry. Because of this specialty the Anasazi in the early stages of their development are identified by anthropologists as the Basketmakers. Their culture dates from roughly A.D. 300, when they accomplished the transition from a nomadic existence to a sedentary way of life. Their groups were small, probably representing no more than an extended family of 20 or 30 people. The size of the group reflected the economic imperatives implicit in their previous nomadic lifestyle; it was difficult for hunters and gatherers to feed a larger group in the arid Southwest.

These early Anasazi were scattered from southern Utah and Colorado to the upper Rio Grande Valley of New Mexico, with a sprinkling of settlements in Chaco Canyon. The Chaco people were still primarily hunters and gatherers, although they cultivated corn and squash. Their crops constituted only a small portion of their diet, and they continued to migrate seasonally in search of game and wild plants. Apparently the Anasazi soon recognized the blessings that even limited agriculture bestowed, and wasted little time abandoning the daily pursuit of dinner over the next horizon.

About A.D. 450 or 500 the Anasazi of Chaco began to enjoy more amenities. They made crude pottery in which they could cook and store their agricultural produce. They also built mud and wood houses with saucer-shaped floors, and had a place they could call home. Of the advances that ensued during the next 400 years, the most important was probably the acquisition of the common bean (*Phaseolus vulgaris*), which supplemented their diet of corn and squash. In addition to being a staple easy to keep without spoiling, the bean provided a dependable source of protein. The Anasazi also improved their pottery and began to use it more extensively, perhaps in response to the challenge of the bean. The beans had to be soaked overnight and then boiled for hours more to tenderize them. Knowing

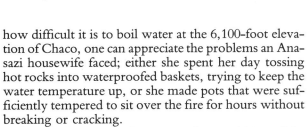

The well-preserved sack, basket, sash (probably a carrying strap), and sandals shown at left, below, were woven of yucca by the Anasazi 1,500 years ago. Much later they began to make pottery, using the coil technique, then applying slips, and brushing on pigments with a bold, steady hand. The Mimbres polychrome bowl above, featuring a ceremonial figure, dates from 1100. Such bowls, with a "kill hole" near the center to allow the soul to escape, were placed over the head of the deceased. At right is an Anasazi jar, with shell and turquoise jewelry thought to have been made by neighboring peoples culturally related to the Anasazi.

how difficult it is to boil water at the 6,100-foot elevation of Chaco, one can appreciate the problems an Anasazi housewife faced; either she spent her day tossing hot rocks into waterproofed baskets, trying to keep the water temperature up, or she made pots that were sufficiently tempered to sit over the fire for hours without breaking or cracking.

Another important change was the acquisition of the bow and arrow. Until this weapon came into their hands, the Anasazi had hunted with the atlatl and spear. The atlatl, a throwing stick with a hook at the end to cup a spear butt, was hard to master and awkward to use in ambush. The bow and arrow not only had triple the target range, but it could be used in the woodlands of the high elevations. Suddenly it was easier to put meat in the pot.

Perhaps the most striking development was in housing. The pit-house, which began as a humble shelter from the elements, gradually evolved into an elaborate,

formalized structure that ultimately became the ceremonial and religious center of Anasazi life. The earliest version was excavated into the soil so that some portion of its walls was made of earth. The superstructure consisted of wood and mud with interior posts to support the roof, which was thatched with brush and small branches and smeared with clay and mud. A fire pit was laid in the middle of the floor under a centrally located hole in the roof, which served both as a vent and as an entry via a ladder.

As the Anasazi dropped their nomadic ways, the pit-houses of Chaco began to reflect a larger investment of labor. A family that knows it won't be leaving soon is more inclined to provide some creature comforts; consequently pit-houses were dug deeper and larger and lined with stone slabs to hold down the dust and reduce dampness. Eventually it was usual for pit-houses to be 30 feet in diameter and 3 feet deep, with roof beams raised 7 or more feet above the floor. Poles were laid on the beams, thatched with brush, and heavily plastered with clay to provide a watertight roof.

Antechambers that served as entrances were added, connecting to the main room by a short passage. This feature provided air circulation, creating a mild draft through the smoke hole that made living with a fire much more pleasant. Small compartments were cut in the walls for storage. Dug in the floor alongside the fire pit was a small hole that served no practical purpose but had symbolic importance.

In present-day Pueblo religion, this hole represents Shipap, the hole from the lower earth through which the ancestors emerged into the current world. It is a small symbol, with a meaning perhaps impossible to trace scientifically from the Anasazi to the Pueblo Indians, but it represents a concept so fundamental to their beliefs that no man who respected his father and had hopes for his children could forget it or misuse it.

As the Anasazi of Chaco began to build more elaborate houses, they also began to congregate into larger

A century before the Chacoans were leaving their canyon, the Anasazi of Mesa Verde in present-day Colorado were moving from their homes on the tableland to alcoves in sandstone canyon walls. In these confines, damp and dismally dark for half the day, they built pueblos with small rooms, kivas, and tiered storage areas. But after only a hundred years the Anasazi abandoned their cliff dwellings. Perhaps the most spectacular of the Mesa Verde pueblos is Cliff Palace (above), containing more than 200 rooms and 23 kivas. At Spruce Tree House (right), a pueblo with 114 rooms, ladders disappear into kivas whose stone-paved roofs form a plaza.

villages. Although it is impossible to know whether these groups were more than extended families or clans, it is safe to assume that a degree of specialization of labor began to appear. The specialists might have included builders, hunters, farmers, and potters as well as religious and civic leaders.

During the 7th and 8th centuries the Chacoans continued to farm as their ancestors had, planting in the spring on likely soil; leaving the plants several feet apart and keeping the weeds down so the corn, beans, and squash wouldn't have to compete for moisture; and praying for rain in the summer and a late frost in the fall. Although no dramatic innovations revolutionized agriculture during this era, apparently the Chaco people began to find the areas where a gentle runoff of rain increased yields, and learned to time their spring planting to avoid frost at both ends of the season. They also had more people available to tend more fields. This is surmised because they began to erect storage buildings behind their pit-houses.

Initially these storage buildings were wattle-and-daub huts — poles stabbed into the ground in a circle, pulled in and laced together, and covered with mud — but soon they became more permanent and substantial structures, built at first with stone slabs and later with layered rock and stout beam ceilings. Some time after 850 or 900 some Chacoans found that the storage houses were thermally efficient, and moved in. At this point, the Basketmaker era ended and, in anthropological terminology, the era of the "Developmental Pueblo" began; by his lights an Anasazi probably just became more comfortable and wondered why he had not thought of it before. He kept his pit-house, and because of strong associations with the past it became his ceremonial center and men's club — in short, a kiva.

The Chacoans were neither the first nor the only Anasazi to begin the transition to building in stone, but what they did with the concept in size, design, craftsmanship, or speed of construction was unmatched by any of the other Anasazi. Why the people of Chaco evinced such a striking cultural dynamism is not known. At one time it was thought that they had received an infusion of new blood — that a more advanced people had moved in among them — because sometime after 850 a physical change became apparent: the heads of the Anasazi were becoming shorter from front to back. A genetic invasion seemed to make sense as an explanation for both the physiological change and the advance in dwelling arrangements, until it was discovered that the modification of skull shape was due instead to a change in child-rearing technique: the Anasazi had adopted the use of a hard cradle board, which flattened the malleable skulls of their infants. Archeologists were back to square one in trying to explain the impetus shown by the Anasazi.

The early Pueblo dwellings in Chaco were not built on a grand scale. Most were simply expansions or refinements of the food-storage warehouse idea: several single-story rooms linked together in a straight line or curve, with perhaps a small plaza attached, and one or more pit-houses in front. Pueblo Bonito itself began this way sometime around 920 with a small, curving group of buildings near the north bluff of the canyon. The construction was crude by later standards, employing large slabs of sandstone mortared rather indifferently with mud. But the fundamental design feature of a south-facing crescent backed by the bluff was retained during subsequent expansion. The design and location may have been fortuitously accidental or brilliantly calculated, for the overall result was a community protected from knifing winter winds by the high bluff and oriented to capture the maximum warmth from a low winter sun beaming on individual stoops, roofs, and communal plazas.

Throughout the canyon, small villages of this type were raised, preferably near the fertile bottom lands. Agriculture was increasingly important to the Chacoans, although they were still active gatherers and hunters, and they may have made early efforts to divert some rain runoff towards their fields. Also at this time the Anasazi acquired the turkey, which joined the dog as the only domesticated animals in Chaco. There is scant evidence to suggest that the Anasazi ate the birds, however; rather, they kept them for their decorative feathers. Domesticated turkeys are a constant aggravation, not to mention a threat to stored food, and the smallest children of the household may have been kept busy herding the birds out from under foot.

Building a Grander Town

For reasons we may never understand, in the late part of the 11th century Pueblo Bonito was launched on a building campaign that continued on and off for 25 to 40 years and was intense for part of that time. Possibly the size of the original pueblo was almost doubled. Although several distinctive masonry types were used and some of the oldest rooms were filled in and surmounted, the construction of Pueblo Bonito proceeded in a planned, organized fashion. It was almost as if someone knew what he wanted and persuaded everyone to cooperate.

In addition to the growth of Pueblo Bonito, its classic building phase was distinguished by more sophisticated masonry work. During this period, the masons of Pueblo Bonito used a veneer-and-rubble technique, in which a core of stone and mortar was finished both inside and out with a veneer of carefully layered and mortared sandstone ashlars. In some sections of wall the veneer was characterized by large sandstone blocks chinked around by groups of small stones. In other sections, bands of large blocks were layered with bands of small pieces of sandstone slabs placed in very even, carefully laid courses, with very little mortar visible. In still other places the masons eliminated the large blocks and used only flat slabs in a veneer with very thin joints and scarcely any exposed mortar. Sometimes several

veneer styles were employed side by side. Scholars are not sure whether the various masonry styles were used sequentially or whether they overlapped in time.

Why the styles varied has been a source of considerable speculation, with explanations ranging from a simple change in fashion to the arrival of new immigrants who took control and introduced new techniques. The answer may simply be that some styles were found to be more stable and quicker to lay, once the stones were shaped — a task that could be delegated to less-skilled apprentices. There is no doubt that the later veneers are more carefully fitted, with smooth, straight walls. Whatever the masonry style, the walls were covered with a smooth plaster. These were obviously concerned craftsmen who were determined to do a job right even if it didn't show.

Another feature of the classic building phase at Chaco that distinguished it from earlier efforts was the in-

corporation of the kivas within the housing block proper. Pueblo Bonito, when completed, had 30 small kivas and 2 great kivas. Although the small kivas appear to be subterranean, they were actually built above ground like the rest of the village. The Chacoans filled in the spaces between the kivas with earth and rubble, creating a level court, so that only the rims of their masonry walls and the ladders protruding from the entrances indicated their presence.

Drawing upon ethnographic comparisons to modern Pueblo Indians, particularly the Hopi and Zuni, anthropologists have made some assumptions about the ownership and function of kivas among the Anasazi, but they are only speculative. The smaller kivas probably belonged to clans or secret societies that assumed responsibility for specific religious rites. They may have been places for contemplation, or simply for "getting away from it all." Or they may have served as

Home for groups of Anasazi for centuries, Arizona's Canyon de Chelly and Canyon del Muerto may also have been refuges for Anasazi from Mesa Verde and Chaco Canyon in the late 11th century. By 1300 the Anasazi had abandoned the area. At left, pueblo ruins in breathtakingly beautiful Canyon del Muerto. Nearby are Anasazi pictographs (right) of human figures and spirals that may have been sun or clan symbols; the petroglyphs above, from Canyon de Chelly, apparently depict hunters and their prey.

fraternal social lodges, not unlike the lodges of the Elks or Moose today. But in all likelihood, the function of kivas was primarily religious. If that is so, the people of Chaco were extraordinarily reverent. The entire valley is strewn with kivas, in numbers out of proportion to the number of residents, when compared with the ratios found in other Anasazi population centers. This fact has raised speculation that Chaco was a religious center, visited by pilgrims from other areas. Unfortunately, no evidence has ever been uncovered that either proves or disproves this thesis.

Some of the great kivas in Chaco Canyon are over 60 feet in diameter. The initial impression is that they are merely overgrown clan kivas, but subtle construction differences indicate that the Anasazi made a distinction between the two. The roofs of great kivas were raised several feet above ground level, whereas the roofs of the smaller clan kivas were flush with the ground. Access to great kivas was by stairs, usually at the north and south sides of the structure, while clan kivas retained the ladder through the smoke hole. Great kivas had a central, raised firebox flanked by paired masonry boxes on the floor, while clan kivas had clay-lined hearths and eschewed any floor boxes.

There were other differences in roof construction and ventilation; also, great kivas had benches around the perimeter. These may have been only concessions to strength or simplicity of construction or to work capacity. Then again, they may not have been. The point is, we don't know. Were the great kivas for large religious functions? Was their purpose merely social? Did they play some role in maintaining cohesion within the large communities that characterized Chaco? Did they somehow bind the people of the outliers to the central towns? And why were there two in Pueblo Bonito — did they signify a social or religious rivalry in the community? Unfortunately, answers are difficult to formulate and impossible to prove.

Through the classic period at Pueblo Bonito, from 1000 to 1120, the population continued to grow. Estimates range from less than 600 residents to about 1,200 town residents, and reach as high as 7,000 for the population of the entire canyon, although about 5,500 seems more likely. Population size is difficult to determine exactly because small villages were built, abandoned, rebuilt, and destroyed by fire almost endlessly, while large sites like Pueblo Bonito were constantly subjected to remodeling and new construction programs. How

Pueblo Bonito

Beneath the towering rock walls of New Mexico's Chaco Canyon the children of light seem dwarfed by their vast pueblo, its 660 rooms and 32 kivas covering more than three acres. This multi-storied complex, the heart of the Anasazi settlement in the canyon, was erected in the 11th century, as ancient builders enlarged Pueblo Bonito's nucleus into a coordinated design housing some 1,000 residents. They skillfully engineered sandstone quarried from the eroded cliffs and massive beams from distant forests into a distinctive communal fortress, with clan units surrounding two central plazas. The great kivas, up to 60 feet wide, were used for community functions, the smaller ones for clan ceremonies. Overpopulation, a possible reason for the unexplained abandonment of the site, is evidenced by the trash pits in the foreground. Tons of refuse had overflowed the retaining walls by the time the Anasazi left their once "beautiful village."

Doorways leading into Pueblo Bonito's interior rooms reveal their sturdy masonry walls. The small doorways with their high sills facilitated heat retention and were easy to close off with a curtain of matting or a slab of stone.

who wrestled the logs home. Smaller logs were used for the cribbed roofs of kivas, but one intact kiva revealed 350 such poles in the roof. Altogether the Anasazi must have lugged home about 200,000 beams. That called for a good many trips to the mountains.

The population also had to be fed, and herein lay the curse or the blessing of irrigation: it was a curse if increased productivity merely attracted more people, but it was a blessing if the people were already there and irrigation simply made it possible to feed them. Whatever the sequence of events, successful agriculture was critical to survival in Chaco, and tending the fields must have absorbed most of the energies of the residents and much of their time.

Creating a Valley of Gardens

Irrigation made agriculture reliable, and the citizens of Pueblo Bonito and Chaco Canyon developed it to a high order. Irrigation in Chaco did not mean damming the wash and rechanneling the water to fields; rather, the system grew naturally from the practice of utilizing the runoff from summer storms. In the beginning a man might place his garden plot to take advantage of the water that ran down a small gully, but soon he would build small diversion dams to slow the water and push it out to fields farther to the side. Small ditches would be dug to carry the water farther still, and soon bigger dams would be erected to fill bigger ditches. The practice was doubly beneficial, because it not only trapped water but also reduced soil erosion. The ditches distributed water to a grid of rock-bordered gardens that edged Chaco Wash, permitting the water to be used over and over as it sought the bottom of the canyon. Canals were enlarged until some measured five feet wide and five feet deep. Gwinn Vivian, the acknowledged authority on irrigation in Chaco, estimates that around 10,000 bordered gardens covered 1,000 acres on the north side of the canyon floor, and that another 1,000 acres of farmland were unirrigated.

Not only did irrigation increase the productivity of the ground within the system, it also encouraged farmers to take a chance on marginal land. A man might not be willing to take the risk of planting on shallow soil where runoff could not be collected, gambling on timely and benevolent rains, knowing that a failed crop meant starvation. But with survival assured, he could take such a chance; if the weather cooperated, he could harvest an abundant crop.

The irrigated land dictated that a large population be close at hand, not only to plant and harvest, but to control the water when it came. A limited runoff from a small shower had to be carefully husbanded, and the cascading torrents from a gully-washer had to be diverted to prevent the fields from being washed out. Irrigation created an intimate relationship between man and water, making it difficult to determine whether the large towns such as Pueblo Bonito were there because of the abundance of food they were able to produce or

much living space and storage space coexisted at any one time is impossible to determine.

Even if the population was a modest 600 for Pueblo Bonito and 5,500 or so for Chaco as a whole, such a concentration of people bred enormous problems. It has been estimated that a population of 1,000 would deplete the usable wood in a 3½ mile radius in one generation and would consume its way to a radius of 6 miles before any meaningful regrowth could occur. For people with no pack animals and five times the population, fetching firewood would have become a monumental undertaking.

Heavy timbers for roof construction also presented a problem. The huge Ponderosa pine and Douglas fir beams that supported the thatch and plaster had to be carried 20 miles from the Chuska Mountains or 60 miles from the San Juan Mountains, and the Chaco people never cut corners in the use of support beams. The 660 rooms of Pueblo Bonito must have represented an unrelenting nightmare for generations of men

whether the presence of a large population was required to keep the irrigation system operating.

The development of Chaco Canyon was an extraordinary achievement, from the extensive irrigation system to the craftsmanship shown in the huge and ordered construction of Pueblo Bonito. (It was the largest apartment complex in North America until the 19th century.) But associated with it are many mysteries.

There are roads radiating out from Chaco that run for scores of miles before the trace is lost. These aren't simple meandering paths widened by time, but 30-foot-wide thoroughfares with curbs that run inexorably in straight lines, disregarding the contour of the land. These people had no wheeled vehicles and no draft animals, so why did they need broad, surfaced roads? Any pack animal will instinctively follow the contour of the land, going farther on a gentle grade rather than assault a short, steep hill, and the Chacoans were their own pack animals. Were they merely trying to impress outsiders with their mastery of the environment? Was this an instance of "it pays to advertise" in a trade war? Were they trying to make it easier to move logs or agricultural products or craft goods coming in from, or going out to, the outliers? Or were these make-work projects to keep idle construction workers and farmhands out of mischief?

None of the explanations is completely satisfactory when one considers the enormous investment of time and energy necessary for construction and the apparent uselessness of a broad, uncontoured highway. It has been argued that the roads represent an attempt to bind other regional communities to Chaco in trade alliances. By establishing the habit of trading food, even when it wasn't necessary, and by setting themselves up as a regional redistribution center, the people of Pueblo Bonito and Chaco were ensuring that when crop failures struck them there was an operating system in place to guarantee a food supply through the lean years. This kind of interdependence makes sense and would seem consistent with what we know of the Anasazi tradition of sharing both work and resources within a village. It is not too large a logical leap to speculate that such cooperation might extend between villages, but it also presupposes a level of centralized authority that many researchers find hard to credit.

Another question that arises is the anomaly of the scattered villages, particularly on the south side of the valley, that coexisted during the classic building phase of Pueblo Bonito. The stonework in these small villages was much cruder than that of Pueblo Bonito, and there was a higher proportion of kivas to apartment rooms. Were the villagers hardscrabble poor relations

On the summer solstice the rising sun pierces an aperture in the wall of Casa Rinconada, located on a ridge across Chaco Canyon from Pueblo Bonito. The largest of the canyon's great kivas, it may have served as a center for ceremonies attended by several villages. It may also have been used for solar observations to mark off the seasons.

exiled to the boondocks to farm the marginal land? If so, they weren't removed very far. Or were they simply the ragged, rugged individualists that many societies generate? It has been suggested that the real source of power and influence originated in the villages. Was Pueblo Bonito created as a ceremonial center for the elite? An answer to any of these questions might snap the whole shape of Chacoan society into focus, but the answers have not yet been unearthed.

Unanswered Questions

Other questions persist, and perhaps the most frustrating of them concerns the location of the cemetery. Most Anasazi buried their dead close to home, sending the deceased on his way with a few gifts that scholars have often found revealing. But at Pueblo Bonito, and Chaco generally, few bodies have been found. If there was a communal graveyard, it should have been discovered by now. In view of this, archeologists are wondering what went on here. A major departure in burial practice would indicate a radical redirection of culture. We know the Chaco culture developed more rapidly than that of other Anasazi peoples, but did it develop differently as well?

There is also undeniable evidence of trade with Mexico, as well as with other Anasazi people, but there is no indication whether this trade was direct or indirect, or who undertook the traveling required for trade. Turquoise, the nearest source of which is in the Southwest 115 miles from Chaco Canyon, is so abundant in finished items at Chaco that some authorities have proposed that it might have been a medium of exchange. This would strengthen the arguments of some scholars that Chaco was a trade center and suggest the existence of a strong, centralized government.

Another "artifact of trade" with Mexico, or perhaps an extraordinary local development, is the astronomical accomplishment of the Anasazi. An observatory of sorts was recently discovered atop Fajada Butte on the south edge of Chaco, with large stone slabs that regulate the sunlight falling on several spiral-shaped petroglyphs. The arrangement indicates that the Chacoans could mark the spring and fall equinoxes as well as the summer and winter solstices. In Pueblo Bonito itself, the rising sun at the winter solstice passes through two particular openings to strike the far corner of the rooms behind — only on a few days does this happen. Perhaps it is coincidence, but the orientation of the openings coupled with the observatory on Fajada Butte leads some to wonder. It has also been suggested that the largest of Chaco Canyon's great kivas — Casa Rinconada — may have been planned in part as a solar observatory. Unfortunately, no evidence exists to indicate whether the Anasazi astronomers were trained in the south or discovered celestial order on their own.

Pottery raises another question about the people of Chaco. For nearly 1,000 years the Anasazi made their pottery in a reducing atmosphere (a firing process that prohibits the free circulation of air) that resulted in predominantly black, gray, and white colors. They could have learned another method easily enough, for the Mogollon and Hohokam fired pottery in an oxidizing atmosphere (a process allowing air circulation), that produced red, orange, and buff colors. About 1100, perhaps a scant 50 years before abandoning the great edifices they had labored to build, the Anasazi themselves quite inexplicably began producing red and orange pottery, which they decorated with black and white pigments. These warm, earth colors necessitated firing in an oxidizing atmosphere. Why did Chaco potters suddenly broaden their techniques after so many centuries of steadfast loyalty to a reducing process? The answer might illuminate the era just before Pueblo Bonito was abandoned.

Pueblo Bonito, the beautiful village, which had housed a population of hundreds, was vacated by the middle of the 12th century. While the exodus did not occur overnight, the Chacoans did not waste much time leaving. In light of the magnificent buildings they abandoned, modern visitors find the departure mysterious and inexplicable. But considering what Chaco had become it may have made good sense.

A once popular notion was that the Chacoans were driven out by raiding Navajo, a theory supported by the fact that all the doors and windows on the lower level of Pueblo Bonito were bricked up, suggesting attempts at defense. There may have been raiders, but without horses they would have been readily crushed by well-fed and numerous Anasazi fighting from defensive positions. It is just as likely that the doors and windows were closed to provide better support for the massive weight of additional floors built above.

Movement was not an alien concept to the Anasazi; except for Chaco, most sites were only occupied for 35 or 40 years before the land wore out or famine struck. Considering the size of the population in Chaco and the intensive agriculture that was practiced there, the pressures to move must have been considerable. Wood was hard to come by and getting scarcer; the removal of ground cover probably increased erosion and the cutting of arroyos; and waste disposal was undoubtedly a problem, making disease a constant threat. It is also theorized that the irrigation practices, which conserved soil and water so effectively, trapped the alkali naturally present in the soils until the concentration of salts finally rendered the soil sterile.

Also, the climate that nurtured the rapid growth of Chaco changed, affecting the frequency and amplitude of rain. Previous to A.D. 900 the area had experienced frequent alternations between wet and dry years, but it was never very wet or very dry. But during the years when Chaco was at its height the periods of wetness and dryness were longer.

Some time after 1150 the rainfall pattern returned to the shorter cycles, and there were more frequent periods of drought as a result. In the face of these physical

and climatic problems, social pressures could only increase. Priests or clans might have been blamed for failing to propitiate the gods properly, causing a schism in the community. Families, clans, or neighborhoods might have begun squabbling over title to the diminishing supply of food or the limited natural resources. If there was a strong central authority, it may have collapsed in the face of howling outrage from a populace angered by the erosion of their quality of life.

The departure was not abrupt, but by 1300 the Anasazi had left Chaco Canyon, and eventually the land was occupied by the Navajo. The people of Chaco would move on, by stages, and commingling with their cultural neighbors at Mesa Verde and with other Anasazi, they would become the Pueblo Indians who still stride the Southwest from eastern New Mexico to northern Arizona. Long afterward, in 1896, an American trader and amateur archeologist named Richard Wetherill arrived and used beams from Pueblo Bonito to build his trading post.

The real mystery of Chaco is not so much why the Anasazi left but why they came, and what sort of people they must have been to build what they did. Chaco was never again to see the glory that it once knew, but perhaps that is fitting. The Anasazi of Chaco Canyon and Pueblo Bonito had their day in the sun, and what they built still glows with an incandescence that stirs the beholder.

The once-magnificent complex of Pueblo Bonito lies in ruins, demolished in part by the collapse in 1941 of Threatening Rock, an enormous free-standing slab of sandstone that had worried the Chacoans centuries earlier. Nature has also destroyed the timber and earthen roofs of the kivas, exposing the important ceremonial chambers to the eyes of strangers.

259

A SLEEPING TOWN AWAKES

Destroyed by the Spaniards nearly 400 years ago, a terraced settlement in Colombia's mountains was reclaimed by the jungle and only recently rediscovered. Local Indians may have the clue to its forgotten past.

César Sepúlveda was one of thousands of rural Colombians known as *huaqueros* ("grave robbers") in the business of digging up old ceramics, potsherds, and other pre-Columbian treasures to sell to smugglers along Colombia's Caribbean coast. One day in 1975 he was scavenging deep in the jungle of the Sierra Nevada de Santa Marta, one and a half days' walking distance from his home, when he discovered a stone road. Believing he had found the route to one of the fabled Tairona villages, where people were said to have buried their dead with hordes of gold, he started to look for graves.

Another *huaquero* interrupted his search, challenged him for possession of the claim, and fired five shots into Sepúlveda's chest. Friends and family members with Sepúlveda chased the attacker into the woods and killed him. They then returned to the fallen Sepúlveda and buried him beneath the rocks of a terrace.

Until the day Sepúlveda paid for his find with his life, nearly four centuries had passed since "The Lost City in the Jungle" had been brutally depopulated by the Spanish conquistadors and abandoned, to be silently reclaimed by the jungle. Now once again the place fell quiet beneath the shade of the 120-foot-tall tagua palms; the sleeping town remained the sole preserve of parrots, monkeys, ocelots, tapirs, peccaries, snakes, and other creatures of the subtropical escarpment.

But word of the jungle shoot-out soon reached the coastal city of Santa Marta, and Gilberto Cadavid of the Colombian Institute of Anthropology's field station there became interested. Thanks to earlier archeological studies and to the vivid writings of the Spanish chroniclers, the Tairona culture was quite well known. Other sites in less remote areas had already been found and excavated, and their architecture along with examples of their pottery and extraordinary gold ornaments had revealed that they were among the foremost engineers and craftsmen of the pre-Columbian world. Researchers knew of the existence of the lost town, but not its location. "One problem for us," comments Alvaro Soto Holguín, former director of the Colombian Institute of Anthropology, "was that the chroniclers were often poets, and they would freely change the data to maintain the meter of their verse."

In their mountain fastness the Tairona built a spacious village with terraces that grace the slopes like hanging gardens. Stone stairways and roads link the terraces, which once supported thatched houses like the reconstructions in this photograph.

In March 1976, Cadavid mounted an expedition into the Sierra Nevada. After six days he arrived at the spot where Sepúlveda had died. A week's digging convinced Cadavid that he was sifting through significant history, and the Colombian Institute of Culture quickly set up simple housing in the jungle for researchers, workers, and a division of the National Guard (assigned to protect the place from looters). Thus began the enormous labor of digging out and preserving one of the largest pre-Columbian population centers discovered since Hiram Bingham found the Inca city of Machu Picchu in 1911. The site, initially called *El Infierno* ("Hell") because of its inaccessible location, was given the prosaic name of "Buritaca 200" in reference to the Buritaca River flowing close by, and to the number of archeological sites already explored in the area. (What the Indians called the place remains unknown.) In charge of the project was Soto Holguín.

The importance of the lost town's exploration extends well beyond the discovery of hidden treasure. Unlike some of the other major New World civilizations — such as the wide-ranging empires of the Aztec and Inca — the Tairona, one of Colombia's indigenous peoples, stayed close to home, establishing a self-sufficient network of interdependent villages. For almost a millennium before the Spanish Conquest, they managed to support a large population on crops grown on their unique mountain terraces without harming the environment. In today's South America the rain forest is being destroyed by an influx of settlers, and the soil leached and eroded away, threatening agricultural disaster. It is felt that the achievement of the Tairona may contain lessons in ecological survival.

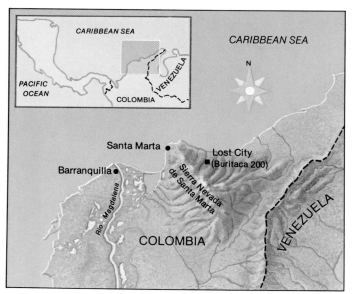

The "Lost City" was one of many Tairona villages in the Sierra Nevada de Santa Marta, an isolated mountain range that rises abruptly from Colombia's coastal plains.

Situated on a ridge 3,700 feet up on the northern slope of the Sierra Nevada de Santa Marta, the highest coastal range in the world, the lost town can be reached only by helicopter or by a five-day mule trip. The isolation of the site is impressive from the air. Eyes strain for the hint of a path, but nothing is revealed. The slopes and valleys below are a seamless green. Only when the aircraft makes a pass over the settlement can one detect a collection of circular stone foundations and terraces scalloped into the hillside, suggesting barnacles on a long-submerged log. The helicopter settles gently on the largest of the terraces and its passengers step out onto a lofty bluff. Long ago the site of the heliport was the great ceremonial center of the lost town. The 20th-century visitor is at first seized by the quiet. Too far away to be heard, a waterfall glides silently down a neighboring mountainside. The horizon hangs suspended above an undulating range of mountain ridges that surround the valley like a garland. Below, the Buritaca River courses its way through the jungle floor to the sea.

The descent from the high ground is easy, on stairways that have withstood time well. The only difficulty is in negotiating the narrow steps — the Indians of the period clearly had smaller feet and, according to the Spanish chroniclers, they didn't wear shoes.

Reaching the first level, one can look back at the skillful reinforcing of the hummock itself, a vivid example of how the Indians had capitalized on the topography. Artfully buttressed by thousands of stones, the knoll descends in layers and finally reaches a flagstone-paved esplanade, now framed by towering tagua palms whose exposed roots splay out like electrical cables.

Descending the flanks of the mountain from the esplanade, the circular lily-pad terraces fan out, protected from erosion by drainage gutters laid around their peripheries and connected by walkways to the main roads. One marvels at the feats of engineering performed by these people, who quarried their own rock with homemade implements.

The royally commissioned chroniclers who accompanied the Spanish to Colombia in the 16th and 17th centuries described in detail scores of villages throughout this mountainous area, peopled by Indians of a highly colorful and religious culture, whom they called Tairona. (The name comes from the word *tairo*, which in the Chibcha language means "goldworkers." The Spanish chroniclers also reported finding a gold foundry in the Sierra Nevada area, but contemporary excavators have failed to locate it.)

"The valley is crowned all around by high mountains . . . ," Father Pedro Simón wrote of one place, "their ridge lines broken by soft, golden streams (which, like crystal snakes, slither down from the mountain tops to the valley), with hills and clefts occupied by large villages, Indian places which one can see from anywhere along the mountain flanks — a pleasant view of over 1,000 large houses, each inhabited by

Terraces scallop the flanks of a ridge encircled by mountains at the Buritaca site. Resembling a dragonfly on a lily pad (left), a helicopter rests on a terrace that was once a ceremonial center. In the foreground is a shelter for fieldworkers.

kinfolk. . . . Finally, throughout the Caldera valley, everything was festivities, dances, games of skill, delicacies, and leisure, since they needed to do scant work to obtain ample food and clothing.

"Their cloths were painted many colors and made on looms," noted Father Pedro. "There weren't any Indians without jewelry. They wore all sorts of beads, gold necklaces, crowns, and nose ornaments, some set with precious and well-cut stones. All the girls wore four or six small pieces of gold around their necks and dressed in two separate garments of painted cloth. They carried fans made from palm wood and feathers . . . . In fact, they had so many curious things made of feathers that it is impossible to describe: short capes with hoods, [decorative] flowers, waistcoats covered with feathers, large and small fans. They even had clothes made of tiger skins. They kept parrots in order to have feathers."

Anthropologists are inclined to believe that the Tairona were descendants of Indians who originally lived on the broad plains of the lower Magdalena River valley on the inland side of the Sierra Nevada. The plains' long annual dry season, lasting more than six months, made it almost impossible to grow crops there. Probably the Indians found the almost constant rainfall at altitudes of 3,000 to 4,000 feet more favorable to agriculture. Also the prevalence of tropical diseases on the plains in pre-Columbian times may have prompted them to move to the cooler and healthier uplands.

According to Donald W. Lathrap, an American anthropologist widely known in the field for his work in

263

South America, the Tairona's ascent to the Buritaca site was the result of two occurrences. The first was the development of "high-yield" corn, which enabled the Indians to produce more of the grain on terrain previously considered unsuitable for crops. And, secondly — if the Tairona had any hesitation about taking their civilization to new heights — the threat of other warlike Indians in their home territory very likely strengthened their resolve. The Tairona were skilled in guerrilla warfare, but the steep slopes provided a more defensible location.

Once settled, Lathrap contends, the Tairona were forced by the ruggedness of the mountains to employ all their technological and agricultural ingenuity. In order to provide flat lands for growing their crops, they built terraces, which they constantly filled with cuttings and green mulch. "Theirs was a stable system," suggests Lathrap, "artificially maintained by a high level of human endeavor."

The Tairona's diet was surprisingly varied for people living on such rugged and challenging terrain. They kept bees for honey and planted manioc, beans, avocados, sweet potatoes, peppers, fruit, and, principally, corn. They hunted game, probably traded for fish with people dwelling nearer the ocean, and like many Indi-

ans even today, they chewed coca leaves both as a source of energy and as an appetite suppressant.

The Tairona culture thrived until its bloody encounter with the Spanish. The conquistadors made a landfall at Santa Marta in approximately 1525 and quickly began their subjugation of the Indian tribes in the region. But the Tairona society was strong and cohesive. Each of its numerous cities had an independent hierarchical political organization. Thus, in contrast to the highly centralized Inca and Aztec empires, there was no single leader whose downfall would throw the populace into chaos. Using spears and arrows, the Tairona resisted European firepower for almost 100 years, often attacking the invaders in the Sierra Nevada as well as successfully protecting their village redoubts.

Other tribes did not hold out as long against the Spanish. The Muisca on the savanna of Bogotá, for example, weakened and surrendered their valuable land in the course of only 30 years. "The Spanish asked them for their gold, and they gave it. The Tairona fought back," says Soto Holguín.

Finally, in 1600, the Spanish penetrated the Tairona defenses and, judging by the amount of charcoal archeologists are now finding, put the torch to the carefully designed village centers and the thatched houses and

killed those occupants who had not fled. "They had to exterminate the Tairona because they were such a strong culture," adds Soto Holguín.

The battle at the lost town must have been as spectacular as it was fearsome, with the bearded Spanish armored with boat-shaped helmets, round shields, and padded coats, warding off the rain of missiles that fell on them as they climbed the broad granite and slate stairway to the jungle capital. They discharged their blunderbusses and crossbows, while the smooth-cheeked, feathered Indians shot their arrows and hurled spears, darts, and stones at the advancing troops. Only when the Spanish brought their horses up from the rear did the Indians flee.

After the Spanish had overrun the settlement, taken as much gold as they could find, and effectively destroyed what had been a sophisticated metropolis for most of a millennium, they abandoned the site. By the time César Sepúlveda came upon it in 1975, some two feet of earth covered the ancient roads and terraces.

By 1980, the scientific team billeted at the site had unearthed nearly 300 miles of stone roads and 260 house sites spreading over 1,000 acres or so of gorges, slopes, and plateaus. Making what they term "very conservative" estimates, the archeologists believe that

Accomplished Tairona goldsmiths fashioned splendid figurines and pieces of jewelry that were coveted by the Spanish. Among the finest examples of their goldwork are hollow, or opencast, anthropomorphic figurines like these. The fantastic being above has a headdress incorporating serpent or dragon motifs. The warrior god at the left wears a bat headdress and holds a two-headed serpent belt. Such pieces were worked in either pure gold or tumbaga, a gold-rich copper alloy.

the lost town's population was at least 3,000 and that the network of Tairona settlements contained at least 300,000 inhabitants.

Although it is smaller than Machu Picchu, the Buritaca site is as old and its archeological yield is great. But its major significance lies in what it reveals about the Tairona's architecture and their skill at using the land. While the Inca surpassed the Tairona in stonework, it is evident that they were no match for the Indians of the Sierra Nevada in planning for both a high quality of community life and environmental protection. Long before the arrival of the Spanish, the Tairona had developed a spacious urban complex by constructing terraces that graced the steep slopes like hanging gardens. So skillfully had they engineered all this that they were able to develop a densely populous, permanent society without upsetting the ecology of their region.

Learning from the Tairona

Today, scattered settlers have hacked down jungle growth to clear a few acres for yucca, coffee, and plaintain fields, only to see their plots erode away. The Tairona "must have known something," says Soto Holguín. "Pure science is not so feasible for a poor country like Colombia, and what we are doing with archeology is trying to learn something from our past to apply to our present."

For eight months, from April through November, it rains every day at Buritaca 200. To prevent floods and erosion, the Tairona constructed an extensive drainage system with stone-lined ditches, reservoirs, and underground sluices. After many centuries of pelting rains and accumulating soil and debris, their stonework is still intact and the drains still function.

The Tairona's main access to the village was a road — actually a wide stairway utilizing natural rock formations — that started by the river and ascended about 500 feet to a plateau where the first terraces and houses apparently were built. From there the main artery branches out into a network of roads and stairways linking the clusters of houses. Small stone bridges span rivulets. The major roads are surfaced with carefully fitted slabs of slate or granite laid on a bed of gravel, while the secondary roads are built of unpolished rock set into the ground. By far the most impressive roadway is the avenue that climbs the hillside past several distinct neighborhoods, finally reaching what is believed to have been a ceremonial square. A large upended rock tablet beside the main avenue is covered with carved indentations that were traced by researchers and found to approximate the plan of the community and probably constituted a map. According to the chronicles, trade with other villages was brisk, and one can easily conjure up visions of Indian merchants ascending and descending the avenue, passing residents busily going about their daily errands.

The community was divided into residential neighborhoods, work areas and farm fields, and sectors for religious and civic functions. Those living on the higher terraces grew corn and wove textiles, while the Indians on the lower levels, near the routes to the coast, carried on a trade that may possibly have extended to Peru and Mexico. A city so well organized had to have a highly structured social system and hierarchy, and accordingly, certain streets boast more spacious house sites, where the elite presumably lived. One group of terraces had two stones blocking the entryway and restricting access. Several stairways that end abruptly puzzled diggers at the site until someone suggested that they might have been public comfort stations, placed discreetly out of view of the houses and thoroughfares.

By codifying artifacts with a computer, the archeologists were able to reconstruct a Tairona household. The circular walls of the Tairona houses were made of wood lashed to four main pilings and six smaller ones secured at the foundation with stones; the roofs were palm thatch. Most of the houses were from 14 to 39 feet in diameter, depending on the status of the family in the social hierarchy. Each dwelling had two entrances facing each other, and a fireplace toward the back. One small house with no sign of a hearth in it may have lodged youths fasting during their initiation rites into adulthood. Built with no interior partitions, the typical house was divided into "masculine" and "feminine" areas, with hunting and farming tools in the first and cooking utensils and decorative objects in

the second. Half of a pot deliberately broken in two was buried in one section and the other half of the same vessel was placed in the opposite area.

The Tairona used river sand as temper for their clay pots, which they turned out with an earth-red, black, or beige finish and decorated with a simple incised design or with appliqués of clay. Most of the ware that has been recovered is the plain but pleasingly shaped red pottery apparently made for domestic use. Tairona ceramics were either utilitarian or ceremonial. Ceremonial pots were not fired in the same kilns as domestic pots — a sign of respect. It is the ceremonial vessels, used in celebrations and burials, that show the great artistry of the Tairona. The elaborately shaped bowls, cups, and jars were given a handsome burnished black finish and ornamented with modeled representations of human faces, jaguars, snakes, turtles, and other creatures, often with protruding fangs and tongues. Among the most unusual pieces are clay ocarinas (small wind instruments) shaped like birds, warriors, or priests with headdresses. A number of small carvings of granite, carnelian, agate, and quartz have been found in graves, and at ceremonial sites.

Gold artifacts found in their funerary arrays — figurines and ornaments such as earrings, nose rings, beads, and pendants — show that the Tairona were also superb metallurgists who used both the lost-wax and the hammered techniques to fashion the pieces. The arti-

Archeologist Soto Holguín treats and labels ceramic artifacts. Most of the pottery found at Buritaca is the red ware for everyday use, but the Tairona also made vessels with a beige finish and special pieces with a shiny black surface.

A fieldworker uses chalk to outline an ancient petroglyph found at Pueblo Bello, a village near Buritaca 200. Representations of fantastic beings like this may have had religious significance, but more likely they were "doodles."

sans worked with both pure gold and a gold-rich tumbaga, an alloy of gold and copper with a reddish hue. To give the tumbaga a golden color they treated it with acid obtained from a plant juice that dissolved out the surface copper. Gold washes and gold leaf were also occasionally used for a rich effect.

In the words of Gerardo Reichel-Dolmatoff, an anthropologist who has written extensively about the indigenous peoples of Colombia, "Life in a Tairona village must have been colorful and busy. Here were a people who loved to manufacture with care and taste the simplest utensils of everyday life, to decorate them and to individualize them. They took pleasure in the smooth and shining surfaces of their black pottery, of their stone artifacts, and of their gold and copper trinkets. There must assuredly have been skilled artisans in many different crafts: potters, goldsmiths, stone carvers, masons, and we can imagine the artistry of their wood carvings, textiles, and featherwork which gained the admiration of the Spaniards."

It is the view of Donald Lathrap that the decorative use of linear patterns, featuring rows of triangles, and the custom of beveling out the backgrounds of ceramic designs show the influences of earlier Indian cultures in northern South America but reveal no apparent connection to more widely known civilizations.

The team in charge of the dig includes archeologists, anthropologists, and engineers who supervise 25 to 30 workers, many of whom had initially been soldiers on guard duty and had returned to join in the work. In the process of excavating house sites they have constructed grids of tautly strung wire, marking off yard-square segments to be dusted and sifted with delicate tools in the search for artifacts.

The research has taken anthropologists to the villages of the Kogi Indians who, they have found, still practice many of the old customs indicated by the findings at Buritaca 200. The Kogi live farther from the coast than other Colombian tribes and are therefore less touched by modern influences. They wear flowing handwoven cotton garments as did the Tairona, according to descriptions in the Spanish Chronicles, and their settlements incorporate similar construction patterns.

This cultural continuity has been an invaluable help to the field workers mystified by some of their finds at the Tairona digs. At a number of house sites, for example, they have found lidded pottery vessels buried beneath the floor or the doorsill. Far from being caches of treasure, as one might have expected them to be, the pots contained only some pebbles or stone beads. Researchers wondered why the Tairona would secrete pots with pebbles in this manner until they found a parallel custom among the Kogi. When the Kogi begin work on a new house they ceremonially bury in the foundation a vessel with a pebble for each member of the household. The shape, color, and size of the pebble link it to the particular person it represents. When a new child is born the pot is dug up and another pebble

Traditionally dressed Kogi Indians walk beneath tall tagua palms in one of the towns built centuries ago by their forefathers, the Tairona. The Kogi carry supplies on their backs in cloth sacks supported by shoulderstraps or headbands.

Lost City in the Jungle

White-clad Tairona Indians stroll among the stone terraces of their mountain settlement in the years before the Spanish conquest. A gentle, pastoral people with a deep respect for the earth and a reverence for the natural order, they had been driven from inland valleys to the steep slopes of Colombia's Sierra Nevada de Santa Marta by population pressure and the lure of more fertile land. Settling on ridges, they carved platforms for their houses and agricultural plots out of the mountainside and linked them with paths and stairways. Aqueducts diverted jungle rainfall to sluice each platform, irrigate gardens, and maintain a water supply. Although they put up a fierce resistance to the conquistadors, the Tairona were overrun, their culture destroyed, and their settlements left to be reclaimed by the jungle.

is added. In this way "all the inhabitants are identified and taken under the protection of the spirits which are the guardians of the dwelling," explains Reichel-Dolmatoff. The Kogi also place stones outside their houses to designate the sexes of the occupants — stones with holes denote females, those with no holes, males.

Equally puzzling were the "thin, wing-shaped bars" of polished stone found in Tairona sites. At first it was assumed that they were worn as pendants. But it was learned from the Kogi that the objects are musical instruments used in ceremonial dances. Dangling in pairs from the raised arms of a dancing priest, the thin plates produce a light tinkle.

Researchers also wondered what to make of a jaguar's skull they found near the entrance of a Tairona ceremonial house they excavated. Again the explanation came from the Kogi. It is their tradition to dedicate ceremonial houses to the jaguar-god, and in earlier times jaguar skulls ornamented the doorways.

The jaguar cult of the Kogi is only a part of a very complex system of religious and metaphysical beliefs, and the Kogi priests, far from being practitioners of magic, are "men of high moral stature and acute intellectual ability, measured by any standards," says Reichel-Dolmatoff. The Kogi perceive themselves to be the possessors of the one true religion. They believe in a supreme Mother Goddess who created the cosmos and stratified it into nine worlds of which the fifth and centermost is ours.

They also hold that the world is animated by solar energy that is strongly manifested at the time of the solstices and equinoxes. Amazingly, anthropologists have found that the central house in a Kogi complex is built in such a way that on two days in the year a ray of sunlight shines down through a hole in the roof and, as the day progresses, traces an equatorial line across the floor between the opposing doors of the building. The days in question are the spring and fall equinoxes. The priests have the responsibility of seeing to it that the sun and moon stay on course and that the seasons and fertility cycles are preserved.

The Kogi, an introspective and religious people, believe in the coexistence of Good and Evil and hold that the purpose of knowledge is to "find a balance between Good and Evil and to reach old age in a state of wisdom and tolerance," explains Reichel-Dolmatoff. They consider themselves to be the "elder brothers" of mankind whose mission in life is to protect the health of the universe. They themselves have learned to use such God-given gifts as agriculture and tools and to live in harmony with their environment. The priests, who are not only their spiritual leaders but the true power of the community, are apprehensive that the ways and inventions of foreign cultures will prove to be destructive. It is the role of the Kogi, in their view, to resist the onslaught of modern civilization so that in the event of a worldwide holocaust they can start life anew.

Study of the customs and religion of the modern-day Kogi has not only helped with the interpretation of Tairona culture — it has also shed some light on outside influences at work in its earliest phases. According to Reichel-Dolmatoff, it seems likely that the Tairona culture "received strong Meso- and Central American influences, most probably by oversea contact." And he

Living in a small village seemingly lost in the vastness of the Sierra Nevada de Santa Marta (far left), the Kogi cling to the old ways and wisdoms of their ancestors even as the modern world encroaches. Not only are their circular thatched houses and their hand-loomed garments (left) similar to those of the Tairona, but the Kogi seem to have retained many of their customs and beliefs. Because of this, the Kogi have been able to help archeologists in their efforts to understand the Tairona culture and interpret their finds at Buritaca 200.

Filling her gourd with water drawn from a log conduit, a girl of Colombia's Sierra Nevada de Santa Marta follows a daily routine that has changed little in the centuries since the Spanish Conquest.

points out that the "most arresting parallels" with Mesoamerican culture are in the whole complex of religious beliefs and practices of the Tairona, evidenced by those of the Kogi today.

The Colombian Institute of Culture and those directly connected with the Buritaca 200 project are fiercely committed to protecting their discovery from treasure hunters. The site was preserved in the past because of its remoteness — looters intrepid enough to penetrate the depths of the jungle were unable to linger because of the lack of food. Colombians have had the painful experience of seeing other archeological sites almost totally destroyed by *huaqueros,* and so they are determined that visitors to "The Lost City in the Jungle" will be admitted only in the most "controlled" manner.

"We haven't talked much about Buritaca 200 on purpose," says Soto Holguín. "We don't want thousands of visitors here. We don't want to build a road or even a footpath to it. Around the Lost City there is vast land in very good condition, and we want to protect it as well as the city sites. The only way to get here will remain by helicopter. One day you will go to Santa Marta, board a plane, come here, see slides and films about the Tairona culture and the results of our project, tour the city and return the same day. We want it to be a learning experience."

The Tairona aren't around anymore to do the teaching, but their probable descendants, the Kogi, think we have a lot to learn. "They consider us little brothers," Soto Holguín observes. "They think our machines are toys, and they actually have compassion for the fact that we are not in close touch with the world."

NECROPOLIS OF A GOLDEN EMPIRE

On the fertile north coast of Peru lived a people whose legacy of sumptuous gold artifacts and a rigidly stratified yet superbly functioning society belied their curious preoccupation with theft and burial.

It was the largest, most populous city of pre-Columbian South America — the powerful capital of an extensive empire. But most of Chan Chan's citizens, its backbone underclass of artisans and builders, lived in tiny windowless rooms, in neighborhoods as crammed and frantically busy as beehives.

Nor did this great cultural center of the severe Chimú civilization — its ceramics, jewelry, and woven goods famous and influential for centuries — boast wide avenues or imposing temples or spacious plazas, like so many of the smaller, less wealthy cities and towns of the Andean region.

Chan Chan was, in fact, a city uniquely closed in upon itself, despite an intricately functioning bureaucracy that administered a territory including two-thirds of northern Peru's irrigated coast lands. It was a city in which a quasi-divine aristocracy, perhaps no more than a tenth of the population, lived in sybaritic isolation inside huge walled compounds. It was a city for which law and religion were synonymous, joined in a grimly peculiar preoccupation with theft. And, what must have been most paradoxical of all, this bustling manufacturing city was gradually becoming the province of the dead. With the demise of each Chimú ruler, his property was sealed off. Down through the genera-

tions, as the common people in the barrios continued to produce the goods and services essential to the maintenance of a despotic state, their capital city became increasingly rich and strange, a vast spreading necropolis — its silent compounds honeycombed with vaults of golden funerary treasure.

What beliefs, what cultural precedents, what historical and geographical circumstances led to the rise and consolidation of Chimú hegemony in 14th-century coastal Peru?

In large part, we can never know. There was no writing. Tales gathered by Spanish chroniclers decades after the collapse of Chan Chan might have some basis in fact, but most have the soft focus of legend. *Yunga,* the language of the empire, has apparently vanished. In the cycle of conquest and assimilation that characterized pre-Columbian South America, the Chimú would eventually succumb to the all-powerful Inca, who skillfully brought in their own bureaucratic institutions

These hammered gold hands and forearms, which probably adorned a Chimú mummy, are a striking testament to the metalworking skills of the artists of pre-Columbian Peru. The geometric designs are thought to represent tattooing.

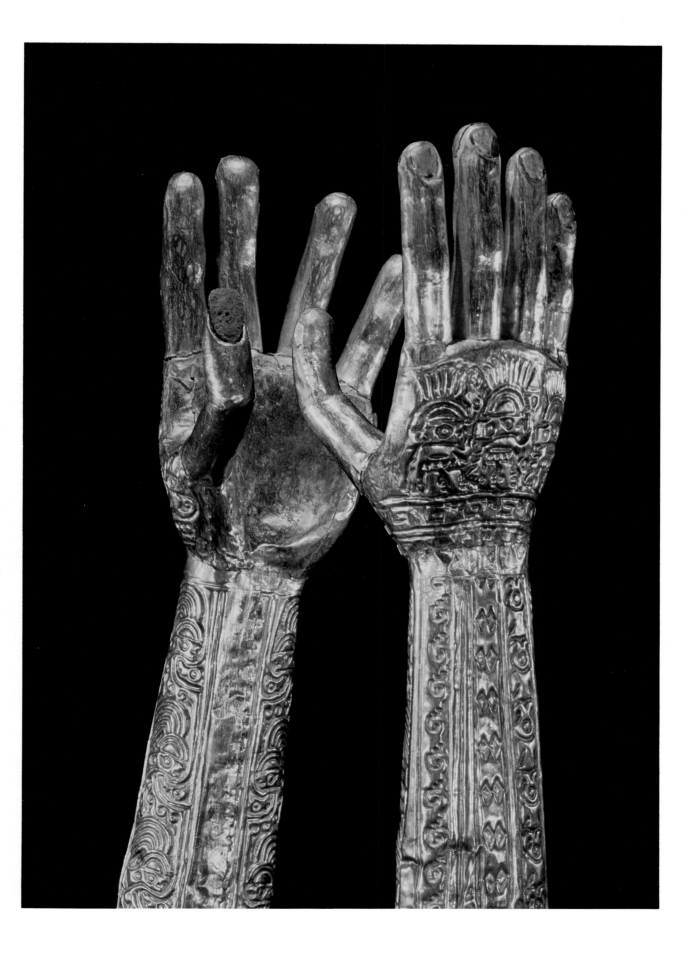

while co-opting the defeated empire's leadership.

Ironically, it is this very process, however, that gives scholars insight into the history of the many civilizations that succeeded one after the other in ancient Peru. In other words, it seems probable that no one culture is entirely, or even significantly, distinct from all the others. Each seems to have been an expression of ways of viewing life, of responding to the challenges and resources of the Peruvian environment, even of societal and kinship concepts, that survived in the region for hundreds, and perhaps thousands, of years. Typically, the conqueror learned from the conquered. New ideas took their place alongside, rather than supplanted, the traditional views.

The story of Chan Chan, therefore, is to a large extent the story of its site, the Moche or Santa Catalina Valley, and of the region that surrounded it. The history of the Chimú empire is inseparable from that of the peoples who had preceded and would follow it.

Archeologists agree that settlement patterns in the Moche Valley over the centuries show an early dependence upon the sea for food, then a gradual transfer of energies to agriculture. This critical change, according to most scholars, could have occurred only as a result of large-scale, highly organized communal effort, owing to the characteristic features of the northern coast.

As in the Nile Valley, great expanses of arable land lie near abundant sources of water, but human energy is required to exploit this resource. At Chan Chan, the foothills of the Andean cordillera, which tumble down to the edge of the Pacific along parts of the coast, are set miles back from the sea. The large wedge-shaped plain watered by the Moche River is suitable for irrigation agriculture, as settlers in the region may have discovered as early as 1800 B.C. The key is the dependable water supply. Although there is virtually no rainfall along the coast, the Moche, which originates in the mountains about a mile above sea level, is well fed by tributaries that catch the regular annual rainfall of the Continental Divide. In addition, because the Andes are subject to severe erosion, the river carries an alluvial flow that rapidly forms soil on reclaimed land and re-supplies nutrients to fields under cultivation.

At least 57 valleys along the Peruvian coastline benefit from the Andean runoff, but the Moche Valley is unusual topographically, a circumstance that may well have caused the development of distinctive methods and policies of irrigation. The river lies asymmetrically along the south edge of the valley, so that the north side of the drainage area slopes gently down to the riverbank while the southern area is jaggedly hilly.

The practical consequences are several. The steeply rising southern land, though less potentially arable, can be reclaimed with short lead-off canals, while reclamation of the much more arable northern areas requires rather long lead-off canals. The lowlands, furthermore, were farmed as sunken gardens designed to tap the high water table. Hydraulic engineering developed so rapidly in the area that by about A.D. 1000 Chimú engineers were making use of concepts not discovered by Western scientists until a century ago.

Historically, irrigation systems in the valley have been built on both banks of the river, forming a network rather than acting as independent canals. In social terms, such a concentration of construction effort was undoubtedly favorable to the development of a single political structure in the valley.

Thus, periodically, the valley gave rise to a culture that gained ascendancy over a much larger region and over much larger populations. Perhaps a century before or after the beginning of the Christian era, for example, pyramids of the Sun and Moon built south of the river served as a center of power for a culture that has variously been called the Moche or the proto-Chimú. Digs in these great platform mounds have unearthed evidence of a society with many characteristics that flowered more fully in Chimú times.

First, the Moche culture (100 B.C. – A.D. 750) was vigorously expansionist, moving out from the well-organized agricultural system of the valley to form extensive trade networks. Second, as befits an authoritarian state, economic control was in the hands of a sophisticated bureaucracy; workers fell into specialized occupation categories; and there was a labor tax imposed upon communities or kinship groups for the building and repair of the canals, city walls, and other municipal projects. Third, as proved by the variations in grave goods and domestic architecture, there were clear-cut social distinctions in Moche culture. The evidence seems to suggest that there were two separate social classes, or castes: the ruling nobility and the commoners, mainly farmers and fishermen.

Scenes from Life

Much of this information may seem somewhat abstract, and it is true that archeological knowledge, to date, has not adequately filled several wide gaps in the record. The Moche come to life for the average observer, however, because of their unrivaled, inimitable legacy of ceramic sculpture. Little as vibrant, as colorful, and as individualistic has been found in the art of any other New World civilization.

Some academics caution that we probably cannot grasp the true meanings of the painted pottery. We may be tempted to see the various scenes and remarkable characters as typical of everyday life, but scholars point out that many mundane activities are not shown. We see warfare and hunting, but not cooking and farming. Perhaps the pottery was not intended as a record of cultural manners and mores but has, instead, a religious or symbolic significance that is lost to us.

Nonetheless, it is fair to say that there is an evocation of exuberant life, perhaps even of individuality, that belies the otherwise monochromatic evidence of the archeological dig. These people were citizens in an efficiently functioning despotic state; yet, they do not

The vast grid of Chan Chan's buildings, now heavily eroded by periodic El Niño rains, shows clearly in this aerial view. Situated just inland from the Pacific on Peru's north coast (see map at right), the city once was surrounded by fields irrigated by the Moche River.

seem to have lived as if there were nothing to life but to act like a cog on a wheel. We see laughter, pain, surprise, and terror. We see implacable birth and grotesque death. Because of the uniquely compelling images of the Moche ceramics, in fact, we catch our only glimpse of the lot of the commoner, before the formidable Chimú ranged into that ancient valley and set up the second most powerful empire (after the Inca) ever to exist in pre-Columbian South America. As one writer has suggested, the Moche would be to the Chimú as the creative, precedent-setting Greeks were to the cleverly assimilating Romans.

Where did they originate, this people that would build at Chan Chan the largest adobe city in history and forge a cohesive empire stretching for over 600 miles along the Peruvian coast?

The Chimú themselves believed that their history began with the mysterious appearance of Taycanamo, an aristocratic figure of undisclosed origin who floated to shore on a balsa log. Lord of certain religious rituals that he performed with "yellow powders," this presumedly charismatic leader explained to the awed natives of the Moche Valley that he had been commissioned to govern them by "a great lord from across the sea." In any event, he was accepted as ruler, thereby founding a dynasty that controlled the region for some

500 years, or until the time of the Inca conquest.

No doubt both legend and the propaganda of statecraft play important roles in this tale. Still, it appears that a dynasty was reigning from the city of Chan Chan by the year A.D. 1000. One historical record credits Taycanamo's son, Guacri-caur, and a grandson, Ñançen-pinco, with conquests to expand the burgeoning empire during their successive reigns. As the empire grew, so did the dogma that monarchy, successfully supplanting the rule of scattered village chiefs, was bringing the fortunate coastal valleys the benefits of order as opposed to anarchy.

What certainly developed in Chan Chan, and throughout the empire, was one of history's most rigidly structured societies. Apparently, the great majority of the populace believed, or at least quietly accepted, the idea that the families of the ruling aristocracy were entirely different beings, superior to ordinary humans. Commoners were supposedly descended from two planets, but their lords claimed a lineage that went back to two stars. This separation of classes, along with differences of rank within each class, affected the very building of Chan Chan.

By the time of its defeat by the Inca about the year 1470, the city contained 10 large rectangular enclosures, or *ciudadelas* (citadels), loosely arranged around the center of the metropolis. Each was surrounded by adobe walls that might have a base as thick as 6 feet and reach almost as high as 30 feet. A single entrance in the north wall gave access to an enclosed world of entry courts, corridors, storerooms, a kitchen, and numerous U-shaped rooms known as *audiencias*. It seems indisputable that a *ciudadela* was the royal residence of the reigning monarch and his family and retainers. Palace officials insured that the storerooms were kept well stocked. Distribution of stores apparently took place in the *audiencias*, whose single entrance and artful placement deep within the mazelike corridors of the compound made theft difficult if not impossible. The high walls enforced the fundamental division between Chimú aristocrats and their inferiors outside.

But the life of the royal compound revolved around the ruler, and when he died, his *ciudadela* became his lasting tomb. In funeral ceremonies that must have been lavish, the deceased ruler was buried with his rarest personal treasures, and scores of young women were sacrificed, or sacrificed themselves, to join him in his next life. Meanwhile, the new ruler commissioned the construction of a new compound for his imperial household. Enlisted in this construction effort, the common people were exhorted to work their hardest, as "the scorned ones of fortune," to help the new ruler take advantage of an odd system of inheritance.

"Split inheritance," which was also the law in the Inca empire, gave the rights of divine authority to one heir, the succeeding ruler. These rights, in practical terms, included the mandate to govern, the power to wage war, and the ability to levy taxes. The right to own the former monarch's property, however, passed to a *panaqa* — literally, a corporation made up of secondary heirs. This group took over the management of his compound and other property, collected revenue from taxes he had imposed, and maintained the cult that grew up around his memory.

It followed, of course, that the ruler's successor had to bestir himself to amass his own material wealth, an enterprise most swiftly accomplished by enlarging the empire by conquest and taxing anew the existing provinces under his rule. It also seems likely that the members of the new ruler's household would be very loyal and highly supportive of his adventures, since the wealth of the corporation that they and their children would inherit would be in direct proportion to the worldly success of his reign.

Although some scholars advise against accepting Moche ceramics as accurate representations of everyday life, one cannot deny the charm and individuality of examples such as the bowl above showing workers smelting metal by blowing through tubes to force air into a furnace; or the funerary object at right, which may have represented a subject offering as tribute a shirt decorated with birds, possibly cormorants.

Where, in this arrangement, were the commoners? The urban lower class in the capital city lived in small apartments which archeologists term "small irregularly agglutinated rooms." Approximately 20,000 people were housed in about 250 acres of such rooms. Socially, they were said to "look upon themselves not as natural equals to the privileged." Economically, they were crucial to the empire, an urban proletariat that produced goods for their own use, to exchange for other goods and services, and for ceremony and trade.

This class was not, however, undifferentiated. Metalworkers, for example, were so specialized that some prepared sheet metal from ingots or fabricated simple artifacts while others tackled more delicate assignments. Archeological excavations show that the elaborate textiles, woodwork, and other crafted goods were produced in different areas of the barrios, a discovery that could imply a social organization based upon both kinship and occupational interest. These urban commoners were arguably more privileged than the lower class in rural areas, who furnished the state's supply of agricultural and construction labor and did not have easy, frequent access to state supplies. Social segmentation — the ruler, the nobility, the urban craftsmen, the rural commoners — was the basis of organization in Chimú society. Its impressive socioeconomic system was a model of preindustrial efficiency, but much of its strength seems to have come from the skillful balancing of social and political privilege among the classes. Unattractive as certain aspects of the social model may seem to the contemporary reader, it succeeded on its own terms for generations.

Was the Chimú state repressive? The question is not easily answered. Its extraordinarily well-organized economy left little room for the commoner with an entrepreneurial bent, but we have no reason to believe that the citizen of Chan Chan found that circumstance confining. Since government and religion were essentially inseparable, so far as we can determine, it might be that one could hardly demand political change without having to face the possibility that one's fundamental religious beliefs could be in error.

Gold and silver, mined in the mountains some distance from Chan Chan, were quite literally "noble" metals, distributed among the privileged for use in clothing, jewelry, or such basic domestic items as drinking vessels. The glittering pieces that survive include a child's boots covered with gold plaques, exquisitely worked gold necklaces and armbands, gold staffs of office, ceremonial cups, and several examples of a uniquely Chimú crown or headdress. These rich pieces may have been displayed before the astonished public, or they may simply have been intended for the shared enjoyment of the members of the aristocracy as they played out a life of comparative ease within the walled compounds. The goldsmith, for his achievements, was given food and clothing by the state bureaucracy, but he could not keep any examples of his craft. His function was to fashion precious objects for the enjoyment or ritual obligations of a superior class of beings.

Perhaps every member of society was brought together in the shared rituals and beliefs of the state religion. Worship often took the form of great feasts and dances, at which the gods appeared to their supplicants.

The drinking of maize beer, or *chicha,* and the chewing of the coca leaf increased the participants' receptivity to the supernatural mysteries being celebrated.

Unlike other major civilizations of the ancient Americas, the Chimú apparently did not believe in a single creator, although some commentators thought that the religion was suffused with a reverence for a kind of universal spiritual principle, perhaps an ineffable supernatural force that animates the visible world. Specific deities, however, had important roles. The most honored was *Si,* the female divinity of the moon, who had control of the weather and of agricultural growth as well as a particular interest in the punishment of thieves. Curiously, in a part of the world where sun worship thrived, the Chimú reasoned that the moon was the more powerful, because she could be seen both by night and by day. An eclipse of the sun was celebrated as a victory of the moon; mournful dances were performed when the moon was in eclipse. To this greatest of the gods, animals, birds, and five-year-old children were sacrificed.

Our sketchy knowledge of Chimú religion indicates that, as was typical in pre-Columbian South America, the state religion always coexisted comfortably with innumerable local religions and ancient cults. A common citizen of Chan Chan, perhaps, would not have seen a conflict between worshiping the state divinities and remaining faithful, as well, to the cult of the village where he was born.

Superstition, religion, state ritual — it is clear that the aggressive, materialistic, well-machined state of Chimú was also a world of oracle and divination, and of what we term "magic." It was a world in which one might ask a shaman to use his skills to attract one's guardian spirits, in which one would think it reasonable to force the household pets and domesticated livestock to join the family in a few days of ritual fasting. In such a world, of course, there was no perception of medicine as distinct from magic.

But, as always in Chimú society, there was a level of state control, even in the practice of medicine. Official curers, or *oquetlupuc,* were trained herbalists paid by the government. They were expected to be experts in the received wisdom of the day. If one was judged responsible for a patient's death because of ignorance, he was beaten and stoned to death, his body linked by rope to the buried corpse of the patient but left exposed to scavenger birds.

Punishment for crime, in fact, should reveal much about the beliefs or fears of any society. Chimú justice may strike us as unusually brutal. Someone guilty of civil disobedience, for example, was interred alive with the bones of traitors and unclean animals. Those found in adultery were flung from a cliff. Men and women were assigned separate footpaths; someone taking the wrong path could be punished as severely as an attempted rapist.

Theft, however, is the crime that seems most to have

Chimú folk healers believed in the curative properties of small beach stones that had been swallowed by sea lions. The drawing above (taken from the Moche stirrup pot at right), shows the animals being hunted to retrieve this magical remedy.

concerned the rulers of the Chimú, who were firm in the conviction that property itself is a divine right of the aristocracy. To find a thief, there were sacrifices to *Si,* and in other ways the case was pursued as equally a religious and civil problem. A captured thief, as well as his father and brothers, would be executed by the injured party; the same fate awaited anyone guilty of hiding the thief. Does the harshness of the punishment for theft indicate that robbery was not unusual and a strong deterrent was necessary? Or does it, on the contrary, indicate that the crime was so unusual that it merited special attention?

How unappealing life in Chan Chan can sound if we concentrate on the draconian legal code, the monolithic state, the inflexible caste system. But the Chimú civilization could not have been completely exploitative of a downtrodden people. For one thing, most evidence seems to indicate that women had nearly equal rights with men — a social ideal not achieved by the Inca, who followed. In certain districts, perhaps because of traditions predating Chimú hegemony, women occasionally even served as village heads. For another, Chan Chan may have seemed more pleasant to its citizens than it might to later observers, purely on esthetic grounds. The amount of individual living space may not seem generous, but, after all, immediately outside the city stretched a great, wide alluvial plain against a stunning backdrop of rocky mountains, whose peaks caught the first and last rays of the day's sun. This setting was, and is, a veritable cathedral of nature.

And the city itself offered features that were unusual for the age — perfectly straight streets, the occasional irrigated garden within the city walls, and fantastic friezes of animal figures and repeated arabesques on many walls of the royal compounds. Tiny as the living quarters of the barrios might seem to our eyes, they were well planned for communal living, with shared kitchens and wells nearby.

The great site has not attracted as much interest as some others of pre-Columbian America, at least in the popular imagination. This is simply because at Chan Chan there were no grand ruins of carved stone, in the classic style of ancient Greece, Rome, and Egypt, as there are at Cuzco, Tikal, and Monte Albán. But the architectural achievements of the capital and the many lesser cities of the Chimú empire are impressive in their mass alone, a testimony to the competently managed labor force of a great preindustrial economic system.

Also, it is not too reckless to assume that the common people shared in the reflected glory of the aristocracy above them. They may have been barred from owning the precious objects produced in their workshops, but they owned highly decorative jewelry made from translucent shell fragments, bright turquoise, and other semiprecious gems. It is true that, to the art critic, most of the pottery, weaving, and other crafted goods seem esthetically inferior to those of the Moche and other Andean cultures. Somewhat sneeringly, scholars write of the Chimú "corporate style," which is characterized by a uniformity that is reminiscent of the comparatively recent concept of "quality control." Nonetheless, the artisans were able to produce at a high standard and in great volume, making available to the urban proletariat skillfully executed ceramics, metal utensils, carved wood objects, clothing, and other textiles. In short, life for the typical citizen of Chan Chan probably offered comfort, security, and a guaranteed role in a formidably capable society. These qualities were far from characteristic of daily life for non-Chimú common people in pre-Columbian Peru.

The Chimú civilization lives in history, however, in its legacy, albeit a somewhat unwilling one, to the Inca. Much of what has entered the popular literature as typically Inca, in fact, can be traced to the lords of Chan Chan, their bureaucrats, and their artisans.

Perhaps above all else, the conquering Inca had refined the Andean art of assimilation. A preeminently practical people, the Inca did not merely imitate the successes of the Chimú corporate style in ceramics and textiles; they removed the artisans from Chan Chan to their own capital of Cuzco and set them to work there. Some scholars think that fundamental concepts of Inca law, though not quite so cruel as Chimú justice, were taken whole cloth from this empire they admired and envied enough to conquer. Much of the famous Inca gold, including the millions of dollars worth of treasure accumulated for the aborted ransom of Atahuallpa, probably came from Chan Chan. And a large number of the region's incomparable gold pieces to be seen in museums today come from the Chan Chan area.

Although the Chimú learned much from the Moche, no culture in that part of the world had ever brought to realization such an imposing list of governmental activities: great public works such as the stucco cities and the extensive canal systems for irrigation agriculture, the mass production of technically proficient goods coupled with an almost paternalistic system of attaching artisans to the state, and an ability to administer conquered territories so that the subject district felt a certain autonomy while still paying tribute to the empire. At any time in history, these accomplishments would have been extraordinary. The Inca were, understandably, willing pupils; consequently, much of what is known about the Chimú has easily been inferred from the obvious borrowings that the Spaniards later found in Inca society.

Two of the most significant social concepts that the Inca refined from Chimú practices were the *mit'a,* or

An Empire Tied Up in Knots

"He who attempts to count the stars, not even knowing how to count the knots and marks of the *quipus,* should be held in derision," said the great Inca ruler Pachacuti. Because the Inca — like the Chimú — had no written language, an understanding of their record-keeping system of brightly colored strings with strategically placed knots called *quipus* (which literally means "knots") was considered tantamount to literacy. The system used a main or base cord to which were attached strings of different colors, lengths, and thicknesses. Knots on such strings represented the numerical equivalents of items being counted. No two *quipus* were exactly alike because

they were designed with a slightly different code of tallying, which nonetheless could be interpreted by *quipu camayocs* ("keepers of the *quipus*").

Experts have determined that certain colors designated different data or events (black was supposed to signify time as in the recording of historical happenings and red to represent war or warriors). But modern-day interpreters cannot be certain what the myriad permutations of strings and knots on each *quipu* actually mean. Although the ancient art of the *quipu* is still practiced today in the Andean highlands of Peru, most of the Inca's surviving "silent strings" are still impossible to decipher.

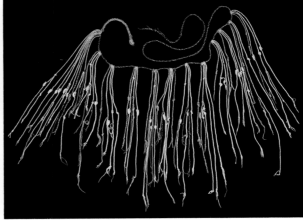

The modern-day quipu camayoc *at left, dressed in the brightly colored shirt and hat of his region, uses a* quipu *to account for the agricultural output of his hamlet. The 500-year-old* quipu *above was used by his ancestors.*

labor tax, and the idea of reciprocity, based upon a mutual commitment between the state and the citizen.

To the Inca, the *mit'a* requirement meant that all males were to devote regular periods of service to the state and females were to produce a certain quantity of woven goods for the state storehouses, religious ceremonies, or the use of the nobility. Long before the Chimú, some form of labor tax had been in existence, but the centuries of Chimú domination of the north saw subtle refinements of the basic concept.

The Chimú saw that the *mit'a* could have two functions. First, a sizable work force could be utilized to construct and manage large corporate agricultural projects, such as the canals of the Moche and other valleys. The labor tax, in other words, became an investment in economic growth, since it was used to create new areas of arable land as an additional productive resource. Second, by redirecting the labor tax into conquest — that is to say, by mobilizing the *mit'a* forces into armies of the empire — the Chimú similarly added to their productive resources by acquiring more taxable land.

Furthermore, the Inca learned about the subdivision of energies from the Chimú. According to the findings of archeologist Michael E. Moseley, the irrigation canals, great adobe structures, and monumental walls of Chan Chan were constructed in independent sections. In his view, each segment was the fulfillment of the *mit'a* imposed upon a particular group. Subsequently, the sections of each project were linked.

Borrowing from the Past

In the historical development of the *mit'a* concept we see yet again that remarkable Andean tendency to learn from and improve upon the past, as concretely exemplified in the practices of the culture a conquering state has just vanquished. Borrow and refine, borrow and refine — this is an admirably pragmatic, if not necessarily humanitarian, approach to conquest.

Reciprocity, too, in its Chimú form impressed the Inca. Although earlier states had demanded various services from their citizens, it appears that the Chimú empire was one of the first great Andean cultures to recognize the value of guaranteeing the citizen something in return. The state took care of the needs and basic desires, the bread and the circuses, if the individual citizen fulfilled his role, say, in the manufacturing life of Chan Chan.

Probably, however, it was the actual nuts and bolts of the administration of the principle of reciprocity more than the basic concept that roused Inca admiration. One must keep in mind that achieving reciprocity would have been a highly complex undertaking, particularly in a sprawling empire that did not use the wheel for transportation, had no form of writing for record-keeping, and probably had developed only such slow forms of counting as the use of different-colored beans. Yet it was necessary to bring large amounts of food from outlying farms to such centers as Chan

Chan and to conduct trade efficiently enough to satisfy subject peoples who lived miles away. Presumably, exchange had to be swift, accurate, and fair. Somehow, the bureaucracy of the state had to insure that those fulfilling their *mit'a* obligations would be adequately reciprocated for their services. Somehow, each artisan who received gold for the making of royal jewelry had to be recorded as returning the correct amount of the precious metal, and so forth. Had the Chimú bureaucracy not functioned with unusual dispatch and effectiveness, reciprocity would not have worked. There were simply too many variables. But reciprocity did work in Chimú times, as it did later in Inca times. The tradition was continued.

The conquest by the Inca does suggest something of a paradox. The Chimú empire was powerful, efficient, and unified, but collapsed quickly, apparently incapable of offering, or desiring to offer, substantial opposition to the invader from the south. Some scholars speculate that there was already a kind of decay in the empire, that perhaps the much vaunted political techniques were beginning to lose their efficacy. Some see evidence of an unexplained decline in population.

It was the last of Chan Chan's dynastic rulers, the ambitious conqueror Minchançaman, who would be overpowered and taken in captivity to Cuzco about 1470. Earlier, he had extended the empire to the northern limits of the desert coast, but, despite a series of victories, the Chimú advance was halted in the south by a great army assembled in the Lima Valley.

Not long afterward, a twist of fate set in motion events that led to the Chimú ruler's downfall. About 1461, the Inca ruler Pachacuti had ordered a half-brother, Capac Yupanqui, on an exploratory raid into central Peru, with orders to advance no farther than the Yanamayo River. On the expedition, some disruption led to the desertion of a group of auxiliary soldiers, the Chancas. Apparently, Capac Yupanqui, fearful of returning to his sovereign with the news that the deserters had made good their escape, decided to redeem himself by storming northward to conquer the thriving state of Cajamarca, which was allied with Minchançaman. Chimú troops were sent to help counter the Inca threat, but Capac Yupanqui emerged victorious.

His was a short-lived moment of glory. Like many a warrior before and after him, he was to suffer the consequences of taking action that resulted in changing state policy. His victory had brought South America's two largest states into open conflict. Pachacuti felt committed to a rapid follow-up. Furious, he ordered Capac Yupanqui executed and soon sent a relief force to Cajamarca under the command of his bastard son, Topa Capac. For strategic reasons, the decision was made to meet head-on the smoldering threat of the Chimú empire. Topa Capac sent the bulk of his crack forces down the Moche River and, despite Minchançaman's determined defense, conquered Chan Chan. After a year or so of campaigns that reached as far north as

present-day Ecuador, the Inca returned to the Moche Valley, looted Chan Chan, and took the ruler and many of his retainers and goldworkers back to Cuzco.

Descendants of Minchançaman retained some power in the Moche Valley for decades to come, but only by cooperating with the shrewd Inca administrators and, in the following century, with the Spanish colonial administration. The Chimú empire itself, however, was no more. Chan Chan, a city which by its very nature required the frequent and large-scale efforts of outside labor to repair its stucco walls and dredge its canals free of silt and alluvial flow, quickly fell into ruins.

To those who assumed power in the region, Chan Chan became little more than a treasure house. First, the Inca melted down gold ornaments to make statues of their own gods and to decorate the walls of important temples. More than 70 years later, the Spaniards looted the city's royal tombs and then diverted the Moche River to wash through the pyramids of the Sun and Moon nearby, revealing the splendid goldwork buried beneath the crumbling platforms. Of the city itself and its great irrigation canals, little remained.

It is fitting, perhaps, that the ruins of Chan Chan do not have the grand, brooding aspect of many other pre-Columbian cities. To understand the Chimú, we should probably give more weight to their social accomplishments than to their esthetic or monumental achievements. Arguably, they embodied Andean ideas at their height — the mutual contract between individual and state, the immutability of social class, a special interpretation of the nature of property, the comprehensiveness and eclecticism of religion.

The Chimú did not contribute as profoundly to the history of architecture and art as did some pre-Columbian cultures, although their skill in hydraulic engineering and metallurgy was astonishing. Principally, however, they made a major contribution to what is still man's most troubling problem — the question of how to create a society that insures a stable order and a sense of security for all of its members.

OF GODS AND MEN

THE AZTEC AND THEIR FIERCE DEITIES

Gods and goddesses of the sun, moon, corn, war, and rain dominated the pantheon of the Aztec. To sustain life on earth, their religion demanded that certain deities be appeased with the sacrifice of human blood.

For nearly two centuries leading up to the Spanish Conquest in 1521 the Aztec were a powerful presence in Mexico. At the time of the Spanish landfall their empire stretched from the Gulf Coast to the Pacific, with influence reaching far to the south. The legendary emperor Moctezuma sat in the seat of power in the beautiful capital city of Tenochtitlán.

As in other Mesoamerican cultures, religion was the ruling force in the daily life of the people — from sunrise to sunrise, from birth to death, every activity was regulated by gods and religious ritual.

In Aztec belief, four different creations preceded the present world. Each was ruled over by its own Sun, and each in turn was destroyed by a different cataclysm. This myth did not originate with the Aztec; similar stories of multiple creations were also cherished by the Maya, who predated the Aztec in the annals of Mesoamerican history.

The fifth world of the Aztec, or Fifth Sun, came into being when the twin gods Quetzalcoatl, whose name in Nahuatl, the language of the Aztec, means "Plumed" or " Precious Serpent," and Tezcatlipoca, or "Smoking Mirror," descended from the heavens with the earth goddess Tlaltecuhtli. She appeared in the form of a monstrous toad with jaguar fangs and claws and with ferocious snapping mouths at the joints of her arms and legs. Seeing this awesome creature floating on the otherwise lifeless primordial waters, the two creator gods transformed themselves into giant serpents, grasped the goddess in their coils, and tore her in two. With one half they made the new earth; the other half they took back to the heavens, where it brought forth many gods.

When these gods saw the earth goddess's mutilated body and heard her anguished cries, they descended to earth to console her and soothe her wounds. To repay her for her sacrifice, they decreed that thenceforth from her body would originate all the fruits needed to sustain the humans that would soon populate the earth. From her hair and skin would spring the trees, flowers, herbs, and all manner of plant life; from her eyes, ponds and springs; from her mouth, rivers and caverns; from her nose, valleys and mountains.

The page at right from a post-Conquest codex commemorates the Aztec legend in which the people were told to build their capital at the place where an eagle landed on a cactus. The eagle is surrounded by ancestors associated with the city's founding, while at the bottom, warriors topple rivals' towns.

A. Thenet cosmographe *numero de anos . LI .*
du Roi

tenochtitlan

colhuacan. pueblo.   tenayucan. pueblo.

Thus the fifth world was made ready for the new race of humans, whom Quetzalcoatl — venerated as a god and culture hero by other Mesoamerican peoples long before the Aztec — would refashion from the bones of the dead of the previous creation. But in the night the wounded goddess continued to cry piteously. She demanded that in return for providing sustenance to humankind she herself be sustained not only with the dead buried in the earth but also with the hearts and blood of living victims.

With the earth complete, the gods, one after the other, threw themselves into a sacred fire to determine which of them would become the new ruling Sun. Those with conceit and pride were rejected by the purifying fire. The one selected as the sun god was a poor and miserable youth, his body covered with pustules. To ensure that he would have the strength for the cycle of birth, death, and rebirth that would take him each day from east to west across the great sky vault and from west to east on a perilous nocturnal journey through the womb of his mother, the earth, he too was guaranteed an unending supply of the most precious gift humans could offer their gods as nourishment: their own life blood.

Thus, in the religion of the Aztec, even before there was a new race of people, the divine earth and sun had decreed a sacred compact between gods and men: the sacrifice of human hearts and blood in exchange for the corn and other foods on which mankind depended, and for light and warmth. If ever men ceased to honor that contract, the earth would withhold sustenance, the sky would darken, and humanity would be doomed. It was a powerful reason for carrying out the bloody practice of human sacrifice, for without it there would be no earth, no life, no future.

The Aztec were latecomers to the Valley of Mexico, settling there in the 12th or 13th century A.D., following a long and arduous migration from the north. After passing through and briefly settling at Tula, the Toltec capital abandoned about A.D. 1000, these ragged nomads hired themselves out for a time as mercenaries and servants to the relatively rich, established towns and cities near the great lake that formerly covered much of the central basin of Mexico. Like Tula, these towns had inherited, or at least aspired to, some of the power and splendor that was Teotihuacán, the great sacred center of Mexico from about A.D. 150 to 650.

The Aztec were driven by belief that they had been divinely chosen to conquer Mexico by their tribal god, Huitzilopochtli, "Hummingbird to the Left" or "Left-Handed Hummingbird." It was this tribal deity who in Aztec cosmology became the divine Sun and also the god of war, and to whom captured enemy warriors or slaves were offered in sacrificial rites. To the Aztec the sacrifice of human blood represented a deification rite in which the victim became apotheosized into the very god to whom the offering was being made.

According to their legend, Huitzilopochtli had given

Digging up Mexico City's Past

It was the needs of a modern city that brought to light the hallowed precincts of Aztec Tenochtitlán, after a sleep of four centuries. In the early morning hours of February 24, 1978, as Mexico City's public utility was installing a new electrical cable line, a workman's spade struck a stone slab that lay 15 feet below street level. Within four days, a team of archeologists had dug out a magnificent oval relief of the moon goddess. Over the next three years, they removed layer after layer of rubble to reveal the remains of a complex of pyramids and temples, striking representations of gods and goddesses, a sacrificial stone, and numerous smaller objects ranging from beads to masks, all of which had somehow escaped the ravages of the Spanish Conquest.

Archeologists have long known that Mexico City was constructed over the broken bones of Aztec monuments and that its streets were cobbled with splintered fragments of ancient art. Over the past 200 years, monuments have emerged by chance as the city was built and rebuilt. But the *Proyecto Templo Mayor* — as the excavation came to be known — was the first systematic effort to disinter what had once been the symbolic heart of a great empire.

Here, in a walled area not much more than 1,300 feet square, stood a commanding double pyramid with two temples, one dedicated to Huitzilopochtli, the god of the sun and of war, the other to Tlaloc, god of rain. A double flight of steps led to each temple. The green sacrificial stone — found *in situ* — occupied a prominent place at the entrance to Huitzilopochtli's shrine, precisely at the head of the steep stairway, down which priests threw the bodies of their victims. Other temples stood on the site, among them a circular structure dedicated to Quetzalcoatl. The whole complex vibrated with color, and traces of red and white paint in abstract design have survived the centuries.

Among the richest rewards of the *Proyecto Templo Mayor* are caches of ritual offerings, brought to Tenochtitlán by pilgrims from the farthest reaches of the Aztec empire. In homage to their gods, they buried humble objects in great number, among them copper bells, shells, turquoise beads, and the remains of fishes and animals. But they also offered up valued stone masks and ornate ceramic vessels, the inheritance of the great civilizations of their past. Altogether about 80 such caches were uncovered, yielding more than 5,500 objects, and numbering among them some of the most spectacular works of art of ancient Mesoamerica.

Clouds cast a somber shadow on the excavations of the Templo Mayor (right, above), putting the rubble into sharp contrast with Mexico City. As she sketches, an archeologist (near right) appears to be unconsciously mimicking the pose of a painted chacmool, a figure whose role in the Aztec pantheon still remains a mystery. Other finds (far right) include a crumbling stone skull with gaping jaws, an ornately carved head of a god, and a crouched figure wearing a crown.

them an omen: their long journey would end when they saw an eagle lighting on a cactus. In A.D. 1325, after about 150 years of wandering, they came to a place where, true to the divine prophecy, they saw the eagle perched on a cactus. They founded their first settlement, a miserable collection of reed huts, on a swampy island in the shallow waters of Lake Texcoco, today a dry lake just east of Mexico City. They called it México-Tenochtitlán, "place of the Mexica and Tenochca," two groups that made up the new arrivals.

The Aztec were desert folk barely acquainted with agriculture. From their neighbors along the lake shore they learned to construct enormously fertile raised fields, called *chinampas*, on which to grow corn, beans, squash, tomatoes, chili peppers, and other staples, and to harvest the wealth in migratory fowl, fish, shrimp, insect eggs and larvae, and the protein-rich blue-green algae that grew along the lake's edge. (The remnants of the *chinampas* survive today as the Floating Gardens of the Mexico City suburb of Xochimilco.)

Over the next 200 years leading up to the Conquest, the pitiful collection of huts grew into one of the greatest urban centers of the ancient world. Tenochtitlán was a city of palaces and temples, as well as humbler dwellings, crisscrossed by canals instead of streets, filled with canoe traffic, and linked to dry land by several long, raised causeways. It was a city so beautiful to the eyes of the conquistadors, who first saw it in 1519 from the surrounding 10,000-foot-high mountains, that not even Venice compared with it, nor the most resplendent royal palace in Spain with that of the emperor Moctezuma. Within little more than a century of the founding of their capital, by superior statecraft, diplomatic stratagems, long-distance trade, and above all, skilled and fierce warfare, the Aztec had made themselves masters of the central valley and eventually of much of what is now Mexico. Only the Tarascan in the west, the Maya in the south, and the Tlaxcalan, the linguistic and cultural cousins of the Aztec, in the north, remained free of their domination. To feed and

288

clothe the 200,000 or so people living in their capital, the Aztec added enormous stores of tribute from all over their "empire" to the wild and cultivated products of Lake Texcoco and its environs.

In the process they had also greatly expanded their cosmology, pantheon, and ceremonial life. They had added deities and rites from subjugated or dependent peoples to their own, in part perhaps to bolster their might but also in large measure to serve their new existence as an urban, imperial, and expansionist nation. Their evolution from nomads to farmers required new gods to oversee new technologies. With the fruits of agriculture as the mainstay of life, knowing the seasons and their patron deities, and the proper times and rituals for each farming activity — and all other human actions — became the overriding concern of priest, noble, and peasant alike. For as the gods had decreed at the beginning of the world, the survival of Aztec society — indeed of all humanity and the natural and supernatural environment — was at stake. Had not all creation been destroyed on four previous occasions?

Clearly, the tales accounting for the origin of the present world and for the cult of human sacrifice that so shocked and fascinated the conquistadors, themselves driven by avarice and steeped in blood and cruelty, are merely pieces of much longer myths that provided Aztec religious ritual with its literary foundation. Their survival even in fragmentary form is largely due to the intellectual curiosity of a handful of Spanish friars, in particular the Franciscan chronicler Bernardino de Sahagún. These European churchmen went beyond their quest for souls to record the religion of the Aztec

Human sacrifice was central to Aztec religious rituals, as vividly illustrated in the scene at left from a 16th-century codex. The priest at the top of the temple steps removes the heart of one victim while another lies at the bottom of the stairs. The still-beating hearts, used to propitiate the gods, were placed in stone receptacles such as the one above, a more than seven-foot-long carved jaguar, weighing over six tons.

even as they strove to wipe its practices from the newly conquered colony.

Whereas Hernán Cortés and his soldiers had come primarily for material gain — land, gold, and slaves — Sahagún brought to New Spain a tradition of humanism. He exhibited an encyclopedic interest in the magnificent civilization the conquistadors had brought down in the final conquest and destruction of the Aztec capital, Tenochtitlán, in 1521.

Interpreting Aztec Rituals

Sahagún's purpose in compiling his great work on the Aztec civilization, the Florentine Codex, was ostensibly to instruct other friars in what they needed to know to combat the old religion, for, as he put it, a doctor cannot cure a disease until he knows its symptoms. But for him, interest in the Indian civilization, especially its religion, seems to have gone far beyond the original intent of facilitating conversion to Christianity. Like a modern ethnographer, Sahagún devised detailed questionnaires on all aspects of native life and enlisted the aid of educated and literate Indians with firsthand knowledge of their culture. Closeted in a convent constructed on the ruins of the old ceremonial center of Tlatelolco, neighbor and ally of Aztec Tenochtitlán, Sahagún and his Indian scribes composed a 12-volume codex covering virtually every aspect of life, from religion, calendars, history, and moral philosophy to foods and natural resources. Fluent in Nahuatl, he set down what the Indians told him in both their native tongue and Spanish translation, almost as if to preserve the knowledge as much for the Indians themselves as for the Spanish clergy. Indeed, his intense interest so disturbed the Spanish authorities in Mexico that for a time the Florentine Codex was suppressed and almost destroyed, a possibility which its author forestalled by making several copies. At that, the work escaped being burned only through the intervention of a sympathetic superior in the Franciscan order.

Other chroniclers of the time found the ways of Indian religion far less congenial. They sprinkled their descriptions with liberal doses of editorial comment and Christian doctrine. Even Sahagún could not free himself altogether of his European religious education and his calling as priest and missionary charged with the saving of pagan souls. Thus much of what we know about the Aztec and their religion comes filtered through Spanish minds that could not help but seize on practices most shocking to, and least understood by, them. Across an enormous gulf of language, culture, religion, and ways of organizing the world, the Spaniards tried to reconstruct a coherent system of Aztec beliefs and rituals. Inevitably this attempt led to misinterpretation, oversimplification, distortion, and exaggeration — especially in regard to human sacrifice, and its corollary, ritual cannibalism.

In Aztec tradition, sacrificial death signified a merging with the gods, and small portions of the victim's flesh were eaten with other sacred foods, presumably so that the selected communicants might absorb some of the gods' divine qualities. It was here, especially, that some friars detected the Devil's hand, for not only was eating human flesh abhorrent to them but they saw in the practice the cynical mockery of the most holy rite of the Catholic Church — the more so because the Spaniards thought the Aztec gods were really the Devil and his cohorts in disguise. To them the Aztec custom of fashioning effigies of the sun god Huitzilopochtli from amaranth seeds and honey was an equally fiendish parody of Holy Communion, for these images, sprinkled with sacrificial blood, were broken into pieces and fed to the worshipers by the native priests in the manner of the Host. The Spaniards were so perturbed by this custom, which they could not eradicate, that in desperation they outlawed the cultivation of amaranth, which was, after corn and beans, one of the most important staples of ancient Mexico.

Difficulties in comprehending the mysteries of Aztec religion arose in part from the nature of Sahagún's informants, who were mainly drawn from the Aztec elite of just one community, Tlatelolco. Women or members of the lower classes, who might have had a very different view of their civilization, were not consulted. There were probably discrepancies also between what the informants actually knew and what they were willing to divulge to foreigners. It is very probable that the Aztec chose not to reveal all their secrets.

Thus, what Sahagún has deeded to history is less a logical and comprehensive picture of the complex beliefs and rituals that motivated Aztec civilization as a whole than a collection of fragmentary versions of rites associated not just with major deities and temples in Tenochtitlán but with gods of local neighborhoods and towns. His work also included descriptions of land features and weather phenomena, of professions, even of different ethnic groups — a mixture of myths, gods, and ceremonies that really were "Aztec" and those the conquering Aztec shared with other peoples. Still, thanks to Sahagún, we know much more about the Aztec than about any other of the Indian civilizations whose eventual doom was sealed on that fateful morning of October 12, 1492, when Rodrigo de Triana, a sailor aboard the *Pinta,* first announced the sight of what proved to be the New World. As for the Aztec, time began to run out when Cortés took his band of 600 men, eager for conquest and spoils, ashore at Veracruz on March 4, 1519. The Indians, who had never seen horses or heard the deadly thunder of iron cannon, at first took him to be the god Quetzalcoatl returning from the heavens to Mexico, as prophesied by an old legend. By coincidence, Cortés's landing fell on the calendrical date 1 Reed, on which the legendary Quetzalcoatl was believed to have been born. By the time they realized their mistake — that Cortés was not Quetzalcoatl and that his arrival was not the divinely decreed end of a cosmic era — it was too late.

Because religion pervaded the lives of the Aztec, their artists did some of their finest work in honor of their gods. The head of the goddess Coyolxauhqui (top left) symbolizes her decapitation by her angry son — her lowered eyelids and slightly open mouth evoke her pain. With etched reliefs of flowers decorating his body, Xochipilli, the Flower Prince (bottom left), is thought by some scholars to be associated with hallucinogenic mushrooms. A priest or penitent wearing the flayed skin of a sacrificial victim is thereby transformed into the god Xipe Totec (above), healer of skin and eye diseases.

To the Aztec, as to all ancient Mesoamerican peoples, time proceeded not linearly but in cycles. As among the Maya, two calendars functioning side by side regulated their ritual and everyday activities. This calendrical system may have been first established by the Olmec around 1000 B.C. or even earlier. One calendar measured the solar year of 18 "months," each with 20 days, to which the Aztec added 5 unnamed days to make 365. This 5-day period was an uncertain, fearful time, fraught with supernatural danger. These solar years were grouped together in 52-year units, comparable to our "centuries." The other "year" was a divinatory count of 260 days, each with its special name and discrete, divinatory significance as good, bad, or neutral, for birth, marriage, and other activities. The ceremonies of the solar year were largely, though not exclusively, related to the seasons and food-producing activities, whereas the divinatory year also regulated commemorations of mythic events believed to have occurred on a specific day in the primordial past or private and public rites unconnected to agriculture or the hunt. The 260-day time count, the province of trained calendar priests, or diviners, was called *tonalámatl*, from *tonál*, loosely meaning "fate." This concept is still alive among some Mexican Indians today.

Just as the world was created, destroyed, and recreated time and again, so smaller units of time repeated themselves. The year and every new cycle began with the lighting of fires in the temples and even on the hearth, for the end of one and beginning of another was a time of uncertainty. The most fearful period was the end of one 52-year cycle, for the Aztec believed that if the present world era was to come to a cataclysmic end, it would happen then.

Each of the 18 months of the Aztec solar year was marked by ceremonies that gave the month its name and defined its special qualities and its relationship to seasonal phenomena or activities and deities considered crucial to their success. A look at some of these 18 ceremonies reveals something of the complexity, beauty, and richness of Aztec ceremonial life and also the extreme interdependence that characterized the Aztec relationship to the environment and the gods.

The first of the 18 months in the solar year coincided with February in the European calendar. It was a time of fervent prayer for the spring rains needed to prepare the thirsty fields for planting. And so it was dedicated to the gods and goddesses of rain and terrestrial water and also to Quetzalcoatl in one of his guises as the god of the wind, who pushes the rain-laden clouds before him. Because the rain deities lived in the mountains, children were carried to their summits, where they assumed the identities of the mountain deities and were sacrificed in their names to hasten the onset of rain.

A grisly ritual marked the second month, in honor of the god Xipe Totec, "Our Lord the Flayed One." Prisoners taken in war were clad in the garments of this god and made to fight mock skirmishes with Aztec warriors. When it came time for the sacrifice, men who had captured the prisoners and who addressed them reverently as their own blood kin, led them before the temple of the Aztec god of the sun and of war, Huitzilopochtli. Here some prisoners were sacrificed by having their hearts removed with a flint knife. Others were tied to a wooden frame and shot to death with arrows. Aged priests dismembered the dead captives, to be apportioned later for a sacrificial meal. Actually, flesh was taken only from the limbs, with small portions being ritually eaten in a stew made of dried corn.

The dead impersonators of Xipe—one of the gods the Aztec inherited from other peoples—were then flayed and their skins presented to their captors. The captors could either wear these skins themselves — thus "becoming" the god all over again — or they

The scene at right, from a pre-Conquest or early colonial codex, shows the feathered serpent god, Quetzalcoatl (left), with his brother, Tezcatlipoca, god of chance and fortune. Tezcatlipoca was venerated once a year in a ceremony in which a perfect young man was chosen to personify him as the epitome of Aztec beauty and be sacrificed in his name. The young man's head was placed on a skull rack, which probably rested on a carved stone platform like the one below, an eerie symbol of the sacrificial rites practiced by this society.

could give them to others in need of healing. The wearing of the skin and its ceremonial removal and disposal by fire or burial was actually a curing ritual, designed to do away with skin and eye disorders through magical analogy to the rattlesnake, which sheds its blemishes together with its skin.

The most important sacrifices of the third month were flowers, dedicated to the great mother goddess in her — to us — terrifying manifestation of Coatlícue, "She of the Serpent Skirt." As Coatlícue she wore a necklace of human hearts and hands, human skulls on her serpent belt, a skirt woven of intertwining rattlesnakes, and like Tlaltecuhtli, another of her manifestations, jaguar claws on hands and feet. Her breasts were empty because she had given all her milk to her children, the people of the earth. The flowers offered to her symbolized the first fruits of springtime, and until this ritual had been performed, the people were forbidden even to smell the flowers. According to Sahagún, great numbers of people poured out of the city on this day to gather flowers for the goddess in the fields and meadows, or if unable to do that, they traded for them with the flower sellers who came to the market. There are echoes of this beautiful ceremony to this day in the Mexicans' love for brightly colored flowers, real and paper, and in the custom of offering flowers to the Virgin of Guadalupe as inheritor of the ancient cult of the mother goddess.

If the first rites of the ceremonial round were most concerned with the rains and with rebirth of the earth's fertility, the fourth month was dedicated to Cintéotl, the young male corn god who embodied the tender new ear of corn, and to his mother, Chicomecoatl, or "7 Serpent," the goddess who personified the maternal corn plant. Here again the offerings were not human life but the fruits of the earth.

Sacrifice to Tezcatlipoca

In the fifth month there followed a ceremony that has served to epitomize the mixture of supreme poetic beauty and sacrificial death that seems so often to typify Aztec ritual. This was the sacrifice of the great god Tezcatlipoca, "Smoking Mirror," Quetzalcoatl's twin in the creation story, and for some of the peoples of Mexico the most important of the gods. A year earlier, the elders had already chosen a young man to personify Tezcatlipoca and to die in his name. He had to be perfect in every respect, fitting the highest Aztec ideal of masculine beauty. His skin had to be without blemish, his hair long and straight, his speech that of the educated Aztec, his eyes bright and clear, his expression pleasant and proud, his fingers long and sensitive, his body without scars, wrinkles, or unsightly bulges. He knew how to play the flute sweetly, and everywhere he went he took his flute, flowers, and smoking pipe, for tobacco was the sacred food of the gods. Everyone he met took him for the living god. The ruler Moctezuma himself provided the young man's

clothing and ornaments, among them ear pendants of precious shell and gold and a pectoral of white sea shell.

Toward the end of his year he was married to four young women, with whom he lived only 20 days, for the preordained end was near. One after the other he abandoned his ornaments as he walked about the city. Five days before he was to die, he went on a ceremonial circuit of the sacred places, singing and dancing. Moctezuma, in the meantime, shut himself away in his palace, in mourning for the coming death of the god. On the fifth day, accompanied by his wives and companions, he traveled by dugout canoe to a small temple in the lake, where he was left alone to meet his death. As he slowly ascended the temple steps, he played his sacred flutes and other instruments, breaking one at each successive level. At the summit he was seized by four priests who swiftly removed his heart and offered it to the Sun. Four men reverently carried his body down the temple steps, and his severed head was placed on the *tzompantli*, the wooden rack that held the skulls of dead warriors and sacrificial victims.

The rain deities, whose goodwill was now essential to the sprouting of the new corn, beans, amaranth, squash, and other fruits, and the goddess of salt, considered their elder sister, were the objects of the rites of the sixth and seventh months.

In the eighth month, just before the new harvest, a woman dressed as Xilónen, goddess of the tender new corn plant, was sacrificed. This was a time when reserves of food had run out for many people, especially the poor. And so on this day the poor were fed out of the public treasury, receiving corn and beans and other staples from the great royal storehouses filled with the surplus of Aztec agriculture and the foodstuffs sent as tribute by conquered and vassal peoples.

The festivities in the 9th month were in honor of Huitzilopochtli, and in the 10th month, of the old fire god, Xiutecuhtli, in rites that included sacrifice of slaves. The power of Xiutecuhtli, long depicted by different peoples in stone and clay as a wrinkled old man bearing a large brazier on his head, was personified in the living volcanoes that had so often spewed their fire and lava over the Mexican land.

In the 11th month the rites were dedicated to the old mother goddess, in which a woman past child-bearing age assumed this deity's identity and name and, ritually reenacting the mythic events that marked the goddess's life in the primordial past, also repeated her violent death by being herself decapitated. Her place was taken by a male priest dressed in her flayed skin, clothing, and accoutrements, and he was addressed by her female names, as though to emphasize the unity of male and female in the natural and supernatural universe that in the Aztec mind was the essential precondition for fertility and fecundity.

In the 12th month, the rebirth of the gods was solemnly reenacted. In the 13th there followed yet another feast, in honor of sacred mountains and their patron deities. On that occasion snakes were revered as symbols of lightning, and one man and four women were offered in sacrifice, for these mountains were considered to be female and the lone male was seen as the substitute of a spirit of the fields. In the 14th month the Aztec paid respect with communal hunts to the god of the hunt, Camaxtli-Mixcoatl, personification of the Milky Way and mythological father of Quetzalcoatl in the Toltec mythology that also inspired the Aztec. As befits so important a god, Huitzilopochtli was once more honored in the 15th month, the rain and earth deity Tlaloc, in the 16th, and the earth goddess, in her form as Tonan, "Our Mother," in the 17th.

The final month of the solar year was again dedicated to the old fire god. The old men of the temples were honored as reflecting the god's great age and wisdom, while young boys brought them offerings of small animals and snakes. The old men were also given *pulque*, the fermented sap of the maguey cactus, which for the Aztec was a sacred drink and is still a popular beverage for many Mexicans.

The year was now dying. Special *tamales* of corn dough wrapped in cornhusk and stuffed with greens were made in great numbers for ceremonious presentation in the temples to neighbors and symbolic dedication to others who lived far away. The people gathered in circles, made offerings of five tamales to the hearth fire, and consecrated gifts of this special food also to their dead. Thus, in the final days of the old year, they entered into communion with their dead and their gods, in the fervent hope that their world would not end, that another year would be born and the cycle of life would start all over again.

Death and Burial Rites

If life was impermanent for the Aztec, so, in the last analysis, was death. Life contained the inevitability of death, but death held within it the certainty of rebirth. For the Aztec, as for other native American peoples, death meant passage from earthly life to another existence on a different plane in a multilevel universe, and for some, even the possibility of return to earth, though in a different form. Eternity was, moreover, a neutral sort of place ruled by fate, as determined by the gods and the calendrical date of one's birth, or by the nature of one's death, rather than by moral connotations of reward for virtue or punishment for evil.

According to the writings of Sahagún, there were three different places to which the soul might travel after death. Beneath the earth, toward the frigid north, lay Mictlan, the Land of the Dead, ruled over by the skeletal Mictlantecuhtli and Mictlanciuatl, master and mistress of Mictlan. Mictlan was the destination of all — young and old, chiefs and vassals — who died a natural death or from some sickness. A second possible destination of the soul was a subterranean paradise toward the east, Tlalócan, Land of the Tlaloc, realm of the rain deities. It was a splendid place, lush, green, and warm, a land of eternal spring. It was the dwelling place of those who had been struck by lightning during thunderstorms or who drowned in the rivers and lakes, or who had suffered from diseases blamed on water — for example, dropsy or suppurating boils and sores. A third abode for the dead lay in the heavens. This was the destination of warriors who died in war or by sacrifice and also of women who died in childbirth.

Much of the elaborate and lengthy death ritual of the Aztec was concerned with lifting the burden of sorrow from the bereaved and easing the passage of the deceased to the afterlife. For the journey to the beyond, the corpse was laid out in funerary wrappings and covered with paper made of beaten bark, a much valued material with many symbolic meanings for the Aztec and other Mesoamerican peoples. Poetic orations were delivered to remind everyone that life on earth lasted but a moment in time and that the abode of the dead, Mictlan, was "where we all come to our fate." Bereaved children were reminded that the gods had willed the death, that no one had the power to prolong life even for a day, and that they now had new mothers and fathers who had lamented in their behalf, had brought them gifts, and would cherish and support them in place of the mother or father who was about to embark for the Land of the Dead.

Along its way to Mictlan the soul had to pass through a narrow place between clashing rocks or mountains that threatened to crush it (a familiar motif in heroic and funerary mythology the world over), past a green lizard and the snapping jaws of a great serpent, over eight parched deserts, across eight mountains, through a region of fierce winds, and across a great water, which was the final barrier to the nine levels of the Land of the Dead. To shield the deceased against the razor-sharp obsidian blades of the wind, personal belongings — shields, weapons, and clothing of warriors, baskets, belts, textiles, and backstrap looms of the women — were ritually burned, so that their smoke might magically envelop their former owner like protective armor. The soul also carried a small dog, who would join the other dogs in the underworld and, provided it had been treated well on earth, carry its owner across the river before the Land of the Dead. Thus, according to Aztec belief, four years after death the soul finally reached its destination.

Not only was the personal property of the deceased burned but also the corpse and the dog that had been sacrificed as the companion on the road to Mictlan. Burning of belongings, as protection or provender on the long underworld journey or as gifts to the lord and lady of Mictlan, continued for four years from the time of death. A green stone — turquoise or jade for nobles, a lesser greenish mineral or a piece of green obsidian for peasants and other commoners — was placed in the mouth of the corpse. It was believed that these bits of stone became their hearts in their new lives. A lock of hair was cut from the top of the head and preserved

Looking as brilliantly plumed as the birds that inspire their name, these quetzales, *or quetzal dancers, at Cuetzalan, Puebla, Mexico, perform a simple dance that is probably* derived from a pre-Hispanic ritual. In this annual ceremony, the participants wear headgear made of paper or silk and bordered by feathers that measures up to five feet in diameter.

with a few other sacred relics of the deceased in lidded boxes carved of basalt or wood. The charred bones were interred in a jar beneath the floor of the home or family temple of the deceased. If the deceased had been a man of authority, status, and wealth, slaves might be sacrificed as well, to serve chocolate and foods to their master in death as they had in life.

According to Sahagún, only those destined to journey to Mictlan were cremated; those who would live as disembodied souls in the agricultural paradise of the Tlaloc were buried in the earth, their faces adorned with liquid rubber, a paste made from amaranth seeds, and blue paint. Their bodies were shrouded with capes of paper made from the beaten bark of fig and mulberry trees, and in their hands their kin placed long staves

of wood — the insignia of travelers — perhaps to identify them to anyone they might encounter in their journey to the beyond.

It was the fate of the dead who dwelt in Mictlan, and perhaps of those residing with the makers of rain in Tlalócan, to remain in their ghostly abodes — presumably to the end of the present world era and the beginning of the next, when once again a creator god might descend to fashion their bones into a new race of humans. But those who became companions of the Sun had a different destiny. Four years after death they were transformed, returning to the earth as gorgeously feathered hummingbirds and other multicolored birds and butterflies that lived on the sweet nectar of flowering plants and trees.

OLD GODS IN NEW GUISES

A multitude of gods ruled the lives of the ancient Americans, and it was the role of the shamans, or medicine men, and the priests to interpret their will to the people. To this day vestiges of the old rituals mingle with Christian ceremonies.

The conquistadors encountered two great empires in the New World, the Aztec in Mexico and the Inca in Peru. They also found prosperous smaller states to conquer, with none as eager to join the Spanish side against their local enemies as the Tlaxcalan, whose territory north of Tenochtitlán was surrounded on all sides by the Aztec. But these states, too, were easily vanquished by superior Spanish arms. An unexpected contributing factor to the downfall of the Indian cultures was the sweep of devastating smallpox epidemics, which also raged through the Antilles, killing most of the native population within 50 years of their discovery by Columbus.

In the wake of military conquest the Spaniards mounted a determined assault against the native religions. Temples were razed and their stones recycled to construct the palaces and churches of the conquerors. Sacred images were smashed, burned, or thrown into the canals that skirted the Aztec ceremonial precinct in the center of Tenochtitlán. Local priests who were not murdered were subjected to public humiliation and forcible conversion. In their zeal to wipe out the pagan religions, the Spaniards destroyed much of the historical record of the people. The Inca had no formal writing, but in Mexico the Spaniards systematically hunted down and burned hundreds of Maya and Aztec codices, or screenfold pictorial manuscripts, recorded histories of noble families, and divinatory almanacs filled with esoteric knowledge whose reading and interpretation required years of specialized schooling. Today these works would be considered literary treasures of inestimable value.

Before their bloody defeat, the Aztec and Inca empires, with millions of people under their control, were highly stratified societies distinguished by differences in status and living standards among rulers, nobles, warriors, and commoners. In earlier times, the occasional services of the village shaman or seer — guardian and singer of the tribal traditions — were all the people needed to maintain spiritual balance between the natural and supernatural worlds and to minister to the sick. But as great cities developed, the complexity of urban life spawned a separate class of professional, full-time priests to tend to the hundreds of activities prescribed

This grotesque clay effigy figure of a Maya god of the underworld, cradling a representation of a human skull, probably served as a ceremonial incense burner. It was discovered in a tomb at Tikal and dates from the 4th or 5th century.

by divinatory calendars to honor the multitude of gods. So thoroughly intertwined were the daily affairs and rites of the great state religions, and so unceasing were the demands on the priesthood, that schools were established to train novices in the esoteric knowledge and practice of those religions. The urban dwellers, in turn, expressed their religious fervor in the annual rounds of festivals tied to the calendar and attended by thousands, even tens of thousands, of people.

Yet crowded as the cities were, most of the population still lived in the countryside as farmers, artisans, and on occasion, hunters and gatherers of wild foods. Their religious passion was no less intense than that of the urban folk, but it was more private, more directly associated with common human concerns such as weather, crop failures, sickness, and death than with the great cosmic uncertainties that so preoccupied the official priesthood.

Even for many urban dwellers, however, a more personal, shamanistic religion — one centered on the deities of the household — probably served their daily needs as well or better than the great and often bloody rituals of the annual ceremonial round performed by priests on the summits of the temple pyramids. The shaman's visions of the supernatural and his techniques of the ecstatic trance — attributed to his use of sacred plants — never quite disappeared even from the complex system of beliefs that evolved as hamlets grew into cities and household altars into temple pyramids. And as the Spaniards were to discover, the old ways of the shaman proved far more difficult to eliminate in the countryside than those of the priest in the city.

It was in the countryside, too, that some of the old gods found refuge, though dressed in the new clothing of the Christian faith. The sun god became transformed into Jesus Christ. And almost everywhere the old mother goddesses reemerged as the Virgin Mary in her different guises, the most famous of them the Virgin of Guadalupe. In 1531, 10 years after the fall of Tenochtitlán, at the precise spot where an Aztec temple to the young mother goddess Xochiquetzal, "Precious Flower," had stood before the Conquest, the Virgin appeared in a vision to a poor and simple Indian convert, asking in Aztec that a temple be built there in her honor. Her cult swept through the Mexican countryside and eventually to all of Spanish America.

The rural Indians also had no difficulty embracing as their own some of the symbols of the Christian faith that seemed especially familiar, in form if not in meaning. Thus, the pre-Conquest cult of the skull as seat of the soul found renewed life in Christian images of the skull as *memento mori* in the hands of St. Francis and St. Jerome. And for people familiar with sacrificial death by bow and arrow in rites of curing and rebirth dedicated to the Aztec god of the flayed skin, Xipe Totec, paintings and statues depicting the martyrdom of St. Sebastian in a hail of Roman arrows might strike a familiar chord. The Indians could even claim the cross as their own, for did it not depict their concept of a four-quartered universe with its sacred center?

If all that confronted the Spanish clergy were old gods in new guises, they might rightly have claimed victory. Instead, after a century of mass conversions and the most determined, often cruel, pursuit of every trace of the old religions, the most realistic of their number were forced to concede that spiritual conquest was far from complete. They feared that their missionary work among the natives might never be fully accomplished if the Indians persisted in customs the Spaniards could only attribute to pacts with the Devil.

The World of the Shaman

What the 16th-century Florentine Codex did to preserve the state religion of the Aztec for posterity, a humbler work, the "Treatise on Indian Superstitions" by Hernando Ruiz de Alarcón did to immortalize the beliefs and rituals of the village shaman. Written between 1617 and 1629, it described the religious customs and beliefs of Aztec-speaking villagers in colonial Mexico. Fluent in Aztec, Ruiz de Alarcón had been appointed ecclesiastical judge for northern Guerrero and neighboring Morelos. Charged with investigating and suppressing pagan beliefs and customs among the Indians, he was forced to admit failure after more than a dozen years of diligent effort; he wrote his work in the hope that his experience would help other missionaries to greater success. Although several editions of his manuscript were copied by hand in the 17th century, its existence remained virtually unknown to scholars until it was discovered and published in the 20th century.

The "Treatise" records in great detail the workings of the supernatural universe of shamans and diviners. It tells about their use of magic and transformation, the nature of their helping spirits, and the rich metaphoric language of their incantations and spells, which summoned the help of supernatural powers in such specific pursuits as fishing with nets, hooks, or traps; gathering honey from wild bees; cutting wood; or making lime — to name but a few. The author also recounts his unceasing but unsuccessful war against the use of magical plants by which shamans and diviners sought to establish communication with pagan gods and spirits and transcend the limitations of the human condition. "One should point out," he wrote, "that almost every time they are moved to offer sacrifice to their imagined gods, there springs up from the other Indians some satrap, doctor, sorcerer, or diviner to so order and arrange it; most of these ground themselves in their spells, or else are made foolish by the drink they call *ololiuhqui,* or peyote or tobacco. . . . "

Ruiz de Alarcón was particularly disturbed by the stubborn refusal of his converts to give up their much-venerated *ololiuhqui,* the Nahuatl name for the potent hallucinogenic seeds of the morning glory plant. When drunk as infusions, he wrote, *ololiuhqui* "deprives one of reason. One can only marvel at the faith which these

In this 8th-century Maya bas-relief a richly dressed noblewoman pierces her tongue with a spiked cord while the ruler Shield Jaguar holds a torch over her head. Sting ray spines were also commonly used in bloodletting rituals whose purpose was to nourish the gods and make contact with the supernatural. Some scholars now propose that extreme pain most likely causes hallucinations, which might explain why the Maya believed they could actually speak to their gods.

In today's Peru the owl is used by folk healers to combat witchcraft. In Moche times it may have had the same significance, and artisans created ceramic stirrup spout pots like the one below to symbolize curers performing their medicinal magic. Experts suggest that the "owl woman" may be holding a slice of San Pedro, an hallucinogenic cactus still used today in shamanistic rituals, as it was before the Conquest. The figure on the base of the pot, a tethered llama, was probably another symbol of magical curing.

wretched natives have in this seed, for on drinking it they consult it as an oracle for all those things that they wish to know, even those which human knowledge cannot reach." Some shamans who specialized in curing diseases themselves drank *ololiuhqui*, believing they would learn the cause of illness, or else they prescribed it for their patients and then interpreted the meaning of their hallucinatory visions. The fear and respect "they hold for the said *ololiuhqui* or for the deity that they believe resides in it" was greater, the priest noted with frustrated astonishment, than any fear they might have had of punishment by the Holy Office or the civil authorities for refusing to reveal their secret stores of the potent seeds. He set about to uproot "this harmful superstition" by destroying thickets of morning glory vines that grew in abundance by streams and rivers and consigning great quantities of confiscated seeds to the flames. But much more remained hidden, and the divinatory use of *ololiuhqui* continued as before.

Although Ruiz de Alarcón's account suggests that some hallucinogenic plants employed by Indians in ritual setting had medicinal uses, it was the ecstatic vi-

Burial Rites in the Andes

The cult of the dead, an integral part of Inca religion, was deeply rooted in Andean tradition, dating back some 15 centuries before the creation of the Inca empire in 1430. In fact, the Inca not only revered their ancestors, they believed the remains held residual power. If, for instance, the body fell into the hands of an evildoer, such a person could impose his wishes on the dead man's descendants.

Perhaps at no other time in his life was an Inca as venerated and as honored as at his death. To the Inca, death symbolized a rite of passage from the natural to the supernatural world, and it was solemnized with elaborate ceremony and great displays of public grief. The family and friends of the deceased dressed in black, and the women of the household cut their hair, painted their faces black, and covered their heads with shawls. The funeral rituals, which continued for almost eight days, included elaborate feasts where songs were sung to remind the assemblage of the good deeds of the deceased. There followed a period of mourning, which could last up to a year for members of the nobility.

One scholar has suggested that Inca burials should rightly be called entombments because most of their dead were placed in beehive-shaped, above-ground tombs constructed of stone or clay. Regardless of whether the corpse was entombed or buried, the Inca, much like the Egyptians, placed a special significance on the material possessions that accompanied the corpse to the grave. No Inca, whether rich or poor, went naked from this world; higher status in society simply meant more elaborate grave furnishings. The body was wrapped in many layers of beautifully woven cloth and was seated in an upright position. The grave was furnished with pottery, gold and silver works of art, jewelry, and food. Sometimes — but only among the elite — a man's secondary wives and his servants were sacrificed at his death and entombed with him. An Inca was also often buried with the tools he had used during his lifetime: a fisherman with his nets or a weaver

with spindles and unspun cotton. More recently, archeologists have discovered frozen, lifelike corpses in the frigid temperatures of the Andean mountain peaks where they were placed hundreds of years ago probably following sacrificial ceremonies.

The Inca death cult was not as involved as that of the Egyptians, but it resembled it in several respects. In one Inca ritual the mummies of rulers and other important persons were paraded throughout the land so that all the people could pay their respects. This practice was abandoned in the 16th century, but the reverence for their deceased ancestors continues to this day among the native inhabitants of the Andes.

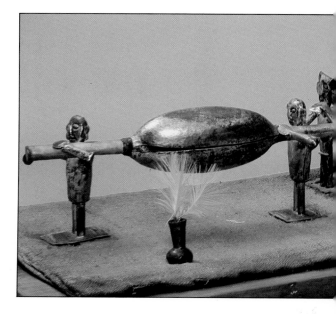

---

sionary trance they produced that most concerned the Spanish clergy. As they and other European colonists soon discovered, the ecstatic trance was nearly universal throughout the Americas, apparently an essential part of service to the Indian gods. Trances played a role in puberty initiations, in the training and practice of medicine men, and in prophecy and divination. Had the Spaniards known that there were worlds beyond the ones they conquered or explored, they would have recognized the ecstatic trance among Arctic Eskimos, among settled farmers deep in the tropical forests of South America, and among the fishing people and guanaco hunters of the Tierra del Fuego.

Although the ecstatic trance was nearly universal, the techniques employed to attain it varied from culture to culture. Eskimo shamans (whose environment in any event lacked suitable intoxicating plants) brought on

trances by the hypnotizing rhythmic pounding of a drum. Plains Indians of North America sought visions and supernatural guardians through fasts, prolonged wakefulness, exposure to the elements, and even self-inflicted pain. Many other Indian peoples, or at least their shamans, employed hallucinogens to explore or confirm in ecstatic dreams the meaning of tribal mythology. The hallucinogenic San Pedro cactus, still used in modern Peruvian folk medicine, is depicted again and again for over 2,000 years in the ceremonial art of successive Peruvian civilizations. The oldest example is a recently found carving of a fanged and clawed god with serpentine hair and a serpent belt — which later became the principal deity of Chavín, Peru's first civilization —who is grasping the tall, columnar San Pedro cactus in his outstretched right hand. Archeologists date the work to about 1300 B.C. The

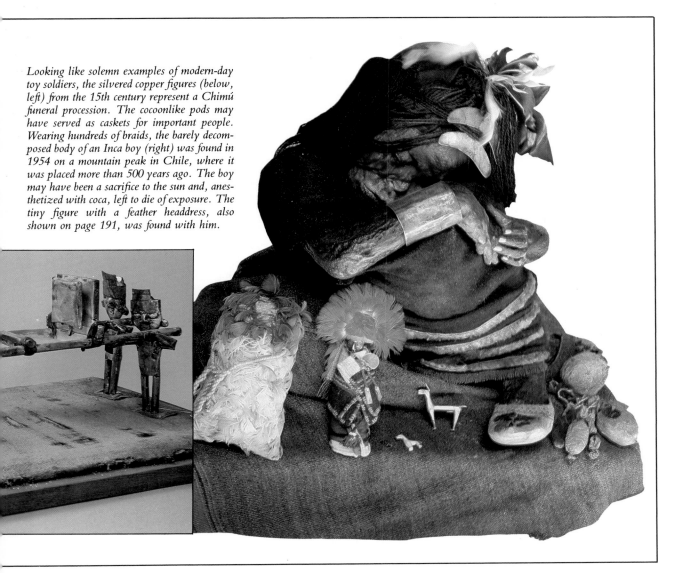

Looking like solemn examples of modern-day toy soldiers, the silvered copper figures (below, left) from the 15th century represent a Chimú funeral procession. The cocoonlike pods may have served as caskets for important people. Wearing hundreds of braids, the barely decomposed body of an Inca boy (right) was found in 1954 on a mountain peak in Chile, where it was placed more than 500 years ago. The boy may have been a sacrifice to the sun and, anesthetized with coca, left to die of exposure. The tiny figure with a feather headdress, also shown on page 191, was found with him.

cactus was also pictured in textiles and on painted funerary pottery of the Moche civilization, which rose on the north coast of Peru in the final centuries of the first millennium B.C., enduring for nearly 1,000 years, until about A.D 750. The potters and vase painters of the Nazca civilization, which flourished at about the same time in southern Peru, outdid their northern contemporaries in modeled polychrome depictions not just of the sacred cactus but also of a San Pedro deity with the cactus sprouting from his shoulders and his forehead.

From South America come the oldest known paraphernalia for taking snuff — a whalebone tablet and birdbone tube excavated in an ancient preagricultural fishing village on the Peruvian coast, dated about 1700 to 1500 B.C. Two 2,000-year-old ceramic sculptures of men putting themselves into a trance by taking snuff have turned up in burials in western Mexico. But it is

from Texas that we have the earliest evidence for a widespread use of psychotropic plants. Here, some 10,000 years old, protected in dry caves from the ravages of the elements, quantities of the so-called mescal bean (the hallucinogenic seeds of the flowering *Sophora secundiflora* bush) have been discovered. The oldest were found in a cave called Bonfire Shelter, dated between 8440 and 8120 B.C., a time when giant bison and mammoth still roamed the grasslands of the southern Plains. In other rock shelters, every occupation layer, from about 7000 B.C. to A.D. 1000, yielded the potent little seeds whose use was not without a certain risk, for they are capable of causing convulsions and even respiratory failure. Mescal beans were widely traded among Indians living in Texas at the time of Cabéza de Vaca's visit in 1539, and as recently as the late 19th century they were still used among Indians of the southern

301

Plains in the ecstatic initiation rituals of shamanistic medicine societies. In these ceremonies, after imbibing a powerful drink made from the bean, the neophytes suffered symbolic death as children to be reborn upon awakening from their ecstatic trance as fully initiated members of adult society. The 17th-century traveler Robert Beverly reported virtually the same phenomenon in Virginia, although there the young Indian initiates were ritually intoxicated with jimsonweed, whose effects could be every bit as dangerous as those of the mescal bean.

The tropical flora of South America is especially rich in psychotropic plants, and the agricultural peoples of the region and even some hunter-gatherers so effectively explored their environments that they discovered a whole range of plants to induce ritual intoxication. They even knew which species to combine where one alone did not suffice for the desired effect.

Cohóba snuff, made from the seeds of a leguminous tree related to the acacias and mimosas, was an early discovery, carried to the West Indies from the South American mainland by the ancestors of the Arawakan tribe encountered by Columbus. In 1492, Columbus noted that in certain rites the inhabitants of the Antilles placed a powder on the heads of wooden idols. When the Arawakans inhaled it through Y-shaped nose pipes, they "go out of their minds and become as if intoxicated." In 1496, Father Román Pané, a Spanish priest on

Columbus's second expedition, wrote that the Indians called their snuff *cohóba,* or *cogioba,* adding that "it is a certain powder which they sometimes take to purge themselves and for other effects."

The Spaniards initially mistook *cohóba* for tobacco, which they also saw the Indians use in their religious rites. Soon to sweep the Old World as a pleasure-giving drug, tobacco was everywhere sacred among Indians as the sustenance of the gods. The Indians believed that it had been a precious gift of the higher powers, never to be used lightly or outside its proper sanctified context. North American Indians generally burned tobacco and offered the smoke to their gods. In the South American tropics, tobacco often served for ritual intoxication, being smoked, taken as snuff, or even boiled and drunk in liquid form, by itself or together with other psychotropic plants.

Cohóba and tobacco were only a small portion of the available hallucinogenic plants. In addition to species described by early chroniclers and explorers, scholars have identified 100 or so other plants with intoxicating properties that Indians used in pre-Columbian times or are still employing today. Modern chemistry, meanwhile, has patiently isolated their psychoactive principles in the laboratory. Where the Spanish perceived in these plants only the Devil at work, and scholars concentrated on ritual and psychopharmacology, the Indians had their own perspective: as Ruiz de Alarcón re-

ported from Guerrero, the indigenous peoples believed there were gods in all these plants. Not for nothing did the Aztecs call their sacred mushrooms *teonanácatl,* meaning "god's flesh." To eat these fragile, tawny-colored fungi or drink their pressed-out juice, reverently, surrounded by taboo, as some Mexican Indians still do in divinatory curing rites, was to partake of divine substance and experience magical flight into the presence of the higher powers. Conversion to Christianity altered this magical world only superficially, by shifting the ceremonies from pagan gods to the Christian divinity: Oaxacan Indians today identify the *teonanácatl* of the Aztec with the flesh and blood of Christ, and when healing shamans consult it in their mushroom-induced trance, its "diagnosis" is accepted by healer and patient alike as the word of the Christian God.

Of all the Mexican Indians who still employ hallucinogens in religious rites and divinatory curing, only one tribe, the Huicholes of the rugged Sierra Madre Occidental, have successfully held out against conversion to Christianity. The principal deities of these Indians, whose language is distantly related to Aztec, are still the old fire god, addressed as "Our Grandfather,"

the white-haired old earth goddess, "Our Grandmother," and the Sun, "Our Father." Their sacred hallucinogen is the peyote cactus (the same plant that serves as a sacrament for the quarter million adherents of the pan-Indian Native American Church).

For the Huicholes, peyote is neither Christ nor saint but remains, as it must have been before the Conquest, a transformed deer god. In the founding myth of the Huichol peyote ritual, a party of divine ancestors — the ancestral gods — set out to search for the peyote cactus under the leadership of their shaman, the old fire god himself. They traveled for 20 days, enduring hunger, thirst, and other hardships, when at last they reached the desert where the peyote grew. There they saw not peyote but a deer and shot it with their bows and arrows. Dying, the deer transformed itself into peyote, and when members of the party tasted its flesh, they became intoxicated. In their ecstatic dreams they saw the truth and beauty of the ancient Huichol way. As the Indians tell it, "they found their life."

Some 12,000 of these most traditional of all Mexican Indians make their lives today in the Sierra Madre Occidental as subsistence farmers, planting corn, beans, and squash with the traditional digging stick, reciting myths, and observing ceremonies that sometimes resemble those of the Aztec, sometimes those of the Pueblo Indians of the Southwest. And each year, at the height of the dry season, small parties of these Indians set out to reenact the peyote myth in pilgrimages that take them on a 300-mile journey to a sacred territory they call *Wirikuta,* the home of the divine peyote in the high desert of north-central Mexico. This ritual "hunt" for peyote with bows and arrows as their only weapons is truly a window on the past — one of the last indigenous ceremonials that is an apparent survival of pre-Conquest ecstatic Indian religion in Mexico.

"Vine of the Souls"

Aside from the Huicholes in Mexico, it is now mainly in lowland South America that hallucinogenic plants can still be seen used as they might have been in their pre-Columbian setting. Even there the old ways are changing fast, as the rain forests fall to the population explosion and agricultural and industrial development.

The best described of the traditional hallucinogens of Amazonia is a potent brew made from a jungle vine of the genus *Banisteriopsis.* Its dramatic effects on the mind play a crucial role in the ceremonies of many Indian tribes, especially in Brazil and the Upper Amazon. In Quechua, the language of the pre-Hispanic Inca and of millions of Andean Indians today, it is known as *ayahuasca,* "vine of the souls." Tukanoan-speakers of the Vaupés of Colombia call it *yajé.* Among the Desana, one of many Tujanoan peoples, the *yajé* ritual and its complex cosmological and social functions have been most vividly described by the Colombian anthropologist Gerardo Reichel-Dolmatoff. Like the peyote ritual among the Huicholes, the communal *yajé* trance

Hallucinogenic plants played a major role in shamanistic rituals. A mural replica from Teotihuacán (far left) shows a mother goddess with the vines of the sacred morning glory plant towering over her. The ceramic hunchback dwarf figure from the Colima culture of western Mexico (near left) holds a peyote cactus in each hand. Discovered in a tomb in Oaxaca, Mexico, the pedestal cup above was probably a symbolic vessel for drinking pulque, *a mild alcoholic beverage.*

serves, above all, for social integration by mystical means, to confirm the beauty, truth, and validity of the tribal culture and its mythological history. The ritual is held at night, in a communal house whose architecture replicates the Indian universe in microcosm. To the accompaniment of sacred chants and the rhythmic sound of percussion instruments, and after long instruction in the sacred tribal lore, initiates into adult society "see" for themselves in their ecstatic trance how the social order was established. They "see" how the reciprocity that regulates relations among humans, animals, plants, and spirit beings was supernaturally sanctioned — even how the material objects in daily use came into being long ago through magical acts of supernatural ancestral culture heroes. The images of these visions, in turn, become the symbols the Indians paint on their houses and utensils.

To have bright and pleasant visions one must have abstained from sex and eaten only lightly on the preceding days. At intervals a shaman describes his visions and interprets them publicly: "That red color is the Master of the Animals," or "This trembling is the winds of the Milky Way." The Milky Way is the home of the supernatural Master of the hallucinogens, to which the shamans ascend in their ecstatic trance and from whom most of them derive their principal spirit

power. He, in turn, guides the shamans to the abode of the red-colored Master and protector of game animals and fish, on whose good will success in hunting and fishing depends. In return for the gift of game, the shaman promises to turn over to the world of animals the soul of any Desana who has violated the rules of life. According to the Indians, nothing else will right the balance their hunting has upset.

In 1970, Richard Evans Schultes, a noted botanist and ranking authority on New World hallucinogens, wondered in print why American Indians, of all the peoples of the world, had been so fascinated with the effects on the mind of certain plants that they explored their territory for them and adopted perhaps 100 species into their religious practices. Yet in the Old World, settled far longer by human beings and probably as rich in psychotropic flora as the New, only a dozen or so such plants are known to have been used. Why such a dramatic difference?

If the question was one of statistics, the answer was one of culture. It came, appropriately, from a distinguished ethnologist and student of religion, Weston La Barre, author of a classic work on peyote as the 20th-century sacrament of the Native American Church. The ancestors of American Indians were, after all, people out of Asia. Far from "primitive," they were fully

Although the Spanish conquerors converted the Indians to Catholicism, many of the Christian ceremonies practiced in the Americas today still reflect ancient rituals of a bygone faith. Thousands of pilgrims form a human snake (far left) as they climb to the peak of the 18,118-foot mountain, Colquepunku, in Peru, in an annual festival at a sanctuary called Qoyullur Rit'i, or "Star of the Snow." Here they celebrate both the Christian feast of Corpus Christi and the disappearance of the constellation Pleiades from the night sky. During an Easter ceremony in western Mexico a masked carnival dancer carrying rattles (near left) represents a Judas character who is redeemed when the bells of the church in the background announce the miracle of the Resurrection; another dancer (above) wears a deer headdress in a dance that reenacts a deer hunt.

modern human beings, who had participated in a long tradition of Asiatic shamanism and who carried that tradition with them into the New World. The hallmark of shamanism was then as now the ecstatic trance as a personal pathway to the supernatural, whatever the technique by which it is triggered. Modified in new environments, adapted to new social, economic, and cultural realities, even transformed into complex theologies where simpler societies evolved into the great Indian civilizations, shamanism and its techniques of ecstasy nevertheless remained the base religion of all American Indians. Accordingly, if not the earliest migrating hunting bands who might have come across Beringia perhaps 30,000 years ago, then perhaps the shamans of subsequent arrivals began from the start to explore their new surroundings for plants that might transport men into the company of the higher powers.

Of course this is speculation. But so is much of what we reconstruct of the ancient past. Still, if it is true that the traditional religions of Indian America are rooted in the shamanism of Siberian forest peoples, as the many correspondences between them indicate, the spiritual ancestor of all New World hallucinogens may well have been that quintessential hallucinogen of the shamans of Siberia and the north Eurasian forest belt — the fly agaric or *Amanita muscaria*, the "magic mushroom" of European folklore and Alice in Wonderland.

A final thought: The striking similarities between the world view of American Indians and that of the tribal peoples of Siberia and the Artic, down to some basic cosmological beliefs and symbols, suggest a very ancient common ancestry. (The anthropological term *shaman* is a Tungus word, derived from the language of Siberia's reindeer hunters.) Is it possible, then, that at least some of the intellectual foundations of the great native civilizations, beginning with that of the Olmec about 1200 B.C., may have been present already in the shamanistic religions of early hunters who, in the pursuit of game, became the real discoverers of the New World tens of thousands of years before Columbus?

Bibliography

ADAMS, RICHARD E. W., ed. *The Origins of Maya Civilization.* Albuquerque: University of New Mexico Press, 1977.

ASHE, GEOFFREY. *Land to the West: St. Brendan's Voyage to America.* New York: The Viking Press, 1962.

ASHE, GEOFFREY, THOR HEYERDAHL, HELGE INGSTAD, J.V. LUCE, BETTY J. MEGGERS, and BIRGITTA L. WALLACE. *The Quest for America.* New York, Washington, London: Praeger Publishers, 1971.

AVENI, ANTHONY F., ed. *Native American Astronomy.* Austin and London: University of Texas Press, 1977.

BENNETT, ROSS., ed. *Lost Empires, Living Tribes.* Washington, D.C.: National Geographic Society, 1982.

BENNETT, WENDELL C. *Ancient Arts of the Andes.* New York: The Museum of Modern Art, 1954.

BENNETT, WENDELL C., and JUNIUS B. BIRD. *Andean Culture History.* Garden City, N.Y.: The Natural History Press, 1964.

BENSON, ELIZABETH P., ed. *Death and the Afterlife in Pre-Columbian America.* Washington, D.C.: Dumbarton Oaks Research Library and Collections, Trustees for Harvard University, 1975.

BENSON, ELIZABETH P. *The Olmec & Their Neighbors.* Washington, D.C.: Dumbarton Oaks Research Library and Collections, Trustees for Harvard University, 1981.

BERNAL, IGNACIO. *The Olmec World.* Translated by Doris Heyden and Fernando Horcasitas. Berkeley, Los Angeles, London: University of California Press, 1969.

BERNAL, IGNACIO. *3000 Years of Art and Life in Mexico.* Translated by Carolyn B. Czitrom. New York: Harry N. Abrams, Inc., Publishers, 1968.

BLACKER, IRWIN R. *Cortes and the Aztec Conquest.* New York: American Heritage Publishing Co., Inc., 1965.

BRAY, WARWICK. *Gold of El Dorado.* New York: American Museum of Natural History/Harry N. Abrams, Inc., Publishers, 1979.

BUSHNELL, G. H. S. *Ancient Arts of the Americas.* New York: Frederick A. Praeger, Publishers, 1965.

CASSON, LIONEL, ROBERT CLAIBORNE, BRIAN FAGAN, and WALTER KARP. *Mysteries of the Past.* New York: American Heritage Publishing Co., Inc.,1977.

CASTILLO, BERNAL DÍAZ DEL. *The Discovery and Conquest of Mexico, 1517–1521.* New York: Octagon Books, 1970.

CATLIN, GEORGE, *Letters and Notes on the Manners, Customs, and Conditions of the North American Indians.* New York: Dover Publications, Inc., 1973.

CERAM, C. W. *The First American: A Story of North American Archeology.* New York: Harcourt Brace Jovanovich, Inc., 1971.

CERAM, C. W., ed. *Hands on the Past: Pioneer Archaeologists Tell Their Own Story.* New York: Alfred A. Knopf, 1966.

CHURCHWARD, COLONEL JAMES. *The Lost Continent of Mu.* New York: Ives Washburn, Publisher, 1931.

CLAIRBORNE, ROBERT, and the Editors of Time-Life Books. *The Emergence of Man: The First Americans.* New York: Time-Life Books, 1973.

COE, MICHAEL D. *America's First Civilization.* New York: American Heritage Publishing Co., Inc., in association with The Smithsonian Institution, 1968.

COE, MICHAEL D., and RICHARD A. DIEHL. *In the Land of the Olmec: The Archaeology of San Lorenzo Tenochtitlán,* Vol. 1. Austin and London: University of Texas Press, 1980.

COE, MICHAEL D. *The Jaguar's Children: Pre-Classic Central Mexico.* New York: The Museum of Primitive Art, 1965.

COE, MICHAEL D. *The Maya.* New York, Thames and Hudson, Inc., 1980.

COVARRUBIAS, MIGUEL. *Indian Art of Mexico and Central America.* New York: Alfred A. Knopf, 1957.

CULBERT, PATRICK T., ed. *The Classic Maya Collapse.* Albuquerque: University of New Mexico Press, 1977.

DAVIES, NIGEL. *Voyagers to the New World.* New York: William Morrow and Company, Inc., 1979.

DEACON, RICHARD. *Madoc and the Discovery of America: Some New Light on an Old Controversy.* New York: George Braziller, 1966.

DEUEL, LEO. *Conquistadors without Swords: Archaeologists in the Americas.* New York: St. Martin's Press, Inc., 1967.

DIGBY, ADRIAN. *Maya Jades.* London: British Museum Publications, Ltd, 1964.

DISSELHOFF, H. D., and S. LINNÉ. *The Art of Ancient America: Civilizations of Central and South America.* New York: Crown Publishers, Inc., 1960.

D'OLWER, LUIS NICOLAU, and HOWARD F. CLINE. "Bernadino de Sahagun, 1499–1590," *Handbook of Middle American Indians,* vol. 13. Austin: University of Texas Press, 1973.

DONNAN, CHRISTOPHER B. *Moche Art of Peru: Pre-Columbian Symbolic Communication.* Los Angeles: Museum of Cultural History, University of California, 1978.

DONOVAN, FRANK R. *The Vikings.* New York: American Heritage Publishing Co., Inc., 1964.

DURAN, FRAY DIEGO. *The Aztecs: The History of the Indies of New Spain.* Translated by Doris Heyden and Fernando Horcasitas. New York: Orion Press, 1964.

EASBY, ELIZABETH KENNEDY. *Ancient Art of Latin America: From the Collection of Jay C. Leff.* New York: The Brooklyn Museum, 1966.

EASBY, ELIZABETH KENNEDY, and JOHN F. SCOTT. *Before Cortés: Sculpture of Middle America.* New York: The Metropolitan Museum of Art, 1970.

EMMERICH, ANDRÉ. *Before Columbus.* New York: Simon and Schuster, 1963.

EMMERICH, ANDRÉ. *Sweat of the Sun and Tears of the Moon.* New York: Hacker Art Books, 1977.

FERGUSON, WILLIAM M., and JOHN Q. ROYCE. *Maya Ruins of Mexico in Color.* Norman: University of Oklahoma Press, 1977.

FURST, JILL LESLIE, and PETER T. FURST. *Pre-Columbian Art of Mexico.* New York: Abbeville Press Publishers, 1980.

GALLENKAMP, CHARLES. *Maya: The Riddle and Rediscovery of a Lost Civilization.* 2nd rev. ed. New York: David McKay Company, Inc., 1981.

HAMMOND, NORMAN. *Ancient Maya Civilization.* New Brunswick, N.J.: Rutgers University Press, 1982.

HEISER, CHARLES B., JR. *Seed to Civilization: The Story of Man's Food.* San Francisco: W.H. Freeman and Company, 1973.

HEMMING, JOHN. *The Conquest of the Incas.* New York: Harcourt Brace Jovanovich, Inc., 1970.

HEMMING, JOHN. *Monuments of the Incas.* Boston: Little, Brown and Company, 1982.

HONOUR, HUGH. *The New Golden Land: European Images of America from the Discoveries to the Present Time.* New York: Pantheon Books, 1975.

HINDLEY, GEOFFREY. *A History of Roads.* Secaucus, N.J.: The Citadel Press, 1972.

HUNTER, C. BRUCE. *A Guide to Ancient Maya Ruins.* Norman: University of Oklahoma Press, 1974.

INGSTAD, ANNE STINE. *The Discovery of a Norse Settlement in America.* Olso, Norway: Universitetsforlaget, 1977.

JENNINGS, JESSE D., ed. *Ancient North Americans.* Salt Lake City: W. H. Freeman and Company, Inc., 1983.

JENNINGS, JESSE D., ed. *Ancient South Americans.* San Francisco: W. H. Freeman and Company, 1978.

JENNINGS, JESSE D. *Prehistory of North America,* 2nd ed. New York: McGraw-Hill Book Company, 1968.

JONES, JULIE. *Art of Empire: The Inca of Peru.* New York: The Museum of Primitive Art, 1964.

JOSEPHY, ALVIN M., Jr., ed. *The American Heritage Book of Indians.* New York: American Heritage Publishing Co., Inc., 1961.

KATZ, LOIS, ed. *The Art of the Andes: Pre-Columbian Sculptured and Painted Ceramics from the Arthur M. Sackler Collections.* Washington, D.C.: Arthur M. Sackler Foundation, 1983.

KELEMEN, PÁL. *Medieval American Art: Masterpieces of the New World Before Columbus:* Vol I. New York: Dover Publications, Inc., 1969.

KRUPP, E. C., ed. *In Search of Ancient Astronomies.* New York: McGraw-Hill Book Company, 1978.

KUBLER, GEORGE. *The Art and Architecture of Ancient America: The Mexican, Maya, and Andean Peoples.* Baltimore: Penguin Books, Inc., 1962.

LA FAY, HOWARD. *The Vikings.* Washington, D.C.: National Geographic Society, 1972

LOTHROP, S. K. *Treasures of Ancient America: The Arts of the Pre-Columbian Civilizations from Mexico to Peru.* Geneva, Switzerland: Editions d'Art Albert Skira, 1964.

LUCE, J. V. *Lost Atlantis: New Light on an Old Legend.* New York, St. Louis, San Francisco: McGraw-Hill Book Company, 1969.

LUMBRERAS, LUIS G. *The Peoples and Cultures of Ancient Peru.* Translated by Betty J. Meggers. Washington, D.C.: Smithsonian Institution Press, 1974.

MAGNUSSON, MAGNUS. *Vikings!* New York: E.P. Dutton, Elsevier-Dutton Publishing Co., Inc., 1980.

MANGELSDORF, PAUL C. *Corn: Its Origin, Evolution, and Improvement.* Cambridge, Mass.: The Belknap Press of Harvard University Press, 1974.

MASON, J. ALDEN. *The Ancient Civilizations of Peru,* rev. ed. New York: Penguin Books, 1968.

MASON, RONALD J. *Great Lakes Archaeology.* New York: Academic Press, 1981.

McINTYRE, LOREN. *The Incredible Incas and Their Timeless Land.* Washington, D.C.: National Geographic Society, 1975.

MEYER, KARL E. *Teotihuacán.* New York: Newsweek, 1973.

MORISON, SAMUEL ELIOT. *The European Discovery of America: The Northern Voyages,* A.D. *500–1600.* New York: Oxford University Press, 1971.

MOSELEY, MICHAEL EDWARD. *The Maritime Foundations of Andean Civilization.* Menlo Park, Calif., of Reading, Mass., London, Amsterdam, Don Mills, Ontario, Sydney: The Benjamin/Cummings Publishing Company, 1975.

MOSELEY, MICHAEL E., and KENT C. DAY, eds. *Chan Chan: Andean Desert City.* Albuquerque: University of New Mexico Press, 1982.

NICHOLSON, H. B., with ELOISE QUIÑONES KEBER. *Art of Aztec Mexico: Treasures of Tenochtitlan.* Washington, D.C.: National Gallery of Art, 1983.

ORTIZ, ALFONSO A., ed. *Handbook of North American Indians.* Washington, D.C.: Smithsonian Institution, 1980.

PASZTORY, ESTHER. *Aztec Art.* New York: Harry N. Abrams, Inc., Publishers, 1983.

PIKE, DONALD G. *Anasazi: Ancient People of the Rock.* New York: Crown Publishers, Inc., 1974.

PRESCOTT, WILLIAM H. *History of the Conquest of Mexico and History of the Conquest of Peru.* New York: The Modern Library, Random House.

PROSKOURIAKOFF, TATIANA. *An Album of Maya Architecture.* Norman: University of Oklahoma Press, 1963.

RAGGHIANTI, CARLO LUDOVICO, and LICIA RAGGHIANTI COLLOBI. *National Museum of Anthropology Mexico City.* New York and Milan: Newsweek, Inc. & Arnoldo Mondadori Editore, 1970.

REED, CHARLES A., ed. *Origins of Agriculture.* The Hague, Paris: Mouton Publishers, 1977.

RILEY, CARROLL L., J. CHARLES KELLEY, CAMPBELL W. PENNINGTON, and ROBERT L. RANDS, eds. *Man Across the Sea: Problems of Pre-Columbian Contacts.* Austin and London: University of Texas Press, 1971.

Bibliography (continued)

ROBERTSON, MERLE GREENE, *The Sculpture of Palenque: The Temple of the Inscriptions*, Vol. I. Princeton, N.J.: Princeton University Press, 1983.

SAHAGÚN, FRAY BERNADINO DE, *Florentine Codex: General History of the Things of New Spain*, 12 vols. Translated and edited by A.J.O. Anderson and C. E. Dibble. Santa Fe, N. Mex.: University of Utah and The School of American Research, 1969.

SAWYER, ALAN R. *Mastercraftsmen of Ancient Peru*. New York: The Solomon R. Guggenheim Foundation, 1968.

SEVERIN, TIM. *The Brendan Voyage*. New York: McGraw-Hill Book Company, 1978.

SILVERBERG, ROBERT. *Mound Builders of Ancient America: The Archaeology of a Myth*. Greenwich, Conn.: New York Graphic Society Ltd., 1968.

SNOW, DEAN. *The Archaeology of North America*. New York: The Viking Press, 1976.

SMITH, BRADLEY. *Mexico: A History In Art*. Garden City, N.Y.: Doubleday & Company, Inc., 1968.

SOUSTELLE, JACQUES. *The Route of the Incas*. New York: The Viking Press, 1977.

STEPHENS, JOHN L. *Incidents of Travel in Central America, Chiapas, and Yucatán*, Vols. I & II. New York: Dover Publications, Inc., 1969.

STEPHENS, JOHN LLOYD. *Incidents of Travel in Yucatán*, Vol. II. Norman: University of Oklahoma Press, 1962.

STIERLIN, HENRI. *Art of the Aztecs and Its Origins*. Translated by Betty and Peter Ross. New York: Rizzoli, 1982.

STIERLIN, HENRI, *Art of the Incas and Its Origins*. Translation by Betty and Peter Ross. New York: Rizzoli, 1984.

STIERLIN, HENRI, *Art of the Maya: From the Olmecs to the Toltec-Maya*. Translated by Peter Graham, New York: Rizzoli International Publications, Inc., 1981.

THOMPSON, J. ERIC S. *The Rise and Fall of Maya Civilization*. Norman: University of Oklahoma Press, 1954.

TOMPKINS, PETER. *Mysteries of the Mexican Pyramids*. New York: Harper & Row, Publishers, Inc., 1976.

Tribes and Temples, A Record of the Expedition to Middle America Conducted by the Tulane University of Louisiana in 1925. New Orleans: The Tulane University of Louisiana, 1926.

TUSHINGHAM, A. D., *Gold for the Gods*. Toronto, Ont.: Royal Ontario Museum, 1976.

The Vinland Sagas: The Norse Discovery of America. Translated with an introduction by Magnus Magnusson and Hermann Pálsson. New York: Penguin Books, 1965.

VON HAGEN, VICTOR WOLFGANG, ed. *The Incas of Pedro de Cieza de León*. Translated by Harriet de Onis. Norman: University of Oklahoma Press, 1959.

WAUCHOPE, ROBERT. *Lost Tribes & Sunken Continents: Myth and Method in the Study of American Indians*. Chicago and London: The University of Chicago Press, 1962.

WEAVER, MURIEL PORTER. *The Aztecs, Maya, and Their Predecessors: Archaeology of Mesoamerica*. New York: Academic Press, 1981.

WEBB, CLARENCE H. *Geoscience and Man, The Poverty Point Culture*, Vol. XVII. Baton Rouge: Louisiana State University School of Geoscience, 1982.

WEDEL, WALDO R. *Prehistoric Man on the Great Plains*. Norman: University of Oklahoma Press, 1961.

WERNICK, ROBERT, *The Vikings*. Alexandria, Va.: Time-Life Books, 1979.

WEST, FREDERICK HADLEIGH. *The Archaeology of Beringia*. New York: Columbia University Press, 1981.

WILLEY, GORDON R. *An Introduction to American Archaeology: North and Middle America*, Vol. 1. Englewood Cliffs, N.J.: Prentice-Hall, Inc., 1966.

WILLEY, GORDON R., ed. *Archaeology of Southern Mesoamerica*. Austin: University of Texas Press, 1965.

The World's Last Mysteries. Pleasantville, N.Y.: The Reader's Digest Association, Inc., 1978.

Acknowledgments

The editors wish to acknowledge the following individuals and institutions for their generous assistance in preparing this volume.

Ambassador Félix Alvarez Brun, Ministry of Foreign Affairs, Lima, Peru; The American Museum of Natural History, New York, N.Y.; James Anderson, Cahokia Mounds Museum, Collinsville, Ill.; Anthony Aveni, Colgate University; Frances F. Berdan, The California State University; James A. Brown, Northwestern University; Carl William Clewlow, Jr., Ancient Enterprises Inc., Santa Monica, Calif.; College of Arts and Sciences, The University of Alabama; Alfonso Espinosa, Embassy of Peru, Washington, D.C.; Robert A. Feldman, Field Museum of Natural History, Chicago, Ill.; Melvin L. Fowler, The University of Wisconsin-Milwaukee; Judith Francis, Brandeis University; David Freidel, Southern Methodist University; Russell Graham, Illinois State Museum; Springfield, Ill. C.R. Harrington, National Museum of Natural Sciences, Ottawa, Ont.; Vance Haynes, University of Arizona; David Hopkins, U.S. Geological Survey, Menlo Park, Calif.; William Iseminger, Cahokia Mounds Museum, Collinsville, Ill.; Federico Kauffmann Doig, Lima, Peru; W. James Judge, Division of Cultural Research, National Park Service, Albuquerque, N. Mex.; Hugo Ludeña, National Institute of Culture, Lima, Peru; Ray T. Matheny, Brigham Young University; Betty J. Meggers, Smithsonian Institution, Washington, D.C.; The Metropolitan Museum of Art, New York, N.Y.; Richard Morlan, National Museum of Man, Ottawa, Ont.; The New York Public Library; Linda Schele, The University of Texas at Austin; Ruth DeEtte Simpson, San Bernardino County Museum, Redlands, Calif.; C. Earl Smith, University of Alabama; Robert Sonin, Art Conservator; Dennis Stanford, Smithsonian Institution, Washington, D.C.; Mercedes Vélez, Colombia Information Service, New York, N.Y.; Birgitta Linderoth Wallace, Parks Canada, Atlantic Region, Halifax, N.S.; Clarence H. Webb, Shreveport, La.; Robert and Judy Zeitlin, Brandeis University.

Credits

Maps by George Buctel: *15, 30, 53, 74, 110, 118, 126, 137, 146, 173, 235, 246, 262, 275.*
Lloyd Kenneth Townsend: *60-6l, 122-123, 154-155, 182-183, 254-255, 268-269*

Special appreciation is extended to the following individuals for their valuable assistance with picture research: Carlos Arostegui; Mrs. Junius B. Bird, Department of Anthropology, American Museum of Natural History; Carol and Lee Boltin; Dr. Elizabeth Boone, Curator of Primitive Art, Dumbarton Oaks; Christopher Donnan, Director, Museum of Cultural History, University of California, Los Angeles; Victor Englebert; Ellen Factor, The Image Bank; Diana Fane, Curator, Department of African, Oceanic, and New World Cultures, The Brooklyn Museum; Nancy Hammerslough, Pictures of Record; Dr. Thor Heyerdahl; David Hiser; Michael Holford; Cathrine Jalayer, André Emmerich Gallery; Dr. Julie Jones, Curator of Primitive Art, The Metropolitan Museum of Art; Dan Jones, Photo Archivist, Peabody Museum, Harvard University; Mary Anne Kenworthy, Photo Archivist, The Universiy Museum, University of Pennsylvania; Barbara and Justin Kerr; Terri Lupo, Marvullo Studios; Loren McIntyre; Martha Otto, Curator, Ohio Historical Society; Pedro Rojas Ponce; Anne Rowe, Curator, The Textile Museum, Washington, D.C.; Barbara Shattuck, National Geographic Society; Dr. Dennis Stanford, Curator, North American Archaeology, Smithsonian Institution; Barbara Stuckenrath, Museum Specialist, Department of Anthropology, Smithsonian Institution; Annette Valeo, The Textile Museum, Washington, D.C.

Grateful acknowledgement is also made to the following offices of The Reader's Digest Association, Inc., for their cooperation with picture requests: Australia, Robyn Hudson; Denmark, Konstantin Giersing; France, Glo Depondt; Italy, Piero Prandoni and Melania Puma; Mexico, Julia Ortiz and Teresa Segovia; The Netherlands, Marianne Dinkeloo; Norway, Per Vokso; Spain, Joaquin Amado; West Germany, Christina Horut.

Binding Design: Mixtec gold breast ornament. Photo © Lee Boltin. *Half-title page:* Pre-Conquest mosaic breast ornament: Mixtec, Mexico. Photo © Lee Boltin (see also page 205). *Title page:* Clay relief from Tomb 104, Monte Albán, Mexico. c. A.D. 500. Photo by Comm-Photo International. *4* Olmec figures. Photo © Lee Boltin (see also pages 106-107). *8-9* "Voyagers of Legend": The *Brendan* en route from Ireland to Newfoundland. Photo by Cotton Coulson/Susan Griggs Agency Ltd. *11* ORONOZ/Museo de América, Madrid. *12* CommPhoto International. *13 left:* © Loren McIntyre, 1982/Woodfin Camp & Associates; *right:* © R. Pereira/The Image Bank. *14 left:* Lee Boltin; *right:* The Brooklyn Museum, A. Augustus Healy Fund. *16* Photo Michael Holford. *17 upper left:* Victor Englebert; *lower right and right:* Thor Heyerdahl. *18 left:* British Museum, Photo Michael Holford; *right:* Musée de l'Homme, Paris. *19* Ida Jane Gallagher. *20 both:* © Kal Muller 1982/Woodfin Camp & Associates. *21* Wesley Holden. *23* © Lee Boltin. *24* The Brooklyn Museum, A. Augustus Healy Fund and Caroline A. L. Pratt Fund. *25 top:* Museo Amano, Lima, Peru/Photo by Pedro Rojas Ponce; *bottom:* Sotheby Parke-Bernet/Photo courtesy American Heritage Publishing Co. *26* The Brooklyn Museum, Dick S. Ramsay Fund. *27 left:* Courtesy of the Freer Gallery of Art, Smithsonian Institution, Washington, D.C. *right:* © Lee Boltin. *29 upper left:* © Lee Boltin; *lower left:* Private Collection/Photo © Lee Boltin; *right:* Sotheby Parke-Bernet/Art Resource. *31 left:* Rita Nanni; *right:* Robert Frerck/Woodfin Camp & Associates. *33* National Museum of American Art (formerly National Collection of Fine Arts), Smithsonian Institution, Gift of Sarah Harrison. *34* Rare Books and Manuscript Division, The New York Public Library. *35* National Museum of American Art (formerly National Collection of Fine Arts), Smithsonian Institution, Gift of Mrs. Joseph Harrison, Jr. *37 both:* Stuart Collection, Rare Books and Manuscript Division, The New York Public Library. *38* Biblioteca Nacional, Madrid. *39 left:* Museo Nacional de Antropologia et Archaeologia, Lima/Photo by Pedro Rojas Ponce; *right:* © Lee Boltin. *40* The Granger Collection. *43* Courtesy of the Biblioteca Estense in Modena/Photo by Roncaglia. *44* Universitäts Bibliothek Heidelberg. *45 upper:* Nathan Benn/

Susan Griggs Agency Ltd.; *lower:* Cotton Coulson/Susan Griggs Agency Ltd. *46 upper and lower right:* Scala/Art Resource/From Gabinetto Disegni, Uffizi, Florence; *lower left:* Giraudon/Art Resource/From Bibliothèque du Ministère des Armées, Paris. *49 left:* Reproduced with the authorization of the Museo de América, Madrid; *top right:* James Churchward, *The Lost Continent of Mu,* New York, Ives Washburn Publisher, 1931. Illustration by James Churchward; *lower right:* James Churchward, *The Children of Mu,* New York, Ives Washburn Publishers, 1931. Map by James Churchward. *51* The Pierpont Morgan Library. *53* Original art by Peter Spier from *Great Adventures That Changed Our World* 1978 © The Reader's Digest Association, Inc. *54-55* Francisco Erize/Bruce Coleman Inc. *57 left:* Alexandria Area Chamber of Commerce; *right:* "The Vinland Map" from *The Vinland Map and the Tartar Relation* by Skeleton, Marston, and Painter, © 1965 by Yale University. Reprinted by permission of Yale University Press. *59* From *Wildflowers of America,* edited by H.W. Rickett, Crown Publishers, Inc., Courtesy of the Gray Herbarium, Harvard University. *60-61 Art reference:* Historic Properties, Parks Canada/Photo by B. Schonback. *62 both:* Nationalmuseum, Denmark. *63* Arnamagnaeanske Institute, Copenhagen University/Photo by Bent Mann-Nielsen. *64 upper* Photo by George F. Mobley © 1964 National Geographic Society; *lower:* Historic Properties, Parks Canada Photo by G. Vandervloogt. *65 left:* Mario Fantin/Photo Researchers; *right:* Nationalmuseum, Denmark. *66-67* "In Search of Early Man": Big and Little Diomede Islands, Bering Strait. Photo by Fred Breummer. *69, 70, and 71:* all © Kerby Smith, 1978. *72 left:* Stephen J. Krasemann/DRK Photo; *right:* Fred Bruemmer. *73 left:* Earth Scenes/Brian Milne; *right:* Stephen J. Krasemann/DRK Photo. *76 and 77:* Photos courtesy of Wilfred Shawcross, The Australian National University, Canberra. *78 left:* Photo by Clayton Howe Barnes/Courtesy Daniel J. Griffin; *upper and lower right:* © Daniel J. Griffin, 1983. *80 and 81:* National Museum of Natural History, Smithsonian Institution/Photos by Chip Clark. *82 left:* San Diego Museum of Man; *right:* © Kerby Smith, 1978. *83 both:* Ecole des Hautes Etudes en Sciences Sociales/Photos Courtesy of Dr. Niède Guidon. *85* National Museum of Natural History, Smithsonian Institution. *86* Denver Museum of Natural History. *87 left:* Dr. James Hester/University of Colorado; *right:* © Kerby Smith, 1977. *88-89* Art by Darrell Sweet, from *America's Fascinating Indian Heritage* 1978, © The Reader's Digest Association, Inc. *90 left:* Art by Vic Kalin, from *America's Fascinating Indian Heritage* 1978 © The Reader's Digest Association, Inc.; *right:* University of Colorado Museum/Photo by Joe Ben Wheat. *91* National Museum of Natural History, Smithsonian Institution. *93 Sunset backdrop:* Four by Five, Inc.; *Corn inset:* Museum für Völkerkunde, Staatliche Museen Preussischer Kulturbesitz, Berlin (West). *95 left:* From *Pre-Columbian Archaeology* by Scientific American, "The Origins of New World Civilization" by Richard S. MacNeish, November 1964; *center right:* Kathy and Alan Linn. *96-97 all:* Kathy and Alan Linn. *98 left:* Kathy and Alan Linn; *right:* Andreas Feininger, Life Magazine © Time Inc., 1967. *99 upper left:* © Justin Kerr, 1978; *lower right and 100:* Courtesy of the Library Services Department, American Museum of Natural History. *101 lower left:* Dr. and Mrs. Franklin D. Murphy/Photo by Christopher Donnan; *upper right:* © Justin Kerr, 1978. *102 left:* Linden-Museum, Stuttgart; *right:* Museo Nacional de Antropologia y Archaeologia, Lima/Photo by Pedro Rojas Ponce; *bottom:* Michael Moseley/Anthro-Photo. *104* © Lee Boltin. *105 upper:* Sergio Larrain. © 1963 Magnum Photos; *lower:* © Robert Frerck/Woodfin Camp & Associates. *106-107* "Stirrings of New World Civilizations": Olmec figures found in 1955 at La Venta, Tabasco, Mexico. Photo © Lee Boltin. *109 top:* Edward Neild collection, Louisiana State Exhibit Museum/Photo by Pictures of Record, Inc.; *left:* Geoffrey R. Lehmann, Mississippi Department of Archives and History; *right:* Louisiana State Museum/Photo by Dennis Harkcom; *bottom:* Beckman and Webb collections, Louisiana State Exhibit Museum/Photo by Pictures of Record, Inc. *110* Courtesy The Library Services Department, American Museum of Natural History/Photo by Junius B. Bird. *111* Map by Clarence H. Webb. From *Geoscience and Man,* volume XVII, © School of Geoscience, Louisiana State University, 1982. *112* Pictures of Record, Inc. *114 left:* Poverty Point Museum/Photo by Pictures of Record, Inc.; *right and 115:* Lloyd Poissenot/

Louisiana Department of Wildlife & Fisheries. *117* © Ric Ergenbright, 1982. *119 upper left:* The Metropolitan Museum of Art, The Michael C. Rockefeller Memorial Collection, Purchase, Nelson A. Rockefeller Gift, 1968; *upper right:* © Lee Boltin; *lower left:* University Museum, University of Pennsylvania; *lower right:* The Metropolitan Museum of Art, The Michael C. Rockefeller Memorial Collection, Purchase, Nelson A. Rockefeller Gift, 1967. *120 left:* © Ric Ergenbright, 1982; *others:* Museo Nacional de Antropologia et Archaeologia, Lima/Photos by Pedro Rojas Ponce. *121* © Ric Ergenbright, 1982. *122-3 Art reference:* Photos courtesy of Alan Sawyer, and Richard L. Burger. *124* Museum of the American Indian, Heye Foundation, New York. *125* Museum für Völkerkunde, Staatliche Museen Preussischer Kulturbestiz, Berlin (West). *128 upper:* The Brooklyn Museum, The Roebling Society Purchase Fund. *lower:* © Lee Boltin. *129* The Metropolitan Museum of Art, Gift of George D. Pratt, 1933. *131* Dallas Museum of Fine Arts/Photo © Justin Kerr, 1981. *133 left:* Photo by Richard H. Stewart © 1939 National Geographic Society; *right:* Farrell Grehan. *134 left:* CommPhoto International; *right:* © George Gerster/Photo Researchers *135 left:* CommPhoto International; *right:* Farrell Grehan. *136 upper left and right:* © Justin Kerr, 1978; *lower left:* © David L. Brill, 1982. *138* The Brooklyn Museum, Lent by the Guennol Collection. *139 upper:* © Justin Kerr, 1979; *lower:* © Lee Boltin. *141* Courtesy of National Museum of Anthropology, Mexico/Photo by Fernando Robles. *142-143* "Pyramid Makers and Mound Builders": House of the Magician, Uxmal, Mexico. Photo Michael Holford. *145* © Lee Boltin. *147* © Justin Kerr, 1978. *148-149* Rare Books and Manuscript Division, The New York Public Library. *150* Shostal Associates. *151 left:* Carl Frank/Photo Researchers; *right:* Colin Wyatt/Photo Researchers. *152 left:* Rare Books and Manuscript Division, The New York Public Library; *right:* Kathy and Alan Linn. *156* © Justin Kerr, 1978. *157* Glyphs drawn by Linda Schele. *158 and 159 both:* Florida State Museum, Gainesville/Photos by Robert Blount. *160* © Justin Kerr, 1979. *161 left:* © Lee Boltin; *right:* Dumbarton Oaks. *162 left:* © David Alan Harvey, 1982/Woodfin Camp & Associates. *163 left:* © Marty Cooper, 1980; *right:* David Hiser Photographers/Aspen. *165* K. Kummels/Shostal Associates; *inset:* Kathy and Alan Linn. *167* Peabody Museum, Harvard University. Photograph by Hillel Burger. *168 left:* The Granger Collection; *168-169* © George Gerster/Photo Researchers. *170-171* The Saint Louis Art Museum, Eliza McMillan Trust Fund. *173 top and center:* Ohio Historical Society/Photo by Roger Phillips; *bottom:* Museum of the American Indian, Heye Foundation, New York. *174* Ohio Historical Society/Photo by Roger Phillips. *175* National Museum of Man/National Museums of Canada. *176* © George Gerster/Photo Researchers, Inc.; *map inset:* The New York Public Library. *177* Walter Rawlings/Robert Harding Picture Library. *178 upper and lower left:* Ohio Historical Society; *right:* Ohio Historical/Photo by Roger Phillips. *179* Milwaukee Public Museum. *181 left:* The Saint Louis Museum of Science and Industry; *right:* Copyright by Southern Living, Inc., July 1982. Used with permission. *184* Photo by Otis Imboden © 1972. National Geographic Society. *185 both:* Museum of the American Indian, Heye Foundation, New York. *187 left:* Copyright by Southern Living Inc., July 1982. Used with permission; *inset:* Museum of the American Indian, Heye Foundation, New York. *188-189* "Ancient Artisans and Master Builders": Embroidered and woven burial mantle, Paracas, Peru. The Textile Museum, Washington, D.C. *191-193 all:* © Lee Boltin. *193 all:* Photos, Michael Holford. *196 both:* © Lee Boltin. *195 upper right and lower left:* © Lee Boltin; *lower right:* Peabody Museum, Harvard University/Photo © Lee Boltin. *197 upper and lower left:* © Justin Kerr, 1978; *right:* Private Collection. *198 left:* Peabody Museum, Harvard University/Photograph by Hillel Burger; *right:* The Textile Museum, Washington, D.C. *199 all:* © Lee Boltin. *200 and 201 top right:* Museum für Völkerkunde, Vienna/Robert Harding Picture Library; *201 top left:* Art from *Fascinating World of Animals* 1971 © The Reader's Digest Association, Inc.; *lower left:* The Metropolitan Museum of Art, Fletcher Fund, 1959; *lower right:* Courtesy, The Edward H. Merrin Gallery, Inc./Photo © Justin Kerr, 1979. *202 left:* © Lee Boltin; *right:* © Justin Kerr, 1983. *203 left:* Smithsonian Institution/Photo © Lee Boltin; *top right:* © Justin Kerr, 1978; *bottom right:* Werner Forman Archive/British Museum, London. *204 left:* © Lee Boltin; *right:* Dumbarton Oaks. *205 all:* © Lee Boltin. *206-207* © Lee Boltin. *207 top:* Werner Forman Archive/City of Liverpool Museum, Liverpool. *208 top:* © Lee Boltin; *bottom two:* © Justin Kerr, 1979. *209 all:* Marc Eto/The Image Bank. *210 both:* © Justin Kerr, 1974. *211 top left and right:* © Lee Boltin; *lower left:* © Justin

Kerr, 1978. *212 left:* The Metropolitan Museum of Art, Purchase, 1900; *right:* Courtesy, André Emmerich Gallery. *213 top left:* Dumbarton Oaks; *bottom left:* Museo Regional de Puebla/Courtesy of National Gallery, Washington/Photo by José Naranjo. *right:* Photo, Michael Holford. *215* Photo by Dick Swift. *216-217* Jean Paul Jallot/Photo Researchers; *217 top left:* Carl Frank/Photo Researchers; *top right:* Eric Carle/Shostal Associates. *218 left:* © Robert W. Mitchess; *right:* CommPhoto International. *219 top:* Farrell Grehan; *bottom:* Photo, Michael Holford. *220* © Gerhard Gscheidle 1983/The Image Bank. *221 top:* Ian Graham/Photo Researchers; *bottom:* © Ric Ergenbright. *222 left:* © Victor Englebert, 1975; *222-223* © Susan McCartney/Photo Researchers. *224-225* Hans W. Silvester/Photo Researchers. *225 top left and right:* Loren McIntyre. *226-227* David Hiser Photographers/Aspen. *227 top left:* Photo by Alfred H. Siemens/The University of British Columbia; *bottom right:* Rare Books and Manuscript Division. The New York Public Library. *228* © David Alan Harvey 1981/Woodfin Camp & Associates. *229 top:* A. Rozier; *bottom:* Photo by Peter T. Furst. Collection of The National Museum of Anthropology, Mexico City. *230-231* "Lost Cities": Ruins of the Maya center of Palenque, Chiapas, Mexico. Shostal Associates. *233* © Lee Boltin. *235 upper:* Charles M. Gordon/West Stock; *lower:* Map adapted from: *Art of the Maya* by Henri Stierlin, Rizzoli International Publications, Inc., 1981. *236 left:* British Museum/Photo courtesy, Peabody Museum, Harvard University; *right:* Robert W. Mitchell. *239* Photograph, Merle Greene Robertson. *240 left:* Drawing by Linda Schele; *right:* Robert W. Mitchell. *242* © David Alan Harvey 1982/Woodfin Camp & Associates. *243* Pete Turner/The Image Bank. *245* Jeff Gnass. *246* Adapted from a map, courtesy of Chaco Canyon National Monument, U.S. Department of the Interior. *247* From the Bob and Tonia Skousen Collection/Photo by Jerry D. Jacka. *248* Courtesy The Library Services Department, American Museum of Natural History/Photo by William Sonntag. *249 both:* From the Bob and Tonia Skousen Collection/Photos by Jerry D. Jacka. *250 upper:* David Muench; *lower:* Jeff Gnass. *252* Jeff Gnass. *253 both:* © Robert W. Mitchell. *256* Jerry D. Jacka. *257* Ray A. Williamson. *259 both:* David Muench. *261* Juan Mayr/Mayr & Cabal Ltd. *263 both:* © Olivier Rebbot, 1980/Woodfin Camp & Associates. *264* The Brooklyn Museum, Dick S. Ramsay Fund and others/Photo courtesy André Emmerich Gallery. *265* © Justin Kerr, 1983. *266 left:* © Olivier Rebbot, 1980/Woodfin Camp & Associates; *right:* Victor Englebert, 1980. *267* Juan Mayr/Mayr & Cabal Ltd. *right:* © Victor Englebert, 1980. *273* © Lee Boltin. *275* David Brill © 1982 National Geographic Society. *276* Private Collection/Photo by Christopher Donnan. *277* Museum of the American Indian, Heye Foundation, New York/Photo by Christopher Donnan. *278 left:* Drawing by Donna McClelland/Photo by Christopher Donnan; *right:* Private Collection/Photo by Christopher Donnan. *279 both:* Loren McIntyre. *281 left:* The Art Institute of Chicago/Photo by Christopher Donnan; *right:* The Metropolitan Museum of Art, Gift and Bequest of Alice K. Bache, 1966 and 1977. *282-283* "Of Gods and Men": Detail of Maya vase showing human sacrificial rites. Photo © Justin Kerr, 1978/Courtesy, Dumbarton Oaks. *285* Library of Congress/Photo courtesy, American Heritage Publishing Co., *287 all:* David Hiser Photographers/Aspen. *288* Photo by George Stuart. From an original codex in the Biblioteca Nazionale Centrale, Florence. *289* National Museum of Anthropology, Mexico/Photo: David Hiser Photographers/Aspen. *290 top:* National Museum of Anthropology, Mexico/Photograph courtesy of National Gallery, Washington. Photo by José Naranjo; *bottom:* National Museum of Anthropology, Mexico/Photo: David Hiser Photographers/Aspen. *291* Courtesy, The Edward H. Merrin Gallery, Inc./Photo © Justin Kerr, 1979. *292 upper:* Bibliothèque de l'Assemblée Nationale, Paris; *lower:* National Museum of Anthropology, Mexico/Photo: David Hiser Photographers/Aspen. *295* David Hiser Photographers/Aspen. *297* © Lee Boltin. *299 top right:* © Lee Boltin; *bottom left:* Peabody Museum, Harvard University/Photo by Christopher Donnan. *300-301* Krannert Art Museum. University of Illinois at Urbana-Champaign. Purchase and gift of Mr. Fred Olsen, 1967/Photo by Wilmer Zehr. *301 right:* Loren McIntyre. *302 left:* Marvullo; *right:* Photo by Peter T. Furst. Private Collection. *303* © Lee Boltin. *304* Loren McIntyre. *305 both:* © David L. Brill, 1982.

Text Permission: "A Sleeping Town Awakes," pages 260-271, adapted from "First Look at a Lost City" by Warren Hoge, The New York Times Magazine, Nov. 30, 1980. Copyright © 1980 The New York Times Company. Reprinted by permission.

Index

Christianity, assimilation by New
World people of deities and
ritual, 298, 303, **305**
Chunkey, Mississippian game, **181**
Church of the Latter Day Saints.
See Mormons.
Churchward, James, 48–49
Cinq-Mars, Jacques, 81
Cintéotl, Aztec corn god, 293
Ciudad Real de Chiapas, 236
Clark, William, 36
Clay in pre-Columbian New World
art, 210, **210, 211.** *See also*
individual cultures and
civilizations.
Cliff Palace, Mesa Verde, Colorado,
250
Clovis people, 71, 86–90, 91
tools and weapons, **84,** 86–87, **86,**
88–89, 90–91, **91**
Coatlícue, Aztec earth goddess,
212, **213,** 293
Coca, ritual use of in the New World,
118–119, 126, 264
Cocijo, Zapotec rain god, **99**
Codices in pre-Columbian New
World art, 206, **206.** *See also*
individual cultures and
civilizations.
Coe, Michael, 132, 133, 137, 138,
139, 140
Cohoba (Cogioba), ritual use of
in the New World, 302
Colima tripod vessel, Mexico, **101**
Colombian Institute of
Anthropology, 260
Colombian Institute of Culture, 271
Colorado College, 80
Colorado Museum of Natural
History, 86
Colossal heads, Olmec, **12,** 132, 133,
133, 134–135, 140
Columbus, Bartolomeo, 147
Columbus, Christopher, 10, 42, 45,
147, 302
Communal labor requirements of
pre-Columbian civilizations,
112, 118, 121–124, 125,
133–134, 214, 216, 220, 222,
279–280
Compass, Olmec, 135
Conquest of the New World by the
Spaniards, 10, **10,** 38, 224,
264–265
assimilation of Christianity by
native people, 298, 303, **305**
destruction of historical
documents and artifacts, 147,
191, 214, 221, 296
recording of New World customs,
141, 147, 260, 262–263,
289–295, 298–299, 302–305
resistance of native people, 162,
264–265

suppression of religions, 289–290,
294, 296, 299–300
Continents and islands, legendary,
14, 42–49, **49**
Convergence, theoretical origin of
pre-Columbian, New World
civilizations, 15–16, 18, 21,
28–29, 31, 92–94, 105, 171,
239, 240
Copán, Honduras, **31,** 148, **151, 152,
213,** 214
ball court, reconstruction,
154–155
Corbelled arch, Maya, 153–154, **219**
Corn (maize), cultivation of, **92,**
94–97, **95, 99,** 161, 162–163,
222, 247, 266
Corn beer *(chicha),* 126, 222
Coronado, Francisco, 26
Corpus Christi ceremony, **305**
Corte Real, João Vaz, 19
Cortés Hernán, 10, **10,** 34, 38, 162,
169, 190, 200, 236, 289, 290
Covarrubias, Miguel, 130–132
Coxcatlan Cave site, Mexico, 96–97,
96. *See also* Tehuacán culture.
Coyolxauhqui, Aztec goddess, **291**
Cranial deformation caused by
binding, 137, 138, 157, 172,
251
Cresterias (roof combs), Palenque,
234
Critias (Plato), 47
Cromwell, Oliver, 36
Cutler, Manasseh, 168
Cuzco site, Peru, **105, 221**

Dating methods, archeological, 71,
75, 77–78, 79, 86, 87, 132,
140, 177
Davenport Tablet, 17
David, Louis, 238
Davis, E. H., 170–171, 175
Death and burial customs, New
World, **99,** 190–191, 210
Adena, **173,** 174, **174**
Anasazi, 258
Aztec, 15, 294–295
Chavín, 127–128
Chimú, 272, **272,** 276, **276**
Hopewell, 171, 176–179, **178**
Inca, **191,** 198
Maya, 151, 198, **198, 199,** 241,
242–243
Mississippian, **184,** 186–187
Olmec, 141
Tairona, 266
Tehuacán, 100–101

Death masks
Lambayeque, **195**
Maya, **203,** 232
Mixtec, **205**
Decker, George 63
Deer mask, Mississippian, **173**
"Del Mar Man," 82, **82**
Del Río, Don Antonio, 237, 238
Dendrochronology (tree-ring
dating), 75
Dent site, Colorado, 86
Desert culture, 247
De Soto, Hernando, 41, 180
De Soto Falls, Alabama, 36
Dick, Herbert, 95
Dickeson, Montroville, **171**
Dickson Mounds site, Illinois, **184**
Dickson Mounds site, Illinois, **184**
Diffusionism, theoretical origin of
pre-Columbian New World
civilizations, 10–21, 22–31,
34–35, 38–50, 103,
104–105, 125, 134, 168–170,
237–238
artifacts and other relics suggesting
cultural ties with overseas
civilizations, **12, 13, 14, 16,
18, 19, 20, 21, 22, 24, 26, 27,
29, 31, 37, 38, 39**
See also Legendary islands and
continents; Lost tribes in
pre-Columbian New World.
Dillehay, Thomas, 82
Diomede, Big and Little,
islands, **66–67**
Domestication of animals,
pre-Columbian, 92–94, 100,
100, 103, 104, 122, 125, 161,
251
Domestication of corn, New World,
92, 94–96, **95, 99**
Ayacucho Valley, Peru, research
project, 104
Tehuacán Valley, Mexico,
research project, 96–104,
96, 105
See also individual cultures and
civilizations.
Drainage, irrigation, and terracing
systems, pre-Columbian, 135,
160, 215, 222, **222,** 226, **227,**
247, 251, 256–257, **260,** 262,
263, 264, 265–269, 288
Drucker, Philip, 134
Drugs and intoxicants, New World,
118–119, **125,** 126, **212,** 222,
264, **291,** 298–299, **299,**
300–305, **303**
Drum, Aztec, **203**
Dupaix, Guillermo, 237
Dürer, Albrecht, 190, 191
Dwarf birch, **73**
Dwarf figure, ceramic, **303**

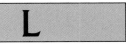

M

Page numbers in **bold** type refer to illustrations.

Reader's Digest Fund for the Blind is publisher of the Large-Type Edition of Reader's Digest. For further information about this special edition, please contact Reader's Digest Fund for the Blind, Inc., Dept. 250, Pleasantville, NY 10570.